THE AMERICAN CANAL IN PANAMA

THE QUEST, THE ACQUISITION

A STORY OF CORRUPTION,
INCOMPETENCE, AND THE EVOLUTION
OF A CANAL EMPLOYEE

photo of Marco Polo

DEDICATION

I WANT TO DEDICATE this book to my wife, Nivia Arce Cepeda de Drummond, my sister-in-law, Melva Montenegro, several Canal Zone union representatives, especially Chuck Wall, several Canal Zone community representatives and activists, especially Mike, Charlene, and Ralph James, several congressmen, Representatives Leonor Sullivan, Ralph Metcalfe, Daniel Flood, and especially John Murphy, and their legislative representatives, especially Terry Modglin, and several senators, especially James Allen, Strom Thurmond, and Jesse Helms, and their legislative representatives. Without the timely help from these people, and others too many to mention, I doubt that I would be alive today to write this trilogy.

ACKNOWLEDGMENTS

I WANT TO THANK Martin Olson, past president of local AFGE 1798, and Hugh Boyle, past secretary-treasurer of AFGE 1798, who, for good or bad, talked me into taking the job as the president of the Canal Zone police union.

I want to especially thank Victor Joseph, the secretary-treasurer of AFGE, and Ricky Royo, now deceased, the first vice president of our union while I was president. Without these men, I could not have accomplished the little that I did. Just as important, my special heartfelt thanks go to all the police and Canal employees who held true to the fight against the Canal giveaway.

OBJECTIVE

THIS TRILOGY IS PARTIALLY written in the first person, but it is not a book, per se, about me. It is a book about the evolution of an employee, any employee, who thought enough about his or her fellow man or woman and their country to try to make a difference.

Several of my children, as well as my friends and acquaintances, have shown an interest in my activities in the Canal Zone. For many people that lived there, the Canal Zone was considered heaven on earth. I was no exception. However, in this trilogy, I have left out most of the good times and personal bad times, unless they helped to tell my story. I have no interest in purposely affecting other lives. This is a trilogy about the political history of the Panama Canal, and by extension, about one man's evolution in his employment, his union, and political activities while living in the Panama Canal Zone from 1964 until 1984. It is an abbreviated political history of the Canal that led up to that time, and after the United States finally left the Canal.

WHY I DID WHAT I DID

I was a local AFGE union president, not well educated, not too bright, and not well liked. I was an unregistered union and anti-treaty lobbyist for a good deal of my employment while living in the Canal Zone. Based upon these inherent negative attributes, one would wonder why any sane man would want to take on this life-destroying endeavor? My answer to that question is, and was, simple.

Aside from the fact that I am, and I was, a creature of impulse, from the beginning of my Canal career, I thought that I was able to make a difference. I knew that no one else would step forward to fill that position as a police-union representative, and because of that position, an anti-treaty lobbyist. Of course, the reader will decide if I was effective or not! Considering the historical facts, I believe I will get the short end of that stick.

I originally wrote this portion of my life while living in the Canal, primarily to inform my children and grandchildren what I did, and what I did not do, in the hope that they would learn from my mistakes. However, after completing the first draft of my autobiography, dealing with my whole life, including my activities in the Canal Zone, I felt that this writing illustrated a more universal, and in some respects, a greater moral and historic value that could benefit others as well.

This writing does not offer any profound solutions to what I considered the waste, fraud, corruption, and incompetence that occurred over the giveaway of the Canal. Waste, fraud, and corruption, and incompetence, I believe, were, and still are, inherent throughout our government.

As I point out, this profound corruption and incompetence did not start with the giveaway of the Panama Canal, and to date, it has not ceased since the Canal giveaway. If anything, the corruption and incompetence have gotten worse. So much for the phrase "practice makes perfect."

To point to a beginning, when corruption and incompetence raised its ugly head and influenced the Canal giveaway, one would have to travel back in time to when the idea of a canal became a conceptual idea within the United States. As soon as our government began using taxpayer funds to alleviate financial crises, or began financing large public–private projects, corruption and incompetence became rampant. I don't believe there is any single solution to such a problem. However, there is a solution that already exists, just waiting to be utilized. Somehow, there has got to be a better way, if our country is to continue to exist for the benefit of us all.

MY SPECIAL THANKS GO OUT TO THE LITTLE MAN WITH BIG IDEAS MILES DUVAL, JR.

My interest in the history of the Panama Canal occurred because of a chance meeting with a man by the name of Miles DuVal, Jr.

I was sitting in a congressional house office in Washington, D.C., occupied by the chairwoman of the House Merchant Marine and Fisheries committee, Leonor Sullivan. I was discussing union business with one of the chairwoman's legislative assistants, Terry Modglin. Mr. DuVal walked into the office and was introduced to me as the special legislative assistant to Congressman Daniel Flood, from Pennsylvania. Mr. DuVal didn't say much. He asked me where I was staying in Washington, passed out some papers related to the Canal, and he left.

At the time, I thought Mr. DuVal and I had no mutual interests and dismissed him as just another single-issue advocate, common in Washington, D.C. I was a union activist, interested only in getting a better deal for my members, and he was a diehard Canal historian, dedicated to modernizing the Canal by having the United States build a third locks system.

That same evening, I received a telephone call from Captain DuVal at my hotel, and he asked me to meet him at the Cosmos Club, where he lived. At the time, I was hesitant to agree. I had spent all day lobbying the hill, and I was about to go down to the hotel bar to unwind. I was pretty sure he didn't have any information that I could use as a union representative. However, knowing that you can get useful information where you least expect it in Washington, I agreed to meet him.

When I arrived at the Cosmos Club and went inside, I was sure I had made a mistake. The place was filled with old men sitting around a large sitting room in high-back overstuffed chairs, smoking cigars or pipes, drinking wine or liquor from fancy glasses, and discussing issues that old men discuss. I recall that the great room was equipped with anterooms on at least one side.

DuVal directed me into one of those empty anterooms and, on a large table, rolled out an engineering drawing of the Canal with the depiction of the third locks. He proceeded to lecture me on the history of the Panama Canal, and the need for a third locks. He also gave me two of his books and told me he was in the process of writing a third book that would complete his trilogy.

He was an old man then, and I thought I would humor him by accepting his gifts and advice. When I returned to the hotel, out of curiosity, I began reading one of his books. I was astonished at how little I knew of the history of the Canal as it related to our Western civilization. It gave me a better understanding of the

Canal, and how important it was to the United States, and indeed to the whole Western world.

I studied Western civilization in the Canal Zone College, but DuVal's history of Western civilization was nothing like the history I studied. All the dates, times, and events were generally the same, but the motivation, the reason for being, was sorely lacking in the history I studied. He brought that history to life.

His history was a history that had a consistent goal, made by men not just eager to get rich, but more importantly, eager to discover, and to build a Canal that would make their country great, or allow it to exist at all.

DuVal's history of civilization isn't just about the past. It is about a civilization striving for the future not yet met. Unless a person understands that idea, they will never understand why the Canal, or any Isthmian canal, was, and still is, important to the United States, and for that matter, the rest of the world.

The Canal story is intricately woven into the inherent motivation and expansion of the Western world at every turn. I learned that an Isthmian route is as important to the United States today as it was even before there was a United States.

In time, I thought of Captain DuVal as my mentor. To me, he was no longer the spry little old man that would dart from one congressional office to the next, delivering papers of one type or another, barely speaking to anyone. To me, he was a giant intellect with few peers. He used to tell me, "Don't accept at face value the information I present in my books. Go to the Library of Congress and fact-check that information. Most of it is all there." I did that, and he was right. Every time I visited Washington, for any reason, I made it a point to visit him. He helped me in so many ways I cannot describe. I don't even know if he liked me. I have always been a hard person to like, but he never passed up a request to help me on one issue or another.

Captain DuVal entitled one of his books *"Cadiz to Catha,"* and it was the first book that I read. That phrase is not unique to Captain DuVal. The phrase encapsulates the motivation for the spread of Western civilization. It is a phrase familiar to most historians, or novices like myself that have taken the time to study the subject. DuVal took those three words and brought them to life in his books. Sometime in June of 1996, provided there is not another delay, Captain DuVal will have gotten his third locks.

Contents

Dedication 3
Acknowledgments 3
Objective 3
Why I Did What I Did 4
My Special Thanks Go Out To The Little Man With Big Ideas Miles Duval, Jr. 5

PREFACE 17
An Inherent Breeding Ground For Incompetence And Corruption 17
Money Means Power 18
Freedom Lost, Power Gained...18
The Almighty Agenda 19
Inherent Self-Interest By The Little And The Great 19

PART ONE: THE QUEST

THE LONG HISTORY OF THE CANAL..23
Pre-Western Civilization History..24
The Mariner's Compass, Mapmaking, And The Fight For Power 25
The Portolan Chart 26
The Mercator Chart 27
The Idea That Changed The Western World...27
Marco Polo 28

CHAPTER ONE: THE ERA OF DISCOVERY 31
The First Step – The Trip Around Africa..31
Christopher Columbus Goes West 33
Spain And Portugal, Two Great Nations In Competition............................34
The Search For Gold And The Search For The North And South Limits Of The American Island...34
Balboa, The Man With A Cloud Over His Head...35

The Quest For Gold And Slaves 37
The Fight To Control The Inland Seas Of Nicaragua... 37
The Mountain Range From Mexico To Colombia 39

CHAPTER TWO: THE COLONIZATION PERIOD 41

The Freebooters Had Arrived And The British Intrusion Began 43
The Woodcutters 44
The Mosquito Land 44
The Freebooters Were Still Not Done 45
The French And Indian War, Or The Seven Years War 45
The Revolutionary War... 47
The War Of 1812 And The Napoleonic Wars...50
1814, The Treaty Of Madrid 53
Canal Projects 53
The Humboldt Study 53
The Last Of The Western Absolute Monarchs.. 54
The Revolt Is On 54
The Holy Alliance And The Reasons For The Monroe Doctrine....................... 55
Slavery Became An Issue.. 56
The Panama Congress 57
Slavery Comes To The Surface Again... 57
The First Panama Canal Giveaway.. 58
The Canal, A Renewed Interest, And The Monroe Doctrine From Surprising Places 59
The Unsettled And Revolutionary Country 60
The British Move To Secure The Nicaragua Route...60
The Mexican–American War, The Political Fight Over Slavery, And The Expansion West 62
The Oregon Territory; Another War Was Brewing 64
The Gold Rush Is On 65
A Return To The Canal Issue, Almost Too Late, And The First Sign Of Crony Capitalism That Nearly Led To War 65
The Panama Railroad 67
A United States Foreign Policy Position, A Disaster For Fifty Years (The Clayton–Bulwer Treaty Of 1850)... 72
The Crimean War, A Distraction For The British... 75
Walker And The Slave States.. 76
In 1856, The British Return To The Isthmus 78

The United States Gets Snookered Again 79
The British Turned To Focus On The Suez Canal, And The French Filled The Void ... 80
Lincoln Comes To Power In Comes Crony Capitalism And The Issue Of Slavery 82
The Civil War 83
What Position Did Europe Take On The Civil War? 85
The Transcontinental Railroad, Crony Capitalism, And Corruption 87
The Need Was There 87
Crony Capitalism Rears Its Ugly Head Again 89
Greed Had No Bounds 90
Lincoln Knew Of This Corruption And Acted Too Late 92
Lincoln's Decision To Solve The Slavery Problem The Ends Justify The Means........... 93
The Chiriquí Panama Transit Line A Solution To The Freed Slaves......................... 93
Riots In Panama 94
The United States Of Colombia 95
The War With Spain Again, Crony Capitalism, Corruption, And An Opportunity Lost ... 95
Grant's Attempt To Salvage The Moment 96

PART TWO: THE ACQUISITION

CHAPTER THREE: THE FRENCH FILL THE VOID 101

The Monroe Doctrine Surfaces Again In America 102
De Lesseps's Miscalculation, And His Unexpected Support................................... 102
The Opposition.. 104
De Lesseps's Supporters 104
The Tehuantepec Transit Route... 105
The French Panama Canal...107
Philippe Bunau-Varilla 107
The Secret Of The Straits.. 109
A New Idea Surfaces.. 109
An Insurrection In Panama 110
Bunau-Varilla, The Manager Of The Panama Canal... 110
The Return To Panama 111
The Return To Nicaragua 112
The First Cleveland Administration 113
The Panic Of 1893 A Second Cleveland Presidency And The Start Of Predatory
    Financing 116

The Spanish–American War 118
Remember The *Maine*... *118*

CHAPTER FOUR: McKINLEY AND ROOSEVELT'S PUSH FOR A CANAL 121

Finally, The End Of The Clayton–Bulwer Treaty, But It Wasn't Easy 121
The Hay–Pauncefote Treaty: One And Two 122
Mckinley Is Assassinated, Roosevelt Is President 123
Bunau-Varilla, Single-Minded, Undaunted After The French Canal Collapse 124
Bunau-Varilla And The Lecture Tour 127
The Creation Of The Panama Canal 128

CHAPTER FIVE: TWO MEN WITH THE SAME GOAL, BUT DIFFERENT MOTIVES 131

The Corruption Begins, And Never Ends 131
Who Was Cromwell? 132
The Americanization Project 135
Financial Supporters Of Cromwell's First Scam 137
Cromwell Was Fired 139
An Abrupt Change From Nicaragua To Panama 139
Cromwell's Second Scam Is Born 140
Conflict Of Interest, Big Time 141
The Political Change To The Panama Route The Conflict Over A Private Or Government Canal 142
The Change Of Position 143

CHAPTER SIX: THE SPOONER COMPROMISE 145

The Negotiations Begin The Spooner Amendment 145
The Spooner Bill Was Not An Easy Act To Pass 146
Pre-Treaty Activities Of Colombia..147
Cromwell's Reinstatement As Council To The New Panama Canal Company...........147
Dr. Silva Represents The Colombian Government.. 149
The 1902 Civil War In Colombia, And A Better Deal Was Made? 150
The Hay–Concha Negotiations 151
The Hay–Herran Negotiations Begin 154

CHAPTER SEVEN: THE SEEDS OF REVOLUTION BEGIN .. 159

Extortion Of A High Order 159

Revolution And Double-Dealing Became The Name Of The Game Cromwell Shows His True Colors 160

Colombia's Attempt To Modify The Hay–Herran Treaty 162

Colombia's Blackmail 163

Obaldia's Appointment To Panama 164

Amador's First Trip To New York 164

Duque's Meeting With Cromwell, Hay, And Herran 165

Amador's Meeting With Cromwell 166

Cromwell And The Worm Has Turned 166

Cromwell's False Narrative 167

Bunau-Varilla Comes To Town, And The Revolution Is Saved 169

Bunau-Varilla's Meeting With Amador 170

Bunau-Varilla Seeks Third-Party Information 170

The Plan Is Hatched Based Upon Past History 172

Bunau-Varilla's Price For His Financial Help 173

Who Supplied The Initial Money For The Revolution 174

The Political Purpose Of The Rainey Hearings 175

The Allegation Of Blackmail That Backfired 175

Back To The Initial Funding Of The Panama Revolution 176

Bunau-Varilla's Personal Financial Worth 177

United States Activities Prior To The Panama Secession 179

The Movement Of United States Forces Close To Panama 179

The Panama And Colombian Activities Prior To The Panama Secession 180

CHAPTER EIGHT: THE PANAMA REVOLUTION 183

The Revolution Begins 183

The Warship That Was Supposed To Seal The Deal 184

The Burning Of Colon 1885 185

General Esteban Huertas 186

The Rebels Carefully Prepared 187

It Took A Woman To Carry On 187

The Plan Well Made 188

Hesitation, Lost Opportunities, And A New Nation Is Born 188

Late Orders Arrived, Rebel Plans Accelerated 189

The Arrest Of The Colombian Generals 190
Great Jubilation And Confusion Reigned 190
Amador's Attempt At Duplicity 191
The Success Of The Revolution Depended Upon The Bribe Of Colonel Torres........192
The Solution That Was No Solution At All..192
Miracles Do Happen, Torres Takes The Bribe..192
No More Money, And A Guarantee Is Made..193
The Independence Movement Started On November 3, 1903, Was Secure By November 6, 1903 The Corruption And Double-Dealing Soon Followed 194
Bunau-Varilla's Right To Negotiate The Canal Treaty 195
The Late Receipt Of Contrary Cables 197
Despite Attempt At Interference Bunau-Varilla Gets His Appointment.................. 198
Bunau-Varilla Appoints J.p. Morgan Panama's Banker 199
The Hay Bunau-Varilla Treaty Negotiations 199
The Treaty Signed.. 202
Bunau-Varilla And The Suicidal Conspirators 203
The Cromwell, Amador, Boyd Conspiracy Of November 17–18, 1903 204
The Infamous November 30, 1903, Cable... 206
World Recognition Of Republic Of Panama.. 207
Bunau-Varilla's Interference In Cromwell's Fiscal Income 207
The Fight To Return The Treaty To Washington 208

CHAPTER NINE: THE TREATY RATIFICATIONS 211

The Hay–Bunau-Varilla Treaty Ratified By Panama.. 211
The Ratification Of The Treaty By The United..211
The Fight 214
The World: "The Panama Revolution, A Stock-Gambler's Plan" 215
Reyes Grievances And 216
 Hay And Root Seek Advice From Bunau 217
United States Forces In Panama 219
The November 30, 1903, Cable And The Reyes' Empty Threats 220
Another Scheme By Cromwell?...221
The Cromwell Compromise, Or Another Scam?..221
General Reyes's Final Defeat... 222
 The Senate Votes On The Hay–Bunau-Varilla Treaty 223
The Hanna, Hay, And Herran Losses 223

The Final Senate Vote 224

The Financial Floodgates Of Corruption Begin To Open The Legal Seeds Of The Corruption Occurred In 1903 But Began As Far Back As 1886–1888................224

President Roosevelt And J.p. Morgan's Influence 225

Cromwell's Informants In Panama And Colombia..226

Bunau-Varilla's Funding Of The Revolution And His Appointment Of J.p. Morgan As "Fiscal Agent" Of Panama...227

Cromwell's Funding Of The Revolution And His Appointment As The Agent Of The Panama Railroad And The Panama Canal Company...................................228

The Collapse Of The Old Canal And The Creation Of The New Canal 229

Cromwell's Conflict Of Interest 231

Summary Of Cromwell's Activities From 1896–1904.....................................233

CHAPTER TEN: WHO GOT THE MONEY 237

Clearing The Decks For The Payout.. 237

How The Money Changed Hands 239

Cromwell's Effort To Again Twice Swindle The United States...................... 240

The Transfer Is Made, And The Money Disappears In France, In Panama, And In The United States 240

President Roosevelt's Re-Election..241

Tracing Where The Money Went Regarding The Panama Railroad, And The Panama Canal Company 244

The Creation Of The New Panama Canal Company 245

Cromwell's Second Scheme More Complex Than Thought 247

Shaw's Caution Regarding Paying The Money.. 247

The Archives Are Lost Forever.. 248

Who Got The $40,000,000 Dollars? To This Day, No One Knows........................ 248

The Whitley Tip..249

CHAPTER ELEVEN: ROOSEVELT'S INDIGNATION AND CROMWELL'S SCHEME UNRAVELS PRESIDENT ROOSEVELT MOVES TO FILE THE CRIMINAL SUIT.. 251

Before The Suit Was Dismissed 252

The Assurances To Assist In France...252

The Final Refusal To Cooperate In France..253

Who Got The $10,000,000 Dollars...254

The First $1,000,000 Dollars Are Concealed..255

What Happened To The $1,000,000 Dollars? 256
What Happened To The Remaining $6,000,000 Dollars? 260
How Cromwell Gained Control Of The $6,000,000 Dollars 260
Cromwell, J.p. Morgan, And Panama 262
The Canal Railroad Employees' Reward 266
The Worm Turned On Cromwell 268
The Great Hog Of The North 268

CHAPTER TWELVE: POLITICS TRUMP PERSONAL POWER 273

Finally, The United States Was Free To Build The Canal, Or Was It? 273
The First Commission Is Created By Act Of Congress 274
The Second Commission Was Created By Executive Order 283
Shonts, Taft, Cromwell, Wallace, And The New York Meeting 286
Gorgas, Magoon, And The Yellow Fever Scare 287
John F. Stevens Replaces Wallace 288
Taft Returns To Panama With Goethals 292
The Sea-Level Canal Or The Locks Canal Was Soon To Be Decided 292
Magoon Is Removed To Occupy A Higher Office 296
Politics Surfaces Again 296
Roosevelt Visits The Canal 297
The Contract That Broke Stevens's Back 299
The Resignation Of Shonts 302
Crony Capitalism Rears Its Head Once, Again And Stevens's Resignation 303

CHAPTER THIRTEEN: PERSONAL POWER AND INCOMPETENCE RULE 307

The Day Goethals Replaces Stevens As Chief Engineer Of The Canal 307
Goethals's First Labor–Management Confrontation And How It Was Handled 309
The First Steam-Shovel Strike 309
Crony Capitalism Again Returns To The Fray 312
Goethals Throws His Workforce Under The Bus 313
Goethals Is Ready To Take Complete Control Of The Canal 315
Goethals's Administrative Reorganization 316
The Canal Record 318
The History Of The Three Ideas Revisited 322

The History Of Bunau-Varilla's Method And The Cost Of Dredging........................323
The Lobnitz Dredge 325
Members Of The Board..325
Roosevelt's Request 326
Bunau-Varilla's Response To The Roosevelt Request "The Key To The Secret Of The Straits"..326
President Taft And Colonel Goethals Respond To The Bunau-Varilla Dredging System 328
Bunau-Varilla's Warning Of The Gatun Dam Problems 331
Bunau-Varilla's Warning Regarding The Culebra Cut 334
No Surprise The Original Cost Of The Canal Was Incorrect..336
Water Available For Canal Traffic 336
The Gatun Lake Stored Water Loss Was Another Problem Ignored By The Consulting Board Minority 337
The Argument Against A Sea-Level Canal By Roosevelt, Goethals, And Taft; Bunau-Varilla's Answer...337
More Problems And Odd Decisions Made By Goethals..340
The Completion Of The Canal...342
The Tolls Issue Was A Congressional And International Problem 344
The History Of The Tolls Problem 345
The Fight Over The Control Of The Canal Operation 347
Trouble Within The Canal Commission 348
The Secretary Of The Treasury Wanted A Piece Of The Pie.. 349
Goethals's Promotion...350
The Safe Lockage Through The Canal 351
August 15, 1914, Formal Opening Of The Canal 353
The Acquisition Summary...353

CHAPTER FOURTEEN: THE AGREEMENT CONCEIVED IN 1904 WAS RATIFIED IN 1926 357

The Tri-Partite Agreement 357

INDEX.. 361

PREFACE

THE PROBLEMS THAT I write about occurred in the Panama Canal Zone, but as I will point out, they also occurred in other agencies within the United States government, and in the history leading up to the giveaway of the Canal.

I have no doubt that the problem of corruption within our government has occurred, and will continue to occur, as long as our government continues to exist.

Ironically, it seems that, the larger our government becomes, under the pretense of protecting the citizens of the United States from one problem or another, the more incompetent and corrupt our government becomes.

I could waste time here and suggest that our Constitution limits what our federal government is required to do, but that is not what occurred, that is not what is occurring today, and no doubt, that is not what will continue to occur in the future.

Today, our federal government has taken on every issue that may or may not affect every person in the United States. As a result, states' rights, indeed, more importantly, individual rights, have been relegated to the whims of the federal government.

AN INHERENT BREEDING GROUND FOR INCOMPETENCE AND CORRUPTION

You have heard this song before, but sometimes it deserves repeating. For a government to grow, it must first identify problems that need to be addressed for the benefit of its citizens. It really doesn't matter if our federal government has a right to address those problems. They do it, and for the most part, they rely on the federal court system to approve of their actions.

As a result, an agency within the government is then created, if it doesn't already exist, and charged with servicing the people that the problem allegedly affects. Once created, the head of that agency must justify the continued existence of that agency to the Congress, to the executive branch, and eventually, to the federal court system, but not necessarily to the citizens of the United States.

MONEY MEANS POWER

The almighty federal budget contains the food that feeds the beast. Have you ever noticed that, no agency is motivated to completely solve the problem that they were created to eliminate? If they did, they would cease to exist.

I don't know of any agencies within our government that have been eliminated within the last fifty years. The name of the agency may change, but as long as the purpose for creating that agency still exists, that agency, or one just like it, will continue to exist. Left to its own devices, that agency will continue to grow.

The reason is simple. Every federal agency head fights to maintain, and eventually increase, his or her budget. The larger the budget, the more personnel the agency has, and the more power the agency head can acquire within the government.

FREEDOM LOST, POWER GAINED

Every president fights to own the objective for which that agency was created, provided the objective meets his or her agenda. Congressmen and congresswomen are motivated for the same reason, because they want that money to be spent in their districts. The more money spent in the congressperson's district, the greater influence they have over their constituency.

The greater effect the federal, local, and state government has on an individual, the less influence and freedom that individual has over his or her own life.

The further removed a person is from his or her direct political influence over these entities, the less political influence individuals have on their own freedom. You need only observe the power the "lobbyist" has at the local, state, and federal level to understand what entity has the greater freedom and power.

Politicians and, increasingly, un-elected bureaucrats decide who will receive the benefit of the taxpayer's dollar. Today, there are nearly as many people that do not pay taxes as there are people that do pay taxes. These people that do not pay taxes also have the right to vote. That dichotomy alone, among all others, has caused this country to become the victim of the politician.

The more dependent upon the whims of a politician a person becomes, the less freedom that person has, and the poorer he or she becomes. In the end, this country will be destroyed because of this one underlying problem. At the very least, we will no longer exist as a republic.

THE ALMIGHTY AGENDA

It is no secret that every president has an agenda that he or she wants to complete by the time they leave office. These people attain office by promising the voters specific actions while in office, which they may or may not fulfill.

Once in office, every president since George Washington has set about completing their agenda, which may or may not be in the best interest of the country, and which may or may not be what they promised to attain that office. Too often, the agenda is a reflection of the politics of the man or woman seeking the office of president.

It is, almost always, an agenda that reflects his or her personality, and/or the mutual agenda of the people surrounding that president. The voter makes his or her decision based upon the promises that may reflect the best interests of the country, but increasingly more often, they decide based upon their own self-interest.

INHERENT SELF-INTEREST BY THE LITTLE AND THE GREAT

This then is a trilogy about the increasing self-interest of men and women, over the greater good of their country and the greater good of their fellow man. It is about men and women in government and business that may have had all good intentions initially but went about trying to solve our foreign policy in such an incompetent and corrupt way that it made matters worse for the United States, the Republic of Panama, and even Central America.

In the aftermath, lives were destroyed, people were murdered and tortured, or forcefully deported from their own country, and the corrupt and self-interested prospered. In the end, the United States was forced to openly go to war with Panama, secretly intervene in Nicaragua, and, perhaps an exaggeration, almost bring down a republican government as a result of "The Iran Contra Affair," because of the incompetent and corrupt mistakes made by a previous government.

This book is not about the good times I had in the Canal Zone. I will describe how I observed, and sometimes participated in, the corruption of the United States government, starting with the individual, the Canal employee, and ending with the President and the Congress of the United States.

Sadly, after leaving the Canal Zone in 1984, I have observed no significant change in how our government behaves toward its own citizens, when conducting its foreign policy, or any other policy for that matter, but that is another story. It is a story that is unfolding to this very day.

PART ONE

THE QUEST

THE LONG HISTORY OF THE CANAL

Before discussing what role, albeit minuscule, the Canal Zone police union may have had regarding the United States' foreign affairs activities related to the Panama Canal, I believe it important to approach the subject from a historical background. The issues I discuss in this writing are not just relationships between the United States and Panama, but they have affected the entire Western world, both commercially, and strategically. The issue of an Isthmian canal evolved over time, long before there was a Panama Canal.

To appreciate the vital importance of the Panama Canal, or any Isthmian canal, to the United States, it is important to understand the history it played, and other transit routes played, and are yet to play, in the development of the Western world.

Now, you may think that statement to be a bit over the top, considering I'm talking about an allegedly obsolete Canal that our government, for whatever reason, gave away to a country that was ruled by a corrupt dictator, who clearly showed disdain for and, at times, was openly hostile toward the United States.

While doing so, we also directly and indirectly closed any opportunity, short of war, to obtain the one best alternative to the Panama Canal, the canal in Nicaragua, should we be threatened with denied access to the Panama Canal.

That is why I have included a brief history of Western civilization's monumental effort to find and eventually build a canal in Central America. It is to clearly expose the false notion that the Canal has lost its importance, commercially, and strategically, for the United States. Without knowing that history, the Panama Canal would forever be described as just another obsolete structure, whose capacity will not accommodate the world's larger and more modern commercial ships and was never able to accommodate our largest warships. Because of this restriction, our government was forced to develop a two-ocean naval fleet, a Pacific fleet and an Atlantic fleet.

PRE-WESTERN CIVILIZATION HISTORY

Of little consequence in writing this book, but of great importance in describing the history of the people that settled in Central and South America, long before there was any knowledge of the North, Central, and South American continent by Europeans, there was a significant Asian quest for discovery, and conquest of the New World. Gavin Menzies, in an article he wrote, described their arrival in the Americas, explaining how "Chinese … with Tartairs, Japanese, and Koreans … crossed the maritime stretch into the Kingdom of Quivira, populating Mexico, Panama, Peru, and other eastern countries of the Indies" long before Vasco Da Gama or Columbus made his trip to the west.

To prove that these discoveries were made, Professor Tulio Arends and Professor Gabriel Novick, and many others, took DNA samples from the Yupa Indians, who lived in the foothills of western Venezuela. They found a compound "in 58% of the Yupa Indians … indistinguishable from Tf Dchi, which is to date, only found in Chinese." "The only other people's whose DNA appears on both sides of the Pacific in the South American Incas (Novick and colleagues) and the Maori (Dr. Geoffrey Chambers) are the Chinese."

There are several detailed published articles describing the Asian influence and obvious settlement in Central and South America, especially in Panama, Nicaragua, and Colombia. Either side of the Atrato River (which flows north from Colombia into the Caribbean) have DNA that Professor Gabriel Novick and colleagues have summarized as follows: "Close similarities between the Chinese and Native Americans suggest recent gene flow from Asia." The same can be said of Professor Novick's description of the Guamiano and Ingano peoples, who live nearby, where the Rio San Juan reaches the Pacific. "The people that live on either side of those rivers … are clustered closer to Japanese people than to other American natives." In short, Gavin Menzies's research, in my opinion, presents sufficient evidence to reinforce the statement of Carlos Prince, who stated: "Chinese, Japanese, and Koreans did indeed populate Panama, as is evidenced by the DNA of today's people."

Why these Asian countries would venture out into the unknown and populate a continent thousands of miles from their shores can only be part of the universal quest of mankind to gain commercial and strategic power over their rivals.

THE MARINER'S COMPASS, MAPMAKING, AND THE FIGHT FOR POWER

Merchant fleets were established. Accurate mapmaking and the mariner's compass, originating from China, were introduced to the Western world. There was a desperate need to balance the power of trade in favor of the Western monarchs. All contributed to the rethinking of how the world would evolve.

In the 13th century, Greek mathematician, geographer, and astronomer Claudius Ptolemy is said to introduce cartography, the art of mapmaking, to the Western world. Until then, any Western naval activity was essentially restricted to navigational routes within the Mediterranean, and the Black Sea. Ptolemy introduced the idea of latitude and longitude geographic locations. Before then a ship captain navigated from port to port and submitted his directions to the ship's log. It was found that each subsequent trip to the same port was always different.

Photo of mariner's compass

THE PORTOLAN CHART

A recent article written in *Discover* magazine, dated June 2014, by Julie Rehmeyer described the research on this subject done by Dr. John Hessler, a curator at the Library of Congress. He described how the portolan chart, a type of chart based upon the study made by Ptolemy, helped solve this problem. Some of the early portolan charts are almost as accurate as the maps we use today. Missing was the correction for declination, the difference between magnetic north and true north at a specific location. The portolan maps did not account for this difference. They also did not account for the ability to chart the earth onto a flat surface without distortions. Comparing the portolan charts with the modern Mercator projections, Hessler found that the 12th-century maps had a uniform declination of 8.5 degrees. "Italy had a declination of 6 degrees, and the Black Sea had a declination of 8.8 degrees." He found that, between the years 1300 and 1350, the chart declination decreased by 2 degrees. "Over the next 150 years, Hessler found the charts shifted again to 11 degrees." This problem had little effect when traveling short distances, but obviously became dangerous when traveling greater distances.

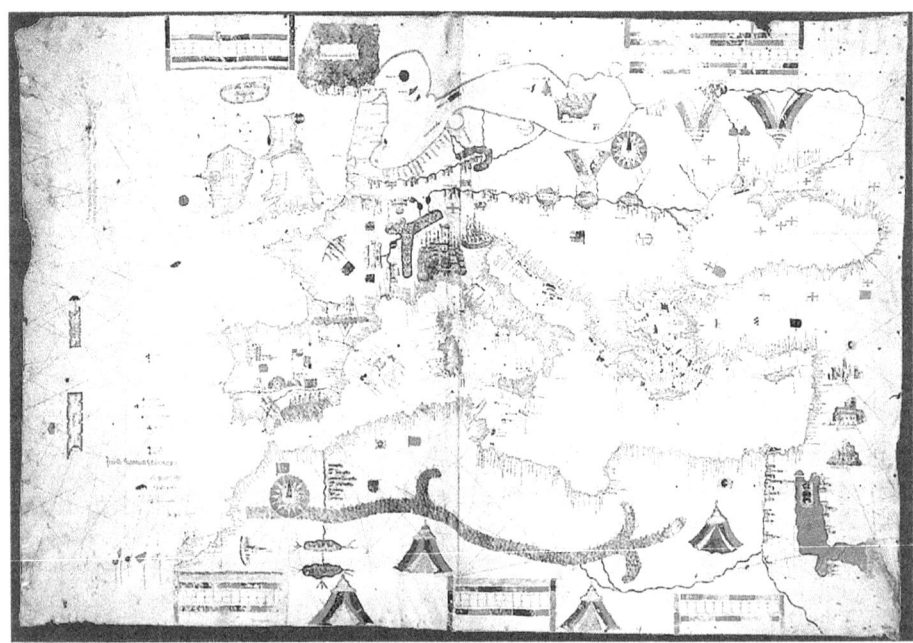

Photo of portolan chart

THE MERCATOR CHART

By the 16th century, Gerardus Mercator introduced his Mercator projections, which accounted for the distortions of accurately projecting a round surface unto a flat chart.

So what has this history to do with the history of the Canal? Did Christopher Columbus first think of finding a canal route to the Far East? The answer, of course, is no, he did not. So, let us go back in time, but not too far back, and point to the very reason for the existence of the Canal, or more precisely, the very reason for the expansion of Western civilization.

There would not have been one without the other.[1]

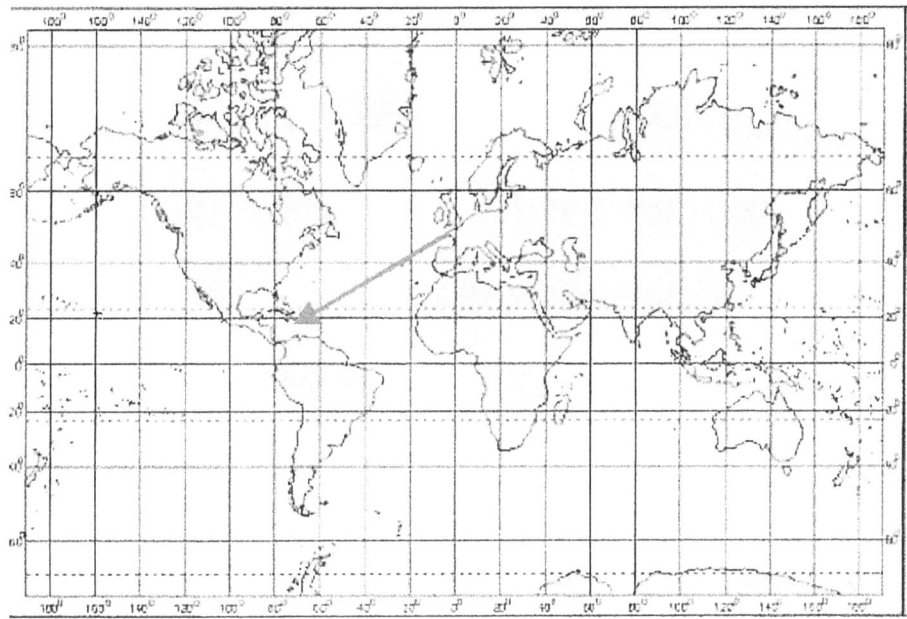

Photo of Mercator Chart

THE IDEA THAT CHANGED THE WESTERN WORLD

In 1253, two brothers, Niccolò and Maffeo, considered rich Venice traders, ventured east to Mongolia. At the time, the Western world was divided into warring city-states. The crusades were still raging. Constantinople had not yet been re-conquered by the Byzantine Empire. The Roman Empire was a thing of the past.

---

[1] June 2014, Julie Rehmeyer, Discover Magazine, "The Mapmaker's Mystery", pp. 44-49.

In 1269, at the request of the great Khubilai Khan, grandson of Genghis Khan, the brothers Polo were sent back to Italy on a goodwill mission to the Pope. They arrived in Venice that same year.

The stories the brothers told of the great wealth and vast lands of the Mongol Empire caused the Pope to send the brothers back to Mongolia. Around 1271, the brothers, accompanied by Niccolò's young son Marco, arrived in Jerusalem, where they picked up papal papers, gifts from Pope Gregory the Tenth, and holy water requested by Khubilai Khan.

In 1275, traveling over the Silk Road, they arrived at Khubilai Khan's summer palace at Xanadu, located in present day China. In 1295, after many years of travel throughout the region, the trio returned home. A year earlier, Khubilai Khan died, and the Mongol Empire disintegrated. Had it not been for a change of fate, the story of the two brothers, Niccolò and Maffeo, and Niccolò's son Marco, and their adventures would have remained local stories, told by old men in local taverns or around the dinner table.

MARCO POLO

However, soon after returning home, Marco Polo was caught up in the Venice–Genoa War and imprisoned. In 1298, undaunted, and while still in prison, Marco Polo, with the help of the adventure writer Rustichello of Pisa, wrote a manuscript entitled *The Description of The World*.

In 1299, due to a peace treaty between Venice and Genoa, Marco Polo was released from prison and returned home. The following year, he married, had three children, and died in 1324. Thankfully, his manuscript did not die with him.

If the Bible is considered the greatest story ever told, and I believe that it is, then *The Description of the World* by Marco Polo, unread and mostly unheard of today, must be the second greatest story ever told. Although, like the Bible, the accuracy of its content has long been questioned, there is no doubt that the manuscript, written by Marco Polo, prompted the expansion of the Western world, indeed the very existence of the United States, and the Panama Canal, as we know it today. The history of the Canal is the economic and strategic history of the Western world.

Photo of Marco Polo

CHAPTER ONE
THE ERA OF DISCOVERY

The Western world changed when Marco Polo, back from his trip to the Orient, described stories of the riches he found there and presented those stories in writing to the monarchs of Europe. We have all been introduced to Marco Polo in our childhood studies of Western civilization, but few of us were taught that his writings, as well as those of Conti and Mandeville, motivated a great rush to find a safe alternative to a land route to the Far East. No European had ever explored the African continent past the northern reaches. To most Western explorers, the world was flat. As long as this thought prevailed, the route to the riches of the East Indies went east, through the land of the fierce Mohammedan and Tartar. That was about to change forever. Henry of Portugal argued that it was possible to sail south, around the western shores of Africa, and eventually come to the eastern shores of India.

The history of the Canal, then, is really a study of the political economy of the Western world in its search to find a quick and safe route to the East Indies. Henry argued that a route that would bypass the hostile Muslim, Mongol, and Turk, would lead the Europeans to the riches of India, China, and Japan.

THE FIRST STEP – THE TRIP AROUND AFRICA

The cautious thinking, then, was that by following down the western coast of Africa, one would eventually round the southern-most tip and come to the southern shores and the riches of India.[1]

Fifty years later, in 1487, Bartholomew Dias, an agent of Portugal, was the first to prove that thinking to be correct. However, he did not prove that the

---
[1] J. K. Ingram, "History of Political Economy." London 1888

world was not flat. That effort was left to the Greeks, the English, the Spanish, and more specifically, a Portuguese pilot, an agent of Spain, known as Magellan.

Photo of Bartholomew Dias

Photo of Magellan.

CHRISTOPHER COLUMBUS GOES WEST

It was the works of the Greeks, Aristotle, Strabo, Ptolemy, and others that convinced Christopher Columbus that he could find a faster water route to the East Indies by sailing west. Columbus's theory was simple. What was not Europe or Africa was the East Indies.

He persuaded the Spanish monarch to allow him to search for this western route. As we all know, in 1492, his first trip carried him to the Bahamas, and he set about naming his discoveries as if they were part of the islands and mainland of Asia.

In 1498, by his third voyage, Columbus was still convinced he had discovered the mainland of the East Indies. His last voyage was in 1502—he died on May 26, 1506—and he was still convinced that he had discovered the shores of the East Indies. His discoveries led him from the islands of the Bahamas to the northern shores of Honduras, and south to, most importantly, the mouth of the San Juan River in Nicaragua. The riches he sought were relegated to the gold he found from the natives inhabiting the lands he discovered. These riches were not nearly enough to fill the coffers of the Spanish monarch, but they did keep him interested. In truth, as we all know, Columbus discovered the islands of the Caribbean and the shores of Central America. His contribution to Western civilization was to stir on further exploration by other explorers in the hope of finding the elusive riches of the Orient.

Photo of Columbus

SPAIN AND PORTUGAL, TWO GREAT NATIONS IN COMPETITION

Portugal and Spain were the two reigning European monarchs competing for the riches of these discoveries, and the Pope was eager to satisfy both by granting papal favors for their discoveries, the Portuguese for their discoveries on the west coast of Africa, and the Spanish for their discoveries on the east coast of Central and South America. In the end, the Treaty of Tordesillas, ratified on June 7, 1494, legally gave Portugal part of South America that once had been opened up to discovery by Spain.

In the year 1500, the king of Portugal further pressed his claim upon the discovery of Brazil by Peter Cabal. That discovery led to further discovery by Portugal along the east coast of South America.

Even as Columbus was making his discoveries, and as late as 1503, other explorers were describing these lands as the New World, and America, after Vespucci. Hojeda and Vespucci explored the shores of South America northward to Venezuela. Vincent Pinzon crossed the mouth of the Amazon to the island of Trinidad. In 1500, Bastidas explored the northern shore of Cap Vela to the Gulf of Darien and the Isthmus of Panama.

In 1502, on his fourth and final voyage, Columbus, off course, explored south to the area at Bluefield's Lagoon and the mouth of the San Juan River in Nicaragua.

THE SEARCH FOR GOLD AND THE SEARCH FOR THE NORTH AND SOUTH LIMITS OF THE AMERICAN ISLAND

The English and French in the north, and the Portuguese in the south concentrated their efforts on finding a route around the vast island that was the New World, while the Spanish concentrated on finding gold from Florida to Colombia.

Ironically, it took Magalhaens, a Portuguese, but an agent of Spain, to prove Columbus's theory was correct. The world was round, and you could sail west to find the East Indies. Magalhaens was not blindly seeking a route to the East Indies by sailing west. He was equipped with the knowledge of a medieval map, published by the mapmaker Waldseemueller, that showed the existence of the straits.

In August of 1519, Magalhaens set out, discovered the Strait of Magellan in

South America, passed through, and ultimately was killed by the natives. However, his men crossed the great Pacific Ocean, where they followed along the west coast of Africa and returned to Spain. Even then, the perception was that Magalhaens had found the southern limit of the vast island of the new land, and not the continent that we know today.

To the Spanish, this discovery had a problem. The Strait of Magellan was too far south to be of much use to them, and it was part of the dominion claimed by the Portuguese. All these explorers described their discoveries as an independent landmass, a huge island lying across the equator with no known north or south limits. It had yet to be considered a continent, as we know it to be today.

BALBOA, THE MAN WITH A CLOUD OVER HIS HEAD

In 1508, King Ferdinand of Spain divided his southern provinces between two of his agents, Diego de Nicuesa, who was assigned an area north of the Darien Gulf called Castillo del Oro, and Alonzo de Hojedo, who was assigned the province south of the gulf called Nombre de Dios. Neither province fared well. In time, Hojedo abandoned the southern province and sailed away. In came the man with a cloud over his head to save the day. He persuaded the colonists to move into the northern province, where the land was more fertile, and the new immigrants formed a rebellion to depose Nicuesa. Balboa was elected the new Alcadia of Santa Maria de la Antigua. The king commissioned Balboa to act as the governor of Castilla de Oro, and Balboa at once set out to make more discoveries for his king.[2] Not bad for a guy whose only claim to fame was as an explorer and ship's captain. On September 1, 1513, Vasco Nunez de Balboa set sail from his base in Antigua and landed at the Caledonia Bay. Balboa was the first to travel overland to Panama and discover the Pacific Ocean. On the 29th of September 1513, he arrived at the coast of San Miguel Gulf and took possession of it for his king.[3]

While he was off making his discovery, detractors in the king's court were busy defaming him. Before he could make a report of his findings, the king appointed Pedro Arias de Avila (Pedrarias Davila) to take his place as governor of Castilla de Oro. The king directed that Balboa be returned to Spain under arrest.

Balboa was eventually acquitted of the charges placed against him and was appointed "leader of the expedition to the Pacific" by the king, but under the

---

[2] Castillo de Oro was the name given the area from the San Juan river, in Nicaragua, to the Atrato river, in present day Colombia.
[3] House Rep. No. 145 (30th Congress, 2nd session, pp. 506-507)

supervision of Avila. As he was to find out, few men that worked under Pedrarias ever fared well.

Photo of Balboa Discovering the Pacific Ocean

In 1516, Balboa once again crossed the Isthmus. This time, with four brigantines, broken down in parts, and reassembled on the Pacific side. After taking possession of the Perlas Islands, off the coast of Panama, he was summoned back to Castilla de Oro by governor Pedrarias Davila, the newly appointed governor of Tierra Firma, put on trial, and in 1517, he was beheaded.

In 1519, a post road was completed, that stretched from the Atrato River on the Atlantic Ocean, over the mountain previously known as the Caledonian route, to the Pacific end at old Panama. This post road became the highway predominantly used to transport gold and silver from Peru, and eventually dry goods and precious timber from other Spanish colonies. In 1597, the Atlantic terminal was moved to Porto Bello, Panama.[4]

A few years after Balboa discovered the Pacific, another expedition conducted by Francisco Hernandez de Cordova left Cuba, and rediscovered the northern shores of Honduras, passed the Gulf of Camechy, and the river Champoton. In 1518, Juan de Grijalva explored along the shores of the Gulf of Mexico as far as the river Tampico. In 1515, Jaun Diaz de Solis explored further south to the Plate River.

THE QUEST FOR GOLD AND SLAVES

For Spain, what started out as an effort to find a passage to the East Indies by sailing West, ended up as the promise of gold and slaves. However, only in the south did Portugal find, both a passage to the East Indies and gold.

The gold discovered by the Spanish in the north was deemed insufficient to satisfy the Spanish monarch. In time, Spain lost interest in its possessions in Florida, preferring the rich gold fields in the south.

When Spain lost interest in the northern conquests, the French filled the vacuum. It became the center of France's colonial activities, and probably the beginning of the declining influence of Spain in the New World. It was the French that proved that there was no northwest passage to the Pacific from Florida to Canada. By the year 1523, the New World proved to be a continent, stretching from Canada to the tip of South America.

THE FIGHT TO CONTROL THE INLAND SEAS OF NICARAGUA

King Charles of Spain, still interested in a western passage to the East Indies, commissioned Gil Gonzalez Davila to continue looking for the western passage.

Pedrarias, true to character, refused to cooperate in the enterprise. In 1522, undaunted, Davila pushed on, as did Balboa before him, crossed the landmass of Panama, and sailed north to Nicaragua on the west coast. He traveled inland to

---
[4] Senate Doc. No. 54 (57th Congress, 1st session.) Part 1, pp. 27-28.

discover the inland lakes, before being forced out by the Indians. When Davila returned to Panama, Pedrarias was waiting to claim Davila's discovery for himself.

In 1524, Pedrarias dispatched Francisco Hernandez de Cordova with secret orders to claim all the land around the inland sea in the name of the governor, Pedrarias, and to search for the strait, or passageway, to the Atlantic Ocean. Cordova was a man soon to go the way of Balboa, but didn't know it yet. Cordova did his job. He found the inland sea by traveling through Costa Rica, and even found the San Juan River that led to the Atlantic Ocean, but he was unable to continue to its mouth, because the river was obstructed by rocks and rapids. In time, after dispatching the hostile Indians, Davila established the City of Granada.[5]

King Charles then commissioned Cortez, the conqueror of Mexico, and a man more dedicated to the king then Pedrarias, to find the western passage to the Pacific. [6]

Cortez immediately dispatched two of his lieutenants south to undertake this effort, only to discover that they could not find such a passage. What his lieutenants did find was an abundance of rich forests that could be used for shipbuilding material. Also, being advised of Davila's discovery of the fresh-water sea in Nicaragua, Cortez dispatched a third lieutenant, Cristoval Olid, to eliminate Cordova and annex the entire Isthmus as far south as Panama.

In the end, not trusting Olid, in 1524, Cortez decided to march south himself to claim this inland sea for his king. Upon his arrival, he found his lieutenants Davila and Casas had dispatched Olid. Cortez had won over Cordova from Pedrarias. However, in 1525, no sooner had he arrived than he was forced to return to Mexico to put down a revolt. Pedrarias saw his chance to reclaim the fresh-water sea. He gathered his forces and marched north, forcing Davila to return to Mexico, and then executing Cordova. Pedrarias also proved, once and for all, that there was no clear western passage from the inland seas.

By 1525, no Pacific Ocean passage could be found in Nicaragua, but there was a passage from Lake Nicaragua to the Caribbean Sea, or Atlantic Ocean. In 1529, Captain Diego Machuca sailed from Lake Nicaragua down the San Juan River to the Atlantic Ocean, and from there, to Nombre de Dios. His discovery established a commercial service from Granada to Spain, Cuba, and South America that lasted until 1537.

As late as 1542, Spanish expeditions were continually commissioned north and south of the Central American Isthmus to find the western passage. It was

---

[5] Senate Doc. No. 54 (57th Congress, 1st session.) , pp. 26-27.
[6] House Executive Doc. No. 107 (47th Congress, 2nd session), 9. 10.

clear by the time of Cortez's death that no western passage to the East Indies existed north of the straits of Magellan. Attention was given even then to the construction of a canal to the Pacific Ocean. As early as 1500, Spanish engineers proposed a canal to the Madrid government. In 1529 Cortez presented canal plans, prepared by Alvaro Saavedra, to the king and queen of Spain with the statement: We have not found yet a passage from Iberia to Cathay, but we must cut it. At no matter what cost, we must build a canal at Panama." None of these plans were ever acted upon. In 1534 Charles V ordered the governor of Tierra Firma, Pascual de Andagoya, to find a favorable route to build a canal to the Pacific Ocean. In response, Andagoya responded by stating: "No prince on earth, however powerful he might be, was capable of forming a junction of both seas… nor of defraying the expenses required for such an undertaking."[7] Others felt differently, but nothing was ever done.

THE MOUNTAIN RANGE FROM MEXICO TO COLOMBIA

What was discovered was an unbroken mountain range that ran from the plains of Mexico to the South American Andes Mountains, with the lowest summits located in Panama and Nicaragua.

Only in Panama, after the discovery of Balboa, in 1513, was a well-constructed post road commissioned across that mountain range by the king of Spain. It was this post road that, for many years, was used by Spain to transport gold, silver, and other goods, from South America, back to Europe.

---

[7] House Report No. 145 (30th Congress, 2nd session) p. 507.

CHAPTER TWO
THE COLONIZATION PERIOD

Having failed to find the western passage, Spain turned her attention to the rich gold and silver fields of Peru and placed the area in the hands of her obedient Spanish viceroy. All these riches were shipped through Porto Bello, an eastern port of Panama, by caravan. Other Spanish colonies were established. To that end, the Kingdom of New Granada was established in 1542, comprising the land north and south of the river Atrato, located in present day Colombia and subject to the Viceroy of Peru.

To ensure that Spain had no competition, special laws were enacted by the viceroy, under the direction of the Spanish king Phillip II, that under the penalty of death, no one should attempt to navigate the river Atrato past the shores of the Darien. Of course, one man's law was another man's opportunity, if he was willing to take a chance. Looking at a modern-day map of Colombia and Panama, there was not much chance of getting caught smuggling goods around the king's directed route to Europe.

In addition, while the Peru and Panama colonies were thriving, so were the colonists in the province of Nicaragua. While the eastern part of Nicaragua was considered inhospitable, the western side of the mountain range was considered rich in gold, silver, forest, and temperate weather. The western plain below the mountain range and around the lakes were fertile and suitable for cultivation of sugar, cotton, tobacco, cocoa, coffee, rice, and corn. The early settlers of this land had migrated from Mexico.

Pedrarias, true to form, destroyed all traces of the early Indian settlers and drove the survivors to the eastern mountains, where they integrated with the more primitive and hostile Indians. Pedrarias also used captured slave labor to work the gold and silver mines. In 1527, Pedrarias was awarded the position of governor over this province, and it was separated from Terra Firma, and formally named Nicaragua.

Because Terra Firma, in Panama, was controlled by his rival, Pedrarias needed another access to the eastern shore and the mouth of the San Juan River, which was controlled by the Indians hostile to him. He set about displacing these Indians, enslaving them when he could, but never fully accomplishing his goal in his lifetime. He died in 1531.

Photo of Pedrarias Davila

His replacement, Contreras, took an opposite approach with the Indians, and he was finally able to open the mouth of the San Juan River for navigation.

In 1542, Contreras was deposed, and the province was integrated into the Presidency of Guatemala. Another attempt was made to subdue the Indians on the eastern coast of Nicaragua, but this attempt was met with resistance by the Indians. In 1560, only six members of the party returned. Finally, in 1574, a colony was established, and the province was added to the Chancellorate of Guatemala.

By 1579, the Nicaragua route became the preferred route for the products of Peru, because of the ease of transport, and the invasion of the Pacific by Frances Drake, who was interfering with traffic through the Panama route. The Nicaragua route was used for the next two hundred years. The Panama route began to disappear. Not mentioned in any detail in this writing, the same was true of the Tehuantepec route, in Mexico. These other routes were turned over to their inhabitants to be ruled as they wished.

In 1550, a need for a canal route to the East Indies again surfaced, and again the Nicaragua route emerged as the preferred route of those discussed. Because of the rivalry in Europe, Spain abandoned any attempt to pursue the matter further.

Between 1585 and 1604, King Phillip II of Spain, a co-monarch of England until 1558, had engaged in an undeclared war with England's other monarch, Queen Elizabeth, over her support for the Dutch revolt against Spain, her protestant faith, and her support of the English freebooters in the New World.

With the blessings of the Pope, in 1588, Spain sent the Spanish Armada, and a large army through the English Channel to dislodge Queen Elizabeth from her throne, only to be turned away and forced to return to Spain. The English sent their own fleet on more than one occasion to defeat the Spanish but were also turned away.

THE FREEBOOTERS HAD ARRIVED AND THE BRITISH INTRUSION BEGAN

Spain had become the enemy of every country in Europe, but still too powerful to openly oppose. Instead France, England, and Holland turned a blind eye to ships of buccaneers, from their countries, that roamed the Spanish Main and the West Indies.

By the year 1630, the English freebooters had cultivated a friendship with the Moscoes, an Indian tribe located along the eastern shore of Nicaragua. The pirates would use the shallow bays and waterways along the eastern coastline and lie in wait for any Spanish ship out of Peru, Mexico, or Central America. Because these English ships were comparatively shallow drafted and fast, they could avoid the heavy draft ships of the Spanish fleet.

Because of the activities of the freebooters, the Spanish were forced to remove their nationals from the offshore islands of the Yucatan, or Belize, and the islands off the coast of Honduras. The pirates lost no time in using these islands as their base of operations.

When the Spanish complained to the British Crown, they were simply told that these pirates were not considered subjects of the British Crown, and the British Crown was not responsible for their actions. The attacks were constant and seemed to escalate.

In 1654, after Oliver Cromwell came to power in England, he ordered a fleet of freebooters to attack Cuba, and in 1655, they gained partial control of Jamaica. By the year 1660, the English were in complete control of that island. Encouraged by the support they were getting from the British Crown, the pirates began moving inland, up the San Juan River, to attack the inland Spanish colonies. In 1665, one band of pirates managed to sack and burn the City of Granada. Realizing the escalating English threat, the Spanish took extraordinary steps to ensure that the inland waters of the San Juan River could no longer be easily used to attack its inland colonies.

THE WOODCUTTERS

In 1678, having gained complete control of the offshore islands and the eastern shore of Central America, from Belize to the mouth of the San Juan River, the English agreed to a treaty with Spain that formally recognized Great Britain's sovereignty in the West Indies and those areas that they were in control of at the time. Because of this treaty, the way of the freebooter was over. These men were now considered British subjects, and most of them took up the trade of peaceful woodcutters. The Spanish colonists were not content with this situation, and still considered these men to be pirates, stealing lumber that rightfully belonged to the Spanish colonies, and they forced the English woodcutters into the areas of Belize and Nicaragua.

THE MOSQUITO LAND

The Moscoes Indians continued to remain friendly with the British woodcutters. To some extent, the Indians had already intermarried with the woodcutters, or freebooters. In addition, in 1650, due to a shipwreck of a Dutch slave ship off the coast of Costa Rica, the Indians intermarried with the Negro slaves that managed to escape to the shore and wander north in search of food and water. The Indian population was no longer an Indian population, but an amalgamation of Indians, Negroes, and Englishmen, known as the Mosquito Indians. The population was continually increased by Negroes coming from Jamaica, until it was considered mostly Negroid. As a result, the population increased until it spread from Honduras to the Bluefields Lagoon in Nicaragua, and the area was later known as the Mosquito Shoreline, or Mosquitoland.

Through several successions of Indian kings, by the year 1687, the Indian lands were taken under the protection of the British Crown. Not meeting success at their first attempt, in 1701 an agreement was finally made between the Mosquito king and the governor of Jamaica. The agreement required that the

Mosquito king provide fifty men to hunt down runaway slaves in Jamaica for money and arms. This treaty, of sorts, was formally ratified in 1720.

THE FREEBOOTERS WERE STILL NOT DONE

In 1680, because the Isthmus of Panama was considered abandoned by the Spanish, a band of British freebooters pushed across the area, looking for gold, and sacked the town of Panama. With the aid of the Darien Indians, the English freebooters attacked two other towns further south. Although these raids failed to bring the riches that were thought to exist, the description of the land encountered by the pirates, comprised of low hills and valleys, sparked renewed interest in an easy transit route across the Isthmus of Panama. In 1695, the Scottish parliament authorized the formation of a colony at Darien, headed by William Paterson, under the name of the Company of Scotland Trading to Africa and the Indies. In 1698, a large Scottish settlement consisting of 1200 men was established at Puerto Escoces at Caledonia Bay. The country was named New Caledonia. The English and the Dutch East India Companies, as well as the Spanish were hostile to the colony. The English and Dutch colonials were prohibited from trading with the colony and it failed to receive support from the British Crown. It was finally dislodged by a group of Spanish marines. All that survived from that colony was the name Caledonia.[1] In 1701, because of his surveys, Paterson wrote that he thought an Isthmian canal could be established in the area with an income of $150,000,000 dollars a year. It would mean, half the voyage time to China, and double the consumption of European commodities in Asia. His attempt at a canal project also failed, and with it, any further attempt for a canal for the major part of the 18th century.[2]

THE FRENCH AND INDIAN WAR, OR THE SEVEN YEARS WAR

The French and Indian War that began in 1754 was a struggle by the British and the French over control of the Ohio River Valley and control of the North American colonies. The Seven Years War was, in fact, a global conflict—involving the British, Prussia, and Hanover, against France, Austria, Sweden, Saxony, Russia, and eventually Spain—that began in 1756 and ended in 1763.

---

[1] Senate Executive Doc. No. 62 (39th Congress, 1st session), p. 12.
[2] 1947, Miles P. Duval Jr., "Cadiz to Cathay.", pp. 10-12.

In 1754, while George Washington, participated in the French and Indian War by attacking a French detachment in the Ohio Valley, the Spanish again attacked the English woodcutters in Belize, but failed to dislodge them. This act caused the English settlers to resume their effort to spread their settlements, and the Spanish were resigned to allow English settlements from the Rio Hondo in the north to the entire eastern coast of Central America, including the offshore islands.

In 1756, the English tried to enlist the Spanish to their side at the beginning of the Seven Years War by offering the Spanish all the settlements along the mainland of Central America, but the Spanish sided with the French. In the end, the British and the American colonists defeated the French in the north, and Spain was forced to give up its holdings in Florida, because of its part in the struggle.[3]

At the end of this struggle, both France and England were financially exhausted. Ironically, it was the end of this war, and the near financial bankruptcy of England, that set up the elements of conflict between the American colonies and Britain some twelve years later. The English decided to look to the American colonies for their financial recovery.

On February 10, 1763, the Treaty of Paris was signed, ensuring England's domination of all of North America east of the Mississippi River, except New Orleans. Spain was given Havana, in exchange for Florida, and in addition, England was required to demolish all of its fortifications in the bay of Honduras, but it allowed the English woodcutters to work anywhere along the eastern shore of Central America.

In 1775, the Mosquitoland formally became a Dependency of Jamaica. In Belize, the woodcutters set up their own government, and resisted any attempt by Spain to remove them. The governor of Jamaica was instructed to protect them as well. The Spanish settlers took this problem into their own hands and went to war with the woodcutters and their Indian allies.

In 1779, Charles III of Spain directed Manuel Galisteo to investigate the possibility of a Nicaragua route to the East Indies. In 1781, he reported that Lake Nicaragua was 134 feet above sea level. (Today it is considered 104 feet above mean sea level.) He reported that high mountains exist between the lake and the Pacific, and a canal was impractical. However, British agents accompanied Galisteo on his expedition and claimed the area they explored as the sovereign territory of the Kingdom of the Mosquito Indians. These agents later declared

---

[3] U.S. Senate Executive Doc. No. 154, loc, cit., pp. 73 ff.

that the Nicaragua canal route was feasible.[4] Even then, the importance of this territory was recognized. Dalling, the governor of Jamaica, said it best by stating: "In order to give a facility to the great object of government, and to fulfill that which is incumbent upon me, I intend to possess the Lake of Nicaragua, by means of our first conquest; which, for the present, may in some degree be looked upon as the inland Gibraltar of Spanish America. As it commands the only water pass between the Lake of Nicaragua and the northern ocean, its situation must ever render it a principle post, to ensure success to our troops forcing their passage to the South Sea; and by our possession of it, Spanish America is severed in two." [5]

THE REVOLUTIONARY WAR

In 1779, Spain again took up arms with France and the American colonies against England. While the war was raging in the north between the British and the northern colonies, the Spanish sent a force to remove the woodcutters from Belize. They were turned away by British warships already dispatched from Jamaica. The British decided, once and for all, to remove the Spanish colonies inland by moving up the San Juan River with eighteen hundred men. Before they could carry out their plan, disease swept the force, and they turned back with 300 survivors.

Having been informed of the British failure, the Spanish governor of Guatemala moved south with a large force of men and forced the woodcutters south into Honduras.

The British fleet engaged the French fleet off the coast of Dominica and dispersed them. Again, on August 28, 1782, with a force of one thousand men, the British marched north to the Black River and forced the Spanish commander to surrender.

The Revolutionary War was coming to an end, and of course, England had lost to the northern colonies. In 1783, at the Treaty of Versailles, the British were forced to give up many of the claims that they had held in Central America. The woodcutters were given the right to cut wood in and around Belize, while the Mosquitolands were to be abandoned by the British settlers.

Spain was to be sovereign over Nicaragua from sea to sea. That treaty was to become enforceable eighteen months after the exchange of the ratification. However, nothing was done, no action was taken by Spain to enforce the treaty.

---

[4] Senate Doc. No. 54 (57th Congress, 1st session). Pp.435-436.
[5] 1947, Miles P. Duval Jr., "Cadiz to Cathay.", pp. 14-15.

After eighteen months, Spain complained to the English government. The British again engaged Spain in modifying the treaty more favorably for the British and the woodcutters, and the treaty, as modified, was finally ratified on July 14, 1786.

An interesting story occurred during the Revolutionary War. On February 14, 1779, Benjamin Franklin, acting as the ambassador to France, was given a letter and a manuscript entitled "Projet de Paix Perpetuelle, par P.A.G.," and was asked to publish it. The author, Pierre-Andre Garza, was a galley slave, serving a twenty-year sentence for murder. The documents were put aside. In March 1781, upon completing his sentence, and in 1782, Garza again approached Franklin. After reading the manuscript, Franklin printed it on his private press in Passy. Aside from his recommendation of encouraging the circulation of money by constructive enterprise rather than war, Garza posed the following: "There is the Isthmus of Panama in America and that of Suez between Asia and Africa; these two isthmuses prevent the junction of four seas and are the reason that to go around the world by water requires about three years and exposes one to stormy and very often icy seas and uninhabitable coasts. Each of these two isthmuses must be cut from one sea to the other by a canal about sixty feet wide, thirty feet deep and about forty leagues long; by means of these two canals one will make the tour of the terrestrial globe, by water, in about ten months, and upon seas that are always good for navigation and very convenient for the establishment upon all the coasts, therefore, new and very beneficial trade between many nations."[6]

Foto de Benjamin Franklin

---

[6] 1947, Miles P. Duval Jr., "Cadiz to Cathay.", pp. 17-18.

After Thomas Jefferson replaced Franklin as minister in Paris, he remained interested in the subject, and sent correspondence, in 1787 and May 27, 1788, on the subject to William Carmichael, the chargé d'affaires at Madrid. His latest letter stated: With respect to the Isthmus of Panama, I am assured by Burgoine (who would not choose to be named, however) that a survey was made, that a canal appeared very practicable, and that the idea was suppressed for political reasons altogether. He has seen and minutely examined the report. This report is to me a vast desideratum, for reasons political and philosophical.

I cannot help suspecting the Spanish squadron to be gone to South America, and that some disturbances have been excited there by the British."[7]

Photo of Thomas Jefferson

---

[7] Thomas Jefferson, Writings, Official and Private, II, 325-326, 397.

Photo of the Revolutionary War

THE WAR OF 1812 AND THE NAPOLEONIC WARS

By 1796, England, Spain, and France were again at war. The British, again moved to displace the Spanish and French settlements along the Caribbean islands. Again the Guatemalan colonists sent a large force to remove the woodcutters from Belize, and again the Jamaican governor sent warships to defeat that Spanish force. The woodcutters, no longer bound by the treaty of 1786, enlarged their area of encroachment into the interior, and declared it theirs by right of conquest.

To the United States, the War of 1812 was centered around the right of free trade with any other country, the British impression of U.S. seamen into its Royal Navy, the British support of American Indian tribes against American expansion to the northwest, and other British insults on the high seas.

The vote to declare war against England was one of the closest in United States history. The United States was divided between the Federalist Party, which favored a strong central government and close ties with England, and the Democratic-Republican Party, which advocated a weak central government, the right to own slaves, expansion into Indian lands, and weaker ties with England. The Federalists were in the northern states, and the Democratic- Republicans were predominately located in the southern states.

The Canadians considered the United States' declaration of war against England as a veiled attempt to absorb Canada as part of the United States.

The prosecution of the War of 1812 resulted in several back and forth battles on the Great Lakes, the burning of York and the village of Newark by the Americans, the burning of Washington and Buffalo by the English, the unsuccessful British attempt to take Baltimore at Fort McHenry, where the lyrics of the "Star Spangled Banner" were first described, and the equally unsuccessful British and American battle at New Orleans. Both the Americans and the British used Native Americans as allies during this war, but it was Andrew Jackson, in March of 1814, that led a force of Indians, Tennessee militia, and U.S. regulars that decimated the Creeks and forced them to surrender. Jackson also participated in the battle of New Orleans on January 8, 1815, in which the British forces were also decimated with little losses by the forces of Jackson.

In the end, the Treaty of Gent was signed by diplomats on December 24, 1814, ratified by the British on December 27, 1814, and by the United States on February 17, 1815. The treaty prescribed that all parties return to their prewar boundaries.

In 1817, the Great Lakes, under the Rush–Baget Treaty, were to be described as neutral, demilitarized territory. The U.S. gained fishing rights on the Saint Lawrence River. Mobile and parts of western Florida remained a part of the United States, despite complaints by Spain. The issues that began the war were ignored. Ironically, several thousand American slaves were able to escape to the British side, and many were given immigration status in Canada, and in 1816, many were given property rights in Trinidad. Also, at the end of the war, the British paid the slave owners reparations, after arbitration by the Czar of Russia.

Photo of Andrew Jackson

The British considered this war as a distraction from the one in Europe, and to a lesser degree, the Caribbean. For the first two years, Britain maintained a defensive posture. They had built the largest navy in the world and used it to establish a successful blockade around Spain and Portugal and the rest of Europe. They also set up a blockade on the east coast of the United States that was not so successful. Their purpose was to destroy the economic power of the French government and remove the Spanish and French colonies from the Caribbean. It wasn't until after the abdication of Napoleon, on April 6, 1814, that the British turned their full attention to the war against the United States.

The French prosecution of the Napoleonic Wars can only be described as the ambition of one man. In 1799, Napoleon installed himself as first consul of France, and in 1804, he was declared emperor. The Peninsular War of 1812 and the French invasion of Russia began the downfall of the emperor's power. By 1813, his forces were defeated and he was exiled to the island of Elba. In 1814, he escaped, returned to power, and was again defeated at the Battle of Waterloo in June of 1815.

Photo of Napoleon

1814, THE TREATY OF MADRID

By 1814, at the Treaty of Madrid between Spain and England, this struggle left the Spanish in control of the Nicaraguan canal route, the Mosquitos still controlled their shores, the woodcutters still controlled the land they seized, but the Spanish monopoly of the Spanish Main and the West Indies was lost forever. In short, all the treaties and all the conflicts that had led up to the 1814 Treaty of Madrid left the Central American area essentially as it was, with the exception that the British had extended their positions, starting in Belize, to Jamaica, the Bahamas, the Barbados, Trinidad, and British Guiana, enclosing the eastern shore of the Caribbean Sea.

CANAL PROJECTS

During the period of all these conflicts, little research was done regarding a possible Isthmian canal. What was done by LaCondamine, Boucuer, and Godin in 1735 and 1740 was nothing more than a scientific foundation. In 1770, the viceroy of Mexico was instructed to devise a plan for a canal across the Isthmus of Tehuantepec, but nothing further was done, and eventually, Charles II of Spain, as stated above, directed his efforts further south to Nicaragua, and he directed a study in Nicaragua. The report was not favorable for Spain.

In 1788, as I mentioned above, the Spanish built a road from the Caledonian Bay, over the Panama divide, and down to the sea. However, when the inhabitants, the Bravos, forced Spain to sign a treaty, even this route was abandoned. Between 1800–1815, the Napoleonic wars caused all interest in an Isthmian canal to cease.

THE HUMBOLDT STUDY

During these years, only the writings of Alexander Von Humboldt, a German scientist, drew any interest related to an Isthmian canal. His work was considered the detailed foundation of all the possible canal routes from the Atlantic to the Pacific Ocean. On March 3, 1793, he described the Nicaragua route as the most favorable.

Ferdinand VII, with the help of the British, was reinstated, and reigned under a constitution, in contrast to the despotism of Bonaparte. Seeking the newfound glory of Spain, Cortez took Humboldt's canal theory, and tried to apply it to the first "Atrato–Napipi" route, located in modern-day Colombia. The effort met with total failure, and it was the last Spanish effort to undertake an Isthmian canal.

THE LAST OF THE WESTERN ABSOLUTE MONARCHS

After the United States Revolution, the rule of the absolute monarchs was coming to an end. First England, and then in 1789, France broke the chains of the monarchs of Europe. Gradually, constitutional monarchs or republics took their place. A new player was starting to emerge in Central and South America. After breaking with England, the United States expanded west. They felt it necessary to defend this continent from any attempted encroachment from the European powers, which were still intent on the establishment of colonies in Central America and the western area of the United States.

THE REVOLT IS ON

The Spanish colonies, dissatisfied with their station, one by one, attempted to revolt from their European rulers while the wars were being waged on the European continent. Under Simon Bolivar, in 1811, the New Grenadians were the first to revolt. After several years of fighting, in 1821, Bolivar finally established the Independent Republic of Colombia, consisting of all the provinces of New Grenada, Venezuela, and Ecuador. Although short lived, the federation put forth the idea that all men were guaranteed freedom, and slavery was abolished.

In September of 1821, the City of Guatemala, followed suit, and declared its independence. In April of 1823, Mexico, under Santa Anna, declared its independence. Under General Filisola, Guatemala, Honduras, San Salvador, Nicaragua, and Costa Rica formed the Independent Federal Republic of the United Provinces of Central America, and they all abolished slavery.

Among these provinces, the concept of slavery was in direct conflict with those of the United States, and it was a major problem in how they viewed the United States for many years to come. However, the United States immediately recognized the complete independence of these countries and sent a formal mission to consult regarding their future actions.

THE HOLY ALLIANCE AND THE REASONS FOR THE MONROE DOCTRINE

The Monarchs in Eastern Europe and the temporarily restored dynasties of Spain and France formed their "Holy Alliance" to crush these rebellions. The Czar of Russia was already encroaching on our own northwestern territories. The intent was to bring these Central American countries back under the rule of the restored Spanish monarchy. The newly restored Bourbons of France had devised their own plan by using the work of Bolivar, who recently declared himself dictator in South America, and Iturbide, who had all but established the same in Mexico. The Bourbons' goal was to establish princes of their own blood to rule over these Spanish American empires.

In 1820, Monroe was reelected, and set about confronting the Holy Alliance and their objectives. Initially, England decided that the Holy Alliance was not in their best interest and suggested that the United States and Britain work together in opposing Spain and France in Central and South America.

Monroe sought the advice of Thomas Jefferson, who in his return letter, emphasized the importance of the situation, and danger to the United States, likening it to no less than the act of independence by the United States from England, and went on to advise Monroe that there should be no European interference in the affairs of the Central, and South American countries, and likewise the United States should not get involved in the affairs of Europe. Taking this advice, Monroe incorporated it into his address to the Congress in 1823, and emphasized that any European country that acted contrary to these principles would be committing an unfriendly act against the United States. By the time of this address, the United States was becoming an economic, and world power. Our country was expanding west rapidly, but we had no effective way to protect our western shores from any country that cared to attack us.

Photo of Monroe

SLAVERY BECAME AN ISSUE

President Adams succeeded Monroe, and as he was known to support Monroe in the principles of his doctrine, Adams reinforced it in every way he could. Congress, on the other hand, did not. After he was elected, Adams brought up the issue before the Congress in the form of a resolution of support, and both houses of Congress refused to pass it. Part of the reason for the congressional lack of support was partisan, and part of that lack of support was the fact that the representatives of the slave states were reluctant to support the Central and South American countries that had declared in their constitution anti-slavery sentiment. These countries had taken a different fork in the road than that taken by the United States. The slave states in the United States depended on slavery for their very existence. The United States depended on these slave states for its very existence when declaring its independence from England.

England, having considered the Monroe Doctrine a threat to its own aspirations in Central America, joined forces with the French cabinet in recognizing the Southern Republics for Great Britain. They then declared the whole of the unoccupied parts of the United States to be open to future settlements by European powers. In short, by 1823, all of Europe lined up against the concept of the Monroe Doctrine put forth by the United States.

All of these Central and South American countries had modeled their institutions after the pattern of the United States, with that one exception, slavery. We had put ourselves on record, on their behalf, and they looked to us for support.

THE PANAMA CONGRESS

Bolivar, intent on creating an empire, proposed a "Congress of American Nations" to meet in Panama. On June 1826, a formal invitation was presented to the United States, as head of the Congress and as the "eldest sister of the new republics." Bolivar needed the support of the United States in order to complete his plan. Adams immediately accepted and nominated envoys to the Congress. However, Adams was quick to inform the United States Congress that there was to be no attempt to form alliances or engage in hostilities with any other nation, but they were instead to engage in commercial and maritime issues, and possibly come to some agreement regarding the Monroe Doctrine with the parties at that meeting.

SLAVERY COMES TO THE SURFACE AGAIN

The House supported the objectives of Adams, which were essentially a watered-down version of the Monroe Doctrine, but the Senate rejected the idea, again on the grounds that the proposed Congress of American Nations also had, as their objective, a discussion on slavery. The southern states had refused to discuss this issue within the Congress of the United States, and they especially did not want any United States representative discussing the issue with other countries outside of the United States. The issue was finally left to the House of Representatives, who watered down the parameters the envoys could discuss even further. It seemed a waste of time even attending the assembly. Any discussion regarding the Monroe Doctrine was removed from the president's plan. However, the issue of an Isthmian canal was raised again by representatives of Panama at the same time the United States Senate was discussing the mission of our envoys to the Panama assembly.

Photo of President Adams

THE FIRST PANAMA CANAL GIVEAWAY

The minister of this new Panama republic, Don Antonio José Canaz, while in Washington, offered the State Department the canal in Panama, in perpetuity, as a joint venture between the United States and Panama. Secretary of State Clay jumped at the proposal and immediately began to set about garnering support for the idea. Knowing that he could not commit to Panama's offer in the name of the United States, and after consulting with the president, Clay profusely thanked the Panama representative, let him know that the United States was deeply interested in his offer, and left the matter open. Clay then ordered his chargé d'affaires in Central America to gather as much information as possible on the proposed canal in Nicaragua. He then worked to ensure that a proposed canal would become an integral part of the Monroe Doctrine. Eventually it was.

On June 22, 1826, the Congress of the American Nations met in Panama. Our envoys never showed. The assembly moved to Mexico, and in the end, it fell flat. Bolivar never got the support of the United States government, and he was never able to put forth his plan to become emperor of South America. The canal issue was once again laid to rest. The fact that Peru and Bolivia broke from the grip of Bolivar was the only redeeming result of this whole matter.

Photo Simon Bolivar

THE CANAL, A RENEWED INTEREST, AND THE MONROE DOCTRINE FROM SURPRISING PLACES

The collapse of the Panama Congress did set in motion the king of Holland's interest in a canal in Panama. He seriously, set about to undertake the project as a private-enterprise activity. On December 30, 1830, the Dutch obtained exclusive right of way across the territory of Central America, and a monopoly of the trade along the coast.[8]

President Jackson, under the Democrats, came to power after Adams failed to gain a second term. Surprisingly, the new United States government vigorously pursued the same foreign policy as Adams, even to the extent of sending letters to the Dutch government stating, in no uncertain terms, that, if a canal was to be built in Central America, it would be built by the United States government. In addition, Jackson directed his minister in the Netherlands to buy up the majority stock of the Holland Company, created to build the canal, so that we would have a monopoly share of the company.[9] Soon after Jackson did this, a revolution took place, and the king and his company were forced to give up the rights in Central America. In the end, it was Jackson who formalized the Monroe Doctrine, and on March 3, 1835, the United States Senate passed a resolution requesting the president to open negotiations with the governments of Central America and Granada to ensure free access to all nations through any canal that may be built

---

[8] House Report No. 322 (25th Congress, 3rd session), pp.20-32
[9] Senate Report No. 1 (57th Congress, 1st Session), p. 61.

there. There were further attempts to build a canal under Jackson's first and second term, but little more was accomplished than a second congressional resolution, passed March 2, 1839.

When president Martin Van Buren succeeded Jackson, he commissioned a detailed survey, which was done by John L. Stevens, who recommended that, if a canal was to be built, it should be built in Nicaragua. He also advised that, even so, capitalists would not rush in to invest in such an "unsettled and revolutionary" country.

THE UNSETTLED AND REVOLUTIONARY COUNTRY

After the death of Bolivar in 1830, the Republic of Colombia broke apart. The Central American Confederation had broken apart by the time Stevens had made his survey, and the Liberals, under Morazon, had moved the seat of power from Guatemala to San Salvador. In 1838, the Conservatives revolted, and open war raged. Eventually, the Conservatives gained the upper hand. The whole of Central and South America became a twelve-year conflict. With the Conservatives more or less in control, and constantly defending their own, each country was left to its own devices. These Conservatives sought support from the Catholic countries in Europe instead of the United States, and canal projects, real and imagined, were again offered. Ironically, it was Napoleon's escape from prison on May 25, 1846, and his ending up in London, where he wrote his famous pamphlet on the canal issue, in which he advocated the Nicaragua route, that changed the British attitude on the matter. Until then, the British government was convinced an Isthmian canal was impossible.

THE BRITISH MOVE TO SECURE THE NICARAGUA ROUTE

After their success in the Napoleonic wars, the breakup of the Spanish American independence movement, and the United States' expansion west, which they took as a threat to their own expansion west, the British moved to aggressively reestablish their dominance of the Mosquitoland and the eastern shores of Nicaragua.

On February 25, 1826, in the will and testament, of the late Mosquito king Robert Charles Frederick, Colonel Macdonald, the English superintendent of Belize, was appointed regent over Mosquitoland. In time, Macdonald appointed his private secretary, Patrick Walker, to act in his stead.

Walker reorganized the administration at Bluefields and set up an all-English Council of State to control the future of this area. Through the help of the Mosquito king, and that king's alliance with the Indian tribes in Costa Rica, the British obtained a large land grant south of the San Juan River that they sold to an English company, who used that grant to establish a large English colony in that area. The Costa Rican government saw this move as an opportunity to develop its commerce rather than as an encroachment, and the English moved to formalize the plan.

On March 14, 1835, Macdonald then called together the legislative assembly of Belize, renamed it British Honduras, and informed the Guatemalan government that they claimed all the land they'd held since the days of the Spanish American independence, from the Rio Hondo in the north to the Rio Sarstoon in the south. In November 1840, Macdonald then declared the laws of England to be enforced in British Honduras, Roatan, and Mosquitia. In 1841, Macdonald sent the British frigate Tweed to the island of Roatan to force the Nicaraguan government to recognize the independence of Mosquitia. The British government had not, as yet, recognized these actions taken by Macdonald, but obviously, they were not opposed to them.

The Nicaraguan government refused to accept the British demands and sought help from the Jackson administration, and later from the Harrison administration. Nothing was done of any importance to enforce the principles of the Monroe Doctrine.[10]

While Costa Rica was in favor of the British encroachment, the government of New Granada claimed jurisdiction over the whole area, including Mosquitia. They issued an order, to the British not to land English settlers, and made their claim not just against England but Costa Rica as well. Ignoring this claim, the British were paying more attention to the United States' territorial expansion to the West Coast.

The Treaty of Paris, in 1783, which settled the Revolutionary War, did not determine the exact boundary between Canada and the United States in Maine. The bloodless Aroostook War of 1838 and 1839, between the British and the State of Maine, led to the settlement known as the Webster–Ashburton Treaty and finally settled the boundary line in this dispute in 1842. However, it did not settle the Oregon Country dispute. The dispute over this territory, once claimed by Spain, Russia, Great Britain, and the United States, was temporarily settled when the United States and Britain signed the Anglo–American Convention of 1818, in

---

[10] U.S. Senate Ex. Doc. No. 27, 32nd Congress, 2nd Session.

which the United States and Britain agreed to a joint occupancy of the territory. Spain and Russia had dropped their claims to the land. However, from 1818 until 1840, the British claimed as their own this territory and all the territory on the west coast of Canada all the way to the boundary of Alaska.

In 1833, the British claimed the Falkland Islands from the Argentine government in order to secure and control the route by sea around South America. The English first landed in the Falklands in 1690, and had continued to claim it as a British territory since then. In addition, the British government finally moved to formalize the actions taken by Colonel Macdonald, their administrator in Belize, or British Honduras, and they were ready to take control of the Nicaraguan canal route. In 1848, the British government informed the government of Nicaragua that the Mosquito king intended to reassume control of the San Juan River. A back-and-forth skirmish took place, but the soldiers of Nicaragua were no match for the overwhelming power of the British naval forces.

Having taken control of the eastern mouth of the proposed canal, the English set about making plans to secure the mouth of the Pacific end of that proposed canal. To do so, they needed to control the Bay of Fonseca, located in Honduras. Ironically, the English were relying on the writings of Napoleon and his description of the best canal route in Nicaragua to direct their actions. Given that they could gain control of the Bay of Fonseca, the English were convinced that they could peacefully negotiate for a right of way in Nicaragua.[11] Our own government was fully aware of the aggressive actions taken by the British against the Nicaraguan government, but the Polk administration chose not to act until it was almost too late.

THE MEXICAN–AMERICAN WAR, THE POLITICAL FIGHT OVER SLAVERY, AND THE EXPANSION WEST

By 1846, the United States was fully involved in the Mexican–American War. It was the annexation of Texas in 1845 that caused Mexico to declare war on the United States, but it was the policy of territorial expansion by the Polk administration behind the annexation of Texas. The Polk government was determined to expand the territory of the United States to the Pacific, and claim Northern California as our own. In 1841, there had been plenty of indications that the English might establish a colony in California and would do so "by all means desirable."

---

[11] 31st Congress, 1st session, house Ex. Doc. No. 75; 32nd Congress, 2nd Session, Senate Ex. Doc. No. 27.

The Oregon Territory had yet to be resolved, and, despite an agreement between the British and the United States for joint occupancy, from 1818 to 1840, the British considered this territory as their own.

In 1842, our own envoy in Mexico suggested that the Mexican government might be willing to cede California to settle some of the debts they had incurred against United States citizens during the Mexican War of Independence. Initially, Polk sent an envoy to Mexico City with an offer of twenty-five million dollars for the Rio Grande border in Texas, and Mexico's Upper California and New Mexico. Polk also offered to forgive the three million owed to the United States by Mexico.

This offer fell on deaf ears. The Mexican government could not negotiate with the United States even if they wanted to. In 1846, the government changed hands four times, and for all practicable purposes, no one seemed to be in charge. Slidell's offer was considered an insult to the Mexican people, and to a new nationalist government that shortly came to power.

The Polk administration was not without its own problems. The country was divided between the Democrats in the South led by Polk, who supported the war, and the northern Whigs who opposed the war. Southern Democrats viewed the war as a right of expansion, and a means of adding slave-owning territory to the country. The Whigs wanted to expand the economy without adding any new land. The Whigs were also adamantly opposed to slavery. It was this war, more than any other that sowed the seeds for the Civil War to come. In the end, the United States won the war with Mexico, and on February 2, 1848, the Treaty of Guadalupe Hidalgo was signed by the American diplomat Nicholas Trist, and the Mexican plenipotentiaries Luis G. Cuevas, Bernardo Couto, and Miguel Atristain. The United States established the border of the United States and Mexico at the Rio Grande River, and gained control of Nevada, Oklahoma, Utah, present-day California, New Mexico, Arizona, Kansas, Wyoming, most of Texas, and Colorado. Mexico received a little over eighteen million dollars, which was less than half what the United States had offered Mexico before the war for even less territory. The United States also agreed to forgive the three million dollars Mexico owed the United States for the Texas–Mexican War of independence. In May 26, 1848, the treaty was ratified with two amendments, one giving Mexicans living in the territories now controlled by the United States the right to become U.S. citizens, and the other denying the legitimacy of Mexican land grants within these United States territories. The United States also pledged the suppression of Indian raids against Mexico, and restitution to the victims of the raids that it could not prevent. On December 30, 1853, the United States was released from this latter pledge when Mexico and the United States signed the Gadsden Purchase Treaty, transferring this northern territory to the jurisdiction of the United States.

Photo of President Polk

THE OREGON TERRITORY; ANOTHER WAR WAS BREWING

While Colonel Macdonald, the British representative in Belize, was busy attempting to secure control over the Nicaraguan canal route and encroaching on the sovereignty of the government of Nicaragua, United States citizens were pouring into the Oregon Territory.[12] The Oregon Trail, created in 1843, made the passage to the West Coast possible by wagon train, and avoided most of the dangers, securing a passage further south through the hostel Indian country on the Great Plains and over the higher reaches of the Rocky Mountains. By 1883 and the "Great Migration," the Oregon Territory was overwhelmed with United States citizens. This migration was met by threats from the House of Commons in Great Britain and the possibility of war. There were many in the United States that would welcome such a confrontation. They raised the cry of "Fifty-four-forty

---
[12] Senate Ex. Doc. 194, 47th congress, 1st session pp 67-81.

or fight," referring to the territory from California to the Alaskan boundary. The people that did settle within the Pacific shores of the United States were violently opposed to the British control in this area. They were aware of the British support of the Indian attacks, in peace and in war, against the United States settlers moving west.

On April 23, 1844, Polk, prior to taking office, and as the leader of the Democrats, clearly expressed his intent to annex Texas, control the Oregon Territory, and remove all British foreign encroachment within the territory of the United States.

It wasn't until the Oregon Treaty of 1846 that the British agreed to give up their claim to this territory and establish the 49th parallel as the official boundary between the United States and Canada in the Northwest. In exchange, Britain was allowed to keep the territory above the 49th parallel to the boundary of Alaska.

THE GOLD RUSH IS ON

One week before the end of the Mexican–American War, gold was discovered in California. This discovery caused an even greater immigration to the Pacific coast by United States citizens eager to strike it rich. There was an even greater need to find a safe and timely route to the Pacific coast of the United States.

A RETURN TO THE CANAL ISSUE, ALMOST TOO LATE, AND THE FIRST SIGN OF CRONY CAPITALISM THAT NEARLY LED TO WAR

While professing ignorance to the actions of the British in Central America, the Polk administration took several actions to ameliorate the problem. After the Mexican–American War, the Polk administration attempted to establish a Tehuantepec right of way across Mexico. Though it was officially accepted by the Mexican government, that government did everything possible to put obstacles in the way of our attempt to build that right of way.

Frustrated by this lack of cooperation by Mexico, the Polk government turned to the New Republic of Granada, which had been involved in over a decade of strife and was eager to enter into a treaty with the United States. Ironically, neither the British nor the French, at this time, thought the lower Isthmus worthy of a canal route effort. The democratic government of Polk was left with a free hand to pursue their goal of expansion. Both the Liberals and the Conservatives in New Granada, now known as Colombia, were anxious, by this time, to save their country from total ruin. On December 12, 1846, the United States and New Granada negotiated the Mallarino–Bidlack Treaty, giving the United States extensive transit rights and the right to militarily intervene in the affairs on the lower Isthmus if any hostility jeopardized those transit rights. The treaty also gave the United States the right to come to the aid of the New Granada government, as the sovereign of the territory, if requested. In short, that treaty gave the United States political control of the San Blas, Panama, Caledonian, and Atrato canal routes, and the neutrality of those routes. This treaty was formally known as the Treaty of Peace, Friendship, Commerce, and Navigation. On June 10, 1848, it was agreed to by the United States, and New Granada.[13]

In addition, even while the Mexican–American War was still raging, the Polk administration appointed Elijah Hise the United States chargé d'affaires to Guatemala to resist British encroachment in Central America, especially in Nicaragua. Hise was also directed to try to negotiate treaties of friendship and commerce with the Central American states interested in opposing British aggression.

In 1849, Hise reported that the British were attempting to control all the known routes through Lake Nicaragua and requested that he be given authority to negotiate a treaty to counteract the British. In the end, Hise negotiated the Hise–Selva Treaty, and signed it on June 21, 1849.[14] The treaty provided for a railroad right of way, or canal, in perpetuity, and guaranteed the integrity of Nicaragua. It established the right of the United States to establish fortresses at the mouth of the San Juan River, and it ignored the Mosquito claims. In short, it confronted the claims of the British in every way.[15] As Hise was being applauded by the press in the United States for his work in Nicaragua, the Polk administration was being replaced by the Whigs, led by the Taylor administration. Taylor's administration was opposed to the expansionist policies of the Polk administration, and took the position that Hise acted without authorization. The Taylor government immediately relieved Hise, and appointed Ephraim G. Squier to take his place. The Hise–Selva Treaty was subsequently rejected by the Nicaragua government, and the treaty was never presented to the Senate for discussion.

Squier was instructed to negotiate with Nicaragua for a commercial treaty in the interest of the "American Atlantic Ship Canal Company," and to secure a canal open to all. He was also instructed not to commit to any alliances, con-

---

[13] U.S. Ex. Doc. No. 69, 30th Congress, 1st session.

[14] Senate Report No. 1 (57th Congress, 1st session), pp. 313-321.

[15] House Ex. Doc. No. 75 (31st Congress, 1st Session), p. 5; Senate rep. No. 1, 57th congress, 1st session pp313-21.

troversies, or speculative schemes.[16] Working against British obstructionism, on August 29, 1849, Squier negotiated a contract with the company of Cornelius Vanderbilt, Joseph L. White, Nathaniel H. Wolfe, and others.[17] On September 23, 1849, through the effort of Squier, the company was able to secure a favorable concession with Nicaragua. The concession enabled the company to establish a canal from Greytown, or any other point on the Atlantic, to any point on the Pacific Ocean. It gave the company the right to establish American colonies along the right of way, and it gave the company exclusive rights to steam navigation on Nicaragua lakes and rivers. Squier also signed a treaty, formally assuring the company of its rights in this contract. Squire included in that treaty the guarantee of neutrality of that canal, and the obligation of the United States to recognize and defend Nicaragua's right of sovereignty, and included a clause offering any other nation the right to negotiate with Nicaragua on the same terms.[18] Also, in September 1849, Squier negotiated a treaty with Honduras, in which Honduras ceded Tiger Island for eighteen months and granted the United States the right to establish a naval base in the Bay of Fonseca. Honduras had been forced to cede the Bay of Fonseca to the British, and they were more than happy to sign a treaty with the United States that would retain their sovereignty over that area.

The British moved to reassert their control in this area. In October 1849, they moved troops to seize Tiger Island, raised the British flag there, and refused to withdraw. Squier gave the British six days to withdraw, and the British evacuated the island in December 1849. Again, war between the British and the United States was avoided.[19]

THE PANAMA RAILROAD

Taking advantage of the Mallarino–Bidlack Treaty of December 12, 1846—agreed to on June 10, 1848—between the United States and New Granada, a contract between the government of New Granada and the Panama Railroad Company was completed. After surveying the best transit route, Colonel George W. Hughes found a depression of only 287 feet between Navy Bay, on the Atlantic side of the Isthmus of Panama, and the town of Panama on the Pacific side of the

---

[16] House Ex Doc. No. 75, 31st Congress, 1st session p 108; pp 119-30.
[17] Senate Report No. 1 (57th Congress, 1st session), pp. 321-327.
[18] 1st House Ex. Doc. No. 75, 31st Congress, 1st, pp 118-185; Senate Ex. Doc. No. 194, 47th Congress session, p.49.
[19] Senate Report No. 1, 57th Congress, 1st session, pp 321-27; Senate Ex. Doc. No.27, 32nd congress, 2nd session pp 13-15.

Isthmus. The distance between the Atlantic and Pacific Oceans was a little over forty-seven miles long, and 263 feet in elevation. The company was essentially a private company. Most of the funding was derived from investments from the northern states, with the British contributing the rest. The promoters of the company were William Henry Aspinwall, the founder of the Pacific Mail Steamship Company, John L. Stevens, Henry Chauncey, and others. But John L. Stevens was considered the motivator of the enterprise. The company was supervised by the engineers Colonel Totten and Mr. Trautwine.

Interestingly, even while the 1848 treaty was being considered, on May 10, 1847, a contract was signed by Jaun de Francisco Martin, on behalf of New Granada, and Mateo Klein, on behalf of a French company, granting Martin a ninety-nine-year concession to build and operate a railroad across the Panama Isthmus. The contract was approved by legislative decree on June 8, 1847. The contract was never carried out and the concession was terminated. On June 12, 1849, the rights were transferred to William Aspinwall and others, who formed the Panama Railroad Company.[20] In 1848, the United States Congress authorized contracts for two steamship lines to provide services to the Isthmus of Panama. The line between New Orleans, New York, and the town of Chagres, on the Atlantic side of the Isthmus, was granted to George Law, and considered profitable. The line between Panama and California and Oregon was granted to Aspinwall and was not considered profitable. Aspinwall took the contract on the basis that he could eventually create a transportation system in which a railroad could connect the two mail lines, and make possible a commercial enterprise connecting the Pacific basin, China, Australia, the East Indies, California, and Oregon.

On April 7, 1849, the company then went to the New York legislature to obtain a charter. The stock was initially set at one million dollars, with the right to raise it to five million dollars. It was later amended to seven million dollars on April 2, 1855.

The lines set for the railroad were generally the same as those laid out in 1827 and 1843: along the Chagres River and running southwest of the Continental Divide. The first controversy encountered by the company resulted from the choice of the Atlantic terminal. George Law, the Atlantic mail contractor, bought up real estate around Porto-Bello, the original selection for the Atlantic terminal, and he expected to sell it at a high price. Instead, the company changed the proposed terminal to Limon Bay, and Manzanillo Island, located just west of the historic City of Porto-Bello.

---

[20] House report 145, 30th Congress, 2nd session pp 1-31.

The original plan of the company was to start the project at Gorgona, located about in the center of the Isthmus, and by working south, the company could eliminate the hazardous pack mule trip to Panama City. However, the company encountered a problem. The river level was too low to accommodate the river steamers used to move along the Chagres River. In August of 1850, the company was forced to start work on the Atlantic side of the Isthmus. They immediately met the first major obstacle encountered by the project. The workers were confronted by an almost insurmountable pestilence of heat, swamps, disease, sand fleas, alligators, mosquitoes, and other bugs that made it almost impossible to work without covering themselves with netting. After work, it was impossible to remain on land, and the workers were forced to retreat to Limon Bay and a floating barracks. Even then, the men refused to sleep below deck, because of the sand fleas and mosquitoes. In a short time, the company was forced to purchase the steamer Telegraph, which was considered less inhospitable.

Realizing that the project was not going to be an easy fifty-mile railroad project they had originally contemplated, on April 15, 1850, Colonel Totten and John L. Stevens negotiated a new contract with the Minister of Foreign Affairs Victoriano de Diego Paredes, who represented the New Granada government. The new contract was approved by the New Granada legislature on June 4, 1850. This contract became the basic contract for the Panama Canal Railroad Company. The gold rush of 1848 also caused a problem in completing the railroad. It forced the company to finish the project as quickly as possible. With the Nicaragua transit route in constant turmoil, many of the "forty-niners," chose the Panama route as a safe and quick route to California. This event changed the project from a long-range project to a short-range profit-motivated project. Even before the railroad was completed, people were clamoring to ride the train no matter how short the ride. Manpower was at a premium, not just because of the competition of the gold fields in California, but also because of the pestilence and diseases prevalent on the Isthmus of Panama. Yellow fever was the disease on everyone's mind, and for good reason. No one knows how many people died building the Panama Railroad. The only records kept were by the railroad company itself, and those records were consistently, and notoriously low.

On February 29, 1852, at a cornerstone building ceremony attended by Stevens, George Law, by then a director of the Railroad Company, Minor C. Story of New York, R. Webb of Manzanillo Island, and Victoriano de Diego Paredes, the ex-foreign affairs minister of New Granada, changed the name of Manzanillo Island on the Limon Bay to the town of Aspinwall. Aspinwall replaced the terminal City of Chagres. At the insistence of the New Granada government, the name of the town of Aspinwall was eventually changed to Colon to honor the explorer Columbus.

Most historians, to illustrate the difficulty encountered in crossing the Isthmus, point to the well documented July 16, 1852, crossing made by then-Captain Ulysses S. Grant and the eight companies, including their families, of the Fourth Infantry that crossed with him. After four weeks on the Isthmus, the regiment reached California. Of the original seven hundred men, eighty men, and as many of the women and children accompanying the regiment, died.[21]

Even John L. Steven succumbed to the pestilence on the Isthmus and died on October 13, 1852. By September 14, 1852, only one tenth of the work on the contract had been completed. The cost of the passage on pack mule increased from two dollars, in 1850, to eighteen dollars in 1853. William C. Young replaced Stevens, and in a short time, Young was replaced by David Hoadley. The company was again reorganized. Everything was imported, included the workforce. Men from almost every country around the world were recruited, but none seemed to withstand the hardships and pestilence of the Panama Isthmus. Only West Indians and Jamaicans seemed to be able to withstand the climate and work for any length of time.

Eventually, the railroad was formally opened on February 15, 1855, and the gold seekers, and others, were able to transit the forty-seven miles of the Panama Isthmus from Aspinwall to Panama City by rail. In 1859, the final cost of completing the construction was about eight million dollars. The final cost in lives, estimated by Colonel Totten, was 6,000. The cost of a one-way transit across the Isthmus was twenty-five dollars.

---

[21] Dr. C.S. Tripler, Report of the regimental Surgeon, Forth Infantry, to Surgeon General, September 14, 1852.

Photo of the beginning of Railroad Construction

Photo of Railroad Locomotive in Panama Canal Railroad

Photo of Box Cars used as living Quarters

A UNITED STATES FOREIGN POLICY POSITION, A DISASTER FOR FIFTY YEARS (THE CLAYTON-BULWER TREATY OF 1850)

The question should be asked, at what price was the war between Britain and the United States avoided. No sooner had Squier won a victory in Nicaragua and Honduras, even if it was a clear sign of crony capitalism, that the Taylor administration immediately acted to undercut its own representative, in favor of the British, in Nicaragua.

President Taylor felt that he could not risk, or he did not want to risk, a confrontation with Britain. One of the major policies of the Whigs was not to expand the influence of the United States outside of our borders. In addition, he was keenly aware that, although the Whigs had won the election, they did not have a majority in the Senate. He did not want the Democrats, whose major policy, apart from slavery, was to enforce the Monroe Doctrine, to force a confrontation with the British and demand reprisals over the British's aggressive behavior in the Bay of Fonseca and Tiger Island in Honduras. To put this matter at rest, President Taylor tasked his secretary of state, Clayton, to enter into negotiations with Britain, and to quickly resolve the issue.

Secretary of State Clayton decided to work in secret with the British minister, and, as an inducement, initially conceded the British claim to the Mosquitoland, and encouraged the cooperation of Britain, like the one exhibited by the construction of the Panama Railroad. When the United States minister to Britain, Mr. Lawrence, was put in place, he also worked to encourage the cooperation of Britain, but he also studied the issue of the British claim to the Mosquitoland and found it to be without merit, and an encroachment to the sovereignty of Nicaragua. [22]

Secretary of State Clayton ignored the advice given to him by Mr. Lawrence, our minister to Britain, buried his lengthy report, and hurriedly worked with the foreign minister of Britain, Henry Bulwer, before the United States Senate could interfere in the process. The British, observing this, took full advantage of the circumstances. In the end, the Clayton–Bulwer Treaty, secretly negotiated, was signed on April 19, 1850, and rushed through the Senate without much debate.

The short version of this treaty was that the British kept their claims in Central America, and the United States was restricted from any attempt at involving itself, unilaterally, in the affairs of Central America. Without any input from the Nicaragua government, the first act taken by the United States was to present the contract made by the American Atlantic Ship Canal Company to the British government for their approval. For over fifty years, because of the duplicity of the Taylor administration and the restrictions outlined in this treaty, the United States was diplomatically crippled from effectively pursuing its own interests in Nicaragua. Instead of notifying the British that the United States would no longer abide by that treaty, the United States spent fifty years trying, unsuccessfully, to interpret the treaty in terms more favorable to our own country.[23]

Taylor died three weeks after promulgating the Clayton–Bulwer Treaty. Millard Fillmore, Clayton's vice president, and a "Whig," took his place and appointed Daniel Webster as secretary of state. Webster and the English representative, Henry Bulwer, agreed that the Squier Treaty could not be effectively enforced

---

[22] Senate Ex. Doc. 194, 47th congress, 1st session pp 67-81, 82-87,88-97 .

[23] Senate Ex. Doc. 194, 47th congress, 1st session, pp 82-87,21-97, 88-97; Senate. Ex.Doc. No. 25, 34th congress, 1st session Doc. I, p4,56,84. Senate Ex. Doc. 25,34th Congress, 1st session Doc. I, p 4.

under the Clayton–Bulwer Treaty. As a result, both the Hise effort and the Squier Treaty were ignored. They also agreed that the United States and Britain would provide joint protection to the American Canal Company. To add insult to injury, the United States presented the American Canal Company's plan for the canal to the British for their approval. [24]

Photo of President Taylor

In August 1851, realizing that they could not move quickly to affect a canal route across Nicaragua, the American Canal Company decided to subcontract, and created the Accessary Transit Company, and gave it the monopoly of all the steamship navigation on all the waterways in Nicaragua. Because of the California gold rush and the massive United States immigration West, the Accessary Transit Company became an immediate success. Although the British were in control of the mouth of the San Juan River, the Accessary Transit Company set up an office at its Atlantic terminal at Greytown. That terminal eventually grew into a predominantly American town, with all the local legal and political organization one would expect of a town in the United States. This town grew up next to the "Anglo-Mosquito" settlement of Greytown. However, the Anglo-Mosquito settlement did not receive any of the benefits of the Accessary Transit Company.

In November 1851, tensions soon grew to an explosive level when the An-

---
[24] Senate Ex. Doc. 25,34th Congress, 1st session Doc. I, p.4.

glo-Mosquito customhouse officials tried to collect port charges from an American vessel, the Prometheus. The charges were refused. An arrest warrant was issued for the Prometheus's captain. Vanderbilt, president of the parent company, paid the charges and the ship was permitted to continue on its way. By December 1851, after complaining to the British, the United States accepted the explanation that the customhouse acted without authority, and the matter was dropped. Because of this incident, the American, British, Costa Rican, Nicaraguan, and even the Honduran governments entered into a protracted back-and-forth argument on the historic rights of each, and how those rights affect the Clayton–Bulwer Treaty and the canal in Nicaragua.[25]

In 1852, the British finally formalized their right to the Bay Islands of Honduras, and the United States pushed back by threatening to renounce the Clayton–Bulwer Treaty. However, nothing of importance was resolved regarding this matter.

THE CRIMEAN WAR, A DISTRACTION FOR THE BRITISH

From 1853 to 1856 the British were involved in the "Crimean War." This was a protracted war against the Russian Empire, and included the British Empire, the French Empire, the Ottoman Empire, and the Kingdom of Sardinia. Britain was forced to turn their attention to their Crimean Peninsula campaign in the east of Europe.

In 1854, while the British were occupied with their confrontation with Russia, another confrontation occurred between the Anglo-Mosquito authorities, and the Accessory Transit Company. After one of the company's ship captains killed a Mosquito Indian, the port authority attempted to arrest the captain for murder. A riot broke out, and the Americans warned the port authority that they would fire on the town if the damages caused by the mob were not paid. In July 1854, the Oyane shelled the town of Greytown and sent American marines ashore to destroy it. The American settlers then worked with the Nicaraguan government to form a provisional municipal government over the port. Because their protector, the British, was preoccupied elsewhere, the Mosquito Indian administration could not do much but complain.

Fillmore's administration was replaced by the Pierce administration and the Democrats, and their expansionist policies. Pierce owed his election to the

---

[25] Senate Ex. Doc. 27, 32nd Congress, 2nd session, Doc. 39, p 102, Doc. 40, p105; Senate Ex. Doc. 25, 34th Congress, 2nd session, Doc. 10, pp28,32-35, 38-40.

"Order of the Lone Star," a secret organization of southern activists bent on the idea of the "manifest destiny" of the United States. Pierce, as an obvious payback, offered to purchase Cuba from Spain, but the Spanish refused to sell their "jewel" of the New World. In response, Pierce let it be known that his administration was willing to take Cuba by force if need be.[26]

WALKER AND THE SLAVE STATES

During this time, Nicaragua was split between Liberals and Conservatives, with the Conservatives progressively gaining power over the Liberals. To regain control of the country, the Liberals aligned themselves with the American settlers, who had chosen a man by the name of William Walker as their leader. Walker was a southerner and an advocate of slavery. In 1855, Walker, with a force of fifty-eight men, secured the capital of Granada from the Conservatives and helped install a Liberal government, under Patricio Rivas as president, and with Walker in control of the forces he had organized. Walker then moved against a smaller opposing force supported by the British and forced them out of Nicaragua. Walker then seized the Transit Company and all its properties.

The British then turned to Costa Rica to confront Walker. With a large force of men, Costa Rica forced Walker into Granada and reclaimed all the properties of the Transit Company.

The American agent in Nicaragua, John Wheeler, sympathetic to Walker's cause, reported the Costa Rican invasion to Washington, and, with documents given to him by Walker, was able to prove that Britain intended to take over the Nicaraguan route by force.

The Monroe Doctrine again came to the fore in the United States Congress, at least verbally. Walker, taking Congress's action as support, removed Rivas as president of Nicaragua, installed himself in his stead, annulled Nicaragua's anti-slavery law, and claimed Nicaragua in the name of the slave states of the United States. The Liberal Nicaraguans immediately abandoned Walker and joined forces with the Conservatives, the Costa Ricans, and Hondurans to oppose him. The United States, embarrassed by his actions, took Walker into custody, and on May 1, 1857, transported him to Panama for trial. Avoiding his trial, in November 1857, Walker returned to New Orleans, recruited another group of men, and

---

[26] Senate Ex. Doc. 9, 35th Congress, 1st Session;.Senate Ex. Doc. 8, 33rd Congress, 1st Session, House Ex. Doc. 85, 33rd Congress, 1st Session; President Pierce, 2nd Annual Message to Congress, 1854.

returned to Nicaragua. He was again arrested, by Commodore Paulding of the United States Navy, and returned to New York.

The southern states, not satisfied with Pierce as their leader, selected Buchanan as their presidential nominee, and he went on to become president. While all this was going on, Nicaragua and Costa Rica returned to their historic confrontation. Costa Rica, at least for a time, was left with complete control of the Transit Company's equipment.

The Buchanan administration finally decided that the Monroe Doctrine must be enforced. He refused to hold Walker prisoner. In turn, Walker, in June of 1860, took up arms again. This time, he landed on the Island of Roatan and was captured by the British and Honduran forces, put on trial, and shot.

By the time Walker was eliminated as a force in Nicaragua, he had destroyed any goodwill the United States may have gained in Nicaragua, and Honduras. Even the British were considered more favorably than the United States.

Photo of William Walker being executed

The transit route through Nicaragua was closed from 1857 to 1862, because of the fighting between the Conservatives and Liberals, the Walker attempt to claim Nicaragua for the slave states, and the subsequent fight to reestablish the Nicaraguan government by, first, Patricio Rivas, the deposed Liberal, then a joint Liberal–Conservative government in 1857, and finally, a Conservative government headed by General Tomas Martinez.

In 1868, the Nicaraguan transit was finally abandoned, partly because of the continued internal Nicaraguan conflict, and partly because of the competition of the Panama Railroad, which became a safer, more stable transit between the Atlantic and Pacific Oceans, patronized by the California gold seekers and immigrants anxious to settle the West Coast of the United States. [27]

IN 1856, THE BRITISH RETURN TO THE ISTHMUS

After extricating themselves from the Crimean War, the British were anxious to return to the Isthmus, and in better shape than when they left, thanks to the bungling of the United States government. It was left to President Buchanan to salvage the position of the United States in that region. He did not fare well at all. After apparently giving up on a joint control of a transit route through Nicaragua, the British, on August 10, 1856, entered two treaties with Honduras. The first declared that the British would leave the Bay Islands, and they were to be free territory with a local government of their own but under the sovereignty of Honduras. The second agreed that the British would abandon her protectorate over the Mosquito Indians in Honduras, provided that the Indians were given a reservation, with self-government, in which Honduras was given nominal sovereignty.

To counter these actions and their perceived weakness concerning the rights of the United States, President Buchanan sent his representative to Britain, George Dallas, to settle this long-standing conflict with England. The British and Dallas immediately entered the Dallas–Clarendon Treaty, and it was sent off to the United States Congress for approval. This treaty, like the two Honduran treaties, gave up control of the Bay Islands, the Mosquito Shore in Honduras, and even limited the Belize settlement. However, all of this was made conditional of the ratification of the two Honduran treaties, and the United States' support

---

[27] United States Senate Ex. Doc. 194, 47th Congress, 1st session, pp. 97-155; United States House Ex. Doc. 24, 26, 35th Congress, 1st session; Unite States Senate Ex. Doc. 9,13, and 63, 35th Congress, 1st session; President Pierce's message to Congress, May 15, 1856.; Congressional Globe 1857,1858, and 1859.

of the British right to construct and control the Honduran railroad. The United States Senate rejected the Dallas–Clarendon Treaty.[28]

After the Senate rejected that treaty, on the 28th of August 1856, President Buchanan addressed the issue in his address to Congress. The Honduran government also rejected the two treaties of 1856. Again, the Buchanan government called for the abrogation of the Clayton–Bulwer Treaty.[29]

THE UNITED STATES GETS SNOOKERED AGAIN

After being rejected over their attempt to come to terms with the United States and Honduras, and above all, to avoid the possibility of abrogating the Clayton–Bulwer Treaty, the British offered to enter arbitration with the United States and another European government. In addition, the British insisted that, if the Clayton–Bulwer Treaty was abrogated, they would fall back on the treaty of 1852, in which the United States recognized the rights of the British on the Bay Islands, British Honduras, then known as Belize, and the Mosquito Shore. The United States was well aware that any arbitration by a European government would bring into question the Monroe Doctrine, opposed by every European country. The move to abrogate the Clayton–Bulwer Treaty was again ignored, or at least lost its steam.

The British, not deterred by its early rejection, worked to gain influence on the Isthmus by helping to settle the Nicaragua–Costa Rica territorial conflict. The result was the Canas–Jerez Treaty signed on April 15, 1858. The British then moved to conclude a treaty with Guatemala, on April 30, 1859, favorable to Britain. This treaty enlarged the land held by the British in British Honduras to four times larger than they claimed in Belize in 1786.

They then concluded another treaty with Honduras on November 28, 1859, giving up all British claims, and recognizing the sovereignty of Honduras, provided the Honduran government never ceded the Bay Islands to any other country. They entered a final treaty with Nicaragua on January 28, 1860, giving up all their claims, with the right of Nicaraguan sovereignty from sea to sea, but with a nominal sovereignty over the Mosquito Indians. The Mosquito Indians were given the right of local self-government, and the administration within Mosquitia. The British made sure that they had a right to interfere in that administration if

---

[28] United States Senate Ex. Doc. 194, 47th Congress, 1st session, p 105.
[29] United States Senate Ex. Doc. 194, 47th Congress, 1st session pp 112-126.

they felt the need. These treaties were sent to the United States for approval.[30] Buchanan, addressing Congress, expressed approval for these treaties on December 3, 1860. [31]

THE BRITISH TURNED TO FOCUS ON THE SUEZ CANAL, AND THE FRENCH FILLED THE VOID

While negotiating these treaties on the Isthmus, the British had turned their attention closer to home. The Frenchman de Lesseps was given a concession from the viceroy of Egypt on November 30, 1854, to build the Suez Canal. In April 1859, the French broke ground, and the British intensified their interest. Ten years later, the Canal was built, and the world was changed. The British felt threatened. As far back as 1834, the British had proposed a railroad through Egypt, and had been turned down by Mohamed Ali Pasha, the Khedive of Egypt. In 1850, the British, with the help of 56,000 pounds, were able to convince Khedive Abbas I, of the merit of a railroad from Alexander to Cairo, 209 kilometers. In 1851, Robert Stephenson was given the contract to break ground on the project. The real work began in 1854 in Alexandria, and the project was completed in Cairo in 1856. This railroad was one of the main sources of income in Egypt before the building of the Suez Canal. Until then, the British had a near monopoly on the India trade.

The British also had the largest navy in the Western world. The British were not about to let the French, even a private French company, interfere in that income source. At the time, the British railroad was the only route to the riches of the West Indies without traveling around the continent of Africa. If a canal was to be built, the British were determined that it had to be under the control of the British government. Eventually, they succeeded in that endeavor. With the Straits of Gibraltar under British control, and the Suez Canal as a Mediterranean transit route under British control, the British route to the Orient could finally be realized in greater capacity than the railroad could ever achieve.

The British interest in an Isthmian canal seemed to take a back seat to the Suez Canal, even to the extent that they were willing to eventually accept the concept of the Monroe Doctrine.

While the British played a part in the Canas–Jerez Treaty of 1858, it was the Frenchman Felix Belly who did the heavy lifting in bringing Nicaragua and Costa Rica to the terms of their negotiated settlement. Belly used the final Nic-

---
[30] United States Senate Ex. Doc. 194, 47th Congress, 1st session, pp 100-105.
[31] United States Senate Ex. Doc. 194, 47th Congress, 1st session, p. 202.

araguan incursion of Walker to convince both Nicaragua and Costa Rica that it was in their best interests to settle their differences and work together. As his reward, in May 1858, Belly obtained a contract from Nicaragua that would run for ninety-nine years and the right to construct and operate a canal route across Nicaragua. He was given the right to all the priority and privileges once held by the American Atlantic and Pacific Ship Canal Company. In addition, the French were given the right to station two warships at each entrance of the canal, or on the lakes or on the San Juan River. [32]

President Buchanan was again faced with a conflict, not with the British, but now with the French. The Monroe Doctrine was again being contested. Buchanan sent his representative General Cass to Nicaragua to protest the Belly contract, and eventually won the day, but not because of the persuasion or even the threatening power of the United States. In time, it became clear that Belly did not have the support of the French government. On March 20, 1861, the Nicaraguan government consented to return the monopoly of the New American Transit Company back to the United States.

Photo of President Buchanan

---

[32] Foreign Affairs of the United States, 1872, p742.

LINCOLN COMES TO POWER
IN COMES CRONY CAPITALISM AND
THE ISSUE OF SLAVERY

In 1864, Lincoln focused on this issue in his address to Congress, and prematurely indicated that the issue the Monroe Doctrine had been settled in favor of the United States.[33] While Lincoln was involved in the War Between the States, Emperor Napoleon, still intent on establishing a transit route on the Isthmus, was busy establishing a monarchy in Mexico, and relying on the southern states to eventually destroy the cohesion of the United States. If Napoleon had succeeded, the Monroe Doctrine would have been a thing of the past. History, of course, caught up with him. By the time General Lee surrendered, and with the United States' pressure to convince the French to leave and give up their ambitions in Mexico and Nicaragua, Napoleon withdrew, leaving General Maximilian to face the brunt of the United States Army.

The success of the Civil War, the Emancipation Proclamation, the Transcontinental Railroad, and the Chiriquí transit line in Panama all depended on the decision of one man, Abraham Lincoln. Lincoln thought that, by making the right decision on three of these issues, he would affect the outcome of the Civil War. Only one of his decisions related to these matters either avoided or shortened the war in any significant way. It was obvious, at least to me, that Lincoln, contrary to the belief of most people today, was a man that believed that the ends justified the means. While some may think that his "real politic" attitude was a valid position during a Civil War, looking back, Lincoln's actions in violating the Constitution and suspension of the right to habeas corpus based upon his own right as commander-in-chief did not shorten the war in any significant way, and did not win him many friends in his own party, or the rest of the country.

The very fact that he was a lawyer, and the fact that he suspended habeas-corpus rights leading up to, and during, the war were minor points, unless you consider that he was well aware of his flagrant assault on the Constitution. You might say he was destroying the Constitution in order to save the Union. This act alone only reinforces my conviction that Lincoln was less concerned with the Constitution than he was determined to maintain the stability of the Union. But then it was not the only act that he did that illustrated his callous attitude toward his opponents and supporters alike. Let me explain.

---

[33] United States Ex. Doc. 56, 32nd Congress, 2nd session; United States Ex. Doc. 104, 47th Congress, 1st session, p 21.

Photo of President Lincoln

THE CIVIL WAR

Before Lincoln was a Republican, he was a Whig and, presumably, against slavery, but more importantly, against the expansion of the United States territories.

From 1800 to 1850, almost all of the territories acquired by the United States, either through purchase, treaty, or conquest, entered the Union as slave states. Building opposition to this expansion, the northern anti-slave states, more specifically the Whigs, felt economically threatened. From 1850 to 1859, the threatened conflict between these two factions became more pronounced. By 1850, the Whigs and the so-called "Know-Nothing parties" split between the northern and southern states and ceased to exist as viable political parties.

The new Republican Party advocated an end to the expansion of the slave states. In 1845 and 1858, Lincoln articulated that position. Almost all of the slave state advocates, and the abolition state advocates, on this one issue, were in agreement. They were convinced that without the expansion of the territories, slavery would eventually cease to exist. If the expansion of the slave states ceased to exist, the economy of the South would receive a deathblow from which the southern states may never recover. The agrarian economy of the South depended on slavery to exist.

To add fuel to the fire, the Supreme Court, in 1857, through the Dred Scott decision, declared that slavery was legal in the territories, as a property right, even if the majority of that territory opposed it. Even the fundamental religions of the day were split, North and South, slave state and non-slave state.

At the base of all this conflict was the simple fact that cotton, and to a lesser degree Tobacco, was king in the domestic and the world market. The slave states produced those crops, at a lower cost than any other state in the union. They could do so because they used slave labor, and the northern states did not. In addition, through the United States' acquisition of new territories, and their increased representation, the slave states, for many years, controlled Congress. They gradually lowered tariffs on predominately southern products, until the northern states could not compete on the world market. However, because of the method of producing these crops, and the destruction of the soil, the slave states needed to expand, or else cease to exist.

In time, the slave states were also aware that the new territories and the Border States were gradually moving toward the free-state position. Eventually, the country was divided into four factions, or uncompromising positions.

The first faction advocated that a historic proportional designation of free and slave territories should be constitutional. The second faction advocated that Congress should decide the question, based upon the due process of the Fifth Amendment. In short, Congress could restrict slavery, but not establish slavery. Lincoln was an advocate of this faction, but in practice, at least initially, he did not practice what he preached. The third faction advocated that the local community had the right to decide this question. The fourth faction advocated that the state had the right to make that decision.

By 1860, the slave states were openly threatening to secede from the Union, if Lincoln was elected.

Even before his election, the southern states were busy seizing federal courthouses, forts, armories, post offices, and treasury buildings located in the South. Before Lincoln took office, on March 4, 1861, seven states declared their secession.

Lincoln's answer to all of this was spelled out in his inauguration address. He declared that secession was "legally void." He promised that he would not invade the South, he would not use force to recover the post offices, and he would withdraw United States marshals and judges from those areas where federal law could not be peacefully enforced. He also stated that he did not intend to end slavery where it already existed.

Before Lincoln's inauguration speech, Buchanan, the outgoing president, was also busy trying to stop the secession from taking place. His argument was that the Dred Scott decision gave the slave states all the power they needed to continue to exist.

Of course, all of this meant nothing when, on April 12–13, 1861, the South captured Fort Sumter. The war was on.

WHAT POSITION DID EUROPE TAKE ON THE CIVIL WAR?

The European powers, for the most part, stayed out of the conflict. The English were still weak from the Crimean War, and the French, more interested in creating an empire in Mexico, were reticent to do anything without the support of the English. The French were convinced the Union would tear itself apart, and that the French could then move in to pick up the pieces.

England was economically more dependent on the food source of the North than they were the cotton and tobacco source of the South. However, early on, the English were supplying the South with arms and ammunition for cotton.

Lincoln knew that just as important to the English and the French was the issue of slavery. The English domestic and foreign relations in Canada and Central and South America were dependent upon their opposition to slavery. If the English were to retain good relations with the governments of Canada and Central and South America, and in fact their own population, they would have to support the North in the Civil War over the issue of slavery. It would seem an easy choice for Lincoln to remove any interference from the European powers by removing the South's ability to produce cotton, and at the same time, produce additional manpower for the North, simply by enlisting the freed slaves.

Working with Secretary of State Seward, Lincoln set about to convince the European powers to stay out of the war. Early on, Seward cautioned Lincoln that the best way to convince the Europeans to stay out of the war was to deliver his Emancipation Proclamation after a decisive victory against the South. The idea was to show that the South could not win the war. That victory came after September 1862, at the battle of Antietam, Maryland. There was a total loss of over 20,000 men in that battle, the greatest one-day battle in the history of the United States, and at the time, indecisive. The fact that the South was turned away was considered a great loss for the South.

The first proclamation was a warning that all the slaves in the South would be liberated by the end of 1862, if the South did not cease their secession by the end of the year. In January 1863, Lincoln signed the order, under his right as commander-in-chief. The freed slaves were considered freemen, but not citizens. Obviously, Lincoln's actions stemmed more from a mentality that "the ends justify the means" than from strong conviction that slavery was wrong. For example, while announcing his Emancipation Proclamation, Lincoln exempted large portions of the South from its enforcement, such as New Orleans, and several other Louisiana parishes, and an area in Virginia later known as West Virginia, and indeed signed presidential decrees of exemption for the four slave states that stayed with the Union, Maryland, Kentucky, Delaware, and Missouri.

On December 6, 1865, the 13th Amendment was ratified. In July 9, 1868 the 14th Amendment was ratified. The 13th Amendment rejected the idea of slavery in the United States, and the 14th Amendment, among other issues, specifically declared that anyone born or naturalized within the United States was considered a Citizen of the United States. The specific purposes of these amendments were to free the slaves, and to allow citizenship to slaves and naturalized foreigners. The amendment gave freed slaves born in a foreign country the right to citizenship. Article 5, of the 14th Amendment states, "The Congress has the power to enforce, by appropriate legislation, the provisions of this article." Even then, under Article 1, section 8, of the Constitution, the Congress has the sole right to determine the right to "uniform naturalization" of a person living in the United States. The 14th Amendment has been enforced, and that enforcement reversed, by the Supreme Court, dealing with the specific issue of the birth of a child by foreign nationals within the United States. Native-born children come to mind. This 14th Amendment problem has again become a recent political issue, over the immigration and related "anchor baby" issue. Clearly the purpose of the 14th Amendment, like the 13th Amendment, was specifically to free the slaves and establish their citizenship, and not to enact citizenship for children born to foreigners while in the United States to gain the benefits given to those children, and their family, by the government of the United States. Few other countries give this dual citizenship to their nationals. To my knowledge, no other country gives this dual citizenship to their nationals unless at least one parent is a citizen of that country.

THE TRANSCONTINENTAL RAILROAD, CRONY CAPITALISM, AND CORRUPTION

The quest for a transcontinental railroad linking the East and West Coasts of the United States, like the quest to link the east and west coasts of Nicaragua by the Whig or Taylor government, was nothing less than crony capitalism.

In the Nicaragua incident, the Taylor government representative, Squier, was specifically instructed to negotiate with Nicaragua for a commercial treaty in the interest of the American Atlantic Ship Canal Company, and to secure a canal open to all. On August 29, 1849, Squier negotiated a contract specifically in favor of the company of Cornelius Vanderbilt, Joseph L. White, Nathaniel H. Wolfe, and others. On September 23, 1849, through the effort of Squier, the company was able to secure a favorable concession with Nicaragua.

The difference between the two was that the United States was engaged in the Civil War, and the transcontinental railroad was expected to play a part, if not a major part, in the North's effort to win that war. What resulted was, again, a clear case of crony capitalism, and a clear decision made by the President of the United States, Abraham Lincoln. That one act, and the congressional need to subsidize that railroad, led to the greatest documented scandal of that time. Greed led to stock manipulation, legislative and congressional corruption, and it eventually called into question the reputation of a President and Vice President of the United States.

THE NEED WAS THERE

Interest in a transcontinental railroad began in 1830, when the steam-powered railroads came into existence in Great Britain. It became more than just interest when the United States obtained the Oregon Territory in 1846, and in 1848, when gold was discovered in California. By 1853, when the United States obtained the Gadsden Purchase, it was no longer a case of whether or not a railroad system connecting the East and West Coast of the United States would happen, but of what route it would take. Before the Civil War, it was a more efficient and safer competitor to the Panama Railroad and the Nicaragua transit route. Eventually, that is just what it became.

There were several advocates for the three routes that the rail line across the United States could take. The northern route was dismissed out of hand, because of the terrible winter weather in the North. The central route was also, initially, considered too far north to be safely traveled in the winter months. With the acquisition of the Gadsden Purchase, the southern route seemed to be the most favorable, at least until the advent of the Civil War. Because of the war, support for the central route shifted decisively. Influential moguls of the day worked to make the railroad happen.

Asa Whitney, one of those moguls, was a strong advocate for the central route. In addition, in 1859, Theodore Judah became the official lobbyist for the Pacific Railroad Convention, and also an advocate for the central route. Judah went one step further, and after discovering a low pass across the Rockies, led a team that showed that the central route was suitable for a central railroad system in all weather. Before 1862, each time a bill was introduced in the Congress to build the railroad, it failed.

Despite all, this interest in a transcontinental railroad across the United States, and the implication of what economic riches it would bring, the southern states refused to support the bill. The slave states were gradually losing the fight to control the territories and the Border States, and they saw the railroad as an instrument used by the North to speed up this problem.

After the secession of the southern states, the Republican Party controlled the Congress, and on May 6, 1862, the House of Representatives passed the Pacific Railroad Act. On June 20, 1862, it passed the Senate. Lincoln signed it into law on July 1, 1862. The act established two mainlines, the Central Pacific from the West, and the Union Pacific from the Midwest.

Each line was required to build fifty miles of track each year. Each line received $16,000 for each mile over level grade, $32,000 a mile over the high plains, and $48,000 over the mountains. The payments were in the form of government bonds, which the companies could resell. The railroads were also given land grants of federal lands. These land grants consisted of 400 feet of right of way, plus ten square miles for every mile of track built. These land grants gave these railroads an area larger than the state of Texas.

The Central Pacific railroad was eventually controlled by four men, who initially invested $1,500 each and formed a board of directors. While the Railroad Act specifically awarded the Eastern contract to the Union Pacific Railroad, the selection of the Eastern terminal had to be selected by the President of the United States. There was no question that the Western terminal would begin in Sacramento. However, the Midwest's, or Union Pacific Railroad's, eastern terminal was being contested by three candidates.

The first candidate was at Council Bluffs/Omaha, proposed by Thomas C.

Durant. Durant controlled the Mississippi and Missouri Railroad. The second contestant was at St. Joseph, Missouri, and the Hannibal and St. Joseph Railroad. The third contestant was at Kansas City, Kansas, via the Leavenworth, Pawnee and Western Railroad, eventually controlled by John C. Fremont.

CRONY CAPITALISM REARS ITS UGLY HEAD AGAIN

The only benefit to the United States that the Nebraska terminal had was that it was the farthest north from the Civil War, and it was being proposed by Thomas C. Durant. In 1862, the closest railroad to Omaha/Council Bluffs was about 150 miles, and it would take five years to connect a feeder line to that location.

The St. Joseph, Missouri, terminal was more centrally located, and could offer feeder lines from Texas and a route servicing Denver, Colorado, the largest desert city in the West, at the time.

Despite all this, Durant was convinced that his proposal would be chosen by President Lincoln, and he began buying up land in Nebraska.

Durant knew something that was not obvious to the average person. In 1857, as a private citizen and lawyer, Lincoln represented the Mississippi and Missouri Railroad, controlled by Durant, against a suit brought by a group of steamship operators in their effort to remove "Government Bridge," the first bridge across the Mississippi River. They argued that the bridge was too low for these boats to pass under the bridge.

In 1859, Lincoln was given a tour of the Mississippi and Missouri Railroad facilities by the railroad's legal representative, Norman Judd. These facilities were to be used to secure a $3,000 dollar loan Lincoln held. Lincoln's ties to Durant were strengthened by the fact that, in 1860, he won the Republican nomination on the third ballot because the Omaha delegation switched its vote to him. In addition, in the 1860 presidential election, Lincoln only got 10% of the Missouri vote. Finally, in the process of making his selection for the eastern terminal, contrary to any of the other contestants, Lincoln spent a good deal of his time with the Mississippi and Missouri Railroad engineer Grenville M. Dodge, discussing the benefits of the Omaha/Council Bluffs terminal. Durant had good reason to be confident that his proposal would be selected, and it was.

Although shut out of the main contract, the Missouri line was given the right to build a feeder line from Atchison, Kansas, and the Kansas Pacific line, as it was later named, was to build a feeder line from Kansas City, Kansas. Both lines were to meet the mainline in central Nebraska. They were given the same subsidies, and land grants as the Union Pacific line.

GREED HAD NO BOUNDS

In contrast to the Central Pacific, the Union Pacific Railroad was immediately steeped in controversy. Durant became rich by selling the land he bought in and around Omaha, but he was not satisfied with that. Durant developed several other schemes that took advantage of the lack of congressional oversight during the Civil War. Although the Congress restricted the control of the Union Pacific to 10% by any one entity, Durant used straw persons, to eventually gain control of most of the Union Pacific stock. He used his control of this stock, his control of the stock of the Mississippi and Missouri Railroad, and the stock of another railroad line that he bought, the Cedar Rapids railroad line, to manipulate the stocks he controlled through fraud, or at best, by spreading false rumors.

For over two years, the Union Pacific Railroad never extended more than forty miles outside of Omaha, Nebraska. Durant built feeder lines that went nowhere, to profit from the government's mileage subsidies and land grants that were given to the railroad. He would float a rumor that the Mississippi and Missouri Railroad would connect to the Union Pacific mainline, running up the stock, and then, while the stock from his other holdings were dirt cheap, he would buy up that stock, and then float the rumor that the Cedar Rapids railroad line would connect to the Union Pacific mainline. After each rumor, he would buy back the depressed stock and start all over again. How many times he did this is unknown, but there is no doubt that this scheme alone made him and his partners rich beyond belief.

After the war and the return of congressional oversight, Durant decided to rehire his former engineer Grenville M. Dodge and finally move to finish the rail line to Promontory Point. However, even the increased congressional oversight was not enough to deter Durant's fraudulent schemes.

He came up with four different schemes. The first, when the railroads would come close to meeting, he would change direction and run his line parallel to the other line and collect the subsidy and land grants from the track mileage that was laid. A second scheme was to sabotage another railroad and claim that land for his own. A third scheme, although probably legal, was to ensure that the rail line ran over the lands that he owned. A fourth scheme, and the one that was the most egregious, and the one that finally brought attention to his corruption—and that of the Congress—was even more devious.

Durant paid $10,000 dollars to Herbert Hoxie to gain control of the Credit Mobilier company. He then subcontracted Credit Mobilier to do the actual track work for the Union Pacific. Durant then directed Credit Mobilier to charge two or more times the actual cost for this track work. He gutted his own company, the Union Pacific, and his stockholders, but pocketed the difference made by the Credit Mobilier, which he controlled.

In the end, on May 10, 1869, the Transcontinental Railroad was joined at Promontory Point, Utah. But it wasn't the Union Pacific that connected the Transcontinental Railroad at Promontory Point. In August 1870, it was the Kansas Pacific rail line that laid the last spike connecting the Denver Pacific line, in Colorado, linking the East Coast and the West Coast.

The Central Pacific built fifteen tunnels as it moved east over the Rockies. Almost all the labor force was composed of immigrant Chinese, supervised by Irish foremen.

Photo of Durant

LINCOLN KNEW OF THIS CORRUPTION AND ACTED TOO LATE

President Lincoln, obviously aware of the Durant corruption, asked congressman Oakes Ames, a member of the railroad committee, to clean it up and get the railroad moving again. Ames appointed his brother Oliver Ames Jr. as the president of the Union Pacific, and he arranged to have himself appointed as president of the Credit Mobilier company. Instead of cleaning up the problem, Ames continued to profit in the corruption. Ames gave stock options to other congressmen, while continuing the overcharging scheme.

In 1872, by the time of the second U.S. Grant election, the scandal was common knowledge and it became a full-blown scandal. The New York Sun published details of the scheme between Durant, Henry S. McComb, and Ames. The following congressional investigation led to an Ames censure, despite the recommendation by the investigation committee that he be expelled, and it implicated Vice President of the United States, Schuyler Colfax, and the incoming president, James Garfield. Ames died three months after he was censured. Durant left the Union Pacific, and because of the panic of 1873, Jay Gould took control of the Union Pacific and the Western Union.

In 1857, Lincoln had an early connection, as a private citizen and railroad lawyer, to the Mississippi and Missouri Railroad, controlled by Durant. He represented Durant against a suit brought by a group of steamship operators. Because of that connection, if made public, his action as president could be considered a conflict of interest. However, Lincoln's $3,000-dollar loan, a considerable sum in those days, and his close ties with the Durant company were a clear conflict of interest. It led to corruption and incompetence, almost beyond belief.

I don't know of any other example that more clearly illustrates what happens when the United States government decides what company should, and what company should not, benefit from a particular government action than this one. However, one need only look at the many other examples of crony capitalism throughout the history of this country to realize that crony capitalism always leads to corruption and scandal.

LINCOLN'S DECISION TO SOLVE THE SLAVERY PROBLEM THE ENDS JUSTIFY THE MEANS

Two years into the Civil War effort, even before his Emancipation Proclamation, Lincoln was looking for a solution to the slavery problem. Freeing the slaves meant that the South could no longer rely on the British's arms and ammunition for their cotton products. Without the slaves, the South didn't have the manpower to economically produce cotton. He obviously saw his problem was not just in the freeing the slaves, but rather what to do with the slaves once they were freed. As a lawyer, he had to know that, once freed, the slaves born in the United States would have the same rights as any other person within the United States. Those slaves not born in the United States were not citizens and were referred to as freemen. He was also aware that representatives of the northern states were afraid that the freed slaves, with no meaningful skills, would invade the North, in order to escape the tyranny of the southern states, and cause economic problems, at best. There was also that problem of the Constitution. Even then, the Congress had the exclusive right to bestow citizenship upon foreign nationals, slave or not. His solution, initially, seemed to be to ship as many freed slaves as he could out of the country.

THE CHIRIQUÍ PANAMA TRANSIT LINE A SOLUTION TO THE FREED SLAVES

Before the lead up to the Civil War, the history of this potential transit line drew little interest from the Spanish, or the Americans, in their quest for a transit route across Panama. The British explored the Chiriquí lagoon in 1839, and it was later explored by the French Navy. Although the proposed terminals boasted of deep-water ports and fertile lands inland, the interior mountain range precluded any realistic attempt at a waterway across Panama in this area.

In May of 1859, Ambrose Thompson organized the Chiriquí improvement Company, and received several concessions from the New Granada government. Because of the nature of the two harbors on the Atlantic and Pacific oceans, and the rich resources in the interior, this transit route also caught the attention of the Buchanan government. On January 6, 1861, a commission reported that the area could be fortified easily, and a railroad across the mountains was feasible. However, because of the advent of the war, the project was dropped.

When Lincoln became aware of this transit route, he revived the project, but not as a transit route. He wanted to establish a colony of freed slaves in the area, but more importantly, he wanted to solve the problem of where to put the slaves once they were freed. Lincoln instructed his representative to investigate the Chiriquí Improvement Company's title to the area and use it for his colonization proposal. Lincoln's proposal was turned over to Solicitor of the Treasury Jordan, and he, in turn, presented a favorable report on the matter. Lincoln then instructed the secretary of the interior to buy up two million acres of the land in that area. On September 12, 1862, a formal contract was signed with the Improvement Company, and on the 22nd of September 1862, Lincoln declared his Emancipation Proclamation, and signed the order on January 1, 1863. However, before that happened, Lincoln changed his mind, and decided to use the freed slaves in the war effort.

Some would say he was willing to use the freed slaves as gun fodder in the war effort. Why he changed his mind is anyone's guess. Perhaps he thought that not enough freed slaves would be willing to leave the United States. In any case, the slaves played a significant part in the history of the United States, and in the advent of the Civil War. Lincoln's initial decision, to ship the freed slaves out of the country, was forgotten in the subsequent history of the war effort.

Ironically, the issue of slavery did not, in itself, determine the act of war between the North and the South. What caused the war was, in fact, the way these slaves impacted the economy of these states, and the rest of the Western world.[34]

RIOTS IN PANAMA

After the Panama Railroad was built in 1855, the United States found itself in a dilemma. On April 15, 1856, a riot broke out in Panama, causing loss of life, and considerable damage to the Panama Railroad, built by a U.S. company. The government of New Granada was not capable of protecting the transit route, and the United States, the Pierce government, did not consider the 1846 treaty between the United States and Granada sufficient to unilaterally use force to protect it. Pierce tried to reinforce the 1846 treaty so that this type of damage could not happen again, but the Grenadian Conservatives in power refused to accept the terms of his proposal. From 1856 to 1861, the Liberals, under Mosquera, staged a revolution, called the war of a "hundred fights."

Eventually, in 1862, the Liberals in Granada gained control of the govern-

---

[34] United States House Ex. Doc. Report 568, 36th Congress, 1st session, p48; United States Senate Ex Doc. No. 41, 36th Congress, 2nd session, pp

ment. In time, Mosquera declared himself dictator, and asked for help to keep the peace in Panama. The Lincoln government, engulfed in our own war, felt that they were in no position to send troops to answer Mosquera's request. In 1863, Mosquera called a truce, and with the help of the Liberals, a new constitution was drawn up, and a new confederation was created.

THE UNITED STATES OF COLOMBIA

The United States of Colombia was comprised of eight semi-independent states, each with its own president. This was the status of Panama for several years to come, and the United States acted as the guarantor of the peace in that area. The Liberals in Central America were back in power.

Lincoln's secretary of state, Seward, contacted the United States minister of Central America, Mr. Dickinson, with plans to establish a railroad transit route across Honduras, and on July 4, 1864, Honduras signed a treaty granting the necessary concessions needed. However, Seward found that all his effort to move ahead on the project was soon blocked by the British, and the Clayton–Bulwer Treaty.[35]

The Mosquito Indian issue was a problem that could not be resolved without the cooperation of the British and the Nicaraguan government. The United States sided with the Nicaraguan government on this issue.

The Liberals in Nicaragua, having obtained this commitment, granted the United States almost identical transit rights to what it had held under the Cass–Yrisarri Treaties. The Dickinson–Ayon Treaty, signed in June 1868, was like the Squire Treaties, with the exception that it avoided an exclusive right by the United States to control the transit route across Nicaragua.

THE WAR WITH SPAIN AGAIN, CRONY CAPITALISM, CORRUPTION, AND AN OPPORTUNITY LOST

As the Colombian Confederacy came to power, the United States and the Confederation became ensnared in a conflict with Chile and Peru against Spain. Spain attempted to use the Panama transit route to transport war material across the Isthmus, and Panama used the 1846–1848 treaty with the United States to force Spain to back off.

Seward referred the matter to the United States attorney general, and received

---

[35] United States Senate Ex. Doc. 194, 47th Congress, 1st session, pp155-157.

an expected favorable opinion, indicating that the United States had the right to intervene in the matter. However, Seward was still not convinced in the 1848 treaty rights of the United States, and he dispatched Caleb Cushing, an experienced diplomat, to Colombia to renegotiate the 1848 treaty.[36]

On January 14, 1869, a treaty was signed giving the United States the sole right to construct a canal within Colombia, with a strip of land ten miles on either side, and the United States was given the right to protect the area by force if necessary. These rights were permanent. Seward's problem was not the Colombians, or the treaty he was able to conclude with Colombia, but rather, it was the United States Republican Congress, caught up in the Durant–Oaks Ames scandal that nearly got their own president tried and convicted for corruption. President Johnson turned the Cushing Treaty over to the Senate for ratification on February 15, 1869, and it failed to get the necessary support.

GRANT'S ATTEMPT TO SALVAGE THE MOMENT

Grant made it clear, upon coming to power, that a forceful American canal policy was needed. He sent General Stephen Hurlbut, resident minister of Colombia, to gain the right to further survey the lower Isthmus and ratify a treaty on the lines of the Cushing Convention. On January 26, 1870, a treaty was signed with all but the right of the United States to use unilateral military force to protect the canal. Grant submitted the treaty to the Senate. However, this time, the Colombian legislature refused to ratify the treaty without an amendment giving Colombia joint protectorate. The United States Senate refused to accept that amendment, and the treaty was not ratified.

Undeterred, Grant decided to redirect his effort toward finding what transit line would be the best possible transit line across the Central American Isthmus. He understood that attempting to obtain treaties would mean nothing if the transit line was unfavorable in one form or another. Over centuries, all of these treaties have been explored, surveyed, and repeatedly negotiated by one country or another, only to fail to be completed, mostly because of politics, but also because the land was never surveyed in detail.

In 1869, Grant enlisted Senator Conness to his cause.[37] Congress passed a resolution that finally provided for the detailed exploration of all the known transit routes. On March 13, 1872, the president appointed an Interoceanic Ca-

---

[36] Diplomatic Correspondence of the United States 1868, Pt. II, p643
[37] United States Senate Ex Doc. 194, 46th Congress, 1st session, pp 157-162.

nal Commission headed by Admiral Ammen of the United States Navy. In time, all the transit routes, from Mexico to Colombia, were surveyed in detail by the United States Navy.[38]

As a result, of all these surveys, only the Nicaragua and the Panama routes were considered worthy of attempting to build a lock canal, and of those two, the report indicated that the Nicaragua route was the most favorable. However, it was pointed out again, that the Nicaragua route held out the diplomatic disadvantage posed by the Clayton–Bulwer Treaty that the Panama route would not necessarily pose. The commission reported their finding to the president on February 7, 1876.[39]

Grant turned his attention to Nicaragua and directed his representative to negotiate a treaty with that country along the lines of the Dickinson–Ayon Convention so that an American company could finally undertake the project. The Nicaraguan representative Seilor Cardenas objected to the terms, but this time claiming the United States should first pay for the bombardment of Greytown in July of 1854. Because of this demand, negotiations ceased.[40] Having failed in his effort to obtain a treaty with Nicaragua, and upon leaving office, Grant made a final, personal appeal to his successor, President Hays, urging him to continue in the effort to obtain a treaty that would give the United States the right to build a canal on the Isthmus.[41]

---

[38] United States Senate Ex. Doc. 15, 46th Congress, 1st session.

[39] United States Senate Ex. Doc. 15, 46th Congress, 1st session.

[40] United States Ex. Doc. 191, 47th Congress, 1st session, pp157; United States House Ex. Doc. 732-43, 43rd Congress, 1st session, 157 & 168, 47th Congress, 1st session, 59-61, 48th Congress, 1st session.

[41] United States Diplomatic Correspondence, October 1871, p 683; United States Senate Ex. Doc. 19,47th Congress, 1st session, pp 157; United States House Ex. Doc. 732-43, 43rd Congress, 1st session, p157,168.

Photo of Grant

PART TWO

THE ACQUISITION

CHAPTER THREE
THE FRENCH FILL THE VOID

HAVING COMPLETED HIS CANAL in Egypt, de Lesseps turned his attention to the Isthmus, thinking that the European powers would never allow Americans to completely control a transit route in that area. He wanted the French to take the lead in this endeavor. However, the French government, while open to such a project, encouraged de Lesseps to create the "Paris Geographic Society" to do the necessary surveys that the United States had already done, but, not printed. The Paris Geographic Society, in turn, created the "Societe Civile Internationale de Canal Interoceanique," directed by a French naval officer by the name of Lucien Napoleon Bonaparte Wyse.

By the time Wyse was appointed to his post, the American survey commission had been published, giving Nicaragua a favorable position for a canal route. Given that position by the Americans, it was not hard for Wyse, on May 28, 1876, to obtain from Colombia a right of way across the Isthmus. In the end, the Wyse exploration group settled on the Panama Canal route, if he could purchase the Panama Canal Railroad, owned by an American company. On May 18, 1878, Wyse got the Colombian government to finalize his grant.

He then turned his attention to his French competition, who were negotiating with the Nicaraguan government for a canal route in that location. On August 11, 1878, when those negotiations fell through, Wyse felt that he was free to report his findings to de Lesseps, describing Panama as the most favorable route for an Isthmian canal.[1]

On May 15, 1879, the International Scientific Congress met to discuss the several canal routes. However, even before this assembly met, de Lesseps had already accepted Wyse's final report in favor of the Panama route. The Congress was composed of many different canal transit supporters.

---
[1] United States Ex. Doc. 194, 47th Congress, 1st session, pp. 166-174.

Of the Panama Canal transit proposals, there were at least two, the Wyse proposal that advocated a sea-level canal, and the Godin de Lipinay idea, which was a lock transit route, with central high lakes used as a water source.

The Godin de Lipinay proposal is the model that is in place today. However, at the time, it was not even discussed by the International Congress. In the end, through the pressure of de Lesseps, on the 8th and 15th of August 1879, the commission adopted the Panama Canal route recommended by Wyse. Initially, de Lesseps tried to reach out to the European powers to guarantee the neutrality of the Canal.

THE MONROE DOCTRINE SURFACES AGAIN IN AMERICA

Having received word of de Lesseps's success in obtaining the Panama concession, and his intent to gain European support to ensure it would remain neutral, the United States Congress moved to pass several resolutions objecting to the project, and specifically declaring that a canal route in Central America must be under the control of the United States. In addition, an American group organized the "Interoceanic Canal Society," supporting the Nicaragua route, and sought a concession to build it. Ex-President Grant was named as a patron of the project.[2] De Lesseps's French detractors were also working against his Panama Canal project, citing the American objections, and the objections made by his own friends.

De LESSEPS'S MISCALCULATION, AND HIS UNEXPECTED SUPPORT

On July 23, 1879, ignoring the opposition to his canal project in the United States, Europe, and France, de Lesseps issued his first stock offer and prospectus for shares worth 15% over the original cost for each share, during the construction, and 10%, after the completion of the canal construction.

This first offer failed to sell enough shares, and de Lesseps was forced to buy back those shares at a large cost. It should have been clear, at least looking back, that the project was not on a sound financial footing from the start. It only got worse as time went on. The reason seemed simple enough. Instead of using the funds to pay for the project expenses, increasingly, the funds solicited were be-

---

[2] United States House report, 48th Congress, 2nd session, United States Misc. Doc. 16, 46th Congress, 3rd session.

ing used to pay off speculators and financiers, whose only interest was to make money, whether through the use of their name, or through the prestige of their financial institution. As time went on, the cost of borrowing money became more prohibitive. De Lesseps was selling the Panama Canal project as if it were an easy task to accomplish.

He had overcome the English interference while building the Suez Canal. He felt that he could do the same with the Americans while building the Panama Canal. He failed to understand that the problems related to the Suez Canal were not the problems related to the Panama Canal. The Panama Canal was a "pesthole" of the first order, with many problems de Lesseps was not even aware of, or equipped, at the time, to solve.

De Lesseps's answer to his first setback was to embark on a public-relations campaign. Realizing that he had made a political mistake in publicly seeking European protection for his project, he publicly renounced his intention to seek that protection, and acknowledged the principles of the Monroe Doctrine. However, he still held on to an overly optimistic prospect in building a canal in Panama. He learned from his first stock offer that without that optimism, he could not sell enough shares.

In August of 1879, with his engineering commission, headed by Wyse and Recluse, de Lesseps decided that he would personally go to Panama to verify the practicality of his plan, and he promised that upon receiving a more detailed survey, the work would start the beginning of the following year. His activities in Panama were more public relations than any serious engineering activity, and they were met with only partial success.

On February 14, 1880, the commission, chosen by de Lesseps, reported that the project was practicable, and that a sea-level canal along the lines laid out by Recluse was also practicable.

De Lesseps's next effort at getting his project off the ground was to visit the United States and attempt to split the opposition lined up against his project. When de Lesseps arrived in the United States, he was faced with a unified strong opposition, from the President of the United States, the supporters of the Nicaragua canal, to the French, and other Europeans that were supporting a Nicaragua canal of their own. The United States Congress was moving forward toward hearings to determine whether the United States would build a canal in Nicaragua.

THE OPPOSITION

The government of President Hays, having failed to secure the Panama Canal route, or even naval depots at either end of that canal route, was aware that, under the Lincoln presidency, the United States had been given the right, under the Chiriquí Improvement Company's contract, to establish naval stations at the Chiriquí and Gulfito ports, located just south of Costa Rica.

Hays ordered the secretary of the navy to establish these coaling stations. The United States Congress passed the funding to establish these Naval stations in Panama but went further by funding these type stations throughout Central America, at both the Atlantic and Pacific coastline.[3] In addition, on March 8, 1880, after meeting with de Lesseps, President Hays presented the Senate with the documents they had called for, related to the Monroe Doctrine, and through a message from the president, he forcefully supported the principles of that document, emphasizing that… "An intercontinental canal across the American Isthmus will essentially change the geographical relations between the Atlantic and Pacific coasts of the United States and the rest of the world. It will be the great ocean thoroughfare between our Atlantic and Pacific shores, and virtually a part of the coastline of the United States. … Our mere commercial interest in it is greater than that of other countries, while its relation to our power and prosperity as a nation, to our means of defense, our unity, peace, and safety, are matters of paramount concern to the people of the United States." [4]

DE LESSEPS'S SUPPORTERS

Undaunted, de Lesseps set about enlisting a formidable cadre of supporters of his own for his project. Because of his success at the Suez Canal, de Lesseps had many influential personal friends in the United States. One of those strong advocates in favor of the Panama project was Mr. Appleton.

A second group of advocates was the stockholders of the Panama Canal Railroad, who stood to gain twenty million dollars if the French canal project got off the ground. Advocating for the French canal was ex-Secretary of the Navy Richard W. Thompson, who was promised $25,000 dollars a year just to promote, and to act as the chairman of an American committee supporting the Panama project.

---

[3] United States Ex. Doc. 46, 49th Congress, 1st session; United States Statute at Large XXI, 448, Appropriations Under the Navy Department.

[4] United States Ex. Doc. No. 112,46th congress, 2nd session; United States Senate Ex. Doc. No. 194, 47th Congress, 1st session, p165.

A third group enlisted by de Lesseps included the banking firms of J.M. Seligman, Drexel Morgan and Co., and Winslow Lanier, whose purpose, on paper, was to act as financial agents of the Panama Canal Company in the United States. They were promised one million and two hundred thousand dollars in commissions, merely for the use of their names and nothing else. These bankers bought up most of the Panama Railroad Company stock, and eventually sold them to the Panama Canal Company at a huge profit.

Photo of J.P. Morgan

THE TEHUANTEPEC TRANSIT ROUTE

An unexpected group of reluctant supporters came into the picture, whose project was based upon an old idea that was long thought dead. The Tehuantepec transit route had always been thought of as a railroad transit, but somehow it had attracted the interest of Captain James B. Eads, who had constructed the bridge across the Mississippi River and proven that he could deepen the lower Mississippi River using jetties. At the time, Eads was considered one of the best engineers the United States had to offer, and one that could demand serious attention from the United States Congress.

Eads proposed a ship railway rather than a canal. He argued that this concept was cheaper than a canal, and could be modified at will. He speculated that the project would cost nineteen million dollars, much cheaper than either the Nicaragua canal, or the Panama Canal. He was soliciting two and one half million dollars a year from the Congress for fifteen years for his project.

Good or bad, Eads's project was just one more competing project in the mix that helped to weaken the support of the Nicaragua route advocates, who were also seeking congressional funds for their project.

De Lesseps's project was not seeking any funds from the United States Congress. His only objective was to ensure that the United States didn't support a competing canal route in Nicaragua. He got his wish. Eventually, the Nicaragua route was passed in the House of Representatives, but not by the two-thirds needed, and no action was taken on the issue again. [5]

Unable to pass any bill related to an Isthmian canal, to a great extent because of the Clayton–Bulwer Treaty, the Congress again moved to have it abrogated. When the Garfield administration came to power, the president, on June 24, 1881, assigned Secretary of State James Blaine to inform all the nations of Europe not to guarantee their protection of the Panama Canal, as it would be an intervention of the powers of American affairs. In short, he reiterated the principles of the Monroe Doctrine.[6]

Blaine then directed his minister in Central America, to try to unite the various Central American countries into a union of states.[7] The Blaine effort met with little support, and the same issues of old surfaced again.

The Garfield administration ended abruptly on July 2, 1881, when he was assassinated. The Arthur administration took up the cause under the secretary of state, Mr. Frelinghuysen. He was met with the same arguments from the British, in their standing fast on the Clayton–Bulwer Treaty.

While the United States was busy arguing over the Clayton–Bulwer Treaty with England, de Lesseps returned to Europe to begin a successful lecture tour to gain support for the Panama Canal project. On November 15, 1880, he announced the cost of the canal would be 102 million dollars, and issued his second prospectus. Unlike his first stock offer, it was met with success.

---

[5] United States House Report 1698, Senate Report 386, 47th congress, 1st session; United States Senate Report 952, 47th congress, 2nd session.

[6] United States House Report 1121, 46th Congress, 2nd session; United States House Report 1698, 47th Congress, 1st session; United States Senate Report 952, 47th Congress, 2nd session.

[7] United States Senate Ex. Doc. 194, 47th Congress, 1st session.

THE FRENCH PANAMA CANAL

He later announced that the canal would open in 1888. In 1881–1882, work on the canal began. De Lesseps made many optimistic projections that could not meet reality. He made those projections, to a great extent, based upon the advice of his major contractors Mr. Couvreux, and Mr. Hersent. When it came time to prove that their advice was sound, they abandoned the project.

Except for the Anglo-Dutch contractors, who brought in large dredges to work the Culebra Cut, de Lesseps used small contractors to work on the canal. De Lesseps was beset with major problems from the start.

One of the first problems he faced was that he had projected 100 million tons of digging as sufficient to excavate the canal, when the actual excavation would require over twice that amount.

The second miscalculation of excavating de Lesseps made was underestimating the impact that disease would have as a debilitating psychological effect on the project. Yellow fever and malaria made it extremely hard to recruit and more difficult to retain labor.

The swamps, mudslides, and the Culebra Cut were just a few of the other major problems standing in the way of completing this project. But none of these problems caused this project to fail. In the end, the project failed because of a lack of financing to see the project through to the finish. There were some that said, Bunau-Varilla among them, the project could have been completed had the last solicitation of funds not been weakened by a false rumor of de Lesseps's death. But that does not change the fact that there was just not enough financial support to finish the project.

PHILIPPE BUNAU-VARILLA

Of the two people most vilified by the men, women, and children of Panama, Philippe Bunau-Varilla must rank first, even above Teddy Roosevelt. And yet, in my view, of the hundreds of people who have attached their names to the Panama Canal enterprise, Bunau-Varilla did more to ensure the future of those children and the many Panamanian children to come. I had often wondered, had Bunau-Varilla been able to look ahead and listen to the diatribe of hate directed against him, would he have thought better in steering a course toward Panama. There can be no doubt that, had he not done so, there would not have been a Panama Canal, and indeed there would not have been an independent Panama, at least not in his lifetime.

It was true that the corruption and deceit involved in building the Canal in Panama was beyond belief. But who were the authors of that corruption and deceit? It can easily be said that the Panama Canal was conceived in corruption, and in the end, the United States lost control of it because of corruption. If I a child born in Panama, I would want to know the truth of this matter, but then, I am not a child of Panama. Nonetheless, let me explain.

By his own recall, Bunau-Varilla became interested in the great works of a canal, any canal, at the inauguration of the Suez Canal on the 17th of November 1869. He was ten years old. Later, in 1880, he had the fortune to listen to de Lesseps give a speech at the military preparation school he was attending just before his graduation. Following his graduation, he entered the corps of "engenieurs de Ponts et Chaussees" and later attended a special engineering school, "Ponts Chaussees," before entering active duty and serving an obligatory five-year government service.

By that time, Bunau-Varilla was determined to work with de Lesseps on the French canal in Panama. His friends and mentors thought him suicidal, if not insane, to want to seek a position in an area that was well known in France to be a pesthole, and where people went to die. It was for that very reason, and his own persistence, that he was given permission to travel to Panama on a leave of absence.

On the 6th of October 1884, he boarded a ship, the *Washington*, in route to Colon, Panama. Also, on that ship was Mr. Dingler, the general manager and chief engineer of the Panama Canal Company. After making his acquaintance, for the next twenty days or so, with the help of Mr. Dingler, Bunau-Varilla studied every aspect of the Panama Canal. By the time he arrived in Panama, he was ready to go to work.

In 1884, Bunau-Varilla was about twenty-five years old and anxious to prove himself. The workforce in the Canal was divided into three divisions. Most of the work, except in Colon, was contracted out to small contractors. Dingler assigned Bunau-Varilla to head up the third division, which encompassed the Culebra and the Pacific slope. The Culebra section was contracted out to the Anglo-Dutch syndicate. Bunau–Varilla was first assigned the task of opening a channel between the mouth of the Rio Grande and the Island of Naos.

While all the contractors predicted he would fail, he found a way to succeed at his task. Within six months, Bunau–Varilla was offered the first division in Colon, in addition to the third division, he already held. In 1884, the wife of Mr. Dingler succumbed to yellow fever. By that time, Dingler had lost his whole family to the pestilence of the Panama Canal.

THE SECRET OF THE STRAITS

The initial work done on the Suez Canal was done by forced labor. To protect their economic monopoly with the Egyptian railroad, and even though, in 1850, they had used the same forced labor to build their railroad, the English convinced the Khedive of Egypt to halt this practice used initially by de Lesseps. De Lesseps was forced to turn to machines and the "dredge" to do the same work slave labor had done. The work on that canal was almost complete until they ran into rock about fifteen miles from the finish. They were forced to finish the work by damming up the cut at each end, and continuing with a dry excavation.

In taking over the Colon division, Bunau–Varilla was faced with the same problem. He found that, although he had more powerful dredges to work with, these dredges could not remove either soft or hard rock. Relying on the engineering experiences he encountered prior to working on the Canal, he incorporated a line of explosives, set a yard apart, in front of the dredges to break up the rock small enough so that the dredges could remove the debris.

Problem solved. His idea, while logical today, was unheard of, and forcefully resisted by the contemporary engineering community of that day. Prior to Bunau–Varilla's experiment, the Panama Canal Company was paying eighty cents a ton to remove soft rock, one dollar and fifty cents a ton to remove hard rock, and four dollars and seventy–five cents a ton to remove rock underwater. In 1885, his experiment proved he could remove rock underwater for fifty–three cents a ton, less than the same cost of removing soft rock under dry excavation.

A NEW IDEA SURFACES

This simple experiment led Bunau–Varilla to propose a new canal scheme that was to compete with de Lesseps's sea-level canal and Godin de Lepinay's lock canal. Bunau-Varilla proposed that the Canal Company construct a lock canal first, and later, with his dredging method, a sea-level canal could be easily constructed while they were already receiving shipping revenues, and this could be done without interfering with ship traffic. A variation of this concept is now being employed by the government of Panama in constructing a third lock system on the Pacific and Atlantic sides of the Isthmus of Panama.

AN INSURRECTION IN PANAMA

In 1885, an insurrection occurred in Panama. The result was that the town of Colon was burned to the ground. Although, initially, the United States made no effort to interfere, eventually under the 1846 treaty with New Granada, the United States moved to protect the canal against violence, no matter the origin. The United States refused to allow the Colombian troops to move against the rebels and refused to allow the rebels to attack the Colombian troops within the Panama Canal transit route. The lessons learned by this incident proved to be of great importance to Bunau-Varilla later in 1903. Some of the players in 1885 were the same players in 1903.

BUNAU-VARILLA, THE MANAGER OF THE PANAMA CANAL

While Bunau-Varilla was working the Colon division, Dingler, who had lost his whole family to yellow fever, left the Canal and never returned. He left his second in command, Mr. Hutin, in charge. In September of 1885, Mr. Hutin left the Canal after contracting yellow fever. By the age of twenty-six, Bunau-Varilla became the general manager of the Panama Canal Company.

Not leaving things to chance with an engineer as young as Bunau-Varilla, the company sent two more engineers to take over two of the vacated divisions. Both men were much older than Bunau-Varilla. Within a week, one, Mr. Sordoillet, came down with a fever. Mr. Petit succumbed within hours of Mr. Sordoillet.

By January of the following year, Bunau-Varilla was removing 1,400,000 cubic yards of dirt from the canal, and was doing it on a consistent basis from January to April of 1886. On January 30, 1886, the company replaced Bunau-Varilla, as general manager, with Mr. Leon Boyer.

Between January 1886 and March 26, 1886, because of Bunau-Varilla's experience, Boyer relied on him to perform the actual function of running the Canal. In March, Bunau-Varilla soon contracted yellow fever, and left the Canal. While Bunau-Varilla survived, within a month, Boyer came down with yellow fever and died before Bunau-Varilla had time to reach France.

On April 17, 1886, Bunau-Varilla had reached France, and immediately began to study the problems confronting the completion of the Canal, and to recover from his illness. He was determined to finish the job he started.

THE RETURN TO PANAMA

Bunau-Varilla was aware that, before he left the Canal, the Culebra Cut had met with little success. After a year and a half, the Anglo-Dutch contractor had failed to solve the problem. During the dry season, they were able to excavate, but during the wet season, the rain and mudslides destroyed any progress they might have made during the dry season. Eventually, as he did with all the other problems he confronted, Bunau-Varilla was able to find a solution to this problem as well.

He initially brought his solution to Charles de Lesseps, the vice president of the company, and proposed that the work should be done by the best company employees available, and that the work should be separated into a special general management, with him as the head. The proposal was turned down by the board of directors.

Eventually, Charles de Lesseps convinced Bunau-Varilla to take on the job as a private contractor, with his brother, Maurice Bunau-Varilla, and two other men, Mr. Artigue and Mr. Sonderegger, both considered excellent engineers. In order to establish this company, Bunau-Varilla had to resign from the position he held in the Corps of Engineers of France, a position he obviously held in high esteem.

The cancellation of the Anglo-Dutch contract was settled by mutual agreement with the Panama Canal Company. Bunau-Varilla refused to take part in the contract negotiations regarding his own company, or the negotiations related in the cancellation of the Anglo-Dutch contract. However, it was the negotiations related to these contracts, and their financial settlements, which brought into question Bunau-Varilla's honesty when the Panama Canal Company eventually failed.

On the 1st of September 1886, Bunau-Varilla returned to Panama and began work. The contract lasted two years, and was successful. During those years they had removed thirty feet from the cut, and the company expected to have just fifteen feet of the cut left to remove by 1891 to finish the job.

By the year 1888, as the Panama Canal Company lost its economic viability, the leaders in that company drew the condemnation of the French people, the politicians, and the court system. Regardless of the fact that there was no violation of French law, both Ferdinand de Lesseps, the president of the company, and Charles de Lesseps, the vice president of the company, were tried, convicted, and sentenced to five years in jail.

The French court eventually vacated the sentences, but the damage was done. While Bunau-Varilla was never charged for any crime, he was considered guilty by association, and the stigma of his activities related to the construction of the French Canal followed him, even while he was fighting to convince the American government to finish the Canal.

Photo of Bunau-Varilla

THE RETURN TO NICARAGUA

Under the Chester Arthur presidency, the Panama Canal project was well underway. The Nicaragua Canal Company's concession had lapsed by September 30, 1884. The Europeans were uniformly opposed to the idea of an exclusive American protection. Arthur was willing to give up control of the Panama route, provided the United States could build a canal in Nicaragua. He proposed to buy the Nicaragua transit route outright, and build a canal, under the complete control of the United States, in Nicaragua. It was thought that, by so doing, he could skirt the problems that had tormented the United States related to the Clayton–Bulwer Treaty. To that end the Frelinghuysen–Zavala Treaty was signed. This treaty gave the United States a strip of land, in fee simple, two and a half miles wide across Nicaragua, with the exclusive right to build and control a canal from sea to sea. In return, the United States guaranteed to protect Nicaragua's territory, and promised a loan of four million dollars.

Upon the completion of the canal, the United States would own the canal jointly with Nicaragua. Nicaragua would receive one third of the revenue, and the United States would receive two thirds of the revenue. Since the previous concessions had expired in September 1884, there was no visible conflict with this treaty, and on December 15, 1884, Secretary of the Navy William E. Chandler ordered Mr. Menocal to decide on a route for the canal.[8]

The work was completed on April 25, 1885. A report was submitted to the secretary of the navy in November, and the Frelinghuysen–Zavala Treaty was sent to the United States Senate for approval.

The Nicaragua legislature approved of the treaty, but the United States Senate, faced with the same problems of the Clayton–Bulwer Treaty, failed to ratify the treaty by the necessary two-thirds majority.

THE FIRST CLEVELAND ADMINISTRATION

Grover Cleveland was considered "an honest Democrat," beyond reproach. He became known as one of the few recognized honest politicians of the time. He was elected mayor of Buffalo in 1881, and governor of New York in 1882 with the help of a split in the state Republican Party. As governor, he vetoed a bill that would raise the fares of the New York City elevated trains. The franchise contractor of the trains, Jay Gould, had been instrumental in taking over the railroad system when it was faced with collapse after the Transcontinental Railroad scandal, and the bill was considered punishment for his actions. Jay Gould was not well liked.

Cleveland considered the bill, although popular, a breach of contract, and a violation of the Constitution. Cleveland's veto was upheld, with the help of Theodore Roosevelt, a member of the New York Assembly, who originally voted for the bill.

In 1884, Cleveland ran for president against the former Speaker of the House, James G. Blaine. Blaine was considered one of the most corrupt Republicans of his time. He was accused of manipulating legislation to favor some stock he had in the Little Rock and Fort Smith Railroad, and the Union Pacific Railroad. Late in the campaign, some documents surfaced that helped substantiate that allegation. In turn, the Blaine campaign accused Cleveland of fathering a child out of wedlock. Being a bachelor, Cleveland admitted to the allegation. With a split in the national Republican Party, Cleveland narrowly won the election.

Domestically, Cleveland set about reforming his administration, moderniz-

---

[8] United States Senate Ex. Doc. 99, 49th Congress. 1st session

ing the navy, reclaiming the public lands the railroads held by government grants, and he vetoed a number of bills that supported subsidies for specific groups, farmers, and veterans, over, what he considered the public good. He was especially opposed to changing the gold standard, favored by Western Republicans and Democrats, and he was opposed to increasing tariffs, favored by the Republicans. It was the issue of the tariffs that helped precipitate the American Civil War. None of these activities drew political friends to his cause.

In addition, in 1885, the Cleveland administration changed the United States foreign relations policy. In his annual address to the Congress, Cleveland proposed a more isolationist approach, and left stand the Clayton–Bulwer Treaty, and the Dickinson–Ayon convention.[9] It was Cleveland's position that private enterprise should build a canal in Nicaragua. However, Central America was constantly in a cycle of civil war against one despot or another, and the United States was forced to protect United States citizens in Honduras and San Salvador.

Finally, on February 16, 1887, the main cause of this unrest, President Barrios of Guatemala, was killed and the wars ended. The five Central American countries involved in these wars signed the treaty of "Perpetual Peace." The terms of this treaty granted each country non-interference in their affairs, and required that, in the event of a conflict, they would be required to submit to international arbitration.

It wasn't long before Nicaragua and Costa Rica availed themselves of the terms of arbitration clause of the Treaty of Perpetual Peace. They requested that the Cleveland administration provide this service. In March 1888, the Cleveland administration decided that both parties would be required to abide by the terms of the Canas–Jerez Treaty of 1858, the terms of which Nicaragua had previously refused to accept. Both parties accepted the terms of the arbitration, which gave Nicaragua the sole right to negotiate a future canal treaty, provided that, if Costa Rica feels that they are injured by the construction of that canal, they would have the right of "positive consent" on the matter. In addition, Costa Rica could not claim any profit from Nicaragua, based upon the rights it may concede.

On August 9, 1888, the Nicaragua Canal Company contract was signed between Menocal and Costa Rica, giving the company the right to build the canal.[10] On January 10, 1888, two bills were introduced in Congress, providing for the

---

[9] United States Senate Ex. Doc. 123, Ex. Doc 99, 49th Congress, 1st session.

[10] United States House Ex. Doc. 59-61, Part I; 48th Congress, 1st session; United States Senate Report 1944, Appendix I, 51st Congress, 1st session; United States Foreign Relations, 1888, "Cleveland's award" United States Diplomatic Correspondence, 1880-1887.

incorporation of the Maritime Canal Company of Nicaragua. On February 20, 1889, both identical bills, approved by the House and the Senate, were signed into law by the president. [11]

In 1889, although he won the popular vote, Cleveland lost his bid for re-election to Benjamin Harrison, a Republican senator from Indiana.

Domestically, the Harrison administration was known for the McKinley tariff increase, The Sherman Anti-Trust Act, and for his annual federal spending, which was the first to exceed a billion dollars annually. The Democrats were able to use these unpopular issues to regain political power during Harrison's 1890 midterm, and his attempt at re-election in 1892.

In 1890, the Maritime Canal Company of Nicaragua was organized, and the concessions of the old company were transferred to the new company. The new Maritime Canal Company of Nicaragua represented the American canal project as a private-enterprise entity. Mr. Hiram Hitchcock was elected president, and Mr. Menocal retained the position of chief engineer. On June 8, 1890, the first construction party began work at Greytown, Nicaragua. Despite the agreement to the Cleveland arbitration, and the fact that they each had separate agreements with the Maritime Canal Company, Costa Rica and Nicaragua each refused to approve the agreement made to the company by the other country. Frustrated, the company appealed to the United States government for help. The secretary of state, Mr. Blaine, directed Mr. Mizner, the minister of Central America for the United States, to settle the matter. Mr. Mizner was able to get both parties to sign the "Treaty of Limits," which was based upon the Cleveland arbitration, and for a time settled the issue. The company resumed preliminary work, establishing its rights of concession under Nicaragua law, but they were also aware that they would need substantial financial support, which they did not have, if they were to finish the project.[12]

In March 1890, the Honorable Warner Miller was elected the president of the company, and a public-relations program was started to convince the public, worldwide, that the project was a worthwhile financial investment.

Although sometime later the company was given a favorable report by Nicaragua, the legitimate rights of the new company were attacked by opponents of the project, who claimed that, historically, the rights to the canal were never released by previous parties—the French and Italians—that had obtained con-

---

[11] United States Senate Ex, Doc. 20, 53rd Congress, 3rd session, pp. 14,70,87.; United States Senate Callander, 378, Report of Senator Morgan, April 14, 1894.

[12] United States Senate Ex. Doc. 5, 51st Congress, 1st session. Report of the Maritime Canal Company to the Secretary of Interior, 1890.

cessions from Nicaragua. The issue was referred to the United States Congress for review, and on August 30, 1890, the Congress reaffirmed the rights given the Maritime Company. On November 6, 1890, the Nicaragua government released its own favorable report. [13]

In addition, on January 10, 1891, the Senate introduced a bill guaranteeing $100,000,000 dollars in company bonds to be used for the Canal's construction, and $70,000,000 to be held by the United States government as security. The bill designated the secretary of the treasury with the power of voting on the expenditures, and the president with the right to name most of the company's board of directors.

Although not voted on, this bill would revert to a government-controlled canal project, under the guise of private enterprise. [14]

Various other state legislatures advocated the support of a canal in Nicaragua. Although there was still the question of whether to build a canal under the control and support of the United States government or through private enterprise, it was clear by the year 1891 that the United States was firmly in favor of a canal in Nicaragua.

On December 23, 1892, the Senate again introduced a bill guaranteeing the Canal Company's bonds, however, this time the House introduced a similar bill that did the same. These bills failed to pass either chamber. Before the Canal Company could move forward on a bond issue, the "Panic of 1893" occurred, and the company was forced to suspend payments. On August 30, 1893, the company went into receivership.

THE PANIC OF 1893
A SECOND CLEVELAND PRESIDENCY AND
THE START OF PREDATORY FINANCING

In 1892, Cleveland again ran for president, and defeated Benjamin Harrison. Cleveland was the only United States president to run for and win two non-consecutive terms for office. At the time, he was the only president to win the popular vote all three times that he ran.

Cleveland was soon confronted with a severe economic depression in 1893 that he seemed unable to correct. The Panic of 1893 was the result of railroad

---

[13] United States Senate Ex. Doc. 4, 52nd Congress, 1st session, p 3.
[14] United States Senate Bill 4827, January 10, 1891; Speech by Senator Morgan, February 6, 1891, United States Senate report 1944, 51st Congress, 1st Session.

overbuilding and questionable financing, which resulted in several railroad and financial failures. Some of these failures were well-known companies, such as the Northern Pacific Railroad, the Union Pacific Railroad, and the Philadelphia and Reading Railroad. As these railroads and financial institutions failed, they were bought up at predatory discount prices. At the time, lasting until 1897, this depression was considered the worst depression in United States history.

President Cleveland was blamed for the problem. He had accepted a deal with J.P. Morgan and the Rothschild syndicate to supply the United States Treasury with 3.5 million ounces of gold, in exchange for a thirty-year bond issue. Cleveland was accused of being too close to the New York banking industry, and he lost support from the Democratic Party.

The New York banks also came under public condemnation. In response to this criticism, or just to hedge their bets, in 1900, Morgan and the other New York bankers heavily backed the Republicans, McKinley and Roosevelt, for president and vice president. Their bet paid off.

The French Panama Canal scandal was also affecting the actions taken by the United States Congress. Information was finally coming to light about the role the ex-secretary of the navy, Mr. Thompson, and the several United States financial institutions played in promoting the old Panama Canal Company within the United States.

A congressional committee concluded that the Panama Canal Railroad Company and the Pacific Mail Company had colluded for fifteen years to restrict commerce between New York and San Francisco across the Isthmus, and they recommended that these companies should be broken up. In addition, the committee, recognizing that the Panama Canal Railroad Company was no longer an American-controlled company, recommended that the United States should absolutely control some Isthmian transit, for competitive purposes, free of foreign stock manipulation.

On January 22, 1894, the Guarantee Bill of 1892 was again introduced by Senator Morgan. The purpose of his bill was to work around the Clayton–Bulwer Treaty, and the problems of Nicaraguan and Costa Rican sovereignty. The House only approved the guarantee part of the Senate bill as amended. Although both the House and the Senate were strong supporters of the canal in Nicaragua, a classic conflict emerged as to how the United States should support that canal. The Senate advocated governmental control. The house advocated private enterprise control with limited governmental financial guarantees.

By the year 1897, the depression brought on by the panic of the Panic of 1893 had run its course. After McKinley became president, and gold was discovered in Alaska, confidence in the economy was restored. It lasted for about ten years.

THE SPANISH–AMERICAN WAR

Leading up to the 1898 Spanish–American War, the United States articulated the principles of the 1823 Monroe Doctrine. Prior to entering the Civil War, the southern states, controlling the United States legislature and the executive branch, instigated a move to buy Cuba from Spain, to add it to the growth of the slave states. Spain turned down the offer. Spain had always considered Cuba as an extension of Spain in the New World. In 1868, the Cuban people started an independence movement against Spain that lasted for ten years and ended with the "Pact of Zayon."

José Marti continued the revolution and was exiled in 1895 after attempting a three-pronged coup that failed. Instead of addressing the problems, the Spanish government used even more repressive methods to quell unrest in Cuba. Negative public sentiment in the United States against Spain grew as the Spanish methods of repression grew.

President McKinley was anxious to avoid conflict with Spain, if for no other reason than to protect United States businesses, which had major economic interests in Cuba.

The president sent Stewart Woodford to Spain to negotiate a solution to the problem. After negotiating with the prime minister of Spain, Praxedes Sagasta, Cuban autonomy was agreed to, and would go into effect on January 1, 1898. However, not relying on this outcome, the United States, which had been building a large navy since 1900, moved its fleet to Key West, Florida, the Gulf of Mexico, off the coast of Spain, and Hong Kong.

REMEMBER THE *MAINE*

The trigger to the war was the sinking of the U.S.S. *Maine* in the Havana Harbor on February 15, 1898, and the death of over 200 sailors. Self-inflicted or sabotage, the American public was incensed, and the fault for the explosion was left for another day.

President McKinley was forced to prepare for war, and requested the funds for defense. On April 23, 1898, Spain declared war against the United States, and on April 25, 1898, the United States Congress declared war against Spain, and declared that it had started on April 21, 1898, when the United States established a blockade around Cuba.

Although the United States had a formidable navy, it was sorely lacking in ground troops, thanks to the previous isolationist Cleveland administration. Then-Assistant Secretary of the Navy Theodore Roosevelt worked with Leonard Wood and raised an all-volunteer cavalry regiment known as the "Rough Riders." Soon the United States recruited volunteers from all over the country. Although the United States had overwhelming forces, they were still using the same frontal tactics of the Civil War, and as a result, many lives were lost.

The first blows of the war by the United States were not struck in Cuba or Puerto Rico. These first blows were struck against Spain in the Philippines and Guam. Only Germany acted, halfheartedly, to interfere in the actions of the United States at the Bay of Manila. In the process of conducting the war, the United States tasked one of its West Coast ships, the *Oregon*, to move to the East Coast. Because the ship was required to travel around the South American coast, it arrived too late to support the Caribbean war effort.

This fact was not lost on the United States, and especially not by the soon-to-be president, Theodore Roosevelt, who was convinced the United States should build and control a canal in Central America and discussed the issue in several of his writings. Roosevelt used the untimely movement of the U.S.S. *Oregon* as a major reason for his Isthmian canal position. He held that position throughout his political career.

On July 1, 1898, Roosevelt resigned as assistant secretary of the navy, and participated in the well-known assault on San Juan Hill. Because of his participation in the Spanish–American War, he was able to transform his popularity into political power, and eventually ran for and won the New York governorship.

On December 10, 1898, the war ended, some sixteen weeks after it began, at the Treaty of Paris. It was ratified on February 6, 1899. It has long been stated that this war healed the wounds opened by the Civil War and expanded the United States' influence in the Pacific and the Caribbean Islands. In addition, this war transformed the United States into a major world power. All and all, as Roosevelt stated, for the United States, it was "a splendid little war." Less known was the fact that this war renewed the effort by the United States to build and control a canal across the Isthmus, not just for commercial interests, but importantly, for strategic interests, as well.

CHAPTER FOUR

McKINLEY AND ROOSEVELT'S PUSH FOR A CANAL

FINALLY, THE END OF THE CLAYTON–BULWER TREATY, BUT IT WASN'T EASY

FROM 1896 TO 1901, the United States again addressed the principles of the Clayton– Bulwer Treaty.[1] In 1896, Secretary of State Richard Olney wrote a memorandum again addressing the need to change the Clayton–Bulwer Treaty. On December 5, 1898, in his annual message to the Congress, President McKinley discussed the need for a canal, but failed to address a route.

He had been advised by John Biglow that he might be interested in the Panama Canal route, rather than the universally preferred Nicaragua canal. The president's speech was followed by a Senate resolution to change the terms of the Clayton–Bulwer Treaty. A few days after the president's speech, Secretary Hay directed the United States chargé d'affaires in England to begin talks with the British. On December 21, 1898, the chargé d'affaires, Mr. White, requested that the British ambassador in Washington, Mr. Pauncefote, be authorized to negotiate a new treaty with Secretary of State Hay.[2] The request was accepted by the British.

In January 1899, Hay submitted Olney's draft amendments to the Clayton– Bulwer Treaty, which had been prepared before the Spanish–American War, when

---

[1] Senate Report 1, 57th Congress, 1st session, p 7; Senate Doc. No. 474, 63rd Congress, 2nd session, p 6.
[2] Senate Doc. No. 474, 63rd Congress, 2nd session, p 3.

the United States had been considered in a much weaker position. In addition, on March 3, 1899, President McKinley appointed the "Isthmian Canal Commission," under the leadership of Rear Admiral Walker, to do a second detailed study of all the known canal routes. This study was completed ten years later.

The British wanted to condition the acceptance of these amendments on the settlement of the Alaska–Canadian boundary dispute, support of the United States regarding the Boer Wars, which had taken a turn considered worse than the Cuban oppression by Spain, and support of the British's Asian policy.

THE HAY-PAUNCEFOTE TREATY: ONE AND TWO

The first Hay–Pauncefote Treaty was signed and sent to the Senate on February 5, 1900. This first treaty was not much different than the Clayton–Bulwer Treaty, and Hay was roundly criticized for his participation in the effort.

A Senate report spelled out the Senate's position on the matter by stating, "Great Britain first closed the Western gate with the Clayton–Bulwer treaty, and then controlled the Eastern gate (The Suez Canal) with her money and keeps it open." [3]

On February 18, 1900, New York Governor Roosevelt wrote a letter to Hay, praising him as a great diplomat, but forcefully presenting his position on the matter. He articulated the problems the United States would have in time of war without a canal and emphasized the recent Spanish–American War as an example, the difficulty experienced by the loss of the use of the U.S.S. Oregon, because there was no canal, and the ability of Spain to use that canal, if there had been a canal that was neutral.

He emphasized the need for a canal, exclusively controlled by the United States, based upon the principals of the Monroe Doctrine.

On May 2, 1900, the Hepburn bill passed the House, providing for the fortification of a future canal. On December 20, 1900, the Senate passed the treaty with three amendments. These amendments required an explicit statement declaring the Clayton–Bulwer Treaty was superseded, the right to protect the canal excluding other powers, and excluding other powers from participating in the adherence of the protection of the canal. In addition, a supplementary treaty was signed giving the British more time to consider the amendments. On May 5, 1901, the British let the proposed treaty lapse.

On April 8, 1901, Hay drafted another treaty, and submitted it to the British

---

[3] Senate Report No. 1, 57th Congress, 1st session, p47.

ambassador. Pauncefote sent it to the British foreign secretary, Lord Lansdowne. On August 3, 1901, Lansdowne sent the British version back to Washington. His position supported the idea that, because the United States alone bore the expense of building the canal, they alone should enforce the neutrality of the canal.

McKINLEY IS ASSASSINATED, ROOSEVELT IS PRESIDENT

While Hay was negotiating this second treaty, President McKinley was assassinated, and Roosevelt became president. He continued Hay's appointment, and on September 21, 1901, he approved the draft treaty submitted by Choate.[4] All of these negotiations were premised upon the idea of a Nicaraguan canal. When the issue of a Panama route surfaced, Pauncefote confronted the issue with Choate. On September 26, Choate assured Pauncefote that Hay was not aware of any such proposal. To ensure that the British were not embarrassed, Lord Lansdowne insisted that the treaty preamble include the phrase "by whatever route may be deemed expedient." [5] The treaty was signed in Washington on November 18, 1901.

On December 3, 1901, President Roosevelt addressed the Congress, announced the completion of the treaty, and discussed the importance of a canal. Like McKinley, Roosevelt did not specify a route. On December 12, 1901, Secretary Hay described the history of the negotiations of the treaty.[6] The treaty was ratified by the Senate on December 16, 1901, and on February 21–22, 1902, the treaty was exchanged and passed into law.

Finally, after fifty years, the United States was free to follow its canal policy unfettered.[7] The significance of the Hay–Pauncefote Treaty cannot be overemphasized.

Since the days of Marco Polo, the Western world had been trying to find, and then build a canal route to the East Indies by traveling west through the Central American Isthmus. The French came close, but went bankrupt. For the last fifty years, the United States was blocked from accomplishing that task. During that time, no other country was willing or able to build a canal without first having the exclusive control of that canal.

Because of the terms of the Monroe Doctrine, no European government was

---

[4] Senate Doc. No. 474, 63rd Congress, 2nd session, pp 27, 42.
[5] Senate Doc. No. 474, 63rd Congress, 2nd session, pp46,292.
[6] Senate Doc. No. 474, 63rd Congress, 2nd session, pp53-68.
[7] Senate Doc. No. 456, 63rd Congress, 2nd session, pp 49-50.

motivated to try. The United States, since its inception, had the most economic and strategic interest in building a canal in Central America. The Clayton–Bulwer Treaty blocked the United States from building that canal for fifty years, short of war. The second Hay–Pauncefote Treaty released the United States from those restrictions and left it with the choice of where to build that canal, either in Panama or Nicaragua.

BUNAU-VARILLA, SINGLE-MINDED, UNDAUNTED AFTER THE FRENCH CANAL COLLAPSE

After the French Canal failed, the world didn't stop moving, and Bunau-Varilla didn't just disappear. When he created his company to work on the Culebra Cut, at the request of the French Panama Canal Company, he was forced to resign his position as an engineer in the French government. After the Canal collapse, he was not able to return to his former position. During the French government's investigation of the Panama Canal failure, Bunau-Varilla was investigated, along with de Lesseps, and the other principles of the company. Bunau-Varilla was accused of bribery and violating the French Department of Public Works' regulations by establishing a private company without the permission of the French government. Eventually, he was found to have been authorized to engage in the activity of setting up a private company while an engineer in the French government by the minister of public works, Mr. Severiano de Heredia.

Not satisfied, the investigative report from the French Commission of Inquiry, issued three major allegations against Bunau-Varilla and the company he founded, the "Artigue, Sonderreger & Co. Society."

The first was that the Panama Canal Company, through the Culebra Company that Bunau-Varilla had created, paid Baron de Reinach a commission, in short, a bribe, to replace the Anglo-Dutch company with Bunau-Varilla's Culebra Company. Baron de Reinach had been involved from the beginning, in one position or another, in all of the financial transaction dealing with the French Panama Canal Company. Demanding high commissions for his services, he was a perfect scapegoat for bribery allegations.

The second allegation was that the Culebra Company had been charging one dollar and twenty-five cents a ton for its excavation, while the old company was charging sixty to eighty-five cents a ton for its excavation.

The third allegation was that the Canal Company had been using escaped convicts to work for them while the company was under the administration of

Bunau-Varilla as chief engineer.

Bunau-Varilla was able to prove through specific documentation, that first, he was not involved in the contract negotiations between the Panama Canal Company and his own company, and that neither he nor anyone in his company had ever met Baron de Reinach. Second, the Panama Canal Company and the Anglo-Dutch Company severed their relationship through mutual consent. He cited the fact that Colombian law required that a company could not remove a contractor without a court order, unless it was done by mutual consent. He further stated that the new company, the Culebra Company, was created at the request of the Panama Canal Company and required to pay a twelve and three-quarter cent indemnity to the Anglo-Dutch company as a condition of the new contract, a condition that he was not a party to. He finally addressed the third allegation, as an absurd lie, that he hired escaped convicts. He showed through his documentation that no administrator or, for that matter, employee had been accepted into the Panama Canal Company without first showing their criminal record. Bunau-Varilla addressed these issues extensively in one of his books.[8] Bunau-Varilla finally argued that these allegations were proven false by Mr. de Lesseps, before the court; second, by himself, before the French parliamentary commission; third, by the liquidator of the company, in a footnote printed by the commission itself in its special report relating to contractors; and forth, by the expert accountant, Flory, who was hired to examine the books of the Panama Canal Company. In the end, no action was taken against Bunau-Varilla related to his activities for the Panama Canal Company, or the Culebra Cut Company that he created.

Despite these allegations, Bunau-Varilla was still a driven man. He was still committed to the Panama Canal Company, and the hope that the French would recommit to the effort to finish the project. To make a living, he took on a railroad construction job in the Belgian Congo, worked on river navigation in Romania, and bought up many stocks in one of the most influential Paris newspapers, Le Matin. In addition, he served as president of the "Madrid, Caceres, Portugal, and West of Spain Railway."

Through his friendship with Auguste Larent Burdeau, a member of the French Chamber of Deputies, Bunau-Varilla continued to seek financial support for the Panama Canal project from the French government. His effort fell on deaf ears. When that failed, he sought the help of the Russian government. He even tried to interest the English in the project. All without success. Bunau-Varilla's

---

[8] Bunau-Varilla, Panama: The Creation, Destruction, And Resurrection, pages 93-138."

appeal was tempting to some in the British government, however, because of the British preoccupation with the unrest that resulted from the first Boer War of 1880, and the lead up to the second Boer War of 1899–1902, they were not interested.

In fact, the British were in the process of negotiating the Clayton–Bulwer Treaty with the United States during the second Boer War. In 1889 Bunau-Varilla ran for a position in the French Chamber of Deputies, in order to help support his Panama Canal obsession, and lost.[9] Shortly after this loss, John Biglow, a long-time friend of Bunau-Varilla, convinced him to write his first book, Panama—The Past, the Present, and the Future.

Biglow was one of the first prominent converts to the Panama Canal project. In 1886, as a member of the New York Chamber of Commerce, he met Bunau-Varilla visiting the Panama Canal. During that time, Bunau-Varilla would give tours and lectures to visiting dignitaries interested in the work being done in the Canal. Biglow was also a long time New York politician and co-owner of the New York Evening Post. Originally a Democrat, Biglow switched parties to support Lincoln, and in 1861, Lincoln appointed him as the American consul in Paris. Working with the United States ambassador in Britain, Charles Francis Adams, Biglow helped to convince the British and the French to stay out of the Civil War conflict. In 1865, Biglow was appointed ambassador to France. He again switched parties in 1872, at the urging of his friend Samuel J. Tilden, and he was elected secretary of state until 1876.

By the time Bunau-Varilla wrote his first book, in 1889–1990, he was convinced that if the Panama route had any chance to be finished, the United States was the only country that could, or would do it. He was also aware that it would be an uphill battle.

The United States was committed to the Nicaragua route. The only two major issues stopping the United States from building that canal were the Clayton–Bulwer Treaty, and the method by which it would be built. In fact, it had been these two issues that had stood in the way of the United States building the canal since 1850. These two issues gave Bunau-Varilla the time to sell the Panama Canal route, on the basis that of its superior engineering, and that it was a more economical route compared to the Nicaragua route.

---

[9] Bunau-Varilla, Nicaragua or Panama, p1.

BUNAU-VARILLA AND THE LECTURE TOUR

For the next few years, Bunau-Varilla embarked upon a concerted lecturing program to convince every influential American of the virtues of the Panama Canal route. In 1901, he published a pamphlet Nicaragua or Panama, which was specifically based upon the report of the Nicaragua Canal Commission of 1897–1899 and the preliminary report of the Isthmian Canal Commission of November 30, 1900. Bunau-Varilla presented the contents of this pamphlet in a series of lectures to the Chamber of Commerce of New York, the Commercial Club of Cincinnati, the Engineers' Club of Cincinnati, the Commercial Club of Boston, and Princeton University of New Jersey.

The result was the introduction to further influential converts that helped Bunau-Varilla convince the American public, and especially the executive and legislative branches of the United States government, that the Panama route was superior to the Nicaragua route.

Among those converts were Frank D. Pavey of Cincinnati, Lieutenant Commander Asher C. Baker of the United States Navy, Colonel Myron T. Herrick, and Francis B. Loomis, who became the assistant secretary of state. It was a friend of Bunau-Varilla, Mr. Percy Peixotto, who introduced him to Lieutenant Commander Asher Baker in 1900. Baker, in turn, directly or indirectly, helped to convince Mr. Reed, speaker of the house, and Mr. Cannon, chairman of the ways and means committee, of the superiority of the Panama Canal route. In 1901, Bunau-Varilla met Mr. Loomis through Sir Edwin Dawes, one of the Suez Canal commissioners. It was Monsignor Schmitz-Didier who advised Bunau-Varilla to seek out the acquaintance of Myron T. Herrick, a friend of Senator Hanna and President McKinley.

On January 16, 1901, Bunau-Varilla finally met Herrick, and through Herrick, Senator Hanna, after his speeches before the Commercial Club and the Society of Civil Engineers of Cincinnati.

Photo of Senator Hanna And President Roosevelt

THE CREATION OF THE PANAMA CANAL

On the following pages, I have gone into detail, explaining how one man, William Nelson Cromwell, could corrupt almost everyone he met, simply for making money and gaining power. It is difficult to determine if J.P. Morgan was Cromwell's mentor or his partner in much of Cromwell's activities, but I don't think that really matters. It was Cromwell that did the legwork, and it is Cromwell that should get most of the credit. The corruption that occurred in the Panama Canal matter was equal to, or greater than, the Intercontinental Railroad scandal, which, ironically, also occurred under a Republican presidency. The details of both scandals were not publicly known until many years later. Both scandals almost destroyed the credibility of both presidents, Lincoln and Roosevelt, their administrations, and the Republican Party for years to come.

Had it not been for Cromwell himself, and the angry animus of President Roosevelt, the details of the Canal scandal may never have surfaced. Almost all of the details of the Panama Canal scandal was gathered and produced within the

United States Foreign Affairs Committee in 1912, under the title of The Story of Panama. It is no surprise that crony capitalism was the key factor that allowed this corruption to occur.

Photo of William Cromwell (AKA the Silver Fox)

CHAPTER FIVE

TWO MEN WITH THE SAME GOAL, BUT DIFFERENT MOTIVES: BUNAU-VARILLA AND WILLIAM NELSON CROMWELL

THE CORRUPTION BEGINS, AND NEVER ENDS

While Bunau-Varilla's goal was to finish the Panama Canal, Cromwell's goal was making money any way that he could. Bunau-Varilla openly did everything he could, by the force of his arguments, to convince everyone he met of the legitimate value of the Panama Canal route, from an engineering perspective, based upon his own experience as the chief engineer of the old French Panama Canal Company.

Prior to the time he became involved in the 1903 Panama Revolution, Bunau-Varilla had no official position in which he could gain access to any officials in the United States, Panama, or Colombia. He approached the issue in an honest, open, and straightforward way. It is remarkable that he was able to do what he did, although he was a foreigner in Panama, Colombia, and the United States. He was unable to convince anyone in France, apart from his friends, of the value of finishing the Panama Canal route.

In contrast, William Nelson Cromwell, an influential American attorney, approached the issue of the Panama Canal route as an official of the New French Panama Canal Company, and an official of the Panama Canal Railroad Company to gain access to the various political actors representing the interested countries involved in the issue.

Through his access to the news media and the American legal system, Cromwell was able to manipulate the officials of the company he represented, and to a great extent, officials in the United States and Colombia. In order to gain his ends, he was willing to initiate a revolution, which if discovered, would discredit the United States, forfeit the properties of his employers, the New Panama Canal Company and the Panama Railroad Company, and possibly cause the death of the people in Panama that relied on him for financial support to accomplish their goal of revolution.

He approached the issue in a duplicative, secretive, and dishonest way. As I have written, much of what Cromwell had done, or not done, during the Panama Canal matter was exposed during the hearing before the Committee on Foreign Affairs in the House of Representatives, chaired by Congressman Pavey in 1912. The subject was called The Story of Panama: Hearings on the Rainey Resolution.

Ironically, much of that information regarding Cromwell came as a result of an allegation by Cromwell that he had been blackmailed by "Panamanians involved in the 1903 revolution." This hearing exposed the scheme, created by Cromwell, that included the brother-in-law of President Roosevelt, J.P. Morgan, and the brother of Secretary of War Taft. The hearing was an attempt to embarrass President Roosevelt, or Taft, Roosevelt's pick for the next president, during the 1908 election season. At the time, when this secret "syndicate of investors" was formed, there had only been rumors of its existence, and Cromwell categorically denied those allegations. Ironically, President Taft continued to rely on Cromwell, and, of course, J.P. Morgan, one of the signatories of this syndicate, on almost every issue related to the Panama Canal.

WHO WAS CROMWELL?

William Nelson Cromwell was born on January 17, 1854. He grew up poor, living with his mother in Brooklyn, New York. He went to public schools, and graduated as an accountant. He was hired as a clerk for the law office of Algernon Sullivan. Sullivan paid for Cromwell's law school education, and in 1879, Cromwell became a junior partner in the firm. In1887, Sullivan died, and Cromwell became the senior partner.

Cromwell practiced in what, today, we would term vulture capitalism. His firm took on large railroads and New York banking centers as clients, whose objectives were the acquisition of ailing or bankrupt companies. His biographers described him as an "arranger," a diminutive, fast-talking "car salesman," dedicated to pursuing his clients' needs, and his own, "moral or not."

He specialized in purchasing and rehabilitating bankrupt companies, creating mergers, restructuring company values, cutting deals with creditors, finding venture capital, and charging large fees for his services. But, to leave his history with just that short description would really do William Nelson Cromwell an injustice.

Even before the issue of the Panama Canal came to his attention, Cromwell had garnered the reputation of inventing the idea of the "holding company," and, with his junior partner, Mr. William J. Curtis, he was able to introduce the idea of the holding company into the New Jersey State corporate laws. [1]

The holding company allowed companies to hide their activities from the public and their competitors. It allowed the company to avoid the restrictions of the Sherman Anti-Trust Act, and allowed the company to hide anti-competitive, and predatory practices. It also created legal separation from the company's subordinate units, thereby avoiding fiscal suit, allowed the corporation to control other firms in other geographic areas, and was well suited to form monopolies.[2]

Early on, Cromwell applied his idea to the Northern Pacific Railroad Company. In 1893, Cromwell was hired to represent the Villard Companies, to buy a controlling interest in the Northern Pacific Railroad Company. After accomplishing his objective, and reorganizing the company, Villard found himself, and the Northern Pacific, on the verge of bankruptcy.

Cromwell managed to secure a 1.15-million-dollar loan with Drexel Morgan and Company. The loan was taken out in the name of Villard's wife. In gratitude, Villard appointed Cromwell in charge of the Northern Pacific Railroad Company. Cromwell and J.P. Morgan immediately set about to consolidate their control of the company.

Villard, born in Germany, had extensive financial contacts there, but it was George Siemens, the president of the Deutsche Bank, Villard's major supporter, which interested Cromwell, and to whom Cromwell wanted direct access.

In 1890, Cromwell incorporated the Oregon & Transcontinental Railroad, and Company, as a holding company, to consolidate control over the Northern Pacific Company. [3]

The financial panic of 1893, caused the Northern Pacific Railroad Corpo-

---

[1] Lisagor and Lipsius, A Law unto Itself, p 27.
[2] Mathew Josephson, The Robber Barons: The Great American Capitalists 1861-1901 (New York: Harcourt. 1962) pp. 100-177, 253-315; Prechel, Big Business and The State, pp. 53-55.
[3] "Henry Villard, a Remarkable Man," The Albany Journal, September 16, 1887.

ration to again face bankruptcy, and Villard's stock interests were sold off, but Cromwell's control of the Northern Pacific continued. He also finally gained direct access to Siemens, and the Deutsche Bank.

Cromwell, with the help of J.P. Morgan, went about removing the old directors of the corporation, and eventually was the last man standing. In the end, the Northern Pacific Railroad would end up in the complete control of J.P. Morgan, due to his original loan to Villard's wife. It was Cromwell's involvement in the railroads that attracted him to the Panama Canal.[4]

It was Cromwell's use of Raymond Poincare as his lawyer in France that helped him garner favorable rulings against Colombia in 1904. Poincare later became president of France.

In 1911, Cromwell was succeeded by John Foster Dulles. Soon after, Allen Dulles joined the firm. Their clients included some of the most influential corporations in the United States, and included the Ford Motor Company, General Motors, IBM, Chase Bank, I.T.&T., Brown Brothers Harriman, I.G. Farben, Standard Oil, and the Bank of International Settlements.[5] After the Second World War, John Foster Dulles served as secretary of state in Eisenhower's administration, and Allen Dulles became the longest-serving CIA director.

Just based upon Cromwell's prior record, one could conclude that he was a notorious self-promoter, manipulator, and a proven first-rate liar. Other than what he made public, much of what he truly did, or did not do, related to the Panama Canal project did not surface until many years later.

In 1893, after the 1888 financial collapse of the old French Panama Canal Company, Cromwell was hired as a counsel and one of the "punitive" directors of the Panama Canal Railroad. Although the railroad was owned by the old French Panama Canal Company, the railroad was incorporated in New York, and by law, Americans were required to serve on the board of directors. There is no record that Cromwell served any meaningful purpose in his position, other than as a place setter in compliance with New York law.

On October 24, 1894, the New French Panama Canal Company was formed. In January 1896, the company hired William Nelson Cromwell as general counsel of the company, because of his work with bankrupt companies, and his alleged connections with American politicians, newsmen, and other men of influence.

From the year 1896 through at least 1904, Cromwell claimed to be the sole

---

[4] David McCullough, The Path Between the Seas; The Creation of the Panama Canal, 1870-1914. (New York; Simon & Schuster, 1977.
[5] Lisagor and Lipsius, A Law unto Itself, p 52.

authority for the actions taken by the Congress of the United States, the United States Isthmian Canal Commission created by the Congress to study and report on the Canal issue, the United States executive branch, the government of Colombia, and the news media leading up to the Hay–Bunau-Varilla Treaty between the United States and Panama.

Cromwell made these allegations in writing, in letters, and statements he used to help support his 1907 claim of $800,000 dollars before an arbitration hearing for the services he provided to the New Panama Canal Company. The arbitrators denied his claims, and he settled for $200,000 dollars instead. Most of the major points of his claim were found to be false, or at best unsubstantiated. This Cromwell document was submitted to the House Foreign Affairs Committee, chaired by Mr. Pavey, in 1912, and was referred to as the Rainey Resolution.

The Cromwell document was addressed—and persuasively found to be false or exaggerated at every major point—in a letter by Bunau-Varilla, sent to the committee, that he described as the "Statement on Behalf of Historical Truth" (1912).

Just one example of Cromwell's false statements started at the beginning of his appointment. Soon after being appointed by the New Panama Canal Company in 1896, Cromwell claimed that, on behalf of the Canal Company, he had convinced the Ludlow Commission, created by the Congress, to report in favor of the Panama route. The problem with Cromwell's allegation was that the "Ludlow Commission Report" was finalized and sitting on the president's desk in late 1895 before Cromwell was an employee of the New Panama Canal Company.

THE AMERICANIZATION PROJECT

Starting in December 1896 with a series of letters sent to the director of the New Panama Canal Company, Mr. Hutin, Cromwell embarked upon an attempt to restructure the company for an eventual takeover by an American company, controlled by Cromwell of course. Within those letters, he emphasized his influence with politicians, newspapers, and men of financial influence within the United States. He advocated the importance of "a different, open, audacious, aggressive" plan of action, to win over the United States to the value of the Panama Canal route.[6] In 1897, Cromwell also wrote Hutin several letters to impress upon him that the United States "wishes to be the virtual owner of the Canal." In January

---

[6] Rainey resolution, p 144; Committee on foreign affairs, House of Representatives. 9.12, 1912, entitled "the story of Panama.

1898, he also urged Hutin to seek the help of Colombia, to remind the United States government of the restrictions of the Clayton–Bulwer Treaty with England, related to the Nicaragua canal, and the principles of the 1846 treaty with New Granada, related to the Panama Canal, and the advantages of United States warships avoiding the long trip around South America if a Canal were built in Panama.

The incident of the Oregon during the Spanish–American War "put to an end all ideas of a canal owned by a private company" subject to the politics of a foreign country.

On June 20, 1898, the Morgan Senate bill, offered to pay $5,500,000 dollars to the Nicaragua Maritime Company in exchange for its capital stock.

Also, in June 1898, in response to the Morgan bill, Cromwell organized an extensive press bureau to help sell the Panama Route to the American public and the United States Congress. On November 18, 1898, just two years after hiring Cromwell, and at his urging, the New Panama Canal Company wrote a letter to the president, offering to sell the company to the United States.

In addition, on November 28, 1898, the New Panama Canal Company sent a commission to New York to discuss the terms of the sale. This offer sparked the interest of the executive branch of the United States but could not be acted upon without the approval of the Congress.[7] On February 27, 1899, Cromwell incorporated his "Americanization project" into his activities.

On March 3, 1899, Congress passed a law creating a new commission, headed by Admiral Walker, to study all the known canal routes.

With the approval of the director general of the New Panama Canal Company, Cromwell wrote to President McKinley, requesting that he not appoint Admiral Walker, Colonel Hains, or Professor Haupt to the commission, as they had previously reported favorably for Nicaragua.[8] On June 9, 1899, the president, ignoring Cromwell's request, appointed Admiral Walker president of the commission, along with Hains, Haupt, Ernst, Pasco, Burr, Noble, Johnson, and Morison. On June 15, 1899, the commission was organized, and they sailed to Paris on August 9, 1899.

On September 7, 1899, Admiral Walker asked the New Panama Company to name a price for the sale of its property. The New Panama Company failed to respond to Walker's request.

---

[7] Rainey resolution, p 146; Committee on foreign affairs, House of Representatives. p.12, 1912, entitled "the story of Panama.
[8] Ibid. p 152.

Instead of responding to Walker's request, on October 19, 1899, the New Panama Canal Company directors approved of an offer to transfer all of its assets to the "Panama Canal Company of America," which Cromwell created in New Jersey on December 27, 1899. The New Panama Canal Company was to receive thirty million dollars in capital from the Panama Canal Company of America and five million dollars in cash for this transaction. True to form, this company was set up as a holding company by Cromwell.

There was no proof that the Panama Canal Company of America had any "capital" with which to make this transaction. There was every indication that this "company" was nothing more than a "paper company" with little or no value. Of the two people present at the signing, Cromwell was listed. The incorporators, William P. Pollock, Harvey W. Clark, and Francis J. Pollock, were all law clerks of Cromwell's company. The company's New Jersey agent was William Brinkerhoff.

FINANCIAL SUPPORTERS OF CROMWELL'S FIRST SCAM

On December 28, 1899, Cromwell released the names of the men supporting the action taken by the New Panama board of directors. These men, as noted by Cromwell in an accompanied news brief, were J. Edward Simmons, Senator Hanna's banker, Kuhn, Loeb & Co., E.C. Converse, Warner Van Worder, August Belmont, H.W. Seligman, Charles P. Flint, George R. Sheldon, Levi Morton, Captain J.R. de la Mar, and Vernon M. Brown, all men "with the most powerful financial influence in the United States." The obvious purpose of this transaction was to obtain the assets of the New Panama Canal Company for pennies on the dollar, and to sell it to the United States for an enormous profit.

Cromwell was obviously acting against the interests of the New Panama Canal Company that hired him in 1896, or at least, the bondholders of the New Panama Canal Company.[9] Fortunately, the French receiver of the New Panama Canal Company, Mr. Sautron, and Mr. Lemarques, the representative of the bondholders, were made aware of the intended actions of the New Panama Canal Company directors. Because of their protest, an umpire, Mr. Betoland, was chosen to rule on the matter. He ruled against the New Panama Canal Company directors.

In December 1899, the New Panama Canal Company directors were forced

---

[9] Rainey resolution, p 154; Committee on foreign affairs, House of Representatives, Feb. 9,12, 1912, entitled "the story of Panama.

to resign. On December 27, 1899, because of the ruling of the umpire, a new board was created on the same date that the "Panama Canal Company of America" was to finalize its corporation documentation. Again, in a letter dated April 10, 1899, Admiral Walker asked the New Panama Canal Company if they were willing to sell the company, and if so, he asked what would be their price.

On April 13, 1899, Senator Morgan introduced a resolution of his Nicaragua bill, without the findings of the Walker Commission. On April 28, Cromwell gave a press statement protesting Morgan's resolution, and on April 30, 1899, sent a letter to the president voicing an official protest, asking the president to present his protest to the Congress. In his letter and news release, Cromwell stated that the New Panama Canal Company had given the Walker Commission all the information that they had asked for.

On May 16, 1900, in response to Cromwell's letter to President McKinley and his news release, the Morgan committee specifically singled out Cromwell for interfering with congressional legislation. Morgan made other scathing remarks directed at Cromwell.

The committee statement continued: "Aside from the fact that said proposal contains suggestions that provide for the robbery of the stockholders of the "Old Company" and the violation of the decrees of the courts of France, it proposes a direct violation of the statutes of related to his letter to the President of Colombia, enacted in granting the concessions to that company, and a breach of our treaty of 1846 with Colombia, which binds us to guarantee the sovereignty of that territory over the state of Panama."[10]

On November 26, 1900, the New Panama Canal Company answered the Walker Commission by stating their desire to incorporate in the United States and allow the American government to establish representatives on the board. In December 1900, unable to get a price on its holdings from the New Panama Canal Company, the Walker Commission released their preliminary report in favor of Nicaragua. They also released an estimate that the Nicaragua route would cost $58,000,000 dollars more to build than the Panama route. [11]

---

[10] Rainey resolution, p 157; Committee on foreign affairs, House of Representatives, Feb. 9,12, 1912, entitled "the story of Panama; Senate Report No. 1337, 56th Congress, 1st session, pp. 9-10.

[11] Rainey resolution, p 72-73; Committee on foreign affairs, House of Representatives, Feb. 9.12, 1912, entitled "the story of Panama.

CROMWELL WAS FIRED

Six months later, on June 19, 1901, the president of the New Panama Canal Company, Maurice Hutin, in a letter of that date, dismissed Cromwell as their representative in the United States. However, his dismissal does not appear to have been because of the deal he hatched with the original directors of the New Panama Canal Company. In fact, Cromwell had unlawfully used the New Panama Canal Company funds, about $60,000 dollars, to change the wording of the 1900 Republican platform in favor of the Panama route, or possibly to support the election of a member of the United States Congress, allegedly congressman Hanna, one of the most influential Republican politicians of the day. At the very least, this amount of money, no small amount in 1900, gave Cromwell access into the political power base of the Republican Party. Cromwell charged this expenditure to the company under "necessary expenses."

The money was not given to Hanna, but was given to the Republican National Committee, of which Senator Hanna was chairman. The year 1900 was an election year, but in his defense, Hanna represented a safe district in a safe Republican state. Whether or not Hanna was persuaded by the superior arguments made to him by Bunau-Varilla, or by the clearly intended felonious bribe that he accepted from Cromwell, it is a documented fact that Hanna, after accepting this money without question from Cromwell, went from a supporter of the Nicaragua route before the election, to a supporter of the Panama route soon after the election.[12]

AN ABRUPT CHANGE FROM NICARAGUA TO PANAMA

After January 1902, the unanimous recommendation of the United States Canal Commission, led by Walker, recommending the Panama route, gave new life to the Panama route. Also, in January 1902, at the request of a long-time friend, and banker, Mr. Edward Simmons, Senator Hanna approached Bunau-Varilla, for getting Cromwell reinstated as the New Panama Canal counsel. Edward Simmons was a major investor in both of Cromwell's Panama scams.

This was no small matter, considering Cromwell was fired for embezzling $60,000 dollars from that same company. Initially, the company refused to entertain the idea. Eventually, on January 27, 1902, the company reinstated Cromwell under strict guidelines. Bunau-Varilla, submitted several letters and documents to the United States Congress, outlining how he went about accomplishing this

---

[12] Rainey resolution, p 72-73; Committee on foreign affairs, House of Representatives, Feb. 9,12, 1912, entitled "the story of Panama.

task. [13]

Cromwell had already embarked on his first scam to take over the assets of the New Panama Canal with the help of influential politicians, bankers, and investors and sell it to the United States.[14] He did not seem to care that, as a representative of a foreign company, he was willing to bribe members of the United States Congress with embezzled money from the company he represented.

Cromwell was questioned about the "Panama Canal Company of America" matter in a Senate hearing, in 1906, and he refused to cooperate, stating that he represented the "Panama Canal Company of America," and it would be a breach of professional secrecy. He didn't mention that he created the "Panama Canal Company of America." His actions were clearly a breach of professional ethics, and a conflict of interest, if not a violation of law. Congress adjourned before any further action was taken on the matter. Because it would have been an embarrassment to the Republican Party, it is doubtful that any action would have been taken anyway.

Undaunted by the French umpire ruling against his first scheme in 1899, and while still working as the New Panama Canal Company legal representative in the United States, Cromwell embarked upon another scheme to cheat the New Panama Canal stockholders. His second scheme, more correctly a scam, bore more fruit, and was again supported by some of the most influential movers and shakers in politics, finance, and business within the United States.

CROMWELL'S SECOND SCAM IS BORN

On May 25, 1900, Cromwell helped create a syndicate of American investors, who pledged to buy up as many shares of the New Panama Canal Company as possible at no more than 20% of the bond's worth, and to sell those shares at no less than 50% of the bond's worth. At the time, these bonds were worth no more than 5% of their original value. For most of these investors—J.P. Morgan, Winslow Lanier and Company, Chauncey M. Depew, Douglas Robinson, brother-in-law of Theodor Roosevelt, Henry W. Taft, brother of the secretary of war, J.R. Hill, G.W. Perkins, and H.J. Satterlee—the scheme was a significant, but not a major speculation compared to their worth. Others who heavily invested in the scheme were, of course, Cromwell, J.E. Simmons, Isaac Seligman, J.B. Delamar,

---

[13] 1912, Bunau-Varilla, Statement on Behalf of Historical Truth, pp. 37-45.
[14] Rainey resolution p. 157; Committee on foreign Affairs, House of Representatives, Feb.9,12 1912, entitled "the story of Panama".

George J. Gould, and, allegedly, Manuel Amador Guerrero, one of the leaders of the Panama Revolution against Colombia, under the name of "F.L. Jeffries." [15]

If, as alleged, Amador was a signatory of this scheme, it would be just more documented proof that, early on, Cromwell was deeply involved in encouraging the revolution in Panama, even while the United States was still negotiating with Colombia over the Hay–Herran Treaty. It would be proof positive that he was double-dealing the New Panama Canal Company, the government of Colombia, and the United States government. Cromwell had sold his scheme to these Wall Street speculators, now he had to buy up the shares, and then sell the New Panama Canal Company to the United States, the only country that would buy it, and he had to do it at a profit. No small matter, even for Cromwell. A major fact, not well known, was that during the time Cromwell was hatching his second scam, most of the bonds, not considered punitive bonds, were changed from registered bonds, or publicly traceable bonds, to bearer bonds, in which the owner could not be traced. Because this was done, Cromwell could and did buy up these bonds in secret.[16] The "punitive" bondholders made up about 38% of the shares, and the small bondholders made up about 62% of the shares. When sold to the United States, the punitive shares were worth $15,000,000 dollars, and the publicly traded shares were worth $25,000.000. There was even an attempt by J.P. Morgan to obtain the "punitive" bondholder shares. Early on, Bunau-Varilla's brother informed his brother that J.P. Morgan had attempted to buy the shares owned by Bunau-Varilla. As stated, Cromwell hatched this scheme and embarked upon its course while still employed by the New Panama Canal Company.

CONFLICT OF INTEREST, BIG TIME

Had the Colombian government found out about Cromwell's scheme to foment revolution, they would have had the right to confiscate the property of the New Panama Canal Company. The United States would have been subject to worldwide embarrassment, at least, and the parties to his scheme, Amador and the other revolutionaries, would have lost their lives and property. Even without this documented proof, there is every indication that Cromwell was deeply involved in inciting the Panama Revolution, even before the rejection of the Hay–Herran Treaty with Colombia. But Cromwell was not through with this matter. Mr. Cromwell's greed, and his zeal for corruption and double-dealing had no bounds.

---

[15] 2003, Ovidio Diaz Espino, How Wall Street Created A Nation, pp. 180-181;
[16] 2003, Ovidio Diaz Espino, How Wall Street Created A Nation, p. 170.

In fact, it was hard to imagine just who Cromwell was not double-dealing. For example, while working for the French Canal Company, and working with Colombia on the Hay–Herran Treaty, and Hanna on selling the Panama route to the United States, he was also employed as the attorney for the Harriman Steamship Co. that operated on the Pacific coast from San Francisco to Panama. This company, and for that matter, most other intercontinental railroads and steamship companies, were opposed to any Central American canal, not just the Panama Canal route.[17]

Like a cancer, Cromwell infected everyone around him with these same negative qualities. Some seventy years later, the reader will meet another Cromwell, by a different name, but with the same objective, the selling of the Panama Canal for personal gain.

THE POLITICAL CHANGE TO THE PANAMA ROUTE THE CONFLICT OVER A PRIVATE OR GOVERNMENT CANAL

In December 1898, it was John Bigelow, an early convert to Panama, and a friend of Secretary Hay, which convinced Hay to advise President McKinley not to commit to the Nicaragua route in his annual address to the Congress.

In January 1899, Senator John T. Morgan, an influential, well-known southern Democrat, obtained a Senate bill authorizing the construction of the Nicaragua canal. The funds to build it would come from the United States Treasury. Created as a private company, the majority of the directors of the Canal would be appointed by the United States government. The Senate bill was sent to the House on the 13th of February 1899.

Colonel Hepburn, an equally influential Republican, supported the idea of a canal in Nicaragua but opposed the Morgan bill. Hepburn introduced his own bill, which advocated that the canal should be built by the United States government, and he vilified the idea that the United States could create a private company under the legal and financial control of the government of the United States. Neither politician would accept the bill of the other, and as a result, no action was taken.

A major argument, although more complex, was who would sponsor the final bill, Morgan and the Democrats, or Hepburn and the Republicans. In 1902, too late to be effective, Morgan agreed to accept the Hepburn Bill, but was unable to pass it in the Senate.

---

[17] Rainey resolution, p 63-64; Committee on foreign affairs, House of Representatives, Feb. 9,12, 1912, entitled "the story of Panama".

As stated, President McKinley forced the Congress to pass a resolution to provide for a new commission, "The Isthmian Canal Commission," chaired by Admiral Walker, to study all the known canal routes, and, the Panama and Nicaragua routes. Twice the Commission recommended the Nicaragua route. In 1900, it released its preliminary report recommending Nicaragua, and again in a final report in 1901. However, on January 21, 1902, the commission reversed its position and recommended the Panama route.

THE CHANGE OF POSITION

A partial reason for this change of position? Members of the commission, Morrison, Burr, and Ernst visited France, and Bunau-Varilla convinced them of the virtues of the Panama Canal. These men were introduced to Bunau-Varilla through his friend Mr. Frank Pavey, a member of the New York Bar and a former senator of the State of New York. In 1912, Pavey chaired the House Committee on Foreign Affairs' hearing on the Rainey Resolution, The Story of Panama. Ernst was also a friend of Bigelow. Bunau-Varilla attributed Mr. Morrison as the person that was able to change the position of the commission in favor of the Panama route.

On December 25, 1901, Senator Hanna sent a cablegram published by the Le Matin, a Paris newspaper associated with Bunau-Varilla, offering to take a second look at the Panama route, if the New Panama Canal Company was willing to sell its holdings for $40,000,000 dollars.

Although he had punitive stock in the company, allegedly worth $400,000 dollars, Bunau-Varilla was no friend of the New Panama Canal Company. However, he knew that a successful Panama Canal route depended upon the directors of the New French Panama Canal Company selling the company at a price close to the estimate given by the Walker Commission. Bunau-Varilla had been trying for months to get the company to make that commitment. Finally, on January 4, 1902, the New Panama Canal president, Marius Bo, sent a message to his representative in the United States, Boeufve, directing him to inform Admiral Walker that the company was willing to sell to the United States government, all of its holdings for $40,000,000 dollars. On January 9, 1902, the company sent a similar cablegram directly to Admiral Walker with a similar offer.

On January 20, 1902, President Roosevelt submitted a report of the Walker Commission to the Congress, recommending the Panama route. [18]

---

[18] Senate Doc. No. 123, 57th Congress, 1st session, p.19.

CHAPTER SIX
THE SPOONER COMPROMISE

THE NEGOTIATIONS BEGIN THE SPOONER AMENDMENT

IN LATE JANUARY 1902, Senator Spooner offered legislation that accepted the findings of the Walker Commission, but also recommended the Nicaragua route if the title could not be obtained from the New Panama Canal Company, and if a satisfactory treaty with Colombia could not be reached. On May 6, 1902, Mount Pele' erupted on the Island of Martinique, and the fight over the Spooner Act began. The debate lasted for about seventeen days.

Bunau-Varilla's activities were well documented, because of his association with the French newspaper Le Matin. He initially used this newspaper to publish his positions on the Panama Canal route. The Times and the Sun, in the United States, reproduced these news releases. Later, these newspapers were to produce their own favorable news releases on the issue. In addition, Bunau-Varilla produced the pamphlet taken from his speeches of 1901, described as "comparative characteristics of Panama, and Nicaragua," which, among other issues, emphasized the volcanic instability in Nicaragua, and he sent every senator a copy of it. Senator Hanna, among others, used the information in this document to argue in favor of the Spooner Act. On May 14, 1902, Mount Momotombo, located in Nicaragua, erupted. The advocates of the Nicaragua route denied the news of the eruption. In response, Bunau-Varilla sent each senator an official Nicaraguan postage stamp depicting the eruption of Mount Momotombo, and on June 19, 1902, the Spooner Resolution was enacted in the Senate.

Even Senator Morgan voted in favor of the act. Bunau-Varilla did the same for each member of the house, and the following day the resolution was passed in the House of Representatives. The president signed it into law on the 29th of June 1902. Several favorable letters were written by the primary author and advocates of the Spooner Act, citing the contribution of Bunau-Varilla regarding this matter.

THE SPOONER BILL WAS NOT AN EASY ACT TO PASS

The Spooner bill, a Senate bill in favor of the Panama route, conflicted with the House's Hepburn bill, which was in favor of the Nicaragua route. On March 1902, the Senate committee presented a report to the Senate rejecting the Spooner bill and voting 7 to 4 in favor of the Nicaragua route. The Hepburn bill passed the House 309 to 2.

In June, a Senate debate began and lasted for two weeks. Senator Hanna and Senator Cullom, who were originally in favor of the Nicaragua route, suddenly supported the Panama route. The issues centered on whether or not Colombia would allow the transfer of the Canal concession to the United States, and whether or not Colombia would agree to an acceptable treaty with the United States. The final vote substituted the Spooner bill—in favor of the Panama route—and the minority Senate report in place of the Hepburn bill, which was in favor of the Nicaragua route. The bill passed by a narrow margin of 42 to 35. The bill was sent to the House and was rejected. Both bills were sent to a conference committee.

The Spooner bill was finally accepted by the House and passed into law. It was signed by the president on June 28, 1902. It provided that Colombia accept a satisfactory treaty with the United States, and it required that the transfer of the Canal title be approved. If either of these issues were not met, then the United States would seek a satisfactory treaty with Nicaragua.

The Spooner amendment was just one more congressional act that Cromwell was eager to claim as his own. Soon after his reinstatement by the New Panama Canal Company, Cromwell sent a message that he had "inspired" the bill that outlined the principles of the Spooner Act or amendment.

In answer to an inquiry by Senator Morgan on the Senate floor, Senator Spooner contradicted Cromwell's claim. Cromwell's claim, contained in his message to the New Panama Canal Company, never became public until several years later, and he never publicly contradicted the statements made by Senator Spooner. In addition to the Spooner Act, Cromwell had alleged that he single-handedly thwarted the Morgan–Hepburn bills of 1898 and 1899, and that he, allegedly, was equally responsible for the creation of the new Walker Commission of June 15, 1899. Of course, none of these allegations were true, but these and other false claims were enough to convince the directors of the New Panama Canal Company and his financial associates of his importance in their cause, both before he was dismissed and after he was reinstated.[1]

PRE-TREATY ACTIVITIES OF COLOMBIA

Soon after the Spooner Resolution was presented in January 1902, attention was directed to Colombia to determine what conditions would be required to obtain the sale of the holding of the New Panama Canal Company.

At the time, Colombia was controlled by President Marroquin, a dictator that was preoccupied in holding onto power within his country. Colombia was beset with constant instances of insurrection.

CROMWELL'S REINSTATEMENT AS COUNCIL TO THE NEW PANAMA CANAL COMPANY

Elsewhere in this book, I have explained when and why Cromwell was dismissed from his position with the New Panama Canal Company on June 19, 1901. On January 27, 1902, Cromwell was reinstated. Bunau-Varilla, at the request of Senator Hanna, helped get Cromwell reinstated. Hanna acted at the request of his long-time banker and friend J. Edward Simmons, an investor, and signatory to Cromwell's first and second schemes to buy up shares of the New Panama Canal Company for pennies on the dollar and sell them to the United States at an enormous profit. Obviously, Cromwell, and the signatories to his second scheme felt a need to have him working from the inside of the New Panama Canal Company, and therefore, in a better position to effect the sale of its holdings to the United States. On the other hand, the New Panama Canal Company was reluctant to have him back. The company's letters and cablegrams to Cromwell on the 27th and 29th, clearly indicate they did not trust him.[2]

Again, true to form, Cromwell attributed his reinstatement to the company's need for his services, which was not at all the reason that they rehired him. In addition, on January 31, 1902, in a letter to the company, Cromwell takes credit

---

[1] 1912, Bunau-Varilla, Statement on Behalf of Historical Truth, pp. 45-56.
[2] Rainey Resolution, pp. 168-169; Bunau-Varilla, Statement on Behalf of Historical Truth, pp. 42-43.

for devising a "program" for the upcoming treaty negotiations between Colombia and the United States, taking credit for the Spooner Act.[3]

There is no doubt that, due to his newfound position as general counsel of the New Panama Canal Company, Cromwell had access to the representatives of Colombia and the United States, especially on the issues related to that company. But Cromwell seemed to imply that he did a lot more. In his statement, inserted in the Rainey Resolution, Cromwell has stated that he convinced Concha, the chargé d'affaires of Colombia, to change his position regarding the sale of the New Panama Canal Company's property to the United States to one that was more conciliatory. He even went further and stated that he helped Concha prepare a treaty that would cover the issues involving the New Panama Canal Company, the issues of international law, the special interests of Colombia, and the treaty of 1846. Outlining his activities, Cromwell stated that he wrote "a new draft known as the Hay–Concha Treaty"—and stated that "in all the negotiations concerning the Hay–Concha agreement, the ministers of the two governments communicated solely through the intermediary of Mr. Cromwell." [4]

All that Cromwell has stated was done with a man, Concha, which refused to leave New York until he was given special instructions from his government. A man, Concha, that genuinely disliked Americans, or any foreigners for that matter, and described Cromwell as a "rat," and not to be trusted. A man, Concha, which was sent to the United States to extract an exorbitant financial reward from the United States and the New Panama Canal Company without giving up its right to sovereignty over the Canal.

True to form, Cromwell laid claim to moving the government of Colombia toward allowing the New Panama Canal Company to sell its holdings to the United States. In his brief to the arbiters of the French Panama Canal Company describing his activities of that time—which was presented to the House Foreign Affairs Committee in 1912—Cromwell stated that, after the failure of the Morgan–Hepburn bills of 1899, the Colombian legation in Washington was closed. In December 1900, Cromwell stated that he met with the consul general of Colombia in New York and convinced him to urge President Marroquin to send a minister to the United States to "deal with the Canal question."

---

[3] Rainey Resolution, p. 169; Bunau-Varilla, Statement on Behalf of Historical Truth, p. 45.

[4] Rainey resolution, pp 175-179; Committee on foreign affairs, House of Representatives, Feb. 9.12, 1912, entitled "the story of Panama".

DR. SILVA REPRESENTS THE COLOMBIAN GOVERNMENT

On December 27, 1900, President Marroquin replied by cable that he was sending Mr. Martinez Silva, and that he would arrive by January 1901.[5]

In February 1901, Silva arrived in New York. On March 7, 1901, Silva sent a message to his government, advising them that, without a press campaign, there was little that he could do. Apparently, he had gotten advice from Cromwell, who wanted Colombia to help pay for his own press campaign.[6] On March 13, 1901, Silva met with Secretary of State Hay. During that meeting, Silva informed Hay that the Colombian government was not opposed to the United States obtaining the holdings of the New Panama Canal Company, provided the terms were satisfactory to Colombia. In the back and forth correspondence between Silva and his government, several issues were discussed.

The first issue was the fear that the favorable conclusion of the Hay–Pauncefote Treaty would move the United States to the Nicaragua route, in which case, the Panama route would be a dead issue. The second issue was the adamant demand that any canal in Panama must be under the sovereignty of Colombia. The third issue was the legality of the Reyes–New Panama Canal Company concession extension of 1904–1910. The fourth issue was what financial gain the Colombian government would get for its cooperation on the matter.

On January 8, 1902, after the Canal Commission pressed him on the Colombian position on the sale of the New Panama Canal Company to the United States, Silva wrote to his government discussing what he thought the Canal Company should pay the Colombian government for giving their permission to sell the company's holdings. In his message, Silva suggests that, without the Colombian permission, the company will lose everything. He goes on to state that the company expects to sell its holdings for $40,000,000 dollars, and he believes Colombia should receive three million dollars from the company. Silva did not receive further instructions but was informed that he would be replaced by another minister, Dr. José Vicente Concha, who would finalize the negotiations.[7]

In addition, on February 11, 1902, Silva received a scathing cablegram from

---

[5] Rainey resolution, pp159-160; Committee on foreign affairs, House of Representatives, Feb. 9.12, 1912, entitled "the story of Panama".

[6] Rainey resolution, pp 160-161; Committee on foreign affairs, House of Representatives, Feb. 9.12, 1912, entitled "the story of Panama".

[7] Rainey resolution, p 167; Committee on foreign affairs, House of Representatives, Feb. 9,12, 1912, entitled "the story of Panama".

the governor pro tempore of the Isthmus, Mr. Arjona, denouncing his perceived understanding that Silva had stipulated the relinquishment of Colombia's sovereignty, and that "it would be better if the negotiations should fail than let that happen." It was clear, from the tone of this cablegram, the position of the Colombian government on the matter.

Bunau-Varilla was also in contact with Silva, attempting to convince Colombia to give permission to the Canal Company to sell its holdings. Allegedly, Silva told Bunau-Varilla that they were of like minds, and that he would be happy to have Bunau-Varilla, who was well known in Colombia because of his work on the old Panama Canal, send a telegram to President Marroquin that would support his own opinion.

Bunau-Varilla sent an extensive cablegram to President Marroquin on the 23rd of February, and Minister Concha arrived in New York on the 24th of February 1902 to replace Silva. Silva died on his way back to Colombia.[8]

On February 27, 1902, the Colombian government gave formal notice to the Panama Canal Company that it could not transfer its property without permission from Colombia. Colombia had five million francs in shares in the company and a representative director on the board. In addition, article 21 and article 22 of the contract of 1878 gave Colombia the right to confiscate the company's property if they tried to sell to a "foreign entity," unless Colombia gave their approval.

On February 28, 1902, the New Panama Canal Company called a general meeting and postponed all action on the sale of its property to the United States until the issue regarding the rights of Colombia was settled.

THE 1902 CIVIL WAR IN COLOMBIA, AND A BETTER DEAL WAS MADE?

The Canal treaty negotiations were not done in a vacuum. The civil unrest in Colombia, and the cost of paying for that civil war was, apparently, uppermost in the mind of the government of Colombia. It was a major cause of the defeat of the Hay–Concha and Hay–Herran treaties.

During the summer of 1902, the head of the Liberal Party in Colombia, Mr. Carlos Lievano, met several times with the United States representative in Colombia, Mr. Hart, to help terminate the civil war in Colombia in favor of the Liberals. The Liberals "had defeated the government of José Manual Marroquin

---

[8] Bunau-Varilla, Panama: The Creation, The Destruction, and the Resurrection, pp.219-210.

almost everywhere except Panama." The Liberals "were at the point of victory with 7,000 troops against a government force of less than 3,000." On September 8, 1902, news reached the United States of the surrender of government forces to the revolutionists after a month's siege at Aguadulce, Panama. Lievano appealed to Hart, indicating that Colombia had already lost 80,000 men, and that if the Liberal Party came into power, they would negotiate a favorable treaty with the United States.[9] Initially, Hart agreed with Lievano. However, within days, he reversed his position, stating, "It's all off; there's no revolution. ... You know we have to build the Canal."

Lievano was informed that the son of General Marroquin, Lorenzo Marroquin, and Aristides Fernandez had also come to request intervention in the civil war on behalf of the Conservatives and pledged the Marroquin government would enter into a satisfactory treaty with the United States. This resulted in "The Treaty of Peace," which was signed on the battleship Wisconsin on November 21, 1902.

General Lucas Caballero signed the treaty of peace on behalf of the Liberals and stated: the American officers openly declared future intervention to assist the Panamanians to win their independence, or the annexation of Panama by the United States if the conflict was not ended. He stated that this was one of the reasons that the Liberals ended their successful war.[10]

On September 12, 1902, the secretary of the navy cabled the commander of the Ranger at Panama not to permit transportation of troops that would convert the Panama Railroad into a theater of hostilities. On September 14, 1902, the Panther sailed from League Island, with 320 marines, and with four rapid-fire guns. The Cincinnati arrived at Colon on September 16, 1902, landed marines and put them aboard Panama Railroad trains.[11]

THE HAY–CONCHA NEGOTIATIONS

On January 22, 1902, Minister Concha was given instructions to negotiate a Canal treaty with the United States, on the best terms for Colombia, and with the strict instructions not to give up sovereignty. On January 27, 1902, he was given further instructions to obtain no less than $20,000,000 dollars from the

---

[9] Raincy resolution, pp. 185; Committee on foreign affairs, House of Representatives, Feb. 9,12, 1912, entitled "the story of Panama".

[10] Ibid: p.184.

[11] Ibid: p.186.

New Panama Canal Company for Colombia's permission to sell its holdings to the United States.[12]

All during the Hay–Concha Treaty negotiations, the United States, under the right of the 1846 treaty, had troops stationed in Panama and restricted Colombian military movements within the railroad right of way. The United States naval forces landed marines and prevented either side from using the Panama Railroad and established a "neutrality" zone. However, it was a well-known fact that the Panama Railroad was aiding the revolutionists by moving their munitions and refusing transportation to the government forces. "Freight tags of the railroad" taken from the "revolutionary ordinance" were used as exhibits by the governor of Panama in a suit he was preparing against the Panama Railroad before his death.[13]

Mr. Hall attributes this double-dealing to the Roosevelt administration. However, it was a well-known fact that Cromwell controlled the Panama Railroad Company, and nothing occurred there without his knowledge and permission.

The cables and letters between Concha, the government of Colombia, and Secretary of State Hay clearly indicate that Concha spent his tenure as representative of Colombia in the United States arguing that his version of Title XXII, of the Hay–Concha Treaty, regarding the interpretation of the 1846 treaty was the correct interpretation. In short, the United States was unlawfully occupying Panama under a false interpretation of the 1846 treaty.

On August 25, 1902, the Colombian government sent Concha a cable telling him to inform the United States that the Colombian government agreed in principle to the amendments presented by the United States, but ratification of the treaty must be done by the Colombian Congress.

The cable further stated, before that can happen, the "pacification of Panama must take place." On September 20, 1902, the Colombian government cabled Concha that they were sending an army to the Isthmus and instructed him to demand from the United States the execution of the treaty of 1846 to assure free passage from Colon to Panama City.

On September 24, 1902, the governor of Panama cabled President Marroquin that American troops had disembarked in Panama City, and that Minister Concha had stated that he would protest the action. On September 25, 1902, the Colombian government cabled Concha, ordering him not to interfere in the

---

[12] Rainey resolution, p 167; Committee on foreign affairs, House of Representatives, Feb. 9.12, 1912, entitled "the story of Panama".

[13] Ibid: p.185.

matter, which would be taken up by the minister of foreign affairs. On October 3, Concha cabled the Colombian government, protesting his orders of September 25, 1902, and stated, "For the fourth time, I resign from this legation."

That same day, he cabled a lengthy message to his government, informing them that the American forces had "established a "de-facto" supreme government in Panama. "Colombian forces are disarmed, their officers travel in the custody of the Americans, and even the governor is escorted like a viceroy." On October 7, 1902, the Colombia government answered Concha's cable: "Your resignation is unpatriotic and inadmissible."[14]

On October 25, 1902, Concha again offered his resignation, and stated that it was "impossible to advance the negotiations of the Panama Canal while there still exists the order prohibiting my discussion of the interpretation of the treaty of 1846-1848, an essential part of the future treaty." On October 30, 1902, Concha sent his government another lengthy cable citing the events that occurred during the insurrection of 1885 in Panama and compared those events to what the United States government was doing in Panama in 1902.

On October 29, 1902, Concha cabled his government that he also sent the foregoing in a letter to Secretary Hay. Hay told him that the United States would adopt the Nicaragua route if the treaty was not signed before the United States Congress met in December.[15] Secretary Hay also cabled the Colombia government and informed them that the United States would act under the Spooner Act, and negotiate a treaty with Nicaragua, if they did not act promptly.

On November 4, 1902, under orders of his government, Concha met with Secretary Hay and demanded that his version of Article XXII that he'd drafted in April, and that Hay had previously accepted, be reinstated. His draft of Article XXII was Concha's interpretation of the 1846 treaty. On November 6, 1902, Concha cabled his government, informing them that he had not received a reply to his demand related to Article XXII. Concha further stated that no matter what Hay's reply may be, he would not sign any treaty while there was an American occupation of the Isthmus. On November 7, 1902, Concha again submitted his resignation. On November 14, 1902, President Marroquin cabled Concha informing him that "the Congress meets 1st of March. Ask all possible advantages in respect to Article XXII. In any case, sign the treaty to save our responsibility. The Congress of Colombia must decide definitely." The president ordered Hay to accept Concha's interpretation of Article XXII. After gaining this concession,

---

[14] Ibid: p. 187.
[15] Ibid: p. 189.

Concha immediately submitted seven additional amendments. On November 18, 1902, Secretary Hay agreed to Mr. Concha's interpretation of XXII, and demanded that Colombia decide Colombia's indemnity by payment of $7,000,000 dollars, and an annuity of $100,000, or $10,000,000, and an annuity of $10,000, and further indicated that Colombia should no longer delay which alternative it would choose.

Concha cabled his government on November 19, 1902, informing them that the United States gave him an ultimatum, refusing an increase of the amount of the indemnity. He stated that they sustained changes in the memorandum of July 18, 1902, denied return to Colombia of government lands, refused to allow the Panama Canal Company to enter into a previous arrangement with the Colombian government, argued that the treaty permits the United States to enter a concession without other conditions, and does not accept that the Canal Company lease has an accepted termination period. He went on to state that he did not believe the treaty was advisable.

Again, on November 19, 1902, Concha addressed the Colombia government in a second cable, stating that he could not agree with the treaty, because "it sacrifices Colombia without even the excuse of pecuniary advantage." He stated that Colombia would receive even less than it now gets from the Panama Railroad alone ($250,000 dollars a year). Finally, Concha stated that his resignation was irrevocable.[16]

On November 22, 1902, Concha sent a lengthy reply to Secretary Hay, addressing the issues he cited in his cable to the Colombian government on November 19, 1902.

On November 28, 1902, Concha finally cabled his government that Dr. Herran would take his place as chargé d'affaires, and left Washington without waiting for his letters of recall or notifying the State Department. His last official act was to send the Hay–Concha Treaty of November 18, 1902, to Colombia without his signature.

THE HAY–HERRAN NEGOTIATIONS BEGIN

On December 11, 1902, Dr. Herran received a cable from Colombia instructing him, "Do all you can to get $10,000,000 dollars cash and $600,000 yearly payment, and all possible advantages as per former instructions." The cable instructed him to obtain a written declaration from the United States government that they will

---

[16] Ibid: pp. 192, 315.

not make any better terms, and if not, "sign the treaty with the stipulation that it will be subject to whatever the Colombian Congress decides." [17]

Both Cromwell and Bunau-Varilla, at least in this one case, were working for the same ends, if not together, in trying to convince the Colombia government, and, President Marroquin, and Vice President of the Colombian Senate General Nel Ospina that they needed to ratify a new acceptable Canal treaty with the United States.[18] Soon after, Bunau-Varilla sent his cables to President Marroquin, and Mr. Concha was recalled and replaced by Mr. Herran as chargé d'affaires for Colombia. In his message to the Congress, dated December 2, 1902, President Roosevelt indicated he would give Colombia a delay before closing the negotiations. Dr. Herran had sent a letter to his government stating that, in an early version of that speech, President Roosevelt had given Colombia until January 5, 1903, to decide on the terms of the treaty.

On December 19, 1902, Dr. Herran sent a letter to the Colombian government, citing Senator Cullom, the chairman of the Foreign Affairs Committee, in which Cullom cites the possibility that the United States may "expropriate" the Canal, justifying this on the grounds of "universal public utility," and pay Colombia later. Herran went on to state that this idea, although far-fetched, was not out of the question, based upon the fact that President Roosevelt was a "determined partisan of the Panama route," and based upon Roosevelt's "impetuous and violent disposition," Senator Cullom's scheme was "not distasteful to him." (Meaning Roosevelt)

On December 25, 1902, Dr. Herran cabled Colombia informing them that he expected an "ultimatum January 5" (1903).

Instead, Secretary Hay sent a letter to Dr. Herran, dated December 30, 1902, requesting the condition of their negotiations, so that he could report the same to the president. On December 31, Dr. Herran replied, again stating that his position was the same regarding the annuity of $600,000 dollars a year. He further suggested that this issue could be resolved by a future contract, since the period when the annuity would begin would take place in the future.

On January 3, 1903, Dr. Herran sent a cable to Colombia, stating that the United States agreed to his proposal to renegotiate the $100,000-dollar annuity after nine years.

Also, on January 3, 1903, the minister of the United States in Colombia in-

---

[17] Ibid: 316.

[18] Bunau-Varilla, Panama: The Creation, The Destruction, and the Resurrection.pp.257-258.

formed Secretary Hay that the Colombia government intended to demand an indemnity from the Panama Canal Company, independent of the treaty negotiations.

On January 8, 1903, Dr. Herran warned his government that President Roosevelt was anxious to procure a treaty with Colombia before March 4, 1903, the close of the United States congressional session, but if that was not possible, he would defer to the Nicaragua route.

It is difficult, at this late date, to discover just how much Cromwell or Bunau-Varilla played in these negotiations. Actually, Cromwell was considered a "rat" by Concha and distrusted completely. How he felt about Bunau-Varilla is anyone's guess. In the case of Dr. Herran, his cables and letters to his government speak for themselves. On January 9, 1903, he sent a long letter to the Colombian government, describing his relationship with Cromwell and Bunau-Varilla. In that letter, he stated that, initially, the common interests of Colombia and the agents of the Panama Canal Company (Cromwell) were "useful," but "now these interests are no longer common, and I am now working independent of our former allies." Also, in that letter, he described Bunau-Varilla as "trying to intervene officiously in this affair, and I know that he has been sending cables to the Colombian government." "This gentleman is an important shareholder of the Canal Company, but he holds no official position in it; his activity is entirely on his own account, and he represents solely his own interests."

Uppermost in Cromwell's mind was not the treaty, but Colombia's insistence to extract an indemnity from the Panama Canal Company, independent of the treaty.

On January 9, 1903, "The secretary positively knew that the reason for the delay was due to the refusal of the Panama Canal Company to negotiate for the consent of Colombia, and to pay the tribute which Colombia was determined to extract."

On January 10, President Marroquin, and Foreign Minister Paul cabled that they understood that the "Concha" amendments were still in the treaty.

On January 16, 1903, the United States minister to Colombia, Mr. Paul, cabled Secretary Hay informing him that "Colombia will not accept the offer of the United States and has given Herran instructions to insist on the terms stated and upon all the Concha amendments; and further, an agent of the Panama Canal Company, in Bogota, must be appointed."

Also, on January 16, 1903, Secretary Hay sent a letter to Dr. Herran informing him that he has told his minister in Colombia that if Colombia persists in its "present attitude, it will make impossible further negotiations."

After much haggling between Hay and Herran, and suggestions and warnings, both written and verbal, by Cromwell and Bunau-Varilla, Hay gave Herran an ultimatum that the United States would agree to giving Colombia $10,000,000 dollars and $250,000 a year in compensation.[19]

On January 22, 1903, Secretary Hay informed Dr. Herran that he had been authorized by the President of the United States to offer $250,000 dollars in annuity, and the time for negotiations had come to a conclusion, and he was not authorized to consider or discuss any other changes.

Also on January 22, 1903, Dr. Herran cabled his government that he had signed the treaty, accepting the ultimatum of ten million dollars, and $250,000 dollars in annuity.

Too late, On January 24, 1903, Dr. Herran received a cable from President Marroquin stating, "Do not sign the treaty." "You will receive instructions in letter of to-day." This letter of instruction was never printed in the Colombian Blue Book.

On February 7, 1903, José Pablo Uribe, the minister of Colombia to France, informed his government that the "Paris Bourse" published a notice that they would not accept a purchase or sale of any shares of the Panama Canal Company except those shares with the number 1 to 600,000. This excluded Colombia's shares, 600,001 to 650,000. This announcement gave added pressure to Colombia to ratify the treaty, as it would render the Colombian shares almost worthless unless they ratified the treaty.

On March 17, 1903, in a special session of the Congress, the treaty for a Panama Canal was ratified by the Senate of the United States by a vote of 73 to 5. [20]

On May 7, 1903, Mr. Mancini, the Canal Company agent in Colombia, stated that the amount Colombia was demanding was 50,000,000 francs.

On April 7, 1903, Secretary Hay sent a cable to his minister in Colombia, directing him to inform the Colombian government that any changes to the treaty would be in conflict with the Spooner Act.

On August 12, 1903, a surprise and embarrassment to the United States government, Colombia rejected the Hay–Herran Treaty.[21]

---

[19] Rainey resolution, pp. 316-321; Committee on foreign affairs, House of Representatives, Feb. 9.12, 1912, entitled "the story of Panama".

[20] Bunau-Varilla, Panama: The Creation, The Destruction, and the Resurrection, p.258.

[21] Rainey resolution, p. 330; Committee on foreign affairs, House of Representatives, Feb. 9,12, 1912, entitled "the story of Panama".

CHAPTER SEVEN
THE SEEDS OF REVOLUTION BEGIN

EXTORTION OF A HIGH ORDER

On August 29, 1903, even after the treaty had been rejected, General Nel Ospina, vice president of the Colombian Senate, with Senators Manuel Maria Rodriguez, and Luis F. Campo, presented a motion on which the treaty could be acceptable to Colombia. Their proposal entailed a demand of $20,000,000 dollars, instead of $10,000,000, from the United States. They also demanded that the annual rental should be $400,000 instead of $250,000 a year until 1967 and increased by 25% every one-hundred years. In addition, the proposal would demand that the New Panama Canal Company would be required to pay $20,000,000 to Colombia before Colombia would allow the New Panama Canal Company to transfer its properties to the United States.

The Hay–Herran Treaty with Colombia would give the United States a ninety-nine-year lease on any future canal. Why that treaty was rejected really doesn't matter. There was no doubt at that time that the United States, and only the United States, was going to build a canal in Panama. The French had already lost interest in the canal with the failure of the sea-level canal in 1889. The English, in agreeing to the Hay–Pauncefote Treaty in 1901, relinquished their interest in that endeavor. These countries were the only other world powers that had shown any serious interest in the enterprise.

Through the negotiation of the Hay–Herran Treaty with Colombia, the United States was clearly showing an effort to resolve the matter peacefully and in good faith. It would have been ludicrous to believe that the United States would pick up their marbles and go home after the Hay–Herran Treaty was rejected by Colombia. The United States was not about to allow a competing power to control a canal on the Isthmus that could threaten the economic expansion and regional influence of the United States.

REVOLUTION AND DOUBLE-DEALING BECAME THE NAME OF THE GAME CROMWELL SHOWS HIS TRUE COLORS

Between March and August of 1903, the news media was abuzz with stories from unnamed sources speculating on what the United States and the people of Panama would do if Colombia rejected the Hay–Herran Treaty.

In July of 1903, huddled around a table in the center of a patio sat some of the most influential people in Panama. They were visitors at a cattle ranch owned by Tomas Arias just outside of Panama City. They had been discussing revolution at least as far back as the collapse of the French Canal Company in 1888. Not knowing the outcome of the Hay–Herran Treaty, they were again discussing what to do if the treaty between the United States and Colombia was not ratified.

Panama, once a prosperous and thriving province of Colombia, was now neglected and impoverished, beset by squalor, decay, and rampant unemployment. The only businesses left in Panama were the Panama Canal Railroad, a caretaker administration from the French Panama Canal, some landowners, bankers, merchants, steamship agents, and newspaper owners. The law enforcement in Panama came from a small contingent of Colombian soldiers that, allegedly, had not been paid for months by the Colombian government. These men had not been given any indication that they would be paid any time soon. Many, if not most, of these soldiers were young, uneducated men, with ragged uniforms, many shoeless, and unhappy with their position. The fire brigade was led by José Gabriel Duque, a Cuban American, owner of the Panama Star & Herald, and the owner of the Panama lottery.

Some of the principal conspirators at that meeting were José Agustin Arango, Manual Amador Guerro, Richardo Arias, Frederico Boyd, Nicanor de Obarrio, Carlos Arosemena, and Manual Espinosa. Also present were Arthur Grudger, the United States consul general in Panama, Herbert Prescott, assistant superintendent of the Panama Railroad, Richard Prescott, H.L. Jeffries, a soldier of fortune, and José Gabriel Duque. The officials of the Panama Canal Railroad were predominantly American citizens.

In addition, the conspirators had enlisted José Agustin Arango, to ask Captain James Beers, the freight agent and port captain of the Pacific terminal of the Panama Railroad, to act as a liaison between them and Nelson Cromwell. Beers was a longtime friend of Arango and was considered a friend of Cromwell. They knew that, without Cromwell's financial support, they could not overthrow the Colombian government. In mid-July, Beers left for New York, and upon his return in early August, he assured everyone that Cromwell would stand by them with financial support and support from the American government.[1] A more detailed depth of this conspiracy and the principals involved can be found in The Rainey Resolution: The Story of Panama.[2]

Little did the conspirators know that the Colombian government was aware of their intentions. In June of 1903, Minister Herran cabled his government that if the Hay–Herran Treaty was not ratified, the probable result would be a revolution in Panama. On July 6, 1903, General Pedro Velez R., of Barranquilla, Colombia, while visiting the United States, sent his brother, Luis Velez R., governor of the department of Bolivar, Colombia, a letter, describing a newspaper report outlining what would happen if the Hay–Herran Treaty was not ratified by Colombia. In it, the report indicated that the United States might take possession of the Canal by force, and that if that did not happen, a revolution would take place, and the United States would recognize the new government. He went on to state that a group of men from Panama arrived in Washington to find out if the United States would support their revolution. The United States, in turn, had made inquiries in Europe for finding out if those countries would object to the revolution if it was immediately followed by the construction of the Canal. The answer was favorable. General Velez recommended sending forces to Panama to subdue any revolution that may occur. This information was relayed to President Marroquin, the minister of foreign affairs, the minister of war, and the president of the Colombian Senate.[3]

Before leaving the United States, General Velez interviewed Nelson Cromwell regarding the Canal question. Cromwell told him that the United States public would not tolerate such an action.[4]

---

[1] 2003, Ovidio Diaz Espino, How Wall Street Created A Nation, pp. 49-52.

[2] Rainey resolution, pp 348-357; Committee on foreign affairs, House of Representatives, Feb.9,12, 1912, entitled "the story of Panama".

[3] Rainey resolution, p.347; Committee on foreign affairs, House of Representatives, Feb. 9,12, 1912, entitled "the story of Panama".

[4] Ibid; p. 347 (US)

While assuring General Velez that the American public would not tolerate the United States government's support of a Panama revolution, Cromwell, after meeting with President Roosevelt, had his press agent submit an article dated July 13, 1903, and published on July 14, 1903, in the New York World.

The article indicated that the president was determined to build a canal in Panama. He had no intention of beginning negotiations for the Nicaragua route, and that to reject the Hay–Herran Treaty would be unfair to the United States after three Colombian representatives worked to sign that treaty. The article went on to state that certain factions of Panama were ready to secede, and ratify a new treaty, if the Colombian Congress did not ratify the Hay–Herran Treaty. The article went into detail how this plan would go into effect.[5] In addition, prior to June 20, 1903, Cromwell decided to meet José Augustin Arango or one of Cromwell's representatives in Jamaica. José Augustin Arango, a reputed friend of Cromwell, was one of the leaders of the Panama conspirators, the attorney and lobbyist of the Panama Railroad Company, and a senator from the Department of Panama to the Colombian Legislature. June 20, 1903 was the date set for the Congress of Colombia to reconvene. At the last minute, Arango received a cable canceling the appointment with Cromwell.[6]

Arango was convinced that Colombia would reject the treaty and decided not to take his seat in the Colombian Congress.[7]

COLOMBIA'S ATTEMPT TO MODIFY THE HAY–HERRAN TREATY

From July to August 1903, there was a back and forth discussion between Secretary Hay, the representative of the United States in Colombia, Minister Beaupre, and the Colombian minister of foreign affairs, regarding the right of Colombia to insert amendments to the Hay–Herran Treaty. It was the position of the United States that it would violate the Spooner Act and the provisions of the treaty of 1846–1848, and the United States would not accept any amendments. It was the position of Colombia that they had a right to make any amendment they felt necessary to protect the rights of their country.[8] From August 12, 1903, the date

---

[5] 1940, Miles P. DuVal, Jr. Cadiz to Cathay, pp. 257-258.
[6] Rainey resolution, p. 348; Committee on foreign affairs, House of Representatives, Feb. 9,12, 1912, entitled "the story of Panama".
[7] Ibid; p. 348 (US)
[8] Ibid; p. 350-351 (US)

the Hay–Herran Treaty was rejected, to the end of August, there was a futile effort by Herran and Cromwell to salvage the treaty.

COLOMBIA'S BLACKMAIL

The issue for Colombia was always the right to extract a price from the New Panama Canal Company and the Panama Canal Railroad Company, independently from the price they wanted from the United States.

The issue for Mr. Cromwell was to avoid paying Colombia these independent charges. The issue for the United States was to negotiate the treaty in good faith, without being subjected to blackmail.

After the failure of the treaty, the Colombian Senate appointed a special committee to address a Canal treaty that would be acceptable to Colombia and the United States. A report was completed but not submitted. Mr. Beaupre, the U.S. minister in Colombia, obtained a "synopsis" of that report, and on September 25, 1903, he sent a cable to Washington describing the report. The report was the first definite expression of Colombia's attempt to blackmail the United States.

The report approved Colombia's rejection of the Hay–Herran Treaty. The financial issues contained in the report provided that the Panama Canal Company would be permitted to transfer its concession to the United States and cancel its 50,000,000 shares of Canal stock owed to Colombia by paying $10,000,000 dollars to the Colombian government. The Panama Canal Railroad concession could continue provided the railroad agreed to pay its $250,000 annual subsidy to Colombia until 1967. After that time, the United States would be given the right to purchase the railroad "at arbitrator's price from Colombia." The United States would pay $150,000 a year until 1967, and $400,000 after that date. The Canal lease would be renewable every hundred years at 25% increase over the last hundred years. The United States must pay Colombia $20,000,000 for the concession upon ratification of the treaty. The report authorized President Marroquin to negotiate a new treaty "without subsequent ratification," subject to the limitations provided in the report. There may be an argument that the Colombian Senate never approved this report. However, based upon the sentiment expressed by most officials in Colombia, it would have passed if presented.

On September 25, 1903, Mr. Beaupre sent a cable to Secretary Hay stating that "most of the prominent Senators avoided me because of the charge frequently made that bribery was being resorted to by the United States and the consequent fear that if seen in conversation with the American minister they would be under suspicion. This was admitted to me after the rejection of the treaty." [9]

OBALDIA'S APPOINTMENT TO PANAMA

President Marroquin decided to appoint José Domingo de Obaldia as governor of Panama. In exchange, Obaldia promised to support Marroquin's handpicked future president, General Rafael Reyes. It was thought that a loyal governor in Panama would make a revolution almost impossible. However, Marroquin was told directly by Obaldia that, if there was a revolution in Panama, he would side with the Panamanians.[10] Obaldia left Bogota on September 3, 1903, and arrived in Panama on September 16, 1903, amid great fanfare, made his home with Dr. Amador, and took up his duties on September 18, 1903.

Most of the initial revolutionary conspirators were employees of the Panama Canal Railroad Company, which was under the control of Nelson Cromwell.

AMADOR'S FIRST TRIP TO NEW YORK

Dr. Amador, employed as the Panama Canal Company doctor, and the informal leader of the conspirators, along with Ricardo Arias, another conspirator, decided to travel to the United States to conduct their expected work there, before and after the revolution. At the last minute, Arias remained in Panama and Amador traveled alone. To leave Panama on legitimate business, Amador wrote his son and told him to send a cable indicating that he was sick and wanted the senior Amador to come to the States.

On August 26, 1903, Dr. Amador left Colon, Panama, on the Panama Canal Railroad steamship Seguranca. The purpose of his mission was to assure the other conspirators of Cromwell's promises; to obtain, if possible, from the secretary of state, the validity of those assurances, immediate recognition, warship protection, and finances; and to obtain support of other forces, money, and arms promised by Cromwell.

Also, on that ship was J. Gabriel Duque, owner of the Panama lottery, and owner of the Panama State & Herald. Duque was considered the richest man on the Isthmus.

Amador left Panama without enough money to pay for his lodging when he arrived in the United States. Had it not been for the fact that he won sufficient

---

[9] Ibid. p. 703
[10] Ibid. pp. 354-355 (US)

money in a ship's poker game, he would not have had enough for his immediate hotel bill upon arriving in New York.[11] Later, he arranged a personal loan with Joshua Lindo, a Panamanian banker located in New York.

DUQUE'S MEETING WITH CROMWELL, HAY, AND HERRAN

Upon arriving in the United States, Mr. Duque met Mr. Roger Farnham, Cromwell's assistant. Farnham told Duque that Cromwell wanted to see him, and they both traveled to Cromwell's office. Cromwell told Duque that he thought the Hay–Herran Treaty would fail, and that Panama should make a revolution and declare its independence. He then asked Duque if leaders in Panama had sufficient funding to support a revolution. Duque told Cromwell that they did not. Cromwell then said that if Duque put up $100,000 dollars, he would furnish the security for such a loan, to be paid after independence. Cromwell further stated that if Duque did this, he would ensure that Duque, a United States citizen, would become the first president of Panama. [12]Cromwell then contacted Secretary Hay and made an appointment in Washington and gave Duque a note of introduction to Mr. Hay. Cromwell's employee Mr. Farnham cautioned Duque not to stay in Washington or register in any hotel.

In fact, after leaving Cromwell's office, Duque met one of his friends, Charles Burdett Hart, a former American minister to Bogota, who offered to introduce Duque to Secretary Hay. Interestingly, Mr. Hart was an information conduit for Mr. Cromwell, allegedly while he was the U.S. minister to Colombia, and certainly after he had been charged and forced to resign. Duque accepted Hart's offer, and they traveled to Washington together on the night train, and ate breakfast at a Washington, D.C., restaurant called "Harvey's."

That morning, Hart introduced Duque, and Hay spent some time explaining that the United States would not allow Colombian troops to occupy Panama based upon the free transit of the railroad under the 1846–1848 treaty with Colombia. Hay was familiar with Duque, and had received several letters from him describing the atmosphere in Panama, and an outline describing how the revolution should take place. Hay refused to answer these letters.[13] Hay offered to arrange a later meeting with the president, but Duque declined the offer, stating

---

[11] Ibid; p. 359 (US)

[12] Ibid; p. 360 (US)

[13] 1940, Miles P. DuVal, Jr. Cadiz to Cathay, p. 271.

he had to sail back to Panama on September 7, 1903.[14]

Troubled by what was discussed with Hay, on September 3, 1903, Duque left Hay's office and marched straight to Minister Herran's office, a friend, and told him everything he had discussed with Hay. This American citizen and long-time resident of Panama chose the Colombian government over the conspirators and the government of the United States. He obviously thought, at the time, the revolution had no chance to succeed.

After receiving this information, on September 4, 1903, Herran passed it on to his government, and hired a detective to spy on Dr. Amador. Herran also wrote Cromwell and the Canal Company in Paris, warning them that the Colombian government would hold them responsible for any secessionist plot on the Isthmus.[15]

AMADOR'S MEETING WITH CROMWELL

Cromwell, after telling Duque that the Hay–Herran Treaty was doomed, met with Amador, on September 1, 1903, and told him the exact opposite. At their first and only meeting, Amador was given every assurance from Cromwell that he would support the revolution. Cromwell asked Amador to return later to discuss the issue.

CROMWELL AND THE WORM HAS TURNED

Shortly after his first meeting with Amador, Cromwell was informed that Duque had gone to Herran immediately after his meeting with Hay. He also received a letter from Herran informing him that the concession of both the Panama Railroad and the Panama Canal Company would be canceled if he took any part in the revolution.[16]

Cromwell's immediate reaction to this letter was to refuse to meet further with Amador. Upon confronting Amador in a waiting room outside of his office, Cromwell refused to discuss the activities of the revolution with him. In response to Amador's persistence to discuss the matter, Cromwell had Farnham practically threw Amador out of his office. On the 10th of September 1903, Cromwell sent

---

[14] Rainey resolution, p.360; Committee on foreign affairs, House of Representatives, Feb. 9,12,1912, entitled "the story of Panama".

[15] Ibid; p. 361 (US)

[16] Ibid; p. 362 (US)

a cable to the superintendent of the Panama Canal Railroad with instructions to make no move that could be considered a pretext for a complaint from the government of Colombia.[17]

Having been frozen out by Cromwell, Amador turned to Secretary of State Hay. Hay's office firmly informed him that the United States would not discuss any issue with anyone involved in a possible secession against a sister nation. Amador was emotionally destroyed, and feeling his cause was lost, prepared to return to Panama.

After refusing to discuss the matter with his own employees for over a month, Cromwell booked passage to Paris on October 15, 1903.

CROMWELL'S FALSE NARRATIVE

Cromwell had finally been threatened by Dr. Herran, in writing, regarding his complicity in the conspiracy to secede from Colombia. Because of his actions, Colombia threatened to confiscate the concessionary rights of the Panama Canal Company and the Panama Canal Railroad Company. Dr. Herran also sent a letter to the Panama Canal Company in Paris to ensure that Colombia's intentions were perfectly clear.

Cromwell knew that, regardless of what he had promised Dr. Amador, he would have to repair his relations with the Panama Canal Company commissioners in Paris, and he would have to convince the government of Colombia that he had abandoned the cause of the revolution.

He had publicly violated the explicit instructions the Panama Canal Company had given him when they had rehired him. Cromwell had to know that he was in danger of being fired again. Cromwell had dodged this same accusation in 1901–1902, while the Hay–Concha and Hay–Herran negotiations were being conducted. Prior to, and throughout these negotiations, the United States had intervened in the Colombian insurrection between the Liberals and the Conservatives headed by General José Manuel Marroquin. The United States backed Marroquin, in exchange for a favorable treaty in Panama. However, while the war was being conducted, the United States occupied the Panama Canal Railroad right of way and refused Colombian transport of men or arms along the rail line between Panama City and the City of Colon.

The railroad employees, working with the Liberals, and in violation of U.S. orders, secretly, transported Liberal arms and men between Panama and Colon.

---

[17] Ibid; p. 362 (US)

The governor of the Colombian district of Panama was about to file a suit against the officers of the Panama Railroad Company when he died. Had the governor lived, no doubt, the Panama Canal Railroad concession would have been forfeited to Colombia. The same railroad cast of characters that were involved in the 1902 secession attempt in Panama were the same cast of characters that participated in Panama's 1903 secession. Neither action could have occurred without permission of Cromwell, or at the very least, without his knowledge.

In September 1903, no doubt having been publicly exposed by his friend Mr. Duque, Cromwell was not prepared to confide with Dr. Amador nor believe that, somehow, without money, he could expect Amador to succeed in a revolution against Colombia.

Cromwell's solution was to cut off contact with Amador, and on September 10, 1903, he sent a cable to Colonel James R. Shaler, superintendent of the Railroad Company, publicly directing the employees in Panama not to take any action that could be considered an action to assist the Panama Revolution.

On September 18 or 19, Mr. Prescott, assistant superintendent of the railroad, and Mr. Hezekiah A. Grudger, the American consul general in Panama, traveled to New York, no doubt in response to the cable sent by Cromwell to Shaler on September 10, 1903.

Grudger met with Cromwell at his office, in private, and swore that no one discussed the revolution. Prescott, while waiting outside Cromwell's office, discussed nothing but the revolution with Mr. Drake, the vice president of the Panama Canal Railroad Company. When Mr. Grudger left the office, Cromwell asked Prescott to return the next day. Upon Prescott's return, he met with Mr. Roger L. Farnham and Mr. Edward B. Hill, both employees of Cromwell, who questioned Prescott extensively about the prospects of the people in Panama pulling off the revolution. Prescott told them that the revolutionists would not attempt a revolt unless they were convinced they were protected by the United States. During the two hours Prescott was at his offices, Cromwell refused to meet with him. During the conversation Prescott had with Drake, he committed himself to the revolution, and Drake informed Cromwell that evening.[18]

Conflicted maybe, but Cromwell was not going to pick up his marbles and slink off to Paris. He was not going to personally finance the revolution, and he was not convinced that the people in Panama could pull off the revolution, but he was going to do what he did best. Just as he did in 1902, he would direct other people to take the action necessary to accomplish his goal, and if they failed, he

---

[18] Ibid; pp. 363-364 (US)

could blame his employees and keep his own hands clean. Prescott and Shaler, and possibly Grudger were being set up as the fall guys. It was time for Cromwell to leave for Paris.

BUNAU-VARILLA COMES TO TOWN, AND THE REVOLUTION IS SAVED

On September 2, 1903, Bunau-Varilla openly suggested—in a published article written in the Le Matin, located in Paris—what would happen if the Hay–Herran Treaty was not ratified by the Colombian government by September 23, 1903. He posed at least two actions the President of the United States could take. Bunau-Varilla suggested that the president could wait until the revolution in Panama took place, in the manner that was done in 1840 and 1856, in which case, they would merely make a treaty with Panama. Another alternative posed by Bunau-Varilla was that the president could declare the international right of eminent domain.

Bunau-Varilla sent a sealed, marked copy of this article to President Roosevelt, and to several of Bunau-Varilla's prominent friends in the United States. This article later gained Bunau-Varilla the title of "the prophet of Panama." Two days after Roosevelt received the article, the president sent a letter to Mr. Hays advising him to do nothing, outlining the several possible courses of actions he could take, and disclosing his disinclination to deal further with Colombia on the matter.[19]

Originally, Bunau-Varilla had decided to remain in Paris, at least until after there was some indication in what direction the president would decide to take the United States regarding the Canal issue. However, at the insistence of his wife, he decided to accompany his family to the United States.

He arrived in New York on September 22, 1903.[20] He met with Joshua Lindo, a friend, of Piza, Nephews & Co., one of the oldest banking firms on the Isthmus. Bunau-Varilla thought that Lindo was the person best suited to give him reliable information in the United States or Panama related to the Canal issue and the possible revolution.

Lindo also had an office in New York, and he was aware of all the activities taking place in the United States. Lindo informed Bunau-Varilla that Amador

---

[19] 1940, Miles P. DuVal, Jr. Cadiz to Cathay, p. 271.
[20] 1914 Philippe Bunau-Varilla, Panama: The Creation, Destruction, And Resurrection, p.288-289.

was in New York and offered to arrange that Amador come to Bunau-Varilla's hotel. Lindo stated that Amador was in despair, and the revolution was without money to support their secession.

BUNAU-VARILLA'S MEETING WITH AMADOR

When Bunau-Varilla returned to his hotel at the Waldorf Astoria, he discovered that Amador had already left two cards requesting to see him. The next day, Bunau-Varilla met with Amador, and Cromwell's deceit was fully revealed.

Amador suggested that it would take six million dollars to affect the secession against Colombia. In addition, Amador stated that his last cable to the conspirators in Panama had been revealed. As a result, he felt that he had exposed his friends in Panama to death.

Bunau-Varilla told Amador that it would be possible to affect the revolution for $100,000 dollars, with the help of the United States, but Bunau-Varilla was not at all sure the United States would get involved in the matter. Not having a plan to resolve the issue, Bunau-Varilla told Amador to remain in New York, not to talk to anyone, and to wait for his further advice within the next few days or weeks.[21]

BUNAU-VARILLA SEEKS THIRD-PARTY INFORMATION

This sequence of events was essentially supported by testimony given by Mr. Hall at a Foreign Affairs Committee hearing in 1912; however, he suggested in his testimony that Bunau-Varilla's activities were done at the request or order of Cromwell.[22] Bunau-Varilla proved that assumption false when he submitted his letter "Statement on Behalf of Historical Truth" (1912) to the same Foreign Affairs Committee. Rather than immediately going directly to Secretary Hay and President Roosevelt to ask them if they would support a revolution in Panama, Bunau-Varilla approached friends of the president's trusted advisors. Bunau-Varilla understood that, other than his public notoriety and expertise in the Panama Canal issue, he had no official position connected to the matter, and so could not expect a meeting with the president or his advisers on the subject, especially a meeting involving a potential revolution against another friendly

---

[21] 1914 Philippe Bunau-Varilla, Panama: The Creation, Destruction, And Resurrection, pp.290-293.

[22] 1912, Rainey resolution, pp. 356-366; Committee on foreign affairs, House of Representatives, Feb. 9,12, 1912, entitled "the story of Panama".

nation. Based upon the actions taken by Cromwell, his rejection of Amador, and his escape to France, Bunau-Varilla felt assured that the United States would not openly support a revolution in Panama. What he did not know was if the United States would act to put down a revolution in favor of Colombia. Or even worse, would Roosevelt decide to turn to Nicaragua, pursuant to the Spooner Act.

To ascertain the answer to his question, Bunau-Varilla sought out a friend, Professor Burr, head of the engineering department of Colombia University. On the 29th of September, Professor Burr, arranged a meeting with Mr. Bassett Moore, a close advisor to the president.

Mr. Moore advocated that the United States had the right, under the international right of eminent domain, to forcefully occupy Panama, and build a canal without the approval of Colombia, based upon the treaty of 1846. When Bunau-Varilla asked him to publish his views in the Sun, Professor Moore declined, stating the idea was not his own and his "conversation with Bunau-Varilla must remain confidential." [23]

In a follow up letter to Professor Moore, dated October 3, 1903, Bunau-Varilla reiterated the conversation they previously had.

That conversation led Bunau-Varilla to conclude that President Roosevelt or Secretary Hay had seriously considered that option and held it as an alternative to Colombia's actions.

After meeting with Mr. Frank Pavey—at the time, a Washington, D.C., lawyer, and friend—Bunau-Varilla learned that the president, while rejecting Cromwell's attempt to involve the United States in a Panama Revolution, was still intent on building a Canal in Panama. The president was intent on using the 1846 treaty to pressure the government to come to terms favorable to the United States.[24]

Bunau-Varilla felt that, because Nicaragua was the only Spooner-Act alternative to a Canal, in the end, the only course of action was a revolution in Panama. He, obviously, felt that Roosevelt would not force an eminent-domain solution to the Panama Canal problem, and would not overtly act to support a revolution in Panama, but would not act to prevent it.[25] In a letter of reply to Senator Hanna, dated October 5, 1903, President Roosevelt spelled out his views regarding this matter, and again he reiterated those views to Doctor Albert Shaw, editor of Re-

---

[23] 1914 Philippe Bunau-Varilla, Panama: The Creation, Destruction, And Resurrection, pp.294-296.
[24] 1914 Philippe Bunau-Varilla, Panama: The Creation, Destruction, And Resurrection, p.297.
[25] 1940, Miles P. DuVal, Jr. Cadiz to Cathay, pp. 296-297.

view of Reviews.[26]

To ensure that he had read the position of the president correctly, on October 9 or October 10, 1903, Bunau-Varilla visited the assistant secretary of state, Mr. Loomis, a friend, but more importantly, a close friend of the president.

Bunau-Varilla informed Loomis that he and his brother had recently bought the Le Matin, the leading newspaper in Paris, France, and they had made the decision to release the so called "Dreyfus Papers" to the public. That letter was the key evidence that eventually brought down the French Republic. Knowing that Roosevelt would be interested in the Dreyfus story from the man that discovered the key evidence in the case, Mr. Loomis arranged a meeting with the president that same day. [27]

When responding to Roosevelt's questions regarding the Canal issue, Bunau-Varilla advised that there will be a revolution in Panama and explained why.

Bunau-Varilla's meeting with Roosevelt apparently changed the President's mind from one of eminent domain, to one of a secessionist observer. On the 10th of October 1903, he again wrote his friend Dr. Albert Shaw, and described his sentiment for a revolution in Panama, but could not publicly voice that sentiment. [28]

Although unaware of the follow up letter Roosevelt had sent to Dr. Shaw, Bunau-Varilla left that meeting convinced Roosevelt would act on his advice. He was not wrong.[29]

THE PLAN IS HATCHED BASED UPON PAST HISTORY

Bunau-Varilla returned to New York on the 13th of October 1903. He met with Dr. Amador at his hotel room in the Waldorf Astoria, and explained to him that there was no need for six million dollars in order to wage a revolution in Panama.

Bunau-Varilla went on to explain that in 1856, the United States had refused to allow Colombian troops to occupy the Panama Canal Railroad property, and again in 1902 when the Colombians threatened to use force to abrogate the extension of the Panama Canal concession. In both cases, the United States used the 1846 treaty as the legal basis for its intervention. In 1902, the United States acted,

---

[26] 1940, Miles P. DuVal, Jr. Cadiz to Cathay, pp. 296-297.
[27] 2003, Ovidio Diaz Espino, How Wall Street Created A Nation, pp. 68-69.
[28] 1914 Philippe Bunau-Varilla, Panama: The Creation, Destruction, And Resurrection, pp.312-313.
[29] 1940, Miles P. DuVal, Jr. Cadiz to Cathay, p. 300.

even while conducting treaty negotiations with Mr. Concha, the Colombian representative.[30] Bunau-Varilla went on to explain that a hundred thousand dollars could be used to bribe the Colombian soldiers.

Initially, Amador refused to accept the plan. He felt that a greater amount of money was needed, and he did not think that the revolution could succeed if only the railroad right of way was separated from the rest of Panama. Bunau-Varilla explained that, with the ten million dollars Panama would receive from the United States when the treaty was ratified, the revolution would have plenty of funds to complete the revolution.

Amador was still unconvinced, and both men parted for the night. The next morning, Amador returned to Bunau-Varilla's hotel room, and after apologizing, accepted the plan.

Having agreed, Bunau-Varilla instructed Amador to prepare to return to Panama on the 20th of October 1903, while he returned to Washington, D.C. He wanted to see Secretary Hay, and possibly find out his position on the matter.

On the 16th of October 1903, Bunau-Varilla again approached Mr. Loomis, and was introduced to Mr. Hay. Mr. Hay was forthcoming in explaining that the United States, while not getting involved in any revolution in Panama, had made the necessary military precautions if that did happen.[31] That was the statement that Bunau-Varilla needed to hear to finalize his plans with Amador.

Bunau-Varilla immediately returned to New York, on the 17th of October 1903, and again met with Amador. Based upon his meeting with Secretary of State Hay, Bunau-Varilla assured Amador that the United States would support the revolution forty-eight hours after it began, and he would supply the one hundred thousand dollars after the revolutionaries had declared their independence. He stated that he would not risk his money or contact the revolution until that goal was met.

BUNAU-VARILLA'S PRICE FOR HIS FINANCIAL HELP

Bunau-Varilla stated that, after Panama declared its independence, he wanted to be declared Panama's representative in Washington, D.C., to finish negotiating the treaty. Bunau-Varilla further insisted that the revolution start by November 3, 1903.

---

[30] 1912, Rainey resolution, p. 366; Committee on foreign affairs, House of Representatives, Feb. 9,12, 1912, entitled "the story of Panama"; 1914 Philippe Bunau-Varilla, Panama: The Creation, Destruction, And Resurrection, pp.312-316.

[31] 1914 Philippe Bunau-Varilla, Panama: The Creation, Destruction, And Resurrection, p.318.

Amador was hesitant to accept either proposal, but Bunau-Varilla insisted that once Panama declared its independence, there would be political pressures from all sides to interfere in the final treaty. He went on to explain that Panama must have an experienced person to negotiate that treaty.

Finally, Bunau-Varilla told Amador that he was free to go his own way on the matter, but if he did, Bunau-Varilla would not be responsible for the outcome.

Reluctantly, Amador agreed to Bunau-Varilla's request. The thrust of this plan, assurances, and agreements were contained in a letter dated October 18, 1903, written by Amador to his son. In that letter, while not naming Bunau-Varilla as the contemplated minister expected to be selected to negotiate the United States–Panama treaty, he seems to hold out the possibility that Bunau-Varilla may not be that minister. Amador was already intent on going back on his word. [32]

WHO SUPPLIED THE INITIAL MONEY FOR THE REVOLUTION

A lot has been written regarding the initial financing of the Panama Revolution. The truth of this matter, and its importance, is fully contained in the 1912 hearings on the Rainey Resolution held by the Committee on Foreign Affairs of House of Representatives, and the 1912 "Statement on Behalf of Historical Truth," sent to the committee by Philippe Bunau-Varilla.

Mr. Hall presented to the 1912 congressional Foreign Affairs Committee that the junta, or revolutionary committee, were not given any money prior to the revolution. He went on to state that $100,000 dollars was sent by the Credit Lyonnaise, for account of the New Panama Canal company, to Heidelbach, Ikleheimer & Company, and credited to Bunau-Varilla. In addition, there was a second "loan" of $100,000 dollars from the Bowling Green Trust Company, with securities deposited by Mr. Cromwell.

However, Mr. Hall stated that the money used to pay for the revolution was advanced by the New Panama Canal Company, the Bank of Ehrman, the senior partner of which, Felix Ehrman, was the vice consul general of the United States in Panama, Isaac Brandon & Brothers, Piza, Nephews & Company, and other bankers located in Panama. [33]

---

[32] 1914 Philippe Bunau-Varilla, Panama: The Creation, Destruction, And Resurrection, p.322; 1912, Rainey resolution, p. 371, Committee on foreign affairs, House of Representatives, Feb. 9,12, 1912, entitled "the story of Panama".

[33] 1912, Rainey resolution, p. 372, Committee on foreign affairs, House of Representatives, Feb. 9,12, 1912, entitled "the story of Panama".

THE POLITICAL PURPOSE OF THE RAINEY HEARINGS

It is important to note that the year 1912 was an election year. I earlier stated that the purpose of the Rainey hearing, at least for some, was to embarrass President Roosevelt, or his support for the prospective president, Taft. To do so, the witnesses, Mr. Hall in particular, had to show that there was a secret Wall Street syndicate, composed by Cromwell, Bunau-Varilla, Roosevelt's brother-in-law, and Taft's brother, and that the Roosevelt administration worked with this syndicate to wrest the Panama Canal from Colombia, and made a small fortune in the process.

Mr. Hall was a staff correspondent of the New York World, and an employee of Joseph Pulitzer, the editor and owner of that newspaper. Mr. Hall spent several years gathering documentation, trying to prove this assertion, all or most of which he presented to the committee for their review, and much of which was incorrect.

THE ALLEGATION OF BLACKMAIL THAT BACKFIRED

This allegation of a secret syndicate surfaced in October 1908, an election year, when the managing editor of the World received a telephone call from Jonas Whitley, an employee of Nelson Cromwell. Mr. Whitley stated that he was aware that the World was about to publish a report "about the Panama Canal involving the President, and Cromwell, which was libelous and inaccurate, and he wanted to set the record straight." [34]

Ironically, the genesis of this story originated from Cromwell himself, when his office complained to the New York District Attorney's office that he, Cromwell, was being blackmailed by some Panamanians, demanding money for their share of the work in the independence of Panama.[35] The State Attorney's Office failed, or refused, to act on this complaint, but the story was leaked to the press. Although the initial story was not going to be published by the World, Cromwell's response to the perceived threat of the story was published. Although there were several follow-up articles written regarding this issue by the World and other newspapers, the president did not respond to the allegations until after the election. He blamed the publication of these articles by the World for the loss of several Republican seats in Congress, and for the attack on his good name. He sued the World for libel. The suit went all the way to the Supreme Court, where it was dismissed.

---

[34] 2003, Ovidio Diaz Espino, "How Wall Street Created A Nation," p. 1.
[35] 2003, Ovidio Diaz Espino, "How Wall Street Created A Nation," p. 2.

Notwithstanding this fact, Mr. Hall's presentation to the 1912 House Foreign Affairs Committee, because it was politically motivated, and faulty at best, unjustly defamed President Roosevelt, his administration, and Mr. Bunau-Varilla.

After almost four years of digging, Mr. Hall was never able to connect President Roosevelt, or his administration, to a Wall Street syndicate dedicated to wresting the Panama Canal from Colombia and making a fortune in the process.

However, there was plenty of documented proof that a secret Wall Street syndicate did exist for the purpose alleged. The names of the participants have since been made public, but the president, the members of his administration, and Mr. Bunau-Varilla have never been connected to that syndicate. There has been plenty of innuendo, supposition, and false rumor devoid of fact alleging that Bunau-Varilla was working in concert with Cromwell, was employed by Cromwell or the New Panama Canal company, but the opposite has been proven to be true.

BACK TO THE INITIAL FUNDING OF THE PANAMA REVOLUTION

The issue of who supplied the initial funding for the Panama Revolution is a perfect example of the faulty allegation made by Mr. Hall, and many others, that Bunau-Varilla was working in concert with Cromwell, or that the New Panama Canal Company was financing the revolution. The same allegation was made by Mr. Ovidio Diaz Espino in his book How Wall Street Created A Nation, published in 2003. I cite Mr. Diaz's book because he has published a copy of the original documents with the names and financial contribution of all the partners of this secret Wall Street syndicate whose purpose was to secretly buy up the worthless French Panama Canal bonds, pennies on the dollar, and sell them back to the United States government at full or greater value. Mr. Bunau-Varilla's name is not among those on that list. Mr. Bunau-Varilla has declared, in the documents he presented to the House Foreign Affairs Committee in 1912, that he alone supplied the initial financing for the revolution, and he has proven the truth of his statement through documentation presented to the House committee, bank transfers and such, that these funds, $100,000 dollars, were derived from his personal bank account at Balser & Company of Brussels, and the branch office of the Credit Lyonnais, A.S. of the Champs Elyse'es. These funds were eventually forwarded to Mr. Bunau-Varilla's account at the New York Bank of Hiedelbach, Ickelheimer & Company.[36] In addition, Mr. Bunau-Varilla has cited, through documented fact,

---

[36] Rainey Resolution; Bunau-Varilla, Statement on Behalf of Historical Truth,

to the House Foreign Affairs Committee of 1912 that Mr. Boyd and Mr. Amador signed an agreement with the "Bowling Green Trust Company" on the securities deposited by Mr. Cromwell on November 25, 1903.[37] This contract happened long after the revolution took place, on November 3, 1903, and indeed after the Hay–Bunau-Varilla Treaty was signed on November 18, 1903.

Notwithstanding the facts that I have cited, there has been the repeated question put forth that if Cromwell did not supply the initial funding for the revolution, or the New Panama Canal Company did not supply the initial funding for the revolution, where did Bunau-Varilla suddenly obtain such a large sum of money.

BUNAU-VARILLA'S PERSONAL FINANCIAL WORTH

Bunau-Varilla's detractors ignore the fact that, in 1903, Bunau-Varilla was not a poor man. His brother and he had recently bought the most prestigious newspaper in France. He had spent several years, since the collapse of the French Canal, building and managing railroads in Europe. In addition, for two years, before the French Canal collapse, he was an owner of the company that worked exclusively on the Culebra Cut, applying an excavation system he'd previously developed that cost his company fifty-five cents a cubic yard, and for which the French Canal Company paid no less than one dollars and twenty-five cents a cubic yard. Previously, the French Canal Company was paying over four dollars a cubic yard for underwater dredging of hard rock.

Prior to succumbing to yellow fever, as one of the French Canal managers, and using his system, Bunau-Varilla was excavating 100,000-200,000 cubic yards a month.

There is no reason to believe he did not attain the same success when he returned to the Canal, and while he was the head of his own company.

In short, his private contract company was making millions of dollars for a period of about two years before the French Canal Company collapsed.[38]

But even ignoring this fact, how Mr. Hall and others would accept the statements of Mr. Cromwell regarding this matter flies in the face of credulity. Obviously, Mr. Hall was blinded by his own political motivation, to the point that

---

[pp.] 89-97.

[37] Ibid. pp. 96-97.

[38] 1914 Philippe Bunau-Varilla, Panama: The Creation, Destruction, And Resurrection, pp. 67-85.

he was willing to accept anything Mr. Cromwell told him. Mr. Cromwell was the same man that embezzled $60,000 dollars from the French Panama Canal Company to bribe the Republican Party to change their party platform, ostensibly in favor of the Panama route. He was the same man that tried to get the Colombian government to pay for his own publicity program. He was the same man that tried to get Mr. Duque, a United States citizen, to pay for the initial funding of the Panama Revolution. This was the same man that promised Mr. Duque, a United States citizen, that Cromwell would make him president of Panama if he would provide the funds for the revolution. This was the same man that turned his back on Dr. Amador after promising financial aid for the revolution, putting Dr. Amador, and the other secessionists in jeopardy for their property and their lives. This was the same man that helped create the first syndicate to swindle the bondholders of the French Canal Company. This was the same man that helped create the second secret Wall Street syndicate to swindle the bondholders of the New French Panama Canal Company. This was a man that had been warned by the Colombian government not to participate in the Panama Revolution, under pain of forfeiture of the Panama Canal Railroad Company and the New Panama Canal Company. This was the same man that, in the face of that threat, seemingly washed his hands of his part in the revolution and retreated to France. This was the same man that initially thought that the United States was either going to take the Canal through eminent domain or drop the matter and move on to the Nicaragua canal. This was the same man that was employed by the French Canal, the Panama Canal Railroad, and a steamship company, all while he worked against them in favor of his own interests and the interests of a secret Wall Street syndicate. Does anyone believe that Cromwell would jeopardize his own finances on the possibility that it would be lost if the revolution failed? This is what Mr. Hall and others would have had the world believe.

In fact, it was Mr. Bunau-Varilla that risked his personal finances, and his good name, in order to salvage the Panama Canal from being lost, probably forever, certainly for years to come. Had Bunau-Varilla not taken that risk, there would not have been a revolution, and there would not have been an independent country of Panama. For his reward, Bunau-Varilla was able to redeem his original $15,000-$20,000 dollars' worth of penalty bonds, and another $10,000 worth of bonds he held in the French Panama Canal Company, the worth of these bonds at the time that they were transferred to his name, prior to any thought of the revolution. In each case, Mr. Bunau-Varilla has explained, in detail, how he came about owning these bonds. In fact, while Bunau-Varilla was minister to Panama, he refused to be paid for his services, and asked that those funds be used to create a monument in honor of Mr. de Lesseps.

UNITED STATES ACTIVITIES PRIOR TO THE PANAMA SECESSION

There was no secret that Roosevelt was convinced that the United States, for commercial, and strategic reasons, must build a canal under exclusive United States control. He was also finally convinced that a canal in Panama was a better alternative to the canal in Nicaragua. In addition, Roosevelt had never denied that he was aware that there was a possibility of a revolution in Panama if the Hay–Herran Treaty was rejected by Colombia. He took reasonable steps to protect the position of the United States should that revolution happen. Also, there is plenty of documentation to show that Roosevelt's initial thought was to acquire the Canal through eminent domain or follow the dictates of the Spooner Act and seek a canal in Nicaragua. However, there is no indication that Roosevelt had finally decided on any course of action on this matter prior to the revolution.

The acts taken by Roosevelt and his administration clearly show, through documentation too lengthy to describe here, that he gave up on the eminent-domain idea, and relied on the treaty of 1846, which gave the United States the right of protection of the Panama Canal Railroad right of way in case there was a revolution in Panama.

Hay's comments to Bunau-Varilla, in which he stated, "We will not be caught napping," were not made without substance. He inferred the same to Mr. Duque, when Duque visited Hay at an earlier date. [39]

THE MOVEMENT OF UNITED STATES FORCES CLOSE TO PANAMA

On October 15, 1903, the Navy Department ordered Admiral Henry Glass, Commander of the Pacific fleet, to move his squadron into position, close to the Panama area, and wait for further instructions. Glass received the first orders prior to Panama's expected secession from Colombia.

On October 16, 1903, President Roosevelt interviewed army officers Captain

---

[39] 1914 Philippe Bunau-Varilla, Panama: The Creation, Destruction, And Resurrection, p.318; 1912, Rainey resolution, p. 360, Committee on foreign affairs, House of Representatives, Feb. 9,12, 1912, entitled "the story of Panama".

Humphrey and Lieutenant Murphy, who had been previously tasked to study the military vulnerabilities on the Isthmus. These men informed the president that there was a real possibility of a revolution in Panama, and that the earliest date substantial amounts of arms and ammunition that could be delivered to that area would be October 20, 1903. They went on to state that a small number of small arms had been smuggled into Panama, and that most Panamanians had some sort of weapon.[40]

On the 23rd of October 1903, the order was given to the Navy Yard in Brooklyn, N.Y. to outfit the U.S.S. Dixie to be ready for sea, and place a contingent of 400 marines on board. The order was tasked to the U.S.S. Atlanta to accompany the Dixie to Guantanamo Bay, Cuba. The president also gave orders to the general staff to prepare for an eventual campaign in Panama.[41] On November 2, 1903, Admiral Glass was ordered to move into the Pacific bay of Panama, and although too late, ensure that Colombia did not disembark any troops. He was to maintain free flow of traffic by the Panama Railroad. The same orders were given to the Wyoming, the Concord, the Marblehead, Glass's flagship, and the Boston.[42]

The same orders were given to the Atlantic squadron, and on November 2, 1903, the U.S.S. Nashville entered the Atlantic harbor of Colon Panama.[43] The U.S.S. Dixie was seen coming into view from Colon, on the 4th of November.

THE PANAMA AND COLOMBIAN ACTIVITIES PRIOR TO THE PANAMA SECESSION

At least by September 4, 1903, through a cable sent to the Colombian government, and a letter sent to the Colombian consul general in New York, Dr. Herran relayed what Mr. Duque had told him, that a general plot by the Panamanians, working with the Panama Canal Railroad company, the French Panama Canal Company, and with the support of the United States, would attempt to secede

---

[40] 1940, Miles P. DuVal, Jr. Cadiz to Cathay, pp. 303-305; 1912, Rainey resolution, p. 367-368, Committee on foreign affairs, House of Representatives, Feb. 9,12, 1912, entitled "the story of Panama". 1912, Rainey resolution, p. 369; Committee on foreign affairs, House of Representatives, Feb. 9,12, 1912, entitled "the story of Panama"

[41] 1912, Rainey resolution, p. 369; Committee on foreign affairs, House of Representatives, Feb. 9,12, 1912, entitled "the story of Panama"

[42] Ibid. P. 371.

[43] 1914 Philippe Bunau-Varilla, Panama: The Creation, Destruction, And Resurrection, p.334; 1912, Rainey resolution, p. 382-383; Committee on foreign affairs, House of Representatives, Feb. 9,12, 1912, entitled "the story of Panama".

from Colombia if the Hay–Herran Treaty was not approved before September 22, 1903. Herran went on to name Dr. Amador, Mr. Tracy Robinson, Mr. G. Lewis, and Mr. Arosemena as the principle conspirators in that plot, with their headquarters in the New York offices of Andreas & Company. [44]

Several follow-up cables and letters were sent back and forth, indicating that the Colombian government was intent on acting on this information. As I have stated, it was this information that caused the Colombian government to warn Cromwell not to get involved in the attempted Panama Revolution.

In the hope that they could weaken the Colombian garrison in Panama, the revolutionists spread a false rumor that a rebel force had invaded Panama from Nicaragua.

On October 25, 1903, Governor Obaldia heard of this rumor, and sent a detachment of Colombian troops, who the rebels thought could not be turned to their cause, from the Panama garrison to "Penonome," a town located in the present province of "Coclé" in the interior, about 140 miles from Panama City. Although Obaldia may have been sympathetic to the revolution— and, in fact, was a life-long friend of Amador's, and living in Amador's home at the time—he was still an official of the Colombian government, personally appointed by President Marroquin, and he was not about to jeopardize his own position on the possibility that the revolution would not succeed.

In an apparent attempt to protect himself, Governor Obaldia, having acted upon this rumor, also relayed the information back to Colombia. In their response, the Colombian government informed Obaldia that they were sending a detachment of soldiers to Panama under the command of General Juan B. Tovar, and General Ramon G. Amaya, to put down the invasion, and he was instructed to send the gunboat Padilla to Buenaventura to pick up more men.

Certainly, an additional problem for the rebels, on October 31, 1903, the Padilla and the Bogota, two Colombian gunboats, arrived in Panama and requested to be refueled with coal. The Panama Canal Railroad Company refused to give it on requisition.

However, the Padilla was refueled after the captain, General Ruben Varon, assured Amador and Arango that he would support the revolution. The cost of this agreement was $35,000 dollars in silver, and with the assurance that the United States would intervene in favor of the rebels.

Governor Obaldia again cabled the Colombian government that the Padilla

---

[44] 1912, Rainey resolution, p. 361; Committee on foreign affairs, House of Representatives, Feb. 9,12, 1912, entitled "the story of Panama"

was ready, but because of the refusal of the Panama Railroad to supply coal on requisition to the Bogota, he cabled the Pacific Mail Company in San Francisco, in order to get coal for the Bogota from their supply in Panama.

Realizing that he made a mistake, endangering the revolution, he also informed the Colombian government that he received further information that there was no invasion from Nicaragua. His hope was that the Colombian government would cancel the orders to send troops to Panama.[45]

---

[45] 1912, Rainey resolution, p. 381; Committee on foreign affairs, House of Representatives, Feb. 9,12, 1912, entitled "the story of Panama"

CHAPTER EIGHT
THE PANAMA REVOLUTION

THE REVOLUTION BEGINS

ON OCTOBER 20, 1903, having been given the promised financial backing of Bunau-Varilla, the perceived backing of the United States government, the necessary independence documents, and a newly created Panama flag, Dr. Amador boarded the Yucatan en route to
Panama.

On October 27, 1903, Amador arrived in Colon, Panama, and was met by Mr. Prescott, a local official of the Panama Railroad Company. Both Prescott and Amador left Colon, traveled to the City of Panama, and to the home of Mr. Frederico Boyd, at the Cathedral Plaza. It was there that he gave his report and outlined his plan to the revolutionary committee.[1]

He was met with extreme pessimism and apprehension. The rebels expected Amador would return with some solid assurances from Hay or Roosevelt that the United States would support their revolution. Instead, Amador could only give them verbal assurances, from Bunau-Varilla, that he would finance them, and that the United States would act to protect the railroad right of way, and by so doing, the revolution.

In addition, the revolutionary committee refused to accept the wording of the document declaring their independence. They refused to accept the flag, also put forth by Bunau-Varilla, stating that it looked too much like the flag of the United States. Ricardo Arias, one of the large landowners, strongly objected to only declaring independence for the strip of land from Colon to Panama City,

---
[1] Ibid, pp.376-377.

which followed the path of the railroad. They all agreed that the revolution should include the whole of Panama, if independence were to take place at all. To accomplish this, the conspirators decided to send men into the interior to gain support for the revolution. [2]

On the 28th of October 1903, Mr. Arias confronted Amador, and informed him that he was withdrawing from the revolution effort. When Amador and Arango tried to convince him otherwise, Arias was said to have told them that they were old men who didn't care if they were hung, but he did care. Amador and Arango knew that Arias 'defection would cause panic among the rebels. Arias, one of the richest men in Panama, was also one of the most influential.

To make matters worse, Governor Obaldia told Amador in confidence that Generals Juan B. Tovar and Ramon G. Amaya had been directed to Panama with a large force of men to put down the invasion from Nicaragua. This turn of events caused Amador great apprehension, and gave him reason to believe that he had failed.

Amador decided not to tell anyone of the impending Colombian activities, and instead, working with Prescott, Amador told the revolutionary committee members that he would send a cable to Bunau-Varilla to get assurance that the United States would indeed send warships to protect them. Prescott asked Arias to hold off on his decision until he got a satisfactory answer from Bunau-Varilla. Arias told Amador that he would hold off his decision to defect, if there were, forthcoming, substantial assurances that would satisfy him.

That cable was sent on October 29, 1903, to Mr. Lindo, located in New York, for Mr. Bunau-Varilla.[3] The message was simple. "An American man-of-war must be sent to Colon." The message also included information that Colombian forces were due on the Atlantic side within five days with over 200 men. [4]

THE WARSHIP THAT WAS SUPPOSED TO SEAL THE DEAL

After receiving this cable. Mr. Bunau-Varilla went to Washington and discussed the 1846 treaty and the 1885 burning of the City of Colon with Assistant Secretary of State Loomis at his home.

---

[2] Ibid, pp. 378-379.

[3] Ibid, pp. 378-380.

[4] 1914 Philippe Bunau-Varilla, Panama: The Creation, Destruction, And Resurrection, p.334; 1912, Rainey resolution, p. 329; Committee on foreign affairs, House of Representatives, Feb. 9,12,1912, entitled "the story of Panama.

THE BURNING OF COLON 1885

Captain Kean, the commander of the Galena, an American man-of-war, was in the Colon Harbor in 1885, and failed to prevent the rebel forces from burning Colon. Captain Kean was rebuked by the United States Congress for his lack of action.

The next day, Bunau-Varilla again met with Loomis, and was told that "it would be deplorable" if that should happen again. Armed with this information, and the fact that Bunau-Varilla knew from news reports that the Dixie and the Nashville were sent to the area, Bunau-Varilla was confident he could reply to Amador's cable.

Of note here is that—Mr. Hall stated this in the 1912 congressional hearing—Bunau-Varilla met with Secretary Hay, and because of his request, an urgent cable was sent to Commander Hubbard, commander of the Nashville, to proceed immediately to Colon with all speed possible. Bunau-Varilla, however, had stated that, although his intention was to do so, he never met with Secretary Hay. On October 30, 1903, Bunau-Varilla sent a cable from Baltimore, stating, in code, that a man-of-war was coming. "All right will reach two days and half; this cablegram is for Amador --- Jones."[5]

Heartened by this message, on November 1, 1903, the rebels Amador, Boyd, and Arango met Mr. Don Porfirio Melendez. They agreed that Melendez should lead the secessionist movement on the Colon side with 300 men to overcome the 150-man police force, if they refused to join the revolution. They decided that the revolution should take place on November 4, 1903, instead of November 3, 1903, as was insisted by Bunau-Varilla. In addition, knowingly or not, they enlisted a previous turncoat, Mr. Duque, and his 287-man fire brigade to help in the movement.

Still in Paris, on October 31, 1903, Cromwell, sent a cable to the President of the United States, offering the support of the New Panama Canal Company and liquidator of the old company, indicating that he would be returning to the United States with full power to complete all the details. Cromwell, apparently, had been kept fully informed of the activities taking place in Panama and the United States, most likely by Mr. Curtis, Cromwell's partner, and felt it safe to return.

Mr. Hall described to the House Foreign Affairs Committee how Mr. Cromwell, according to Cromwell himself, directed almost every detail of the revolution.

---

[5] 1914 Philippe Bunau-Varilla, Panama: The Creation, Destruction, And Resurrection, pp.330-331; 1912, Rainey resolution, p. 381; Committee on foreign affairs, House of Representatives, Feb. 9,12, 1912, entitled "the story of Panama".

However, it should be noted again that Mr. Cromwell was considered a scoundrel by Dr. Amador and the rest of the rebels, before, during, and after the revolution, because he left them high and dry in their greatest need. In fact, there is plenty of documentation to show that, until Amador and Boyd returned to New York after the revolution on November 18, 1903, Cromwell played no part in that revolution. Obviously, the story told the House Foreign Affairs Committee regarding the exploits of Mr. Cromwell directing the revolution, I assume from Paris, was simply fantasy, fabricated by Cromwell, no doubt.[6]

Any activities regarding the revolution by Cromwell, if taken, were taken by the employees of the Panama Canal Railroad Company in Panama. However, the actions taken by these employees could not have been taken without the approval or knowledge of Cromwell.

GENERAL ESTEBAN HUERTAS

At the time of the revolution, General Huertas was a diminutive young man of thirty, who was dedicated to the Colombian Army. He grew up as a runaway, joined the army at the age of eight years old, and at age eight, distinguished himself under fire. During the civil war of 1900, he lost his right arm, and despite his wounds, continued to fight. At the age of twenty-six, he was promoted to general. He was sent to the Panama district to command the Colombian garrison there. While in Panama, Huertas married, had children, and developed personal connections and friends among the secessionists.

The revolutionists knew that they would have to turn Huertas against Colombia, if they expected to avoid bloodshed. They did so step by step.

Initially, Arango approached Huertas, and told him that the generals that were coming to Panama were coming to relieve him of his command, and he would be reassigned to another district, located in the interior of Colombia. Next, Amador approached Huertas and told him that Panama was about to secede from Colombia, under the protection of the United States. Finally, Huertas' closest friend, Pastor Himenez, approached him and solicited his support in the revolution. To all this persuasion, Huertas was non-committal almost to the end.[7]

---

[6] 1912, Rainey resolution, pp. 384-385; Committee on foreign affairs, House of Representatives, Feb. 9,12, 1912, entitled "the story of Panama".
[7] 2003, Ovidio Diaz Espino, How Wall Street Created A Nation, pp. 92-93.

THE REBELS CAREFULLY PREPARED

General Tascon and one hundred of his men had been sent to Penonome on a wild goose chase. The mayor of Panama City, Francisco de Ossa, the brother of Amador's wife, had been turned to the rebel cause. A makeshift force of firefighters under Gabriel Duque had been set up in Panama. Sr. Don Porfirio Melendez had been assigned, with 300 men, to lie in wait along the Panama Railroad line, and possibly, they would be used to overpower the police force in Colon, if they refused to join the revolution. In the end, the secessionists could only wait for the warships from the United States to arrive, as promised by Bunau-Varilla.[8] On the evening of November 2, 1903, the U.S.S. Nashville arrived in Colon, Panama, under Commander Hubbard. The rebels were jubilant. Bunau-Varilla had kept his word. The rebels considered it was a sign that the United States was there to protect them.[9] The rebel jubilation was short-lived. About midnight that same evening, the gunboat Cartagena, carrying General Tovar, General Amaya, General Francisco Castro, and about 500 elite Colombian troops, under the command of Colonel Eliseo Torres, also arrived in Colon, Panama.

Except for a small number of leaders, which had purposely kept this fact from the others, the rebel forces were unaware that Colombia had sent such a large force to Panama. The following morning, as they watched the Colombian forces disembark, and the United States make no effort to stop them, the rebels panicked and abandoned their cause.

Even Amador and Arango were ready to concede that the revolution had failed. They knew that they could not hope to prevail against such a strong force of elite Colombian troops.

IT TOOK A WOMAN TO CARRY ON

Like all Latin American countries, especially at that time, and at least publicly, the district of Panama was a male-dominated society. At home, privately, certain women had more influence than popularly believed. Dona Maria de la Ossa Amador was one of those women.

Marital influence among the conspirators was almost complete. After the flag,

---

[8] Rainey resolution, pp. 384-386; Committee on foreign affairs, House of Representatives, Feb. 9,12, 1912, entitled "the story of Panama".
[9] 2003, Ovidio Diaz Espino, How Wall Street Created A Nation, p. 94; Rainey resolution, p. 386; Committee on foreign affairs, House of Representatives, Feb. 9,12, 1912, entitled "the story of Panama".

supplied by Bunau-Varilla, was rejected by the revolutionaries, Manuel Amador, the son of Amador, designed a new flag. Senorita Maria Amelia de la Ossa was engaged to Richard Prescott, the brother of Mr. Herbert G. Prescott, who was assistant superintendent of the Panama Railroad. Mrs. Amador's daughter Elmira was married to Mr. William Ehrman, nephew to Felix Ehrman, United States consul general in Panama, and head of the Ehrman Bank at the Cathedral Plaza in Panama City. Mrs. Espinosa, Mrs. Lefevre, and the Arango and Arosemena families were all involved in making the Panama flag. All of these women had great influence in the cause of the revolution.

But it was Mrs. Maria de la Ossa Amador that has been accredited with saving the revolution on November 3, 1903, when all but Arango had abandoned Amador and lost heart. Even Amador abandoned the idea, giving up all hope of secession, and retreated to his home to await the consequences of his actions.

THE PLAN WELL MADE

Mrs. Amador convinced her husband to continue, to finish what he had started.

She is also credited with devising the plan to separate the generals from their troops in Colon: transport the generals by train to Panama, effect their arrest, and try to bribe the leader of the Colombian troops in Colon to leave Panama.

If that did not work, the plan was to attack them along the railroad line, if they tried to join up with the generals in Panama.

She also advised her husband to ask Prescott, who was in Panama, to wire Colonel Shaler, the general superintendent of the Railroad, who was in Colon, with a request not to allow any troops to transit to Panama City by use of the railroad.[10]

HESITATION, LOST OPPORTUNITIES, AND A NEW NATION IS BORN

On the evening of November 2, 1903, Commander Hubbard, captain of the U.S.S. Nashville, arrived in Colon, Panama, with a force of less than fifty men. He had no orders to prevent Colombian troops from disembarking in Panama. He reported to his superiors in Washington that the city was calm.

---

[10] Rainey resolution, pp. 384-385; Committee on foreign affairs, House of Representatives, Feb. 9,12, 1912, entitled "the story of Panama"; 2003, Ovidio Diaz Espino, How Wall Street Created A Nation, p. 98.

He had previously made a recent port of call to Panama, and he was aware of the tensions between the citizens of Panama and the government of Colombia over the failure to satisfactorily conclude the Hay–Herran Treaty between Colombia and the United States.

When the Cartagena arrived around midnight on November 2, 1903, with General Tovar, General Amaya, General Francisco Castro, and about 500 elite Colombian troops, under the command of Colonel Eliseo Torres, Commander Hubbard boarded the vessel to ascertain the purpose of the visit. General Tovar informed Hubbard that the purpose of the visit was to relieve the Garrison in Panama, and that he intended to disembark in the morning on November 3, 1903. Satisfied that there was no rebel activity and that the Colombians had a right to disembark peacefully, Commander Hubbard returned to his ship.

In the morning of November 3, 1903, General Tovar repositioned his ship, docked at the Colon Wharf, next to the U.S.S. Nashville, and disembarked with all his men and officers. Tovar was met by General Porfirio Melendez, the prefect of Colon, General Pedro Cuadras, and several other Colon officials. Melendez informed the Colombian generals that the Nicaraguan invasion was a hoax, and he tried to encourage them to return to Colombia. However, Tovar was warned by José Segundo Ruiz, the port captain of Bocas del Toro province, that Ruiz had been told, for certain, that a separatist movement was planned, and the United States was openly in favor of that movement. Suspicious, Tovar questioned General Cuadras, who informed him that the area was quiet, and he had not heard of any planned separatist movement.

As discussed above, Shaler and Melendez were intent on separating the generals from their troops. They did so by promising that the generals would leave Colon on Governor Obaldia's special train car, and the troops would follow soon after. Although initially insisting that the troops leave at the same time, Tovar, despite his suspicion, agreed to leave Colon without his troops. He left Colonel Torres in charge of the troops, with instructions to follow shortly.

LATE ORDERS ARRIVED, REBEL PLANS ACCELERATED

Shortly after Tovar left Colon, and while he was visiting the U.S. consul in Colon, Mr. Oscar Malmros, Commander Hubbard received his late-arriving instructions from Assistant Secretary of the Navy Darling not to allow the Colombian troops to disembark, and to protect the railroad right of way.

Left with the fact that the Colombian troops had already disembarked, Hubbard discussed the matter with Shaler. Hubbard was informed that the railroad would not allow the Colombian troops to be transported to Panama City without the orders of Governor Obaldia. Hubbard returned to his ship to prepare his men, in case the Colombians tried to board the train by force. He also sent a cable to Darling explaining his situation and the fact that the Railroad Company refused to transport Colombian troops without Governor Obaldia's orders. He also sent word that the revolution may take place that same evening.

The rebels also planned to take over the Cartagena, the gunboat Tovar arrived on, by luring the crew off the boat, and manning it with rebels commanded by Melendez.

When Tovar left Colon, although he did not know it yet, he had lost any hope of stopping the revolution. That responsibility rested with Colonel Torres, and as time went on, with all his bluster and threats, he proved that he was not up to the task.[11]

THE ARREST OF THE COLOMBIAN GENERALS

When Tovar arrived in Panama City later that morning on November 3, 1903, he was met by General Huertas, Governor Obaldia, other Panama officials, and the general consul of the United States, Mr. Felix Ehrman. They were all transported to the government house. There, Obaldia produced telegrams proving the invasion from Nicaragua was false, and reassured Tovar that Panama was quiet. Tovar was later transported to the Comandancia General above the post office, where he had his lodgings.

Again, Tovar was warned—by Dr. José Angel Porras, and General José M. Nunez Roca—that the rebels were planning a revolution. Finally taking heed to the warnings, Tovar, too late, took steps to bring his troops to Panama City. Back and forth messages and plots were made, but finally, General Huertas acted, arresting Tovar and all his generals and staff. [12]

GREAT JUBILATION AND CONFUSION REIGNED

As expected, there was a great celebration in Panama over the arrest of the Colombian generals and their staff. Upon discovering the arrest of the generals, the

---

[11] Rainey resolution, pp. 388-389; Committee on foreign affairs, House of Representatives, Feb. 9,12, 1912, entitled "the story of Panama"
[12] Ibid. pp-391-395

general in charge of the Bogota threatened to Bombard Panama City until the Colombians were released. The man in charge of the Colombian troops in Colon, Colonel Torres, threatened to burn down the city and kill every U.S. citizen in Colon if the generals were not released. There were several cables sent back and forth between Felix Ehrman, the U.S. consul general in Panama, and Mr. Loomis, the assistant secretary of state, describing the arrest of the Colombian generals, and the control of Colon by Colonel Torres. Ehrman also sent a cable to the secretary of state describing the bombardment of Panama City by the Colombian gunboat Bogota, and the threat to follow up the following day. Return cables were sent from the State Department and the navy, ordering that the shelling be stopped by force if necessary. Before these orders could be acted upon, the Bogota left the Panama bay area. Mr. Ehrman also sent cables to Mr. Shaler and Commander Hubbard, requesting that the Colombian troops not be transported to Panama City.

AMADOR'S ATTEMPT AT DUPLICITY

Amador sent repeated cables to Bunau-Varilla, requesting he send the $100,000 dollars promised, without mention of the agreement they had made, appointing Bunau-Varilla the representative of Panama. Bunau-Varilla returned cables to Amador and the revolutionary government, stating that he had approved $25,000, and advised that the rebels must gain control of Colon, if they wanted the United States to recognize the new revolutionary government. He also requested his appointment, as agreed to by Amador.

The revolutionary government also sent repeated cables to the U.S. government, requesting quick recognition. The United States sent word to Bunau-Varilla and others that they would not recognize Panama as an independent government until they controlled the whole of Panama City and the City of Colon.

General Huertas sent a letter to Commandant Leoncio Tascon, the commander previously sent on a wild goose chase to Penonome, a city located in the interior of Panama, requesting that he return to Panama City and assist him in ensuring that the revolution succeeds. He further stated that the United States had sent ships to help ensure that fact, and that any effort to resist would be fruitless. [13]

---

[13] Ibid. pp-394-399.

THE SUCCESS OF THE REVOLUTION DEPENDED UPON THE BRIBE OF COLONEL TORRES

The rebels again got "cold feet, and lost hope." They were caught between General Tovar's refusal to order Colonel Torres, in control in Colon, to stand down, the bombardment of Panama City by the Colombian warship Bogota, the refusal of the United States to recognize their fragile government if they did not first take control of Colon, and Bunau-Varilla's refusal to send the rest of the money they would need to finance their revolution. In addition, Colonel Shaler had repeatedly informed Porfirio Melendez that he could not long refuse transporting the Colombian troops without forfeiting the railroad concession. He further informed Melendez that absent the order not to transport the Colombian troops to Panama given to him by the United States government, he would be obliged to comply with Colonel Torres's request. [14]

THE SOLUTION THAT WAS NO SOLUTION AT ALL

Desperate, the rebels decided to send Tovar back to Colon. To comply with the United States' order not to allow Colombian or rebel armed military forces the use of the railroad transit route, the rebels decided they would accompany Tovar, still under arrest, with armed civilians. Their hope was that somehow, together in Colon, they could convince General Tovar and Colonel Torres to leave Panama peacefully. Their plan to separate Tovar from his troops was about to fall apart.

MIRACLES DO HAPPEN, TORRES TAKES THE BRIBE

On the evening of November 5, 1903, General Tovar was sitting in a railroad car in Panama City, guarded by armed civilians, awaiting to be transported to Colon. He had refused to be bribed, and he had refused to give orders to Torres to leave Panama and return to Colombia. Tovar was keenly aware that any one of these actions would have cost him his position as a general in the Colombian Army, and most likely his life.

On the other hand, Colonel Torres was faced with a number of different problems. He was aware that his threats to burn down the City of Colon, without orders from his superior, would lead to personal disaster no matter what the outcome. He could not force his way onto the railroad transit without confronting

---

[14] Rainey resolution, pp. 441,442,454-456; Committee on foreign affairs, House of Representatives, Feb. 9,12, 1912, entitled "the story of Panama"

the United States government troops, which he was not willing to do without orders. In addition, Torres was convinced by Colonel Shaler that 5,000 American troops were on their way to Panama, and if he remained in Colon, he would be captured or killed. Suddenly, the bribe looked awfully good. Colonel Torres finally agreed to accept the $8,000-dollar bribe and leave Panama with his troops aboard the Royal Mail Steam Ship Orinoco. The bribe was paid by Mr. Wardlaw, the cashier of the Panama Railroad Company.

NO MORE MONEY, AND A GUARANTEE IS MADE

The captain of the Orinoco informed the agent of the Royal Mail Company that he could not transport the Colombian troops back to Colombia without first being paid for their passage. The Panama Railroad Company had no more money in their safe, and the rebels were also without funds. Finally, after refusing all other assurances, the captain of the Orinoco accepted about 1,000 pounds and, allegedly, a written guarantee signed by Colonel Shaler and Commander Hubbard and agreed to transport the Colombian troops back to Colombia.

The fact that Commander Hubbard may have signed the guarantee to pay the Royal Mail Company for transporting the Colombian troops back to Colombia was said to be proof positive that the United States was involved in the conspiracy for Panama to secede from Colombia. However, the written guarantee was never produced.

Commander Hubbard reported that he played no part in these negotiations between Colonel Torres and the representatives of the "provisional government." [15] As the Orinoco was preparing to leave Colon, the U.S.S. Dixie arrived, and 400 U.S. marines were sent ashore, and took up positions previously held by the fifty marines from the Nashville.

The following day, the raising of the flag, and the formal Declaration of Independence in Colon was declared at 10:00 A.M., on November 6, 1903. Ironically, Colonel Torres was the only Colombian to lose his life in the rebel confrontation in Colon.

Allegedly, while in route to Jamaica, Torres got drunk, bragged about his bribe, and was thrown overboard by his men. On November 3, 1903, because of the bombardment of the Bogota, a Chinese citizen on Salsipuedes Street in Panama City was killed. [16]

---

[15] Ibid. pp-457-458.
[16] 2003, Ovidio Diaz Espino, How Wall Street Created A Nation, p. 130.

photo of President Amador

THE INDEPENDENCE MOVEMENT STARTED ON NOVEMBER 3, 1903, WAS SECURE BY NOVEMBER 6, 1903 THE CORRUPTION AND DOUBLE-DEALING SOON FOLLOWED

Contrary to what has been taught in Panama and elsewhere, the corruption and double-dealing did not emanate from Philippe Bunau-Varilla. He had made his position clear to Amador early on, and he set his terms for supporting the revolution. Amador reluctantly agreed to his terms, and from their actions after the revolution, so did the other co-conspirators of the revolution.

For those children of Panama who have been incorrectly taught that there was a great revolution emanating from the District of Panama, the fact of the matter is that the revolution emanated from six to twelve Panamanian and American men and women, mostly employees of Cromwell's Panama Railroad Company, and a soldier of fortune, who, for whatever reason, felt that their fortunes were being jeopardized by the actions of the Colombian government.

Bunau-Varilla was intent on finishing the Panama Canal. He was acutely aware that the United States was the only country that could complete that task. He was also aware that the United States, humiliated over the failed Hay–Herran Treaty with Colombia, would not risk completing the Panama Canal without independent control of that canal after it was built. Bunau-Varilla was also convinced that the United States always had an alternative to building a canal in Panama.

On the other hand, the Colombians, the rebels in Panama, and, apparently, Nelson Cromwell were convinced that the United States had to come to terms over the canal in Panama, and any alternative was just a bluff by the United States. The Colombians, and later, the Panamanians were convinced they could extract better terms from the United States than what the United States was prepared to concede. Colombia found out the folly of their position, and Bunau-Varilla was determined not to allow Panama to fall into the same trap.

After the success of the revolution, Amador set about reneging on his agreement with Bunau-Varilla, either because of false pride or through the advice given to him by Cromwell. It was Cromwell that initially convinced Amador and the rest of the conspirators, in July 1903, that he would back their revolution. Later, he promised Duque the same, if he, Duque, would finance the revolution. It was Cromwell that abandoned the revolution after threats from the Colombia government. It was Cromwell, J.P. Morgan, Amador, and the rest of the conspirators that set about stealing the money that should have gone to the people of Panama and the bondholders of the French Canal. There is no evidence that Bunau-Varilla, Roosevelt, or Hay played any part in this corruption.

BUNAU-VARILLA'S RIGHT TO NEGOTIATE THE CANAL TREATY

On November 3, 1903, the provisional, or de-facto, government of Panama was created, composed of José Agustin Arango, Frederico Boyd, and Tomas Arias.

Amador, giving up his right to be president, was selected as the first minister in Washington, and given the task of negotiating the treaty with the United States. Carlos Arosemena, and Ricardo de la Espriella, a lawyer, were selected to assist Amador in his task.

From November 5, 1903, to November 6, 1903, there were several back and forth cables sent between Amador and Bunau-Varilla. On November 3, 1903, Bunau-Varilla received a telegram from Amador requesting 100,000 pesos, or

$50,000 dollars and informed him that the City of Panama had been bombarded by the Bogota. Bunau-Varilla thought the telegram strange, since his agreement with Amador required that the rebels control both sides of the Isthmus before he sent any money. In response, Bunau-Varilla decided to send $25,000, through Mr. Lindo, the following day. On the evening of November 4, 1903, Bunau-Varilla received another confusing telegram from Amador informing him that "tomorrow at daybreak attack will be made Atlantic," and again requesting money, "rabish-thousand dollars—help ships Atlantic Pacific little coal took the flight Padilla—Amador

Bunau-Varilla sent a response, explaining the conditions previously agreed to, that he had opened up an account of $25,000 dollars immediately, and encouraged Amador to take Colon. That evening, Bunau-Varilla received another telegram from Amador, again through Mr. Lindo, which stated, "The hostile troops are re-embarking. Demand from Jones (Bunau-Varilla) $100,000." Signed by Amador.

On the morning of November 6, 1903, Bunau-Varilla again sent a telegram to Amador reminding him of the agreement made on October 20, 1903, explained that this "explicate" agreement through his "official authority" would solve both the financial and political questions needed and "inseparable" to accomplish his mission. Bunau-Varilla stated that he "declined any further responsibility in the future if the Government of the Republic prefers any other solution."

That same morning. Bunau-Varilla received a telegram from the provisional government, signed by Arango, Boyd, and Arias, declaring to the secretary of state that on November 6, 1903, the whole of Panama was under the control of the government of Panama, and requested that Bunau-Varilla "press the recognition of the Republic by the Government." Bunau-Varilla responded to the telegram from the Panama government by stating that he could not act usefully without being first appointed minister plenipotentiary of the Republic of Panama. He requested that they send, by cable, his appointment, and that they notify the American consul in Panama, so that the consul can cable Washington what powers Bunau-Varilla was given. Bunau-Varilla also requested that the Panama government give him the power to appoint the official banker of the Republic in New York, in order to open an immediate credit.

That evening, 6:45 P.M., November 6, 1903, Bunau-Varilla received a telegram from the provisional government appointing him "Envoy Extraordinary and Minister Plenipotentiary" with full powers for political and financial negotiations. The telegram was signed by Boyd, Arango, Arias, and F.V. de la Espriella, minister of exterior relations.

Bunau-Varilla sent a telegram to the Panama government thanking them for his appointment and informing them that the United States had officially recognized the Republic of Panama and had informed Colombia of its decision in a letter dated November 5, 1903. Bunau-Varilla received a reply signed by de la Espriella acknowledging the news, and thanking Bunau-Varilla for his timely news. On November 7, 1903, Bunau-Varilla sent a wire to Secretary Hay that he had been appointed Panama's representative.

THE LATE RECEIPT OF CONTRARY CABLES

Bunau-Varilla returned to Washington on the evening of November 7, 1903, and discovered two telegrams that were sent to him, one by the provisional government, and the other by Amador, dated November 4, 1903, and never forwarded to him after he left for New York. The first telegram, sent by the provisional government, informed Bunau-Varilla that he had been appointed confidential agent to negotiate the recognition of the Republic, and to contract a loan for $200,000 dollars to be deposited where Piza and Nephews would indicate, and requested an answer. The telegram was signed by Arango, Boyd, and Arias. The second telegram signed by Amador, stated, "You will be appointed Confidential agent, only diplomatic office which it is possible to give you." These cables gave Bunau-Varilla good reason to conclude that Amador had gone back on his word.[17]

On November 9, 1903, Secretary Hay sent Bunau-Varilla an invitation for lunch at his home, and Bunau-Varilla used the appointment to press for "de Jure" recognition of Panama, in order that he could be formally received as the representative of Panama.

To be recognized as a "de Jure" government, rather than a de-facto government, the protection of the whole of Panama had to be extended by treaty. So long as the treaty was not signed, only the zone from Colon to Panama was protected by the treaty of 1846. Once the treaty was signed this problem could be resolved. [18] It was for that reason that Hay did not formally invite Bunau-Varilla to the Department of State. These were issues that Bunau-Varilla was well versed in, and that Amador, or the other junta members for that matter, had no concept of.

Regardless of this fact, initially, after recognizing Panama, Roosevelt ordered

---

[17] Bunau-Varilla, Panama: The Creation, The Destruction, and the Resurrection pp.344-354. Rainey resolution, pp. 463-465; Committee on foreign affairs, House of Representatives, Feb. 9,12, 1912, entitled "the story of Panama".

[18] Bunau-Varilla, Panama: The Creation, The Destruction, and the Resurrection p. 355.

the navy to patrol the whole of Panama, without forcing a confrontation with the forces of Colombia unless fired upon.

While at his luncheon with Secretary Hay, Bunau-Varilla impressed upon Hay that the same problem that caused the collapse of the Hay–Herran Treaty would occur in the Panama Treaty, if it was not concluded quickly. Hay informed Bunau-Varilla that he understood that Panama was sending a commission, with Amador at its head, to negotiate the treaty. Bunau-Varilla told Hay that "so long as I am here, Mr. Secretary, you will have to deal exclusively with me." Upon leaving the luncheon with Hay, Bunau-Varilla sent a cablegram to de la Espriella telling him that he, Bunau-Varilla, denied the rumor that a special commission is coming to discuss the treaty, as it would be contrary to his mission. He promised to submit all the articles to de la Espriella in succession, as they are agreed upon. He went on to say that he had been assured that nothing had been done on Panama's side to prevent the rapid drafting of the treaty. He further stated that it was necessary to act rapidly to avoid obstructionism from groups supporting the Nicaraguan and Colombian interests. [19]

DESPITE ATTEMPT AT INTERFERENCE BUNAU-VARILLA GETS HIS APPOINTMENT

That same day, Bunau-Varilla received a cablegram informing him that on November 10, 1903, Amador and Boyd would leave, carrying Bunau-Varilla's "credence."

The following day, November 11, 1903, Bunau-Varilla received a follow up cablegram stating that Amador and Boyd had no "mission" except to communicate the mission sent to you in "yesterday's cablegram to avoid loss of time." On November 12, 1903, Bunau-Varilla received another cablegram restating the same message he received on the 11th of November.

In contrast, conflicting dispatches were sent by the American consul in Panama. On the 10th of November 1903, the consul informed the Department of State that Boyd and Amador were in route to the States to negotiate the treaty. He went on to state that Pablo Arosemana would follow on the next steamer. A follow-up cable dated November 11, 1903, stated, "I am informed that Bunau-Varilla is the authorized party to make treaties. Boyd and Amador have other missions and to assist their minister. ....Ehrman."

On November 11, 1903, Bunau-Varilla sent a follow up cablegram to Min-

---

[19] Ibid; p. 358.

ister de la Espriella, informing him of the government's position as sent on the 11th, and re-affirmed by Consul Ehrman that same date. He further informed de la Espriella that Hay agreed to the proposition Bunau-Varilla expressed on the 9th of November, and invited Bunau-Varilla to the State Department on the 13th of November. In effect, Hay officially would recognize Panama as a government de Jure, rather than a government de facto on that date. [20]

BUNAU-VARILLA APPOINTS J.P. MORGAN PANAMA'S BANKER

Having settled the political issue of his formal position as the representative of Panama, between the 9th and 12th of November, Bunau-Varilla returned to New York to settle the financial interests of Panama.

He visited the banking firm of J.P. Morgan and proposed that the Morgan firm accept the office of financial agent of the Republic of Panama. Bunau-Varilla also requested an immediate loan of $300,000 dollars on behalf of Panama and offered to put up as cash $100,000 to cover the guarantee of the loan. In return, J.P. Morgan would be granted the "exclusive faculty" of cashing the indemnity to be paid by the United States to the Republic of Panama by virtue of the treaty.

Because of an expected time, delay, in addition, Bunau-Varilla requested that Mr. Lindo "place at the disposal of the Panama Government" the $75,000 dollars left of the $100,000 he had promised Amador. Bunau-Varilla also borrowed $25,000 from Lindo to be paid to the J.P. Morgan Company. Lindo was assured that he would be repaid as soon as J.P. Morgan advanced the $100,000 guaranteed by Bunau-Varilla's money.[21]

Having done all that he had promised, politically and financially. for the benefit of Panama, Bunau-Varilla was now left to negotiate the treaty with Secretary Hay.

THE HAY BUNAU-VARILLA TREATY NEGOTIATIONS

Even before he met with Secretary Hay on the 9th of November, the U.S. consul to Colombia informed the State Department in a dispatch dated November 6, 1903, that "if the United States would land troops to preserve Colombian sovereignty, and the transit, Colombia would declare martial law, and will approve by decree

---

[20] Ibid; pp. 359-361
[21] Ibid. p-361.

the ratification of the treaty was signed, or if preferred by the United States, install a friendly congress to approve the treaty next May." The message went on to state that "tomorrow, martial law will be declared, and 1,000 troops will be sent from the Pacific side, and the same number from the Atlantic side."[22] General Reyes was dispatched first to Panama and later to the United States to affect the purpose of this dispatch.

The Panama government begged Bunau-Varilla to arrange to send a delegate aboard an American cruiser to the "Magdalena" to prevent Reyes from coming to the Isthmus. Bunau-Varilla responded by advising de la Espriella that he, de la Espriella, inform General Reyes that he cannot disembark in Colon without proper letters of "credence," as envoy extraordinary and minister plenipotentiary of Colombia to the government of Panama. On November 12, 1903, de la Espriella cabled Bunau-Varilla and informed him that he would take his advice.

On the 13th of November, Bunau-Varilla met with Secretary Hay at the State Department, and later was escorted to the White House to formalize the recognition ceremony. Upon leaving the White house, Bunau-Varilla impressed upon Hay the need to finish the treaty quickly. He mentioned to Hay that there were two problems that could destroy any chance that the canal treaty was ratified. One was the Reyes mission on its way from Colombia, and the other was the Amador mission on its way from Panama.

On November 15, 1903, Bunau-Varilla received Hay's project of a treaty, with a request for any suggestions at "your earliest convenience." Bunau-Varilla approached the subject based upon the problems he observed when the U.S. Senate took up the debate on the Hay–Herran treaty. He was aware that, close to an election, the Democratic Party would work to destroy any chance of a Republican treaty. He also considered that there were several Republican senators "devoted" to Nicaragua that would very likely cause the vote to fall short of the sixty needed for passage, if there was even a small opposition to its ratification. Bunau-Varilla was determined to avoid that possibility. He decided to propose a new treaty, with only four issues that he would defend. The first was neutrality of passage, the second, was the equality of all flags regarding toll charges, third was the attribution and indemnity equal to that agreed upon with Colombia, and the fourth was the protection of Panama. In addition, he proposed a grant of sovereignty en bloc.

That is to grant the United States in the Canal Zone "all the rights, power and authority which the United States would possess and exercise if it were the Sovereign of the Territory; to the entire exclusion of the exercise by the Republic

---

[22] Ibid. p362.

of Panama of any such sovereign rights, power, and authority." With the help of Frank Pavey, Bunau-Varilla's lawyer and friend, his version of the treaty was completed. A letter dated November 16, 1903, was sent to Secretary Hay, annexing his new treaty, and a suggestion that Hay had the decision to accept the framework of the Hay–Herran Treaty or the new drafted treaty at his pleasure.

On November 17, 1903, the delegation from Panama arrived in New York at the same time Bunau-Varilla sent Hay the two versions of the treaty. He sent the delegation a telegram of welcome and apologized for not meeting them in New York because of his duties in Washington. Amador and Boyd returned Bunau-Varilla's telegram with a short note of cordiality.

Bunau-Varilla later learned, through a newspaper release, that the delegates were to meet with Mr. Farnham, Cromwell's employee, and they would meet with Cromwell that same day, keeping the delegates in New York. It was later learned that Cromwell had convinced the delegates to delay their trip to Washington until November 18, 1903. Bunau-Varilla found their meeting with Cromwell strange. He was fully aware that Cromwell had abandoned them in their hour of need and put their lives and fortunes at risk.[23]

Receiving no reply from Secretary Hay on the morning of November 17, 1903, Bunau-Varilla sent a letter to him, requesting that he would like to "terminate the negotiation and sign the treaty tomorrow." He warned Hay that he felt that the newly arrived commission from Panama, now in New York, "was full of intrigue, and the people surrounding them would find great profit in delaying, and palavering, and none in going straight to the end." He informed Hay that he was "writing the commission to stay in New York tomorrow, and not to leave before evening." He then requested to meet Hay that same night, or the next morning. Hay replied that he could meet that same night or the next morning, at Bunau-Varilla's convenience.

They met that same night and worked out their differences over the articles of the treaty. Hay again brought up the issue of indemnity for Colombia, and Bunau-Varilla addressed the issue verbally that night, and later at the meal the next morning in writing, condemning the right of Colombia to any claim of indemnity. That evening, Hay requested that Bunau-Varilla meet him at his house, and proposed a single modification to Article II, in which Hay proposed instead of the words "leases in perpetuity" the words "grants to the United States in perpetuity the use, occupation, and control." Having agreed to the change, both Hay and Bunau-Varilla signed the treaty at 6:40 P.M. on November 18, 1903.[24]

---

[23] Ibid. p371.
[24] Ibid. pp 371-377.

THE TREATY SIGNED

At 7:15 P.M. that same night, Bunau-Varilla telegraphed de la Espriella, Panama's minister of exterior relations, informing him that he signed the treaty, that it contained the same political and financial conditions as the Hay–Herran Treaty, except for "necessary simplifications referring to jurisdictions and analogous stipulations." He informed de la Espriella that Boyd, Amador, and Arosemena left New York en route to Washington, and should arrive within two hours. He then congratulated the minister, the government, and the people of Panama.

When Bunau-Varilla met Amador and Boyd, and told them that the treaty was signed, he was confronted with anger, consternation, and disappointment, even before they knew what was in the treaty.

The next day, November 19, 1903, Bunau-Varilla read the documents Amador, and Boyd brought with them. Those documents indicated that Amador and Boyd were to negotiate the treaty, and Bunau-Varilla was to play a passive role in the negotiations. When Boyd mentioned the idea of "fresh negotiations on certain points," Bunau-Varilla informed him that would not happen, and that the treaty would go to the United States Senate and to the Panama government for approval or non-approval, without change. He further argued that the documents he received from the Panama government gave him the right to negotiate and sign the treaty in their behalf, and that is what he did. He reminded Amador and Boyd that the documents they have brought, were null and void since the treaty had been signed, and even if it had not been signed, the documents carried by Amador and Boyd were superseded by the several cablegrams he had received by the Panama government. "You have, therefore, neither in law nor in fact any reason for intervening, so long as I do not ask for your advice." When Mr. Pavey, who Bunau-Varilla had appointed consul of the legation of Panama, read the treaty to them, Amador exclaimed, "At last, there will be no more yellow fever on the Isthmus."

On the evening of the 19th of November, Bunau-Varilla received a cablegram from de la Espriella, asking him why he signed the treaty before consulting with Amador and Boyd.

The next morning, Bunau-Varilla received a follow-up cable from de la Espriella, stating that he had received an explanation from Amador and Boyd "on the powerful reasons which made you sign the treaty, annuls anterior cable sent to-day on this subject to your excellency." [25]

---

[25] Bunau-Varilla, Panama: The Creation, The Destruction, and the Resurrection. pp. 377-379.

BUNAU-VARILLA AND THE SUICIDAL CONSPIRATORS

If Bunau-Varilla thought that he had brought Amador and Boyd over to his side, he was to learn quickly that was not the case.

Bunau-Varilla's next immediate problem was the impending arrival of the Colombian delegation headed by General Reyes. The Colombian government had already promised the United States a final treaty satisfactory to the United States. The signing of the Panama Treaty, as far as Bunau-Varilla was concerned, was only the first step in countering Colombia's attempt to reclaim its Panama district and the Canal. To nail the coffin shut, Panama needed to ratify that Panama Treaty, if for no other reason than to show the United States that they were reliable partners in that enterprise. Colombia had already shown the United States that they were not.

When Bunau-Varilla introduced Amador and Boyd to Secretary Hay, the first issue Hay mentioned was the Reyes delegation, and the need to ratify the treaty promptly. Their answer was noncommittal, and they informed Hay that they did not have the authority to ratify the treaty alone, and that it was necessary to send the treaty to Panama for ratification. Bunau-Varilla observed that Hay was visibly disturbed by this statement. After leaving Hay's office, Bunau-Varilla asked the delegates, since they have indicated that they approved of the treaty, that they should seek special authority from the government to ratify the treaty. Amador and Boyd refused to do so.

He informed the delegates that, by their actions, they had given Secretary Hay reason to believe that Panama may not ratify the Panama Treaty. The very fact that the United States will not ratify the treaty first, as they had done with Colombia, should have given the delegates cause for concern. Their attitude, conveyed to Hay, may have opened the door for Colombia to succeed in reclaiming Panama, and the Canal as well.

On November 20, 1903, Bunau-Varilla decided to send a lengthy telegram to de la Espriella with the request. De la Espriella refused the request.

On the 24th of November 1903, Bunau-Varilla prepared the treaty documents for passage to Panama, in the City of Washington, and he enlisted the delegates Amador and Boyd in the process. In addition, Bunau-Varilla included a letter to de la Espriella indicating that he would remain at his post until the ratification of the treaty, and no longer.

On November 25, 1903, Bunau-Varilla, undaunted, again sent a final blunt cablegram to de la Espriella, outlining what he had done for Panama, what the United States may do if they were again insulted, what the delegation had done to jeopardize the Panama Treaty, and what Colombia will gain from the hesitation to ratify the Panama Treaty. Bunau-Varilla requested from de la Espriella, in as much as Amador and Boyd had approved of the treaty, to at least cable him with authorization to inform the government of the United States that the government of Panama would ratify the treaty upon receiving it at Colon, Panama. Bunau-Varilla stated that, if the government would not take this small step, he, Bunau-Varilla, would not be responsible for the outcome, "the most probable being the immediate suspension of the United States' protection, and the signature of a final treaty with Bogota, in accordance with the constitutional laws of Colombia in case of war." These were the plans which the Colombian general Reyes was bringing to Washington. He then stated that if he did not receive a positive response from de la Espriella, he wished to submit his resignation.

On November 26, 1903, de la Espriella responded by stating, "In view of the approval given by the delegates Amador and Boyd to the Canal treaty, your excellency is authorized to notify officially the government of the United States that said treaty will be ratified and signed as soon as it is received by the provisional government of the republic." The cable was endorsed by Arango, Arias, and Manuel Espinosa.[26] Bunau-Varilla responded the same day by thanking the government.

In a more personal cable, sent on November 27, 1903, signed only by de la Espriella, absent his title, Bunau-Varilla received the statement, "The situation is saved, the triumph is assured according to your cablegram on 26th." De la Espriella went on to offer any other help the government may give. This was a complete turnaround from the previous correspondence, and an obvious repudiation of the advice the government was getting from Amador and Boyd.

THE CROMWELL, AMADOR, BOYD CONSPIRACY OF NOVEMBER 17–18, 1903

Bunau-Varilla should have realized that Amador and Boyd had not been acting alone. He was aware that the Panama delegation had met with Cromwell, and indeed were detained overnight in New York at Cromwell's request. Bunau-Varilla thought their delay was "strange" but opportune, in that it helped him finish and sign the treaty before they could interfere. However, he was to learn, that upon Cromwell's return from Paris, the Panama Treaty would remain in jeopardy.

---

[26] Bunau-Varilla, Panama: The Creation, The Destruction, and the Resurrection, pp. 382-385; 2003, Ovidio Diaz Espino, How Wall Street Created A Nation, pp. 153-155.

Eventually, at the hands of Cromwell, not at the hands of Bunau-Varilla, the government of Panama would be totally corrupted, for the first time in its infancy, and for decades to come.

Certainly, the meeting, between Boyd, Amador, Arosemena, and Cromwell, which took place between November 17 and November 18, 1903, above all other factors, created the birth of the so-called "Rabi-Blanco" hierarchy class in Panama, if it did not already exist. On November 17, 1903, upon their arrival in New York on the steamer The City of Washington, Mr. Farnham, an attorney and an employee of Cromwell, met the Panama delegation and requested that they meet with Cromwell, who would be arriving in New York on the steamer Kaiser Wilhelm der Grosse that same afternoon. According to the statement of Mr. Arosemena, who was present at least before the Cromwell, Boyd, Amador meeting, Amador vehemently objected to meeting with Cromwell, because Cromwell had abandoned them in their hour of need. Arosemena urged Amador to meet with Cromwell, and cautioned Amador to "not make an enemy of Cromwell in the delicate position in which we are placed." Amador and Boyd agreed to meet with Cromwell that afternoon and extended their stay in New York until November 18, 1903.

What was said at that meeting is undocumented. In fact, at a "World Newspaper Commission" interrogatory hearing, held in Panama in June of 1909, Mr. Boyd repeatedly swore, under oath, that the delegation never met with Mr. Cromwell in New York that day. Cromwell, in his account with the French arbitrators, stated that before leaving Panama, Amador and Boyd "had arranged by cable to meet with him in New York for a conference."

Of course, Mr. Arosemena stated the meeting did take place. In addition, there were hotel records, and other witnesses that confirmed that the meeting occurred.

Not only did Boyd lie to this commission, but he lied to the Panama government when he told them that he and Amador went directly to Washington when they arrived in New York, and of course never met with Cromwell that day. Why did he lie?

Their actions reveal more than what they may have said. By the time the delegation departed for Washington, they had appointed Cromwell fiscal agent, general counsel, and representative of Panama in the United States.[27] Unaware that Bunau-Varilla was in the process of signing the treaty, Cromwell advised

---

[27] 2003, Ovidio Diaz Espino, How Wall Street Created A Nation, p. 145; Rainey resolution, pp. 722-723; Committee on foreign affairs, House of Representatives, Feb. 9,12, 1912, entitled "the story of Panama.".

Amador and Boyd on how to undercut Bunau-Varilla regarding the treaty negotiations in order that Amador could take credit. After they found out that the treaty had been signed, Cromwell may have advised Amador and Boyd on how to attempt a renegotiation of the treaty by having the Panama government reject it. Amador and Boyd may have attempted to do this on their own, but there is no doubt an attempt was made with the help of Cromwell.

THE INFAMOUS NOVEMBER 30, 1903, CABLE

On November 30, 1903, through a cable to his subordinate, Cromwell himself tried to remove Bunau-Varilla from his position.

In addition, on November 25, 1903, after the Panama delegation returned to New York from their trip to Washington, Cromwell arranged to have Amador and Boyd sign a loan agreement with the "Bowling Green Trust Company," in which they pledged the money they expected to receive from the United States, or the custom revenues of the ports of Panama and Colon. The loan was for $100,000 dollars, which the Trust Company made at 6% per annum, payable in four months, and renewable in four months, upon a payment of 3% bonus.

In 1909, Boyd stated, under oath, in Panama, that Amador arranged for the loan, after having been introduced by Mr. Brandon, of Isaac Brandon & Brothers, and that no security was given. Mr. Brandon swore that he had nothing to do with the loan. Mr. Cromwell had reorganized the Bowling Green Trust Company, was its attorney, and one of its directors.

As stated, on November 30, 1903, Mr. Drake, vice president of the Panama Canal Railroad, no doubt on behalf of Cromwell, sent a cable, in cipher, to Captain Beers, Cromwell's eyes and ears in Panama, to confidentially deliver a message to the junta, before the delegates Amador and Boyd could arrive back in Panama. The cable directed Beers to request from the junta that Arosemena be appointed as the representative of Panama to replace Bunau-Varilla. The cable was signed by Drake, but years later it was discovered that Cromwell was the author. Unaware that Bunau-Varilla had already cemented his position with the Panama government on November 26 and November 27, 1903, Cromwell's vitriolic letter fell on deaf ears. However, it did form the basis upon which the critics of the Hay–Bunau-Varilla Treaty would long rely when criticizing Bunau-Varilla and the United States.

WORLD RECOGNITION OF REPUBLIC OF PANAMA

Having cemented his position with the government of Panama, and, at the time, unaware of the November 30, 1903, cable emanating from Cromwell's office, Bunau-Varilla set about seeking formal recognition from other world leaders, in order to ensure that the United States would not back off of its commitment to Panama.

Unlike Cromwell, Bunau-Varilla was not convinced that the Reyes delegation, sent from Colombia, had failed in their efforts.

On November 28, 1903, General Reyes arrived in Washington. Reyes immediately let it be known, through the news media, that Colombia would sign a treaty with the United States and would forego the indemnity. The United States would gain the Canal without cost. As an alternative, Reyes threatened to mass thousands of armed troops and invade Panama through the Darien jungle. However, by the time Reyes arrived in Washington, Panama had been recognized by the United States on the 13th, France on the 16th, China on the 22nd, and Austria-Hungary on the 27th of November 1903. Germany acted on the 30th of November, and Russia on the 7th of December.

BUNAU-VARILLA'S INTERFERENCE IN CROMWELL'S FISCAL INCOME

On November 13, 1903, Bunau-Varilla requested the recognition of France. On November 15, Bunau-Varilla received a reply informing him that France wanted to know the disposition of the Panama government regarding the extension of the Canal concession granted by Colombia. After consulting with the Panama government, Bunau-Varilla assured France that Panama would honor the extension of the Canal concession and honor the Old Panama Canal Company shareholder investments.

England, also, would not extend recognition to Panama, until they received assurances that the debt owed to their bondholders by Colombia would be honored by Panama. After again consulting the Panama government, Bunau-Varilla assured England that Panama would honor that debt "according to a proportion of the population of the respective Republics." England recognized Panama on December 26, 1903. Japan and Italy offered their recognition on the 28th of December. Nicaragua, Cuba, Costa Rica, and Peru all offered their formal recognition. In the space of about twenty-five days most of the world powers had followed the United States in recognizing Panama.

General Reyes was left with the threat of force if Colombia was to reclaim Panama, and they would have to fight the United States, and face the condemnation of the whole world, if they chose to do so.

To gain that recognition, Bunau-Varilla sent numerous letters to these countries in order to convince them that the break with Colombia was just. Of course, it helped his cause that the United States was first on board.[28]

Even given all of this, General Reyes was not through. On November 29, 1903, when asked by a reporter from the New York Herald what he would do, since the treaty had been signed and the world had recognized Panama, General Reyes simply responded that "the treaty had not been ratified."

This statement begs the question, did General Reyes make a deal with Cromwell to ensure that the treaty would not be ratified by Panama? If Cromwell was not working with Reyes, he was doing everything possible to help him. Certainly, Cromwell, by this time, was convinced that the United States would not turn to the Nicaragua canal if the Hay–Bunau-Varilla treaty failed. President Roosevelt had admitted as much in writing.

If that should happen, if the Panama Canal ratification should fail, Cromwell must have thought, the only alternative left for the United States would be to again turn to Colombia and accept Reyes's offer. Had he made a better deal with Reyes after the treaty failed? Thanks to the success of Bunau-Varilla, no one will ever know. But Cromwell was not through trying to deep-six the Bunau-Varilla Treaty. Like the cable that was sent from Cromwell's office on November 30, 1903, what occurred next was done behind the cloak of his subordinates.

THE FIGHT TO RETURN THE TREATY TO WASHINGTON

Bunau-Varilla knew that the treaty was due to arrive in Panama by December 1, 1903, and a steamer controlled by the Panama Canal Railroad Company was due to leave Panama en route to New York the same day.

Bunau-Varilla thought it a simple matter to delay that ship for one day, for the Panama government to promptly ratify the treaty, as promised, and return it to the United States, so that there would be no second thoughts from the American government due to outside pressures, and in time for the contemplated President Roosevelt's address to the Congress, on December 7, 1903, and his message to the Senate and House of Representatives on January 4, 1904.

---

[28] Bunau-Varilla, Panama: The Creation, The Destruction, and the Resurrection, pp. 387-400.

Bunau-Varilla would soon learn that nothing is simple. Bunau-Varilla knew that Cromwell was the legal representative of the New Panama Canal Company in the United States, and the attorney and representative of the Panama Canal Railroad Company. The president of that railroad was the banker J. Edward Simmons, the man who had requested Senator Hanna to use his influence with Bunau-Varilla in ensuring that Cromwell could be reinstated as the Panama Canal Company representative.

Because of his earlier assistance to Cromwell, Bunau-Varilla thought that he would have no problem getting the Panama Railroad Company to delay the steamship out of Colon until the treaty was ratified by Panama and returned to the United States.

Mr. Drake was the vice president of the Railroad Company, whose signature was fixed to the vitriolic November 30, 1903, cable to Mr. Beers, denigrating Bunau-Varilla and the Panama treaty. Drake was considered devoted to Cromwell. Little did Bunau-Varilla know that Cromwell, and Simmons, were also among the many co-conspirators in Cromwell's scheme to rob the French Panama Canal Company bondholders, which was to be sold to the United States for $40,000,000 dollars.

Again, the question has to be asked, why would these people interfere in the treaty process, if it meant that they would lose their share in the profits gained by the sale of the Panama Canal Company to the United States? It stands to reason that they thought they could get a better deal. With or without Simmons's knowledge, but certainly with directions from Cromwell, Drake did his part to kill the Panama Treaty. That is a fact.

On November 28, 1903, Bunau-Varilla wired a request to detain the ship scheduled to leave Colon that next Tuesday, December 1, 1903, until the Panama government could examine, discuss, and ratify the Panama Treaty. He signed the wire with his official title as representative of Panama. For the next two days, Bunau-Varilla received no reply to his wire. After making several excuses why nothing had been done, Drake promised to bring the matter up with Mr. Cromwell and Mr. Simmons and agreed to telegraph Bunau-Varilla before 6:00 P.M. that same day. Mr. Drake failed to keep his promise. The following day, after the steamer Yucatan was scheduled to leave Panama, Bunau-Varilla received a negative response from Mr. Simmons, the president of the Panama Railroad.

Realizing that he had been thwarted by Cromwell, on December 3, 1903, Bunau-Varilla turned to the government of the United States. He sent a cable to Minister of Exterior Relations de la Espriella, requesting that the ratified treaty be deposited in the American State Department bag, and that they entrust the treaty, when ratified, to the American consul. He went on to say that the Panama Railroad could no longer be trusted to guarantee transport of the treaty.

CHAPTER NINE
THE TREATY RATIFICATIONS

THE HAY–BUNAU-VARILLA TREATY RATIFIED BY PANAMA

BUNAU-VARILLA RECEIVED TWO CABLEGRAMS dated December 2, 1903. The first came from de la Espriella stating that "at this moment, at eleven-thirty, the junta or provisional government has just approved and signed the treaty. It was signed by de la Espriella."

Soon to follow was a cable from the Panama government. "It is most agreeable to inform your excellency that, unanimously and without modifications, we have ratified the Canal treaty. This action of the government has attracted unanimous approval. This cable was signed by J.A. Arango, Tomas Arias, and M. Espinoza."[1]

THE RATIFICATION OF THE TREATY BY THE UNITED

Having signed the Hay–Bunau-Varilla Treaty, attained world recognition for Panama, and gotten Panama's ratification of the treaty, despite the opposition of Amador, Boyd, Cromwell, and the Colombian general, Reyes, Bunau-Varilla set about obtaining the United States' ratification of the treaty.

Initially, Bunau-Varilla felt that the United States' ratification would be the easiest part in his effort. While working on the Hay–Herran Treaty, as a private lobbyist, he was aware of the many objections to that treaty, by Republican and Democrat senators alike. It was because of these objections that he'd presented a

---
[1] Bunau-Varilla, Panama: The Creation, The Destruction, and the Resurrection, pp. 401-408; 2003, Ovidio Diaz Espino, How Wall Street Created A Nation, pp. 155-156.

totally new treaty to Hay, while still maintaining the basic structure of the previous Hay–Herran Treaty. He wanted to ensure that the United States Senate would not bring up the same objections when debating the Hay–Bunau-Varilla Treaty.

Bunau-Varilla knew that ratification of the Panama treaty would not only have to overcome Democrat opposition, during an election year, but also members of the Republican party, who were also opposed to the treaty for other reasons. In addition, he would have to overcome a group that objected to what they considered the United States' infringement on the rights of the Colombian government, and the group that adamantly promoted the Nicaragua route, Senator Morgan.

As early as November 23, 1903, Senator Morgan, an influential southern Democrat and avid Nicaragua canal route advocate, had been deriding Bunau-Varilla in scathing descriptions not worthy of a United States Senator, but well within the discourse of the time.[2] Morgan represented the southern states. He was convinced that a Panama Treaty would mean the loss of economic power in the South. In addition, he was fully supported by the Transcontinental Railroad lobby, and the steamship lobbies that were opposed to any Canal. These organizations had long been rumored to have played an important financial part in Colombia's rejection of the Hay–Herran Treaty. They acted on the premise that the enemy of my enemy is my friend.

Interestingly, Cromwell represented one of those steamship companies, and at least one Transcontinental Railroad company, the Northern Pacific Railroad Company, but not surprisingly, almost every action he took in this matter conflicted with the interests of that steamship and railroad company.

Initially, Morgan was asked to join with the governors of the southern states in a plan to construct the Nicaragua canal by means of a private corporation. Morgan rejected this proposal as a diversion to the issue at hand.[3]

One of Bunau-Varilla's first actions, more described as a misstep, was to send Senator Morgan a letter of reconciliation, in the hope of winning his goodwill, if not his support. [4]That one letter, and a news article, that was written by Bunau-Varilla and published in the French newspaper Le Matin, on September 2, 1903, caused a major scandal in Washington. Even the attention of the President of the United States was briefly focused on these issues.

These allegations of collusion by Bunau-Varilla and a secret group of financial investors, of course, were coming from Bunau-Varilla's detractors, partic-

---

[2] Bunau-Varilla, Panama: The Creation, The Destruction, and the Resurrection, p.49.

[3] 2003, Ovidio Diaz Espino, How Wall Street Created A Nation, p140.

[4] Ibid: p. 140.

ularly employees of Cromwell, and anti-treaty advocates, and in addition, they suggested there was collusion between Bunau-Varilla and the president.

Roosevelt dismissed the charges by the opposition, that there was collusion between Bunau-Varilla and the United States government, specifically the president, based upon the content of Bunau-Varilla's September 2, 1903, news article. Allegedly, the president felt that Bunau-Varilla was drawing too much attention to himself, rather than focusing on the treaty. After investigating the matter personally, the president found that the people allegedly involved, never had contact with him until after Bunau-Varilla had written his article of September 2, 1903.

In his letter to Bigelow on January 6, 1904, the president intimated that an article released by R.L. Farnham, formerly a World employee and Cromwell's assistant, published by the New York World from their Washington bureau, on June 13, or 14, 1903, was more prophetic of what Roosevelt was thinking at the time than the article released by Bunau-Varilla.

Prior to releasing that June 13, 1903, article, Cromwell had been in a lengthy discussion with the president. The issues released in the Cromwell article were the same issues Cromwell discussed with the president, and the same issues the Senate was alleging were being colluded on by Bunau-Varilla and the president.

In addition, the president was describing Bunau-Varilla, in writing, as one of the most astute persons he had ever met. In fact, there was no one at the time, in the Congress, or in private life, which had ever met Bunau-Varilla that didn't respect his principled intelligence. [5]

Undaunted by Roosevelt's dismissal of their allegations, the news media, specifically the World, and anti-treaty members of the Congress, particularly members of the Senate, accused Bunau-Varilla of blackmail when discussing his letter to Morgan, and collusion with the president regarding his news article of September 2, 1903, and the Panama Revolution.

The call came out that Bunau-Varilla should be deported for his actions interfering with the Senate negotiations and interfering in the international relations between Colombia and the United States, and, a violation of the treaty of 1846.

---

[5] Roosevelt Papers, Roosevelt to Moore, January 6, 1904. (Letter Books, XIV, 416-417.) Ibid, Roosevelt to Lodge, January 6, 1904, (letter Books, XIV, 414-415), Ibid, Moore to Roosevelt, January 7, 1904, (letter Books, XIV 418-419), Roosevelt Papers, Roosevelt to Bigelow, January 6, 1904, (Letter Books, XIV 411-412); Miles P. DuVal, Jr, Cadiz to Cathay: The Story of the long Diplomatic Struggle for The Panama Canal, pp. 407-410.

THE FIGHT

On December 7, 1903, President Roosevelt presented the Hay–Bunau-Varilla Treaty to the Senate and devoted a great deal of his message to the Panama Canal.[6]

On December 17, 1903 the Senate debate began. Senator Hoar immediately introduced a resolution calling for the Panama Revolution documents.[7] On December 18, 1903, the president sent a report containing the diplomatic correspondence between Colombia and the United States from March 8, 1903, to November 18, 1903. [8]Previously, on December 16, 1903, he had sent the same documents to the House of Representatives.

Soon after starting the debate, the Congress adjourned for the rest of the year, leaving their positions, in favor of or against the treaty, to the news media to carry the day.

On January 4, 1904, the Congress reconvened, and the president sent a special message to the Congress, outlining the administration's position on the Canal matter. He included some of the Hay–Reyes documents, and the historical details related to the issue, some of the naval reports of officials at the scene, and strongly suggested that the time for delay was passed. [9]

In a letter to his friend, the publisher of the Out West, Charles F. Lummis, he likened the government of Colombia to 17th-century Spain, and Spain under Philip II, and went on to say he could not respect such a country. He proffered that he would be willing to make things better, referring to United States–Colombia relations, willing to "build railroads," or even grant them money by act of Congress, but he would not allow Colombia to continue to "tyrannize" Panama, or to "block the pathway of the canal, if I can help it." [10]

On January 4, 1904, Senator Morgan introduced a resolution barring the president or the Senate from waging war without the consent of Congress as a whole, when the "foreign power concerned" is at peace with the United States.[11]

On January 13, 1904, Senator William J. Stone proposed an investigation into Bunau-Varilla's part in the revolution. On January 26, 1904, he introduced a resolution to that effect.

Feeling confident that the resolution would go nowhere, since he was under

---

[6] Senate Doc. No. 32 (58th Congress, 2nd, Session.)
[7] Congressional Record, 58th Congress, 2nd Session, Volume 38, Part 1, pp. 316-324.
[8] Senate Doc. No. 51 (58th Congress, 2nd. Session).
[9] Senate Doc. No. 53, 58th Congress, 2nd Session, pp. 5,30.
[10] Roosevelt Papers, Roosevelt to Lummis, January 4, 1904. (Letter Books XIV 386-387).
[11] Congressional record, 58th Congress, 2nd session, Volume 38, Part 1, p. 426.

diplomatic immunity and beyond any parliamentary inquiry, Bunau-Varilla decided to strike back publicly. He contacted his friend Mr. Mitchell, the editor in chief of the Sun. Bunau-Varilla was aware that Senator Morgan had been a great supporter of the "FREE CUBA" movement, and Estrada Palma, who organized, on United States territory, an insurrection against Spain. On January 27, 1904, the Sun published an article comparing Estrada Palma, and Cuba and Spain, with Bunau-Varilla, and Panama and Colombia. The drive to move forward with a congressional inquiry against Bunau-Varilla was diminished by that one article, but not totally defeated.

THE WORLD: "THE PANAMA REVOLUTION, A STOCK-GAMBLER'S PLAN"

On January 17, 1904, the well-known, at least to Panama historians, and infamous World article was published with the headline "The Panama Revolution, A Stock-Gambler's Plan to Make Millions."

The article specifically accused Bunau-Varilla of leading a "gang" of speculators, and of being behind the revolution, in order to make millions. The article went on to accuse Bunau-Varilla of forcing Panama to appoint him as their minister in Washington.[12]

Bunau-Varilla was furious after reading the article and threatened to sue the World for libel if they didn't retract the article and inform him of the piece's author. He did notice that everyone involved in the conspiracy was named, except the Americans, and of course, Cromwell. The World refused to divulge the author at the time.

Bunau-Varilla, a public figure, was advised not to go forward with his legal action. The World knew, and Bunau-Varilla knew, that he was very likely to lose that suit.

It wasn't until 1912, that Bunau-Varilla discovered the author of the article. That fact was revealed in the Rainey Resolution hearings before the Committee on Foreign Affairs of the House of Representatives.

Earl Harding, a staff writer for the World, testified, referring to the January 17, 1904, article, that "the facts were brought to the World by Jonas Whitley, of Mr. Cromwell's staff of press agents, and the World holds a receipt for $100 for

---

[12] Bunau-Varilla, Panama: The Creation, The Destruction, and the Resurrection. p. 423.

the tip." [13]

By January 18, 1904, President Roosevelt, paying close attention to the public and Senate discourse related to the treaty, was confident that the treaty would safely pass the Senate. In a letter to his friend Cecil Spring Rice, who worked in the British Foreign Office, Roosevelt explained why he felt confident the treaty would pass, and then he could "get on with digging the Canal." [14]

On January 20, 1904, Senator Morgan, apparently out of desperation, introduced a Senate resolution that would effectively annex Panama.

Also on January 20, 1904, Secretary Hay sent a letter to Senator Cullom, chairman of the Senate Foreign Relations Committee. In that letter, he enclosed a letter sent to Hay by Bunau-Varilla with a detailed explanation of why it was necessary to pass the treaty without amendments. [15]

The same day, January 20, 1904, President Roosevelt wrote a letter to Senator Spooner, referencing Bunau-Varilla's letter to Hay, and again, in detail, explained why he was requesting that the Senate not add amendments to the treaty.[16]

On February 10, 1904, President Roosevelt wrote to his son, expressing his confidence that the treaty would pass the Senate. In that letter, he stated, "I think the opposition to Panama is pretty well over, and I shall be surprised if within a week or so we do not have the treaty ratified." [17]

REYES GRIEVANCES AND

As the Panama treaty was coming close to Senate debate, all during the month of December 1903, General Reyes, the special ambassador to Colombia, was engaged in discussions with Secretary Hay over the grievances presented by Colombia against the United States, in violation of the treaty of 1846. He hired Mr. Wayne MacVeagh, the former secretary of justice, in the Cleveland administration, to assist him in these matters. In addition, General Reyes, allegedly hired a mysterious press agent by the name of "Mr. W. Morgate." General Reyes signed an order to pay Mr. Morgate $20,100 dollars in gold on February 9, 1904, just before he left for Europe. The other members of the Reyes Commission stated that

---

[13] Ibid, p. 424.
[14] Roosevelt Papers, Roosevelt to Spring Rice, January 18, 1904. (Letter Books, XV, P. 53-54.)
[15] Cullom, op. Cit., pp.384-385.
[16] Roosevelt Papers, Roosevelt to Spooner, January 20, 1904. (Letter Books, XV,78-81.)
[17] Roosevelt Papers, Roosevelt to Roosevelt Junior, February 10, 1904, (Letter Books, XV, p. 335.)

there were no services of "this nature performed." It has been assumed that Reyes forged the document and the receipt, since there was no record of a Mr. Morgate in Washington. Another possibility is that Cromwell was that press agent. This possibility is not so farfetched.

On December 23, 1903, General Reyes sent a formal letter to Hay outlining his grievances. On January 5, 1904, Secretary Hay answered the complaints, dismissing them.

HAY AND ROOT SEEK ADVICE FROM BUNAU

Both Secretary Hay and Mr. Root, the secretary of war, were not yet convinced that Colombia would not go to war over the Panama issue. Root met with Bunau-Varilla on January 8, 1904, and for more than an hour, Bunau-Varilla tried to convince Root that Reyes's threat of war through the Darien jungle was an empty threat.

On January 12, 1904, Secretary Hay met with Bunau-Varilla to discuss the same issue and requested Bunau-Varilla's advice on the matter when responding to Reyes's recent statement that "General Reyes informs us that war can be avoided if we pay an indemnity to Colombia." He went on to explain that a war would cost far more than an indemnity, and influential people had encouraged the government to pay the indemnity.

Bunau-Varilla reiterated what he had said to Secretary Root, specifically, an invasion of Panama by "land forces" was a farce, and "it will never happen." In addition, he emphasized that it would be "dishonorable" to submit to blackmail in order to gain "tranquility." He went on to say that if Secretary Hay was asking him to cooperate in that blackmail, he would refuse, and if that was "your plan, I would have to resign beforehand."

Hay told Bunau-Varilla that he expected the answer that was given. Then Hay asked what answer should be given to the Reyes request? Bunau-Varilla asked for time to think about the request. After some thought, Bunau-Varilla returned with an answer, which Hay, for the most part, gave to General Reyes.

On January 13, 1904, Secretary Hay submitted a letter to General Reyes stating: "This government is now, as it always has been... most desirous of ... good relations between the Republic of Colombia and that of Panama."

The letter went on to suggest that the people of Panama could submit to a "plebiscite" on whether they preferred to remain a citizen of Colombia or not. An alternative would be to put the question to a special court of arbitration, by agreement.[18]

This reply by Hay convinced Reyes that he had no hope of prevailing in his quest to gain an indemnity from the United States, and he took his grievances to Paris.

What Secretary Root and Secretary Hay and Bunau-Varilla alike did not know was that, as early as November 9, 1903, when General Reyes had received his commission from the Colombian government, he had signed a decree "prohibiting the recruiting and mobilization of troops to retake Panama." He was aware that the United States had saturated all the southern rivers and bays of Panama with over forty warships of every kind. In addition, when he reached Washington, on November 28, 1903, he sent a cable to his government stating, "All conflict with Americans should be avoided. Do not occupy territory of Panama, including Isle of Pines."[19]

Bunau-Varilla's advice to Secretaries Root and Hay, made on January 13, 1904, was clearly supported by the actions of the Colombian government as late as January 28, 1904. According to an article released by the New York Herald, Colombia had amassed many troops at Titumati, located at the shores of the Atrato River, close to the border between Panama and Colombia. Colombia was forced to recall these troops, due to the fact they could not advance "even a mile" through the jungle, and in the end were "decimated" by fever.[20]

It is important to understand that Bunau-Varilla's advice to Hay was given out of his personal experience with the jungle and mountain area of Panama. As the chief engineer of the Panama Canal Company, he had succumbed to yellow fever himself. After living and working in Panama for several years, he was intimately aware of the impossibility of invading Panama through the southern jungle. Even General Reyes was aware of this impossibility, hence his decree on November 9, 1903, and his advice to his government on November 28, 1903. General Reyes was making an empty threat, but no one in the United States possibly could have known that the threat was empty, unless General Reyes took that person into his confidence.

---

[18] Bunau-Varilla, Panama: The Creation, The Destruction, and the Resurrection. pp. 417-420.

[19] Rainey resolution, pp. 727-728; Committee on foreign affairs, House of Representatives, Feb. 9,12, 1912, entitled "the story of Panama".

[20] Bunau-Varilla, Panama: The Creation, The Destruction, and the Resurrection. p. 422.

UNITED STATES FORCES IN PANAMA

From November 3, 1903, until December 17, 1903, the United States abandoned its position of protecting the transit route on the Isthmus, and under orders of President Roosevelt, ensured that no Colombian forces were permitted to land within the limits of the whole "State of Panama." To accomplish this directive, as stated previously, the United States saturated all the bays and rivers located on the Atlantic and Pacific sides of Panama, and even some of the northern bays and rivers of Colombia.[21]

On December 17, 1903, after pressure from several senators, Roosevelt modified his orders to Secretary Moody to "maintain observation only" from the area of the Yavisa. The order continued: "Confine active defense against hostile operations to the vicinity of the railroad line on the Isthmus and for its protection."[22] On December 19, 1903, Secretary Moody passed on these orders to Admiral Glass, the navy official on the ground in Panama.

In the process, there was extensive correspondence back and forth between Admiral Glass and the Navy Department discussing the movements of Colombian forces, and local natives hostile to the activities of the United States Navy in Panama.

On January 12, 1904, Admiral Coghlin cabled the secretary of the navy that there were 4,000 Colombians amassed at Barranquilla, Colombia, and that the Mandingo Indians in Panama were hostile, but that the Indians from Conception Bay south to the Mosquito village in Panama were friendly to the United States.[23]

Again, at the insistence of several senators, and to ensure the passage of the Hay–Bunau-Varilla Treaty, On January 13, 1904, Roosevelt further modified his orders, to restrict defense of the Isthmus to the vicinity of the railroad line, from Colon to Panama City. From January 13, 1904, until March 4, 1904, after the ratification of the treaty, Admiral Glass kept the Navy Department informed of the capability of the United States and of Panama to protect themselves if Colombia attacked. His report indicated that Panama alone could not protect itself if that happened.

Finally, on March 4, 1904, Secretary Moody sent the following cable to the naval forces in Panama, in response to a request from Admiral Coghlan: "Treaty of Panama provides for the maintenance of independence of Republic of Pana-

---

[21] Rainey resolution, pp. 482-496; Committee on foreign affairs, House of Representatives, Feb. 9,12, 1912, entitled "the story of Panama".

[22] Ibid: p.496.

[23] Ibid: pp. 496-502.

ma, not integrity of her soil. … Do not prevent citizens of Colombia landing in Panama unless within the strategic limits of the Canal Zone and with arms and hostile intent." [24]

THE NOVEMBER 30, 1903, CABLE AND THE REYES' EMPTY THREATS

The November 30, 1903, was the cable to Mr. Beers from Mr. Drake, that alleged

Bunau-Varilla's warnings; that quick ratification of the treaty would prevent General Reyes from making a more advantageous treaty with the United States, was false. He stated that Bunau-Villa's statement that Reyes' threats were empty threats, was also false. Certainly. Drake could not have known on November 30, 1903, that General Reyes' invasion threats were not empty threats, unless he was working with Reyes, or that he had access to Colombia's official cables and documents. Bunau-Varilla did not give his advice to Hay and Root until January 13, 1904, alluding to this empty threat.

Certainly, Cromwell—considered the origin of the November 30, 1903, cable—had never set foot in Panama until January 1904 and could not know that the Reyes threat was valid, unless he was in the confidence of General Reyes. Considering Cromwell's documented association with Reyes, after November 30, 1903, the supposition that he was working with Reyes, as early as November 28, 1903, along with Amador, and Boyd, to defeat the Panama treaty, Treaty is no stretch of the imagination. [25]

In addition, Cromwell's own documented account indicates that, as early as May 1903, Reyes was in contact with J.P. Morgan, an associate of Cromwell, and a co-conspirator in one of Cromwell's financial schemes regarding the French Canal Company. It is not difficult to imagine that Reyes discussed the Panama Canal issue with J.P. Morgan, and that Cromwell received that information from J.P. Morgan.

In March of 1903, the United States had ratified the Hay–Herran Treaty, and by May of 1903, the Colombian legislature was debating that treaty. Obviously, the President of the United States had a reason to discuss the matter with General Reyes. Likewise, J.P. Morgan, to protect his financial interest in the French Panama Canal, also had a reason to discuss the matter with Reyes in Cuba. What information J.P. Morgan received from Reyes certainly would have been conveyed to his co-conspirator Cromwell.

---

[24] Ibid: p. 503.

[25] Ibid; p.406.

ANOTHER SCHEME BY CROMWELL?

According to Cromwell's own account, when General Reyes left Washington, having failed in his mission, he went to New York, and "through mutual friends," engaged in several conferences with Cromwell, which ultimately had a "great deal of importance."

Mr. Cromwell suggests that among these mutual friends were J.P. Morgan and Theodore Roosevelt. [26]Mr. Cromwell stated that Roosevelt met Reyes around May 3, 1903, while Reyes was passing through the United States en route to Mexico; Reyes then stopped off in Cuba where he met J.P. Morgan, where Morgan was yachting.

Cromwell stated that he proposed a compromise between Colombia, Panama, and the United States at these discussions. According to Cromwell, Reyes gave these proposals "serious consideration." Cromwell stated that on February 3, 1904, he advised the Canal Company by cable of these proposals, and on February 9, 1904, Cromwell sent Captain Beers to Panama, to explain the compromise to the Panama government, which "authorized its consideration." Cromwell failed to give any details of this compromise, only that it was accepted by all sides.

If true, Cromwell, J.P. Morgan, and the President of the United States, Theodore Roosevelt, were doing all this in secret while the Senate of the United States was still debating the Panama Treaty. That is an absurd proposition at best.

No doubt, Cromwell was engaged, possibly with Reyes and J.P. Morgan, on another scheme to extract money from the United States, Panama, certainly from the Panama Canal Company, or Colombia. However, to include the President of the United States in this scheme, while it can be proven that the president was totally involved in Washington, passing the Panama Treaty, takes more trust in Cromwell's word than he deserves.

This alleged compromise, was included in Cromwell's presentation, given to the arbiters in control of the French New Panama Canal Company. Cromwell was demanding $800,000 dollars as a service fee, for representing the French Canal Company. They settled with a fee of $200.000–$250,000.

THE CROMWELL COMPROMISE, OR ANOTHER SCAM?

What possibly could have been the compromise? Recall that the November 30, 1903, cable sent by Mr. Drake to Mr. Beers refers to several reasons why Bu-

---

[26] Committee on foreign affairs, House of Representatives, Feb. 9,12, 1912, entitled "the story of Panama.". pp. 730-731.

nau-Varilla should be replaced. One of those reasons was Bunau-Varilla was making an agreement to pay the foreign debt, specifically $2,500,000 dollars, owed by Panama to be paid to Colombia for the extension of the Canal Company concession in 1894. Another was the English investments and loans made to Colombia based upon the prospect that there would be a treaty with Colombia and the United States.

Whatever the real reason, according to Cromwell and company, it was grounds to dismiss Bunau-Varilla in November 1903, but in January 1904, it may have been the very important "compromise" allegedly brokered by Cromwell, Panama, the United States, and Reyes in New York. [27]

Indeed, Cromwell may have been taking credit for what Bunau-Varilla had already accomplished first with France, regarding the rights of the shareholders of the Canal Company, on November 16, 1903, and later England on December 26, 1903, after assuring the English ambassador that "Panama would assume her share of the Colombian debt, in proportion to the respective Republics." Both agreements were made by Bunau-Varilla, only after he received the authorization of the Panama government. [28]

GENERAL REYES'S FINAL DEFEAT

Early in February 1904, after failing to accomplish his objective in the United States, and after meeting with Cromwell, according to Cromwell, Reyes pursued his cause in the civil courts of Paris, France. On March 31, 1904, he met with an even greater defeat in the French court.[29]

The purpose of Colombia's suit was to defeat the transfer of the French Panama Canal Company to the United States, and thereby defeat the Panama Treaty with the United States. It was Colombia's position, as the sovereign of the Isthmus, that the treaty of 1846 and the concessionary law of 1878 prohibited the French Panama Canal Company from transferring or selling its property rights without the consent of Colombia.

"The French court ruled that the "obligation" of the French Panama Canal Company toward "Colombia" had been automatically transferred to the new sovereign of the territory," Panama. The ruling was based upon the international

---

[27] Ibid: p. 725.
[28] Bunau-Varilla, Panama: The Creation, The Destruction, and the Resurrection. p. 388.
[29] Committee on foreign affairs, House of Representatives, Feb. 9,12, 1912, entitled "the story of Panama". p. 731.

interpretation of the "real and effective Sovereign of the Isthmus." The court stated that "The Republic of Panama had become the entity formerly designated by the word "Colombia" in the concessionary law of 1878."

The court went on to state that "The United States had been obligated to enforce the treaty of 1846' with the government of 'New Granada,' as the 'effective sovereign' of the Isthmus, and from New Granada to 'Colombia,' when it was replaced by Colombia, and from Colombia to the 'Republic of Panama,' when it replaced Panama."

After his failure in France, Reyes returned home and subsequently, with the help of, you guessed it, Cromwell, became one of the most corrupt presidents of Colombia. In time, Reyes was forced to leave Colombia, under the threat of prosecution from the legislature and court system of Colombia. Reyes and his cronies had effectively bankrupted the country. But that is another story. [30]

THE SENATE VOTES ON THE HAY–BUNAU-VARILLA TREATY

On January 18, 1904, the Senate Committee on Foreign Relations insisted on amendments that would give the United States "greater authority and more complete sanitary control over the terminal ports on the Atlantic and Pacific," and reported out the treaty to the Senate with these amendments. On January 29, 1904, the committee reconsidered its actions, and withdrew its amendments.[31]

In fact, On January 28, 1904, Senator Cullum, chairman of the Senate Foreign Relations Committee, after receiving the letter from Secretary Hay, dated January 20, 1904, asked for the rejection of these amendments, "and the final approval of the treaty without any amendments." [32]

THE HANNA, HAY, AND HERRAN LOSSES

Senator Mark Hanna was one of the most forceful and active Panama Canal treaty advocates. However, he never lived to participate in the Senate debate, and he did not see the treaty come to ratification by the United States. On November 3,

---

[30] Ibid: pp.420-421.
[31] Committee on foreign affairs, House of Representatives, Feb. 9,12, 1912, entitled "the story of Panama". p. 481.
[32] Cullum, op. Cit., pp.384-385; Miles P. DuVal, Jr, Cadiz to Cathay: The Story of the long Diplomatic Struggle for The Panama Canal, p. 415-416

1903, Senator Hanna came down with "typhoid" fever, and retired to a room at the Arlington Hotel, located in Washington. He died on February 16, 1904. His funeral was held in Senate chambers on February 22, 1904. Secretary of State Hay died several weeks later. Hay had previously retired to his home because of exhaustion while the treaty was being debated, and left his assistant secretary, Mr. Loomis, to take over many of his responsibilities.

On February 10, 1904, Dr. Herran, the negotiator of the Hay–Herran Treaty, closed the Colombian legation, "and notified Secretary Hay" that he was returning home with "crushed spirits and broken health." He allegedly died in a New York hotel, before returning home. [33]

THE FINAL SENATE VOTE

On February 23, 1904, after extended debate on the treaty, the Senate voted to accept the Panama Treaty, sixty-six to fourteen, without amendments.[34] Bunau-Varilla cited the ratification was approved by the Senate 75 to 17. The proclamation and exchange of letters of ratification took place on February 25, 1904, and February 26, 1904. [35]

THE FINANCIAL FLOODGATES OF CORRUPTION BEGIN TO OPEN THE LEGAL SEEDS OF THE CORRUPTION OCCURRED IN 1903 BUT BEGAN AS FAR BACK AS 1886–1888

Almost all the financial documentation dealing with loans, and payments to Panama, and the French Panama Canal Company was disclosed after 1909 when the World newspaper was sued by the President of the United States, and the World's investigative reporters were directed to investigate the matter by its owner, Mr. Joseph Pulitzer. Mr. Hall and Mr. Earl Harding were those primary investigative reporters. The result of their investigation was finally publicly exposed.

In 1912, the House Foreign Affairs Committee held their hearing. This hearing, above all else, was held to embarrass President Roosevelt and his choice for his successor, Mr. William Taft.

---

[33] 2003, Ovidio Diaz Espino, How Wall Street Created A Nation, p. 159.; Bunau-Varilla, Panama: The Creation, The Destruction, and the Resurrection, p. 425-426.

[34] 2003, Ovidio Diaz Espino, How Wall Street Created A Nation, p. 159.

[35] Bunau-Varilla, Panama: The Creation, The Destruction, and the Resurrection, pp. 427-428.

PRESIDENT ROOSEVELT AND J.P. MORGAN'S INFLUENCE

President Roosevelt, steeped in New York politics, was a true progressive in his domestic politics, and a hawk in his foreign politics. Even as a New York legislator, he worked against corporate corruption, and became a leader in the reform faction of the New York Republican Party. After he lost his first wife, he left New York for a life out west.

After he failed as a rancher, he returned to federal and New York politics.

This is the story most historians describe. However, upon his return to politics, he was not particularly well liked by the Republican Party. His progressive politics interfered in New York corporate interests. Notwithstanding this, his activities in Cuba as a "Rough Rider" catapulted him into the office of governor of New York.

What most people do not understand is that, after the assassination of McKinley, Roosevelt was inaugurated as president at the age of forty-two, the youngest president ever. In many ways, at least early on, Roosevelt was naive. Roosevelt's first act as president was to keep in place all or most of McKinley's cabinet appointees.

As president, true to form, he did his best to move the Republican Party toward progressivism. He was known for trust busting, and increased regulation on business. His domestic policy was known as the "Square Deal" politics of the time. His foreign policy was known as "speak softly and carry a big stick."

Knowing this, one wonders how anyone could think that Roosevelt would ever knowingly consider getting involved in the alleged corruption charges placed against him by the World newspaper. In addition, one wonders why the New York banking industry would ever consider Roosevelt as a candidate for Vice President of the United States, knowing his domestic politics.

The answer, of course, is that, first, Roosevelt walked into the Oval Office surrounded from the beginning by J.P. Morgan operatives. Second, thanks to Cromwell's "holding company" concept, the banking industry was relatively immune from Roosevelt's "trust busting" activities. J.P. Morgan benefitted from competition because of Roosevelt's domestic political policies.

In fact, it was only due to J.P. Morgan's partner, Mr. George W. Perkins, a signatory to Cromwell's syndicate scheme, that Roosevelt even received the vice-presidential nomination. In gratitude, Roosevelt sponsored a dinner in Perkin's honor.

But J.P. Morgan's influence in Roosevelt's government didn't stop with Perkins.

John Hay's daughter was married to the son of William C. Whitney, who was connected to the Morgan family. Roosevelt's brother-in-law, Douglas Robinson, was a signatory to Cromwell's syndicate, and a director to J.P. Morgan's Astor National Bank. The secretary of war, Elihu Root, was the personal attorney for J.P. Morgan. When William Taft became secretary of war, his brother was a signatory to Cromwell's scheme. Roosevelt's assistant secretary of the navy, Mr. Herbert L. Satterle, was J.P. Morgan's son-in-law, and a signatory to Cromwell's syndicate scheme. It was Senator Hanna, a friend of Roosevelt, and the Senate leader of the Republican Party, who advised Roosevelt to listen to the advice of Cromwell— "He knows these people" in Colombia and Panama "better than anyone." It was Senator Hanna's banker, another signatory to Cromwell's scheme, who helped convince Bunau-Varilla to get Cromwell reinstated as the legal representative of the Panama Canal Company, and no doubt played a part in convincing Hanna to change his position on the Canal issue. These are just a few of the people that Roosevelt relied upon to make his decisions. Is it any wonder that he made the decisions that he did?

CROMWELL'S INFORMANTS IN PANAMA AND COLOMBIA

Senator Hanna's advice to President Roosevelt was not far from the truth, but it is even doubtful that Hanna knew that Cromwell was getting a good deal of his Colombia and Panama information from representatives of the United States government. Hezekiah Gudger—then American consul general in Panama, and later chief justice of the Supreme Court of the Canal Zone, after the treaty—was intimately involved in the Panama Revolution, and in close contact with Cromwell before, during, and after the revolution.

On September 8, 1903, Mr. Gudger and Mr. Prescott, the assistant superintendent of the Panama Railroad, met with Cromwell, and Vice President Drake at Cromwell's office in New York. Gudger spent some time with Cromwell in his office but stated he did not discuss the revolution. Mr. Prescott spent his time with Mr. Drake, discussing nothing but the revolution issue. In addition, Gudger played an important part in the revolution.

Mr. Charles Burdett Hart, the minister of the United States in Colombia from 1902–1903, was also in close contact with Cromwell, even after he resigned from his position, and after answering charges against him by the United States. Returning to the United States on May 30, 1903, he gave Cromwell a detailed report of the situation in Colombia and followed up his report with Mr. Farnham at his home in Virginia.

Hart's son was in business with the son of Gabriel Duque in Colombia. While Mr. Hart was informing Cromwell in New York, Duque's son was lobbying the government of Colombia for the ratification of the Hay–Herran Treaty. [36]

Cromwell's eyes and ears in Panama was Captain Beers. He was Cromwell's primary contact in Panama between the Panama Junta, the U.S. minister in Panama, and the Panama Railroad employees. Mr. Beers was also tasked to spy on United States representatives sent by President Roosevelt to gain independent information in Panama. Mr. Beers was sent a cable from Mr. Drake, containing the following general instructions: "Your telegram is of utmost importance; telegraph as soon as possible when Walker arrives from Washington; find out what action the junta is taking in response to his arrival; the subject of the minister of the Republic of Panama is of vital importance, and we rely on you to keep us informed." [37]

BUNAU-VARILLA'S FUNDING OF THE REVOLUTION AND HIS APPOINTMENT OF J.P. MORGAN AS "FISCAL AGENT" OF PANAMA

As previous documentation has shown, on November 15, 1903, Bunau-Varilla sent a telegram to J.P. Morgan in New York, to establish an immediate credit line of $300,000 dollars for the Republic of Panama. He used his own finances, $100,000, as collateral for this line of credit. On November 16, 1903, he promised to deposit $75,000, and within two or three days deposit the other $25,000 dollars to the firm of J.P. Morgan. Bunau-Varilla stipulated that his collateral would cease "as soon as the account of the Republic will be credited on your books." He requested that $50,000 be disbursed to the Republic of Panama immediately upon the signing and ratification of the Panama Treaty by the government of Panama, and $150,000 upon the ratification of the treaty by the United States.

On November 17, 1903, Heidelbach, Ickelheimer & Company placed $75,000 dollars with J.P. Morgan to the credit of Bunau-Varilla. On the same day, J.P. Morgan transferred the $75,000 to the Piza, Nephews & Company, Mr. Lindo's firm. On November 23, 1903, Bunau-Varilla arranged to borrow $25,000 from

---

[36] Committee on foreign affairs, House of Representatives, Feb. 9,12, 1912, entitled "the story of Panama." p. 336.

[37] Ibid. p. 479.

Mr. Lindo. Mr. Lindo gave Bunau-Varilla the $25,000 dollars, check no. 4507, and on November 24, 1903, Bunau-Varilla endorsed the check to Heidelbach, Ickelheimer, and on November 25, 1903, they transferred the check to J.P. Morgan's bank. On the same date, J.P. Morgan deposited the $25,000 into Lindo's bank.

To add confusion to this transaction, On November 16, 1903, the banking house of Isaac Brandon and Brothers bought a $75,000-dollar draft on Piza, Nephews & Company, from Mr. Lindo's Panama house of Piza, Nephews & Company. This draft was stamped with Piza, Nephews & Company's acceptance on November 23, 1903, payable to the Mechanics and Traders' Bank on November 30, 1903, but was paid, according to Piza, Nephews & Company's books, on November 24, 1903. The Brandon Brothers, allegedly, charged no interest, and required no security for this transaction.

In turn, as the legal representative of the Republic of Panama, Bunau-Varilla, also on November 16, 1903, announced that he had appointed the firm of J.P. Morgan as "fiscal agent" of the Republic of Panama for one year. [38]

CROMWELL'S FUNDING OF THE REVOLUTION AND HIS APPOINTMENT AS THE AGENT OF THE PANAMA RAILROAD AND THE PANAMA CANAL COMPANY

As previous documentation has shown, On November 17–18, 1903, William Nelson Cromwell met with Amador, Arosemena, and Boyd in New York. On November 25, 1903, Mr. Amador and Mr. Boyd signed an agreement for a $100,000-dollar loan with the Bowling Green Trust Company, with collateral based upon the customs revenues of the ports of Colon, and Panama, or the revenues received from the United States treaty with Panama. They agreed to pay 6% per year on the loan, to be paid in four months, renewable for four months at a bonus of 3% per year.

Mr. Cromwell reorganized the Bowling Green Trust Company, was its attorney, and one of its directors. The loan was secured by $90,000 dollars par value of Northern Pacific bonds, the Railroad fully controlled by J.P. Morgan, and $10,000 par value of Baltimore & Ohio bonds. These bonds were deposited in the name of William Griffiths, and witnessed by E.B. Hill, one of Cromwell's staff.

There were some allegations that, previously, Amador made an additional, "loan with a bank," and it was noted by Amador in a letter dated October 18, 1903, to his son, with little or no detail as to that loan. There is a notation of a

---

[38] Committee on foreign affairs, House of Representatives, Feb. 9,12, 1912.

commission of 3% from the Bowling Green loan on the books of Piza, Nephew & Company, on December 27, but it did not indicate to whom it was paid.

The $100,000 dollar loan was transferred to the Piza, Nephews & Company firm. $50,000 on November 27, 1903, and $50,000 on December 1, 1903. The debits on the Piza, Nephews Company shows $30,384.67 on December 4, 1903, for supplies sent to the Republic of Panama on the steamer Alliance. On December 14, 1903, $9,932 was sent to Panama on the Yucatan.

On December 22, 1903, the Brandon banking firm was paid $46,000 dollars through Piza, Nephews & Company.

There was a total of $340,000 repaid to the Brandon Bank, out of the $450,000 they allegedly loaned the Republic of Panama, "and allegedly without security, and partly without interest." [39]

According to Cromwell, and at the request of the "New Panama Canal Company," the delegates Amador and Boyd, "over a period of three days," obtained an official, formal declaration, signed by Amador and Boyd on November 27, 1903, which Cromwell said, "was addressed to us as general counsel of the company," as well as similar declarations for the Railroad Company. The delegates assured him that the New Panama government would "confirm" all of the concessions of the Canal and Railroad Companies and acknowledge and approve the disputed extension to 1910. The Panama government demanded, in turn, "the appointment of a delegate to the board of directors, and the appointment of agents in Panama, in accordance with the concessions…" After the Colombian court claim was decided in Paris in 1904, the Panama government "appointed an agent on the board of the Panama Canal Company, Mr. Poylo, of Paris, in order to show its sovereignty, and the Canal Company recognized Mr. Renaudin, and Mr. Shaler as agents on the Isthmus of the Canal Company and the Railroad Company respectively, under the concessions."

THE COLLAPSE OF THE OLD CANAL AND THE CREATION OF THE NEW CANAL

To get a better understanding of how Cromwell was able to control all the funding through the J.P. Morgan Banking firm, much of which has already been stated in one form or another, one must go back, briefly, to the collapse of the French Panama Canal Company, and the transfer of its assets to the New Panama Canal Company in 1888. The Old Panama Canal Company purchased the Panama Ca-

---

[39] Ibid: p.724.

nal Railroad Company from the J.P. Morgan syndicate for $18,600,000 dollars.

In 1889, the old Panama Canal Company went bankrupt, and was dissolved by the "Tribunal Civile de la Seine," and a receiver, Monsieur Brunet, was appointed.

Among other reasons, the collapse of the Panama Canal invoked renewed interest in the Nicaragua canal. That same year, the United States granted a charter for the construction of the Nicaragua canal.

In February 1890, Achille Monchicourt was appointed co-receiver of the old Panama Canal Company, and Mr. Brunet resigned. In 1893, the Colombian government granted a ten-year extension to the Panama Canal Company, to begin on October 31, 1894.

In 1892, to no avail, the United States' secretary of state, through his representative Mr. Coghlan, urged Colombia not to grant the extension. In July 1893, the French court appointed Mr. Lemarquis as trustee for the bondholders, and Mr. Gautron as the co-receiver. In 1894 Mr. Lemarquis died, and Mr. Gautron remained as the sole receiver.

Before Lemarquis died, he and Gautron were able to reorganize the old company before the October 31, 1894, date. On October 20, 1894, they incorporated the new company under Article 21, of the French law related to companies.

The French government never chartered the new company, nor was it under the supervision of the French government. The capital of the new company was fixed at 65,000,000 francs, divided into 650,000 shares of 100 francs each. Importantly, 5,000,000 francs were set aside for the Republic of Colombia for the extension of the concession, and 40,620,700 francs were taken by the "penitentiary" shareholders. These shares were the penalty given to the major officers of the old Panama Canal, and contractors that allegedly profited from their connection to that canal, in lieu of criminal charges. De Lesseps, his brother Eiffel, and Bunau-Varilla were among those people that were required to buy up these shares. It should be noted that all these Canal Company officials, except Bunau-Varilla, were charged but eventually never prosecuted. The public took up 3,484,300 francs, or 6,000 shareholders, and the balance, 15,895,000 francs, was obtained by the liquidator of the old company.

The assets of the old company included the Panama Railroad and its 68,534 shares out of the 70,000 shares, which, as stated, were purchased for $18,094,000 dollars. A contract was made between the old and new railroad companies which provided that if the Canal were not built, "the new company was to pay 20,000,000 francs for it."

For Bunau-Varilla's part, he was required to purchase $20,000 dollars' worth of shares, and he bought another $10,000 worth of shares due to a personal bet he made with a friend.

In 1906, Cromwell testified that he had been appointed the "general counsel of the Panama Canal Company since 1896."[40] In fact, his official connection with the New Panama Canal Company began in January 1896. Because of his illegal use of company funds—$60,000 dollars—Cromwell was released from the company in late 1901.

Through the effort of Bunau-Varilla, and at the request of Senator Hanna, Cromwell was reinstated by the new company on January 27, 1902, and he was requested to sell the company for $40,000,000 dollars. According to Cromwell, he met Mr. Amador and Mr. Boyd, as special delegates, and Mr. Arosemena, as counsel of the Panama Junta, in New York. On November 18, 1903, the delegates assured Cromwell that the "concessions and property of the Panama Canal Company" would be "fully recognized and protected."

CROMWELL'S CONFLICT OF INTEREST

Extracts from the 1906 Senate committee from the hearing on the interoceanic canal, relative to the refusal of William Nelson Cromwell to answer certain questions, revealed the following: Cromwell asserted that his law firm had been the general counsel of the Panama Canal Company for nine years, and the general counsel for the Panama Railroad for twelve years. He stated that "his employment was made by Mr. Whalen, who was the vice president of the Panama Canal Railroad Company. It was made in June 1886, it was verbal, made in New York, and no record was ever found." Cromwell was then a "stockholder, legal counsel, and director of the Panama Railroad Company." "He was invited by Bayard, another agent of the Panama Canal Company, and the contract had been made by which the Panama Railroad was taken over by the New Panama Canal Railroad Company from the receiver of the old Panama Canal Company." In short, Cromwell was tied to the new Panama Canal Company, through his position as director, and shareholder of the old Panama Railroad Company.

The only way Cromwell could avoid this conflict of interest would be to sell his shares in the Panama Railroad Company. He did not do that. His salary as general counsel was $3,500 dollars a year. In the election of directors, his proxy was 1,100 to 5,900 shares out of a total of 70,000 shares.

---

[40] Ibid: pp. 1139-141.

In 1896, The New Panama Canal Company paid Cromwell $25,000 dollars per year for his services. During that 1906 hearing, the Senate committee developed facts that proved Cromwell never acted as attorney for either the Panama Canal Company or the Panama Canal Railroad, never represented them in a court of law, and was hired solely to convince Colombia to allow the Panama Canal Company to be sold to the United States. When Cromwell realized where the committee was going with its questioning, he invoked his right not to answer questions due to his client-attorney privilege. It was the committee's position that Cromwell could not invoke a client-attorney privilege.[41]

"The privilege only extends to information derived from his client as such, either by oral communications or from books or papers shown to him by his client or placed in his hand in his character of attorney or counsel. ... There is no privilege where the attorney is himself a party to the transaction or agreement which he is called upon to disclose."

By the end of the hearing, the committee had developed a clear case of contempt of Congress against Cromwell but adjourned before any action was taken. Senator Morgan, the main antagonist against Cromwell at that hearing, died soon after the committee adjourned. The Republican Congress did not want to give the president a black eye, and they were convinced that Cromwell had secrets best left undisclosed.[42]

What the Congress didn't know, even in 1906, was that Cromwell and J.P. Morgan, along with Roosevelt's brother-in-law and Taft's brother, had an even more personal reason to sell the Panama Canal Company to the United States, unencumbered with lawsuits. Cromwell had invested $1,333,333 dollars; J.P. Morgan had invested $433,333; Douglas had invested $200,000; Henry Taft had invested $190,000; and, allegedly, Amador (F.L. Jeffries) had invested $750,000, among others, in Cromwell's second secret syndicate, related to his Panama Canal Company scheme.

If, as alleged, F.L. Jeffries is Dr. Amador, his investment would account for his mention to his son of a bank loan ("already has been arranged with a bank") prior to November 3, 1903, but there has never been any fiscal account of that loan.[43] Obviously, prior to 1903, Dr. Amador had no large sums of money, and in fact, was dependent upon his employment with the Panama Railroad Company for his income.

---

[41] Committee on foreign affairs, House of Representatives, Feb. 9,12, 1912, entitled "the story of Panama". pp. 530-531

[42] Ibid: pp. 534-572; Senate Document No. 475, 59th Congress, 1st session.

[43] 2003, Ovidio Diaz Espino, How Wall Street Created A Nation, pp. 174,181.

SUMMARY OF CROMWELL'S ACTIVITIES FROM 1896–1904

Although he never set foot in Panama until 1904, Cromwell's activities related to the Canal dated back to the time de Lesseps purchased the Panama Railroad and took over the "Wyse" concession with Colombia. Because the Panama Railroad was chartered in New York, it was necessary for a board member to be an American.

In addition, as far back as March of 1880, the then secretary of the navy, after resigning his position, became a promoter of the de Lesseps canal company. Mr. Richard W. Thompson, at a salary of $25,000 dollars, formed a committee of New York bankers. Mr. Thompson appointed J.P. Morgan, J. and W. Seligman, Winslow, Lanier & Company, and others as fiscal agents of the committee. They then proceeded to buy up most of the Panama Railroad company shares.[44]

This then was the origin of Cromwell's, or at least J.P. Morgan's, Lanier's and Seligman's entrance into the Panama Canal Railroad and eventual Panama Canal Company schemes Cromwell concocted.

In 1893, at the height of the countries fiscal "1893 Panic," Cromwell also purchased shares in the railroad, and was appointed its general counsel, and later made a director. At the time, the railroad was owned by the New Panama Canal Company. At the time, the shares of the Panama Canal Railroad Company, and the shares of the New Panama Canal Company were at rock bottom.

Mr. Boyard, the general agent of the New Panama Canal Company in the United States, appointed Cromwell as its director. From 1898 until 1900 Cromwell was engaged in convincing Colombia to extend the "Canal Concession" for ten years, starting in 1904. In return, Colombia was promised 5,000,000 francs in shares.

By 1896, as he stated, Cromwell was a shareholder, general counsel, and director of the Panama Railroad Company. He was also appointed the general counsel of the company in the United States and Colombia. The stock of the Panama Railroad Company, purchased by the Old Panama Canal Company, was worth $7,000,000 dollars.

The New Panama Canal Company was transferred the Panama Railroad Company by "decree," with a provision that, if the New Panama Canal Company did not finish the Canal, they would pay to the receiver of the Old Company $5,000,000 dollars for the stock and property of the Panama Railroad Company. The decree went into effect on October 1894. This decree tied the Panama Rail-

---
[44] House Executive Doc. No. 107 (47th Congress, 2nd Session.), pp. 100, 214-219.

road Company and the New Panama Canal Company together as one entity, only and if the Canal was finished.

This decree was a major point of objection by the Colombian government, while discussing the Silva, Concha, and Herran treaty negotiations with the United States.

Colombia complained that the second Canal concession extension was illegal, and that, in any case, they had a right to refuse transfer of the concession to the United States, if they were not satisfied with the results of the negotiations. The Colombian government also wanted the right to extract financial concessions directly from the New Panama Canal Company. All of this would have been detrimental to the Cromwell syndicate's interests.

When Bunau-Varilla signed the November 18, 1903, treaty with the United States, he had already embarked on an effort to gain world recognition for Panama. He assured England and France that Panama would recognize their financial rights based on deals and debts they had originally made with Colombia.

Cromwell immediately saw Bunau-Varilla's actions as a threat to the interests of the syndicate. On November 30, 1903, he had his employee pass on a cable to the Panama Junta, excoriating Bunau-Varilla, and strongly requested that he be removed from office and replaced by Mr. Arosemena, before he, Bunau-Varilla, "causes more trouble."

Cromwell had already made claim to the $40,000,000 dollars for the sale of the Panama Canal Company to the United States through his syndicate scheme. Unsatisfied, he was also looking ahead to the $10,000,000 due to Panama at the ratification of the treaty by the United States and Panama. Cromwell had already made amends with Amador and Boyd by the time Bunau-Varilla signed the Panama Canal treaty. Apart from the cable his company sent to the junta, on November 30, 1903, Cromwell also attempted to reject, or at least delay, the ratification of the treaty by Panama, by refusing to provide a timely turnaround of the ratification documents. On the 18th of November 1903, Cromwell had already attempted to kill or modify that treaty with the help of Amador and Boyd, under the belief that Amador could get better terms from the United States than Bunau-Varilla. Obviously, Cromwell was doing this not for Panama, or the United States, but for the "syndicate" that he secretly represented.

In 1904, having failed in his several attempts to kill the Hay–Bunau-Varilla Treaty, Cromwell, with the help of J.P. Morgan, moved to control the financial transfer of the Panama funds and the Panama Canal Company funds because of that treaty.

J.P. Morgan had already been appointed the fiscal agent of Panama by Bunau-Varilla on November 15, 1903, subject to a limit of one year from the ratification of the treaty. This limit of one year, while not seeming to be a problem at the time, became a major issue after the treaty ratification for the Cromwell syndicate.

CHAPTER TEN

WHO GOT THE MONEY

CLEARING THE DECKS FOR THE PAYOUT

Cromwell was worried that some of the suits being proposed by various entities would last for over one year, or more, and would cause an extended delay in transferring the Canal Company funds to the liquidator of the Panama Canal Company. "The prosecutions in Paris would inevitably entail a delay, possibly for at least a year before the final decisions of the French courts." [1]

On March 2, 1904, the attorney general of the United States, Mr. Knox, sent a cable to Cromwell in his official capacity as the general counsel of the Panama Canal Company, informing him that the government of the United States was ready to carry out the transfer of the company to the United States, and to disburse payment to the liquidator of the company. In order for that to happen, it was necessary to first overcome the several suits pending in France and the United States.

According to the following statements made by Cromwell, the most important of these suits was the Colombian suit, based upon the alleged illegality of transferring the Panama Canal Company in conflict with the treaty of 1846, and the 1878 Wyse concession. This suit was decided by the Tribunal Civile de la Seine in favor of the company on March 31, 1904.

On March 30, 1904, an American citizen, Mr. Wilson, filed a suit against the secretary of the treasury and the company in Washington, D.C., alleging that the payment or the transfer of the company was a violation of the Spooner Act, in

---

[1] Committee on foreign affairs, House of Representatives, Feb. 9,12, 1912, entitled "the story of Panama". p. 288.

that the transfer could only be done if the transfer was done with Colombia, the exact wording of the Spooner Act. After consulting with the attorney general's office, it was agreed to move ahead without regard to this suit.

The matter of the possible claim of the registrar, for transfer and registration fees, 5,000,000 francs, was resolved by indemnifying the company by the United States and having the attorney general's office sign a formal agreement to this effect.

The ratification of the shareholders was given special attention by the representatives and the attorney general's office. This matter was also resolved to the satisfaction of the United States.

The issue of the inventories, plans, and archives in Paris, as well as the inventories of the lands and property titles on the Isthmus, were examined and approved by the United States. In early March 1904, the attorney general asked that the judgments against the liquidator on the Isthmus be resolved before the transfer of the company could be made.

These judgments were made by creditors on properties within the Canal that had been made against the liquidator, and these creditors threatened to appeal any ruling that might occur. This matter was resolved by setting aside 350,000 francs by the company until the matter could be finalized. The attorney general's office agreed to this compromise. The Panama Railroad shares were held under special agreements with the liquidator. Both Cromwell and the Attorney's office came to an agreement as to how to resolve this matter as well. The final matter agreed upon was the power to transfer the Canal Company and Railroad Company. It was agreed that the shareholders would vote to transform the present board of directors into a board of liquidators.

On April 16, 1904, these matters and others were discussed, and it was agreed that all the documents would be signed before the shareholders meeting in order to eliminate further complications and delays, caused by possible further lawsuits.

In addition, the transfer of property outside of the Canal Zone was signed by deed in Paris. The company agreed to sign other deeds from "time to time," as required. To do so, it was necessary to sign a power of attorney, appointing Mr. Renaudin as its proxy agent in Panama. The special assistant to the attorney general requested that an additional proxy be appointed. Mr. Cromwell suggested that he be appointed as this additional proxy. His suggestion, apparently, was accepted. On February 17, 1905, the attorney general required, in writing, that Cromwell transfer buildings located in the City of Panama, as well as the Canal

Company's rights on the Island of Taboga.[2]

On April 23, 1903, the shareholder's meeting arrived, and the shareholders approved the transaction.

HOW THE MONEY CHANGED HANDS

Left to be decided was how the $40,000,000 dollars was to be paid by the United States. The original agreement was that the transfer would be done in Washington, D.C., but Cromwell had other ideas.

Initially, Cromwell proposed that the payment be made in bonds at 2% interest, or by installments in cash at 2% interest for the deferred payments. The secretary informed Cromwell that the Spooner Act did not allow for any change of the payment in full, and that it be paid in Washington, D.C.

To avoid injunctions, seizures, and complications, and more importantly, a potential loss to his syndicate scheme, Cromwell proposed that the funds remain with the United States until their actual payment to selected financial agents, or fiscal agents, who would deposit the funds into the Bank of France on behalf of the United States.

He suggested that the J.P. Morgan Banking Company be appointed as that fiscal agent. In that case, the Bank of France, immune from any civil action, and the funds held by the United States, also immune from civil actions, would retain title to the funds until their arrival in the Bank of France. In payment, J.P. Morgan would receive 175,000 francs, or $35,000 dollars. Of course, no one, publicly, knew what else J.P. Morgan would get from this transaction and his connection to Cromwell's syndicate scheme.

Ironically, but not surprising, it was Cromwell that wrote a series of contracts between the "Canal Company, and the United States, the Canal Company and J.P. Morgan and Company, and J.P. Morgan and the United States." These contracts were signed on April 28, 1904 and agreed to by the attorney general of the United States.[3]

No one was aware that J.P. Morgan was a partner in Cromwell's syndicate. On April 28, 1904, the attorney general's office agreed to Cromwell's proposal.[4]

On April 30, 1904, it was announced in press releases, that President Roosevelt "had made peace with the J.P. Morgan banking company," and appointed it

---

[2] Ibid, p. 296.
[3] Ibid, p. 294.
[4] Ibid. pp. 293-295.

as the disbursing agent for the $40,000,000 dollars. Knowing the background of the people surrounding Roosevelt, his decision is no surprise at all. On May 3, 1904, the cabinet confirmed the selection of J.P. Morgan as the disbursing agent for the United States.

CROMWELL'S EFFORT TO AGAIN TWICE SWINDLE THE UNITED STATES

Even while working with the office of the attorney general in transferring the Panama Canal Company and the Panama Railroad Company to the United States, Cromwell was busy working to squeeze out even more money from the United States.

Not until the Senate took up this issue in 1906, did the Congress discover that Cromwell had found a way to swindle the United States out of hundreds of thousands of dollars weeks before he negotiated the turnover of the Panama Canal Railroad shares to the United States. The committee cited the committee statement of Mr. Wallace, the first United States chief engineer, and the "the minute books" of the Railroad Company to show how Cromwell participated in declaring and paying $1,000,000 dollars in dividends to the stockholder of the Railroad Company in excess of the receipts for the preceding fiscal year."

The recipients of this swindle also included the members of the first and second Cromwell-created syndicate, Cromwell, J.P. Morgan, Seligman, Lanier, and others.

Another swindle was related to the repair of two ships, whereby a heavy debt was imposed upon the United States in the purchase of the railroad, all of which is found in the records of the hearings before the 1906 Morgan committee.[5]

THE TRANSFER IS MADE, AND THE MONEY DISAPPEARS IN FRANCE, IN PANAMA, AND IN THE UNITED STATES

In 1904, $50,000,000 dollars was considered an enormous amount of money. It was the largest international transaction made by the United States, up to that time. Had the American public known, at the time, that most of that money went to a secret syndicate, a few corrupt Panamanian politicians, railroad employees, and William Nelson Cromwell, no doubt the United States government would

---

[5] Ibid, p. 533.

have fallen. Certainly, President Roosevelt would not have been re-elected.

It was not until 1906, at the Senator Morgan hearings, that some of the evidence of this grand swindle surfaced. It was not until after the election of 1908, at the Paris and Panama investigative hearings conducted by the World investigative reporters Mr. Hall, and Mr. Earl Harding, that further evidence on this matter was revealed. However, most of the evidence was finally disclosed in 1912 during the House Foreign Affairs committee, known as the Rainey Hearings. Ironically, it took the belated ego of Cromwell, the son of the late Panamanian President Amador, and several other Panamanian officials, the anger of President Roosevelt, a freelance reporter by the name of Hammond, and the dogged search of the reporters assigned to investigate this matter for the World newspaper, for the full depth of this scandal to be revealed.

These reporters were forced to defend the accusations of the United States President and others that the World newspaper had committed slander against President Roosevelt.

The World had published a newspaper article in 1908 that alleged that Roosevelt and others were involved in a secret syndicate to profit from the sale of the Panama Canal Company to the United States.

However, to this day, there is no positive evidence to show what happened to most of the money the United States spent to purchase the Panama Canal Company and Railroad Company, or the disposition of initial funds paid to the government of Panama for the purchase of these companies.

PRESIDENT ROOSEVELT'S RE-ELECTION

In September of 1904, the ink on the Hay–Bunau-Varilla Treaty had barely dried, but essentially, not one ton of dirt had been dredged from the Canal.

Because of domestic politics, the United States was already in the initial stages of giving away its long-fought effort to obtain one of the greatest commercial enterprises the world had ever known. As President Roosevelt was approaching the November 1904 election, he had, arguably, attained the greatest public accomplishment for the United States of any president since Lincoln. After over fifty years, the United States was about to build one of the greatest wonders of the world. Roosevelt did not want any negative publicity so close to his re-election, but he was about to get some, and Mr. Cromwell was involved.

In September of 1904, after the treaty funds had been distributed to Panama, Dr. Morales and Mr. Arias were appointed special fiscal commissioners of Panama and were sent to New York to arrange the investment of $6,000,000 dollars with Mr. Cromwell. Mr. Obaldia was appointed the minister of Panama to the United States, and he was involved in trying to convince the United States to accede to Panama the same issues Amador and Boyd discussed with Cromwell and Bunau-Varilla on November 18, 1903.

Boyd suggested then that the treaty should be amended to include the rights of Panama, included in Articles 1, and 22, of the Hay–Herran Treaty, not included in the Hay–Bunau-Varilla treaty. These articles addressed the "enforcement of the Dingley tariff in the Canal Zone, the jurisdiction of the ports of Panama and Colon, and other points of minor importance." These issues again surfaced, with the advice of Mr. Cromwell.

In September of 1904, Dr. Morales, who spoke fluent English, and had previously published several articles in other newspapers related to these issues, was commissioned by the North American Review to write an article dealing with the secret history of the signing of the Hay–Bunau-Varilla Treaty. Dr. Morales stated on June 28, 1909, that his article "no doubt" described "revelations against President Roosevelt in connection with the independence of Panama…" The title of his article was "The Panama Canal Treaty: Its History and Interpretation." The article, due to be released to the North America Review on October 20, 1904, was never published, and President Roosevelt went on to win re-election.

What happened to convince Dr. Morales to withdrawal his article never surfaced until 1909. Like much of what Cromwell had done related to the Canal purchase, this article would not have seen the light of day had it not been for the anger expressed by President Roosevelt, and the libel suit he filed against the World newspaper in 1908–1909. Dr. Morales stated that it was Minister Obaldia that convinced him not to publish his article. He went on to state that he had been visited by several GOP officials who "begged" him not to publish the article. These gentlemen told him that they "feared the exposure of the history of the Panama Revolution would defeat Mr. Roosevelt for the presidency…"

They declared that they had been authorized to reimburse him for his article, and that the president would sign any order desired for the adjustment of the differences with Panama, if Dr. Morales would acquiesce. Dr. Morales gave the names of these gentlemen to the World reporters that interviewed him in 1909. Their names were "George A. Burt, formerly the superintendent of the Panama Canal Railroad, and another man by the name of Mr. Anson." They told Dr. Morales that they "represented the Republican campaign collector, and his chief, George Bruce Cortelyou, of the Republican National Chairman."

On the 18th or 19th of October 1904, President Roosevelt sent a letter to the secretary of war, Mr. Taft, instructing him to go to Panama and resolve the issue. Mr. Cromwell accompanied Taft, as his confidential advisor.[6] Mr. Cromwell's first visit to Panama was also the first time he was publicly connected to the secretary of war. Mr. Taft would later become president of the United States. This relationship between Mr. Cromwell and the eventual-President Taft, caused enormous interference in the effort to build the Canal by the United States, and certainly added years in delay over the simple matter of who would oversee building that Canal.

The question should be asked, why would Cromwell be interested in what happened to the Canal after the United States purchased the Panama Canal Company and obtained a treaty with Panama? He and his syndicate partners had received most of the money to be had from these financial transactions.

Most historians attribute his prolonged interest in the Canal and Panama to his desire for power. He controlled the politics in Panama. To one degree or another, he influenced the politics in the United States, related to the Canal, for at least thirty-five years after the treaty was ratified. While most of his syndicate partners had taken their money and disappeared, Cromwell and J.P. Morgan remained.

The answer to that question was touched upon at the Senate hearings in 1906, when Mr. Cromwell's official position was described as: "The Railroad Company thus placed within the control and direction of the New Panama Canal Company, was chartered by the laws of the State of New York. ...having been general counsel of the Panama Canal Railroad Co. since 1893, which office he still holds, and (general counsel) of the New Panama Canal Co., which office he still holds; and having been a stockholder and director of the railroad since 1893, both of which relations still continue; and having been general counsel of the Republic of Panama, representing it in a diplomatic sense in making agreements with the President of the United States, while he still held his offices and relation above stated; and being the fiscal agent of the Republic of Panama in control of certain large investments in bonds and stocks held in the United States; and being the counsel of the legation of Panama to the United States, all of which offices and appointments he still holds; and being the confidential advisor and informant of the secretary of war, and of the President of the United States in very important affairs relating to the Panama Railroad, and the conduct of all the operations of the government in the Canal Zone, from the organization of the forces and to

---

[6] Ibid Pp. 476-477.

examining the qualification of appointees doing the work of construction, sanitation, and preparation; and having been actively engaged, at the request of this government, in making agreements with the government of Panama for changes in the postal affairs of the United States and Panama; and in enacting a tariff law for the Canal Zone; and in arranging with bankers of Panama for supplying coin for the payment of officers, clerks, and laborers who were doing service in Panama for the United States; and in making agreements with Panama in reference to supplying food for persons so employed; and in many other matters disclosed in Cromwell's testimony..." [7] Having held all these roles, Cromwell's power was almost absolute. Why would he give that up?

TRACING WHERE THE MONEY WENT REGARDING THE PANAMA RAILROAD, AND THE PANAMA CANAL COMPANY

No one that I am aware of has ever traced the financial history of the Panama Canal Railroad Company stocks and bonds since the collapse of the Panama Canal Company in 1888. When mentioned in any book, this issue was so disjointed, it never made sense to the average person interested in the subject—or at least, studying the issue, it never made sense to me. No doubt, there was a purpose for this obscurity.

We do know that, prior to the 1888 collapse of the Old Panama Canal Company, in 1880, J.P. Morgan, Mr. Seligman, and Mr. Lanier, all U.S. bankers, and others, bought up most of the shares of the Panama Canal Railroad.

In 1888, the Old Panama Canal Company, acquired the Panama Railroad Company for $18,600,000 dollars, to control building the Canal without paying greater compensation if the R.R. was an independent entity. The J.P. Morgan, Seligman, and Lanier syndicate owned 80–90 % of these shares.

In 1888–1889, the Old Panama Canal went bankrupt. On May 15, 1889, the liquidator, or receiver, Mr. Brunet, of the Old Panama Canal Company suspended work on the Canal. On February 13, 1890, a second receiver, Mr. Monchicourt, was appointed. On March 8, 1890, Mr. Brunet, the previous receiver resigned, and Mr. Monchicourt remained the sole receiver. In addition, Colombia granted an extension, importantly, by legislative approval. The French court, after prolonged discussion, granted the receivers the right to reorganize and dispose of the assets

---

[7] Committee on foreign affairs, House of Representatives, Feb. 9,12, 1912, entitled "the story of Panama". p. 532.

of the company. On April 4, 1893, the Colombian government granted another extension to start in 1894, which was not approved by the Colombian legislature. It was this second extension that the Colombian government has argued, from time to time, was illegal.

In July 1893, the French courts appointed Mr. Lemarquis as trustee for the bondholders, and Mr. Gautron as co-receiver. In 1894, Mr. Monchicourt died, and Mr. Gautron continued as sole receiver.

THE CREATION OF THE NEW PANAMA CANAL COMPANY

Just prior to October 31, 1894, the Old Canal Company was reorganized into the New Panama Canal Company. On October 20, 1894, the New Panama Canal Company had capital of 65,000,000 francs, with 5,000,000 francs set aside for the Colombian government to pay for the second ten-year extension. 40,620,700 francs were owned by the so-called "penitentiary shareholder," 3,484 300 francs were owned by public subscription, and the liquidator held 15,895,000 francs. These penitentiary shareholders turned in their claims, receipts, settlements, and cash to the receiver. The receiver turned in the cash he had on hand, as well as other liquid assets, including the Panama Railroad stock. Mr. Lemarquis, the trustee for the bondholders, transferred the assets of the old company to the new company for 60% of the profits.

These assets included the Panama Canal Railroad shares, 68,534 shares out of 70,000 shares. These shares were deposited with the "Comptoir National d' Escompte," subject to an agreement between the Panama Canal Company and the Panama Canal Railroad Company. In U.S. terms that meant they were put in escrow.

This agreement with the Panama Railroad Company, finally agreed to on March 24, 1900, was made under the condition that the New Panama Canal Company would pay $5,000,000 dollars to the shareholders of the Panama Canal Railroad Company, if the New Company did not complete the Canal within a specific time period. That time limit was extended by Colombia in 1894, for ten years. No money was exchanged in making this agreement with the railroad.

In addition, no realistic effort was ever made to finish the Canal by the New Panama Canal Company after taking control of the Old Panama Canal Company. The objective was to sell the New Canal Company from the beginning, and the United States was the only realistic buyer for this sale.

In recall, 1900 was also the first syndicate scheme between Cromwell, the Panama Canal Company officials, J.P. Morgan, Seligman, Lanier, and others to buy the Panama Canal Company outright as the "American Panama Canal Company" for pennies on the dollar. The $5,000,000 dollars forfeiture if the Canal was not completed was also the same amount of money the Cromwell syndicate invested in their effort to acquire the Panama Canal Company, and part and parcel, the Panama Canal Railroad Company. Had they succeeded, they would have acquired the Panama Canal Company and the Railroad Company for next to nothing.

That effort fell through, due to the complaints of the shareholders of the Panama Canal Company, but not due to the effort of Cromwell.

In 1893, Cromwell bought shares in the Panama Canal Railroad Company, and was appointed director and legal counsel for the company.

Having failed in his first scheme, Cromwell embarked on a second scheme, with the same, but more ambitious, objective, and with the same core investors, only this time with success. Aside from his scheme to control the shares of the Panama Canal Railroad for his syndicate of investors, and also to control the shares of the New Panama Canal, Cromwell's objective was to ensure that his second syndicate's members, J.P. Morgan, Seligman, Lanier, himself, and others, received the $5,000,000 dollars from the $40,000,000 the United States paid for the Panama Canal Company, as well as a substantial portion of the balance of that $40,000,000 in 1904.

As stated, in 1880, the original cost of the Old Panama Canal Railroad Company was around $18,000,000 dollars. The J.P. Morgan syndicate bought up 80%–90% of those shares. In 1888, the shares were sold to the Old Panama Canal Company.

In 1889 the Old Panama Canal Company was dissolved, and the New Panama Canal Company agreed to acquire the Old Panama Railroad Company, and it was capitalized at $7,000,000 dollars. In 1889, if the New Panama Canal Company failed to build the Canal, the New Canal Company would own the Panama Canal Railroad Company upon payment of $5,000,000 to the shareholders of the Panama Canal Railroad Company. In short, on paper, there was a $13,000,000 profit for the purchase of the railroad by the New Panama Canal Company. This special agreement was held in escrow by the liquidator of the New Panama Canal Company.

CROMWELL'S SECOND SCHEME MORE COMPLEX THAN THOUGHT

The way Cromwell was able to pull off his second scheme was to first buy up enough shares of the Panama Canal Railroad Company to control that company, which he did, and then to secretly buy up as many shares of the New Panama Canal Company, which were converted to bearer bonds, so that the shares could not be easily traced, and thus to hide the names of his syndicate investors. Cromwell relied on the laws of the French government to cover his actions, which he did. He effectively kept secret all these objectives for many years. At least one or two of his objectives will never be known.

On May 7, 1904, the majority of the shares of the Panama Canal Railroad Company, 68,887 shares, were turned over to, and acknowledged by, the United States government. In addition, as a result of this action, the United States agreed that the payment was due.

It must be mentioned here that J.P. Morgan was a major player in all of Cromwell's schemes, at least as far back as the acquisition of the Northern Pacific Railroad in 1873, mentioned earlier in this writing. J.P. Morgan was a major player in the acquisition of the Panama Canal Railroad Company in 1880, and Cromwell's many other schemes. Without the support of J.P. Morgan, Cromwell could not have succeeded in the schemes he devised.

SHAW'S CAUTION REGARDING PAYING THE MONEY

In order to complete this transaction, Secretary of the Treasury Shaw requested a legal opinion regarding the impact of the "Spooner Act" upon the transfer from the secretary of state, before he would turn over the $40,000,000 dollars to the Panama Canal Company, or the $10,000,000 to the Republic of Panama. The specific wording of the Spooner Act required that the United States turn over the money to "Colombia," not Panama. In turn, the office of the secretary of state requested a legal opinion from the attorney general, which he later passed on to Secretary Shaw.

On February 26, 1904, the assistant attorney general answered by stating, "The treaty provides for payment to Panama on the exchange of ratification. I do not think that further legislation is necessary, and I regard such legislation as inadvisable."

THE ARCHIVES ARE LOST FOREVER

The United States had purchased all the property and assets of the Panama Canal Company on the Isthmus, including the "technical plans, and commercial archives in Paris." The United States received the property on the Isthmus, and all of the technical plans, but they never received the archives in Paris. The "archives" would contain Mr. Cromwell's confidential reports, all of Mr. Cromwell's accounts, and "most of all," the list of shareholders that received the $40,000,000 dollars. [8]

WHO GOT THE $40,000,000 DOLLARS? TO THIS DAY, NO ONE KNOWS.

On December 15, 1908, in his message to Congress, and on December 1, 1908, in a letter to Mr. Foulke, President Roosevelt invited "if any reputable man" desires to look over any of the documents related to the Panama Canal Company, they "may have free access to these documents and can look over everything himself." On May 6, 1904, President Roosevelt, in a letter, directed payment of the $40,000,000 dollars.

Also, on May 6, 1904, in a letter, the secretary of the treasury wrote the auditor of the State, and other departments, to requisition the warrant for $40,000,000 dollars.

On May 7, 1904, the treasury secretary, Mr. Shaw, signed the treasury warrant for $40,000,000 dollars.

On May 9, 1904, Secretary Shaw delivered the warrant to Charles Steele, of J.P. Morgan and Company, located in New York. Also, on May 9, 1904, a letter was sent from the assistant treasurer at New York to the secretary of state, indicating that J.P. Morgan and Company, as special disbursing agents of the United States Treasury, had deposited $25,000,000 dollars as security.

On May 26, 1904, J.P. Morgan and Company, in a letter to Mr. Hamilton Fish, assistant treasurer at New York, described the process in which they would disburse the $40,000,000 dollars.

J.P. Morgan and Company turned in two receipts showing that 128,600,000 francs were paid, through the Bank of France, to Mr. Pierre Gautron, the liquidator of the Old Panama Canal Company, and 77,400,000 Francs, through the Bank of France, to Mr. Marius Bo and Mr. Georges Martin, representing the New

---

[8] Committee on foreign affairs, House of Representatives, Feb. 9,12, 1912, entitled "the story of Panama". p. 326.

Panama Canal Company.

On June 27, 1904, J.P. Morgan and Company, informed Mr. Hamilton Fish, assistant treasurer at New York, that they had made the final payment of the $40,000,000 dollars.

From that date forward, although an attempt was made in 1906 by the Congress, and again in 1909 by the investigators of the World newspaper, no public record exists to determine what happened to the $40,000,000 dollars. The United States paid for the assets, plans, and archives of the New Panama Canal Company. [9]

In 1906, Senator Morgan questioned Mr. Cromwell extensively regarding his activities from 1893–1905, related to the governments of Colombia, Panama, and the United States, and the Panama Canal Company, and Panama Canal Railroad Company. Other than background information, Mr. Cromwell refused to answer the questions put to him by Senator Morgan and others, to the point that, at the end of the committee hearing, the committee considered charging him with contempt of Congress. [10]

In 1908, the World newspaper, located in New York, was drawn to the 1903–1906 issues related to Mr. Cromwell's refusal to answer the questions put to him by the Senate. They printed six articles, charging that there was a syndicate of American citizens intent on getting their hands on the $40,000,000 dollars paid to the "New Panama Canal Company" by the United States. The newspaper alleged that the American government, and the individuals representing that government, were involved in the 1903 Panama Revolution, to build a canal in Panama.

THE WHITLEY TIP

A portion of the information in these articles was derived from a "tip" given to the World on October 2, 1908, by Jonas Whitley, an employee of Mr. Cromwell. It was a Cromwell blackmail complaint made to the New York district attorney, Mr. Jerome, by Mr. Cromwell's lawyer, Mr. W.J. Curtis, which led to Mr. Whitley's tip. The New York district attorney complaint was never pursued; however, it was leaked to the press. Mr. Cromwell, afraid the press would publish the information contained in the complaint, sent Mr. Whitley to refute Cromwell's participation in the allegation made in the complaint.

---

[9] Ibid. Pp. 522-523.
[10] Ibid. Pp. 530-572.

In the conversation with Mr. Whitley, transcribed by the World, the allegations of a syndicate surfaced, and Charles P. Taft, the brother of presidential nominee, Mr. William Taft, and Douglas Robinson, the brother-in-law of President Roosevelt, were named as members of that syndicate. After receiving the information given to them by Mr. Whitley, the World received a telephone call from Mr. Cromwell, which they also transcribed. Cromwell further informed the World that, in part:

"Neither I nor any one allied with me, either directly or indirectly, at any time or in any place in America or abroad, ever bought, sold, dealt in, or ever made a penny of profit out of any stocks, bonds, or other securities of either the Old Panama Canal Company, or the New Panama Canal Company, or ever received for the same a single dollar of the 40 million paid by the United States."

It was Mr. Cromwell's statement, and his Mr. Whitley's statement to the World that caused the World articles to be printed during the 1908 political campaign. [11]

---

[11] Ibid. p.302.

CHAPTER ELEVEN

ROOSEVELT'S INDIGNATION AND CROMWELL'S SCHEME UNRAVELS PRESIDENT ROOSEVELT MOVES TO FILE THE CRIMINAL SUIT

On December 1, 1908, angered by the accusation, which included members of his government, President Roosevelt denounced the essentially reprinted World article in the Indianapolis News, printed on November 2, 1908. The same essential information was published by the New York Sun. The president went on to state that the $40,000,000 dollars was paid directly to the French government, and that every important document related to this matter had been made public. He stated that he did not know of any syndicate, and that no syndicate had any connection to his government, and it was a slander that any American citizen profited from the sale of the Panama Canal.

In reply to the president's statements, the World called for a congressional investigation. It cited the fact that these other newspapers reprinted the same information gathered originally printed by the World. They argued that the president lied about "who got the money."

In 1909, because of these articles, published during and after the 1908 election year, the World newspaper was the subject of a libel suit filed by President Roosevelt.

On February 17, 1909, under orders of President Roosevelt, Attorney General Bonaparte returned a criminal indictment against the Press Publishing Company, owner and publisher of the World, Mr. Joseph Pulitzer, president of the company, and Mr. Caleb M. Van Hamm and Robert H. Lyman, both editors of the World. In addition, another indictment was filed against the owners and publishers of the Indianapolis News.

The suits were based upon the allegations made against ex-President Roosevelt, President Taft, Charles P. Taft, the president's brother, Mr. Douglas Robinson, the brother-in-law of ex-President Roosevelt, ex-Secretary of State Elihu Root, William Nelson Cromwell, and J.P. Morgan.

The suit against the Indianapolis News was defeated early on. The suit against the World was pursued and, after several defeats at the lower court level, was finally dismissed in the Supreme Court. This dismissal was not made based upon the issues presented by the government, but for the right of a newspaper to publish under the first amendment right of the United States Constitution.

BEFORE THE SUIT WAS DISMISSED

To defend themselves, the World representatives requested court orders to gather information in Panama and France. To get the government's permission to do this, the World had to pay the travel expenses to Paris of U.S. Attorney Wise, and Deputy Attorney General Stuart McNamara, and the travel expenses to Panama of Mr. Knapp, of the attorney general's office.[1]

THE ASSURANCES TO ASSIST IN FRANCE

On July 12, 1909, Mr. Wise informed Mr. De Lancey Nicoll, the World counsel in New York, that he had been directed by the attorney general to request the U.S. ambassador in Paris to cooperate fully with the requests of the World. Mr. Wise also informed Mr. John Lindsay, Mr. De Lancey Nicoll's law partner that, if they needed any documents written by the president—from the French president—then they could contact him.

The State Department also informed Mr. Nicoll that the ambassador to France had been instructed to assist the Coudert brothers, the World's counsel in Paris, in obtaining the authorization of the minister of justice, in order that the examination of witnesses could begin about July 12, 1909.

---

[1] Ibid. Pp.302-308.

THE FINAL REFUSAL TO COOPERATE IN FRANCE

All of these assurances went for nothing. On June 21, 1909, Mr. Nicoll received a cable from the Coudert brothers that the French "government" was "interfering." They wanted to know the nature of the case, the names of the witnesses, and a list of the questions that would be asked.

Mr. Lindsay took the matter up with the attorney general, and the State Department. On July 13, 1909, Mr. Wise wrote a letter to Mr. Lindsey informing him that the French government informed the United States ambassador in France that "no such examination as was contemplated by us can be had." Mr. Wise added that he had requested that an office in the embassy be provided for any witness that may wish to provide information, but he could not force anyone to testify. He went on to state that the Old Panama Canal Company and the New Panama Canal Company deposited all their records into a depository, the "Credit Lyonnais," and were subject to French law, and "no court in France could make any order compelling the Credit Lyonnais or its officers to submit the papers to our examination." "Under the laws of France, such books must remain for a period of 20 years."

On July 15, 1909, Mr. Lindsey wrote to Mr. Wise, requesting that Wise plan "so that I can see tomorrow, if possible, at any time suitable to your convenience, the records of the two companies."

Mr. Wise answered Mr. Lindsay by informing him that he did not have the power to order these companies to show their books.

In addition, the World hired "an eminent British attorney and member of Parliament," who went to Paris to investigate the matter. He reported, in part, "I have never known any corporation ... having so completely disappeared and removed all traces of its existence as the New Panama Canal Company." "I consulted leading French lawyers, and they declared that they knew of no machinery, legal or otherwise, by which its records could be brought to light." "The liquidation of the new company was finally closed on June 30, last." "No record exists here of a single person who received the money or of the proportions in which it was paid." [2]

The disbursement to the shareholders of the New Panama Canal Company and the Old Panama Canal Company took about ten years and were composed of about 100,000 shareholders. In June 1908, the French accounts were liquidated.

Of the $40,000,000 dollars disbursed to shareholders, the New Panama Canal Company, (Compagnie Nouvelle), composed of mostly large shareholders,

---

[2] Ibid. Pp. 326-328, 308, -309.

including the "penitentiary shareholders," received $15,000,000, or 38% of the total. The Old Panama Canal Company (Compagnie Universelle) was composed of small shareholders, who received $25,000,000, or 62% of the total. Only the "penitentiary shareholders" disbursement was made public. It has been documented that Bunau-Varilla was forced to invest $20,000 in penitentiary shares, because of his company's involvement in the Old Panama Canal Company, and he bought another $10,000 in shares, because of a bet he made with his friend in the Old Panama Canal Company.

After the $40,000,000 dollars was disbursed, Bunau-Varilla's company received $440,000, plus another $13,200 in profit. The greater portion of the $39,500,000 balance has been purposely left to obscurity by the Cromwell syndicate. [3]

WHO GOT THE $10,000,000 DOLLARS

As stated above, on December 10, 1903, the minister of Panama, Mr. Bunau-Varilla, informed the secretary of state, Mr. Hay, that he had appointed J.P. Morgan and Company, for one year, as financial agent of the government of Panama.

On December 16, 1903, the acting secretary of state, Mr. Alvey Adee, advised the secretary of the treasury that J.P. Morgan and Company had been appointed as financial agents of the Republic of Panama for one year.

On February 24, 1904, the acting secretary of state, Mr. Adee, sent a letter to the Department of Treasury requesting to know if the $10,000,000 dollars was ready to be paid to Panama.

On February 24, 1904, the secretary of the treasury, Mr. Shaw, acknowledging the inquiry of the acting secretary of state's letter, informed Mr. Adee that he was ready to disburse the money as soon as he got a legal opinion from the attorney general regarding the act of June 28, 1902. "The Spooner Act," which specifically provided that this payment be made to the government of Colombia, not Panama.

On February 26, 1904, the Department of Justice wrote an opinion to the secretary of state, informing him that the secretary can pay the $10,000,000 dollars to Panama, and further legislation was not needed.

On March 3, 1904, an inquiry was made by the secretary of treasury, Mr. Shaw, to the secretary of state, requesting to know how to disburse the $10,000,000 dollars. He wanted to know if the payment should be "payable to Secretary of State,

---

[3] 2003, Ovidio Diaz Espino, How Wall Street Created A Nation, pp. 164-165.

or J.P. Morgan; in one warrant of $10,000,000, or 10 warrants of $1,000,000."

In response, also on March 3, 1904, the secretary of state, Mr. Hay, directed the secretary of the treasury to pay the whole $10,000,000 dollars to J.P. Morgan, but stated that "if the agent" (J.P. Morgan) "does not receive it immediately, it can be deposited in the safe at the State Department."

On April 26, 1904, the secretary of state, Mr. Hay, sent a letter to the secretary of the treasury, indicating that he received a request from the government of Panama to send $1,000,000 dollars to J.P. Morgan and company, and retain a check for $9,000,000 until called for by the minister of Panama.

On April 29, 1904, a letter from the secretary of the treasury, Mr. Shaw, to the secretary of state, Mr. Hay, indicated that they had disbursed a $1,000,000-dollar warrant, number 4674, to J.P. Morgan and Company.

On May 3, 1904, the United States cabinet confirmed J.P. Morgan and Company as disbursing agents of the United States.

On May 4, 1904, J.P. Morgan issued a check, number 31537, to Philippe Bunau-Varilla for five hundred and fifteen thousand francs, the equivalent of $100,000 dollars, the amount of money, Bunau-Varilla said he loaned the Panama Junta.

THE FIRST $1,000,000 DOLLARS ARE CONCEALED

On May 13, 1904, President Amador signed Law Number 48 of the National Assembly of Panama, in which the financial transactions of the revolution were concealed. This law provided the legal basis for the lump-sum expenditures up to and including June 30, 1904.

On May 19, 1904, the acting secretary of state, Frances B. Loomis, sent a letter to the secretary of the treasury, requesting that the $9,000,000 dollars be made out to J.P. Morgan and company, "and deliver the warrant to Mr. Morrison, from this Department."

On May 24, 1904, Mr. Cromwell enclosed a translated copy of a letter from the minister of foreign affairs of Panama to the chargé d'affaires of the United States, Mr. W. W. Russell, stating that because the $9,000,000-dollar transfer of funds was an accomplished fact, the president of Panama had no other course but to accept the situation. The provisional government of Panama had directed that not less than $8,000,000 dollars be invested to secure the finances of Panama, however, "the national convention, as a sovereign body, in actual session, reduced the before-mentioned sum to six million dollars in accordance with Article 138 of the Constitution."

Also, on May 24, 1904, Mr. Cromwell informed the attorney general, Mr. P.C. Cox, on a "subject directed to the Isthmian Canal Commission," and he stated that "the commission has taken up the matter." Cromwell also informed Mr. Cox that the Panama Fiscal Commission would arrive in New York "in a day or two," and that "Mr. Perkins, and I have been in close conference upon the subject and are in full sympathy with the sound advice you gave me on Friday." Cromwell then, in the same cable, informed Mr. Cox that he would be in Washington, D.C., within the next few days.

On May 26, 1904, Mr. Cromwell informed Mr. Cox, the U.S. attorney general, that on the 17th of May 1904, he had been appointed, by decree, "counsel to the special fiscal commission" by the government of Panama. He stated that he had informed the "commission" the reasons of state that influenced the United States government in making payment to the fiscal agent of the balance of $9,000,000 dollars. He further stated that the special commission arrived in New York, that day, and organized under the title of "Special Fiscal Commission of the Republic of Panama," with offices in his building. [4]

WHAT HAPPENED TO THE $1,000,000 DOLLARS?

As long as Mr. Cromwell was not directly involved in the accounting, the World newspaper was more successful in finding out what happened to the $1,000,000 dollars the United States paid Panama to build an Isthmian Canal within their territory.

The above Panama law, Number 48, accounted for the following:

Liquidated accounts of the extinct department of Panama up to and including November 3, 1903   --was $400,000 dollars.

Expenditures of the junta, or provisional government, between November 4, 1903 and February 20, 1904, when the first president was inaugurated   --being $1,200,000.

Expenditures of the organized government between February 21, 1904, and June 30, 1904   --was $1,400,000.

Total in Panamanian silver   --$3,000,000

Total American Gold, at prevailing exchange   --$1,365,000

---

[4] Ibid. Pp. 524-530.

J. Gabriel Duque, owner of the Panama Star & Herald, declared that the accounts showing how the money was disbursed were burned by agreement in a secret session of the Panama National Assembly. All efforts by the World investigators to obtain an entire accounting failed. However, they were able to establish:

Ernesto T. Lefevre, son-in-law and executor of José Agustin Arango, admitted that he had in his possession all the original vouchers signed by Arango as one of the junta leaders. He refused to produce those vouchers, because, he stated, if he did so, the persons compromised would cause his ruin politically.

In 1909, the investigative reporters of the World, found a check from J.P. Morgan made out to Mr. Amador for $100,000 dollars.

The official gazette of the Panama government first appeared on November 14, 1903 and failed to include the accounts for November 1903. The first accounting was for December 1903, which did not appear until March 10, 1904. The World finally obtained a certified statement from the treasury general of Panama that showed:

Balance in the treasury of the old department of Panama, November 1, 1903—was $162,330.45 dollars.

The president of the court of accounts assured the World that the books did not show whether this balance was cash or documents. From other records it was clear that most of this balance was due to documents, not cash.

The certified account showed:

Expenditures from November 1 to 3	--was $22,629.65.
Remaining balance on November 3, 1903	--was $139,812.70.
Receipts, November 4–30 inclusive	--was $53,553.40.
Expenditures, November 4–30 inclusive	--was $4,819.15.
Balance in treasury, November 30, 1903	--was $188,546.95.
Balance in treasury, December 31, 1903	--was $161,486.80.

The apparent balance, in the published accounting, as shown, was $4,158.15 in cash, and $157,328.65 in documents.

It was obvious that first costs of the revolution were not paid out of the treasury, except the $22,629.65 dollars, which, on November 3, 1903, was the amount disbursed to pay for the first bribery payment, a portion of the $35,000 demanded by Colombian Admiral Ruben Varon. The certified accounting for November amounted to $27,448.80.

The published accounting, legalized by the national assembly, in lump sums showed that from December 1903–June 1904:

The military received $840,240.50 dollars.

The other government agencies received $429,932.70.

For a total of: $1,270.173.20.

The military expenditures went from $100,000 and $200,000 dollars a month, in December 1903 to May 1904, to $14,927 in June, and $11,504 in July of 1904.

"Because, any military equipment was furnished before the revolution, these military expenditures were suspect, and most likely were to cover the after expenses of the revolution."

General Esteban Huertas was paid $30,000 dollars in silver soon after the revolution. On May 30, 1904, President Amador signed Law Number 60, awarding General Huertas another $50,000 in gold to travel to Europe and study military organizations. "He went to England, and soon returned to squander the rest of the money."

The American officials of the Panama Railroad Company, who in 1903 had been working in Panama, were paid in sums of $15,000–25,000 dollars in silver, per person, for their part in the revolution "in the spring of 1904." Native patriots were paid similar sums.

When Isadoro Hazera, minister of finance, prepared his first comprehensive report to the national assembly in 1908, "he was told by President Amador not to attempt to straighten out the problem." Dr. Amador stated the "less said the better concerning the first million of the $10,000,000 dollars paid to Panama for the Canal concession."

Of that first $1,000,000 dollars, Mr. Cromwell stated to the Congress on February 26, 1906, that $622,615.52 went to pay drafts on J.P. Morgan. The remainder $377,384.48 of the $1,000,000 approximates the sum unaccounted for by the treasury reports of Panama. [5]

In the February 1904 accounting of the Panama treasury, there appears a receipt for $103,500 silver from the Brandon brothers. "The value of one telegraphic draft for $46,000 American gold, at 125 %." There is also a loan from the Brandons for $11,000 silver.

---

[5] Senate Doc. No. 407, 59th Congress, 2nd Session, p.1043.

In the March 1904 accounting, there are loans of $100,000 and $20,000 dollars in silver from the Brandon brothers, and a receipt from them of $183,000 in silver from a loan of $90,000 in American gold. In the April 1904 accounting, there is a loan of $82,000 in silver from the Brandon brothers.

The May 1904 accounting shows $36,222.50 dollars in silver from J.P. Morgan in small drafts to Panama merchants. There also were advances of $10,000.00 and $40,000.00 silver on loans from the Brandon brothers, and $104,441 in silver that was paid to the army.

The June 1904 accounting shows $107,000 dollars in in silver received from a draft of $50,000 in gold by J.P. Morgan, and payable to General Huertas. There were two other drafts from J.P. Morgan, one payable to J.A. Arango for $5,356.35 silver, and another draft payable to O. Holde for $34,500.35 in silver. A loan of $10,000 in gold was made from the Brandon brothers to the junta on January 20, 1904, and another loan of $25,000 in silver was made on January 25, 1904, to the junta, appearing in the June accounting, and a current loan of $50,000 in silver also from the Brandon brothers.

The July accounting shows $200,000 dollars in gold from J.P. Morgan. A J.P. Morgan draft was made to Governor J.D. Obaldia for $8,566.66 in gold, and five J.P. Morgan drafts to various Panamanian merchants, for sums totaling $25,550 in gold. After July 1904, the Panama leaders stopped publishing treasury statements.

Without a degree in accounting, it would be difficult to follow how the first $1,000,000 dollars was spent by the junta. The bottom line was that the total outgoing accounts of $2,017,657.40, from the $3,000,000, left a balance of $982,342.60 unaccounted for, and that is why President Amador ordered that the first million dollars should not be included in the treasury statements, and why, according to Mr. J.G. Duque, the records were "burned by agreement in a secret session of the Panama National Assembly." [6]

It wasn't until the investigation of the reporters Earl Harding and Mr. Hall, in 1909, that any financial information related to the $10,000,000 dollars paid to Panama came to light. The son of the late Dr. Amador released his father's papers to Earl Harding and testified that the co-conspirators of the revolution were hiding the truth.

Fearing they would be accused of perjury, these co-conspirators began to testify truthfully, and the logjam was broken.

---

[6] Committee on foreign affairs, House of Representatives, Feb. 9,12, 1912, entitled "the story of Panama." pp. 731-734.

In the end, it was learned that the major part of the first $4,000,000 dollars, sent to the government of Panama for the benefit of the people of Panama, went to line the pockets of the junta and their supporters.

WHAT HAPPENED TO THE REMAINING $6,000,000 DOLLARS?

Allegedly, this $6,000,000 dollar, originally set at $8,000,000, originated as a verbal agreement between President Roosevelt, and Dr. Amador, the president of Panama. The only reference to this agreement was referred to during the questioning of Mr. Hall, at the 1912 House Foreign Affairs Committee, entitled The Story of Panama.

Mr. Hall testified that the only reference to this agreement that he was aware of could be attributed to a dispatch sent by Mr. W.W. Russell, the United States minister to Panama. Mr. Hall promised to put the dispatch into the "appendix" of the hearing report.

The purpose of this agreement was to "invest" for "prosperity," for the future of Panama. What took place next could not have been a surprise to anyone who knew Mr. Cromwell. The basis for this transfer into the hands of Mr. Cromwell started in December of 1903.

HOW CROMWELL GAINED CONTROL OF THE $6,000,000 DOLLARS

On December 16, 1903, the acting secretary of state, Mr. Alvey Adee, advised the secretary of the treasury that J.P. Morgan and Company had been appointed as financial agents of the Republic of Panama for one year.

It progressed to a Cromwell-translated cable to Mr. Russell, from the minister of foreign affairs of Panama, that was sent to Mr. Russell, referring to the six million dollars, and another cable to the attorney general, Mr. Cox, that Mr. Cromwell, and Mr. Perkins, an associate of J.P. Morgan and co-conspirator in Cromwell's syndicate scheme, would be meeting a "special Panama commission" to decide how to spend the six million dollars.

Cromwell sent a later cable to Mr. Cox, informing him that, by decree, Cromwell had been appointed counsel to the special fiscal commission by the government of Panama. On May 24, 1904, Mr. Cromwell sent a translated copy of a letter from the minister of foreign affairs of Panama to the chargé d'affaires of the United States, Mr. W. W. Russell, stating that because the $9,000,000-dollar transfer of funds was an accomplished fact, the president of Panama had no other course but to accept the situation.

The provisional government of Panama had directed that not less than $8,000,000 dollars be invested in order to secure the finances of Panama, however, "the national convention, as a sovereign body, in actual session, reduced the before-mentioned sum to six million dollars in accordance with Article 138 of the constitution."

Also, on May 24, 1904, Mr. Cromwell informed the attorney general, Mr. P.C. Cox, on a "subject directed to the Isthmian Canal Commission," and he stated that "the commission has taken up the matter." Cromwell also informed Mr. Cox that the Panama Fiscal Commission would arrive in New York "in a day or two," and that "Mr. Perkins, and I have been in close conference upon the subject and are in full sympathy with the sound advice you gave me on Friday." Cromwell then, in the same cable, informed Mr. Cox that he would be in Washington, D.C., within the next few days.

On May 26, 1904, Mr. Cromwell informed Mr. Cox, that on the 17th of May 1904, he had been appointed, by decree, "counsel to the special fiscal commission" by the government of Panama. He stated that he had informed the "commission" the reasons of state that influenced the United States government in making payment to the fiscal agent (J.P. Morgan) of the balance of $9,000,000 dollars. He further stated that the special commission arrived in New York that day and organized under the title of "Special Fiscal Commission of the Republic of Panama," with offices in his (Cromwell's) building. [7]

Dr. Morales and Mr. Arias were members of the commission sent to New York to arrange with Cromwell for the investment of the $6,000,000 dollars.

Mr. Hall testified in 1912, to the House Foreign Affairs Committee, that 875 Panama Railroad bonds were bought for $919,843.75 dollars, and $4,080,000 was invested in New York real estate.

Cromwell used the real estate firm of Douglas E. Robinson, Roosevelt's brother-in-law, a co-conspirator in Cromwell's syndicate scheme and a director of J.P. Morgan's Astor National Bank, to enact his real estate transactions.

In his testimony to the 1912 House Foreign Affairs Committee, Mr. Hall stated that the Republic of Panama has never published any official report from Cromwell regarding his activities as fiscal agent of the Republic of Panama. A list of the original mortgages was published. "But no one knows where they stand

---

[7] Ibid. pp. 524-530.

today. Most if not all have fallen in and the money has been reinvested by Mr. Cromwell."

In a back and forth questioning with congressman Levy, Mr. Hall stated that, unlike J.P. Morgan, who was bonded by the New York State's attorney general's office, Mr. Cromwell was never bonded; there was no trust agreement, and no security to protect Panama against the loss of the money. He further stated that he understood the money had been reduced to $3,000,000 dollars. [8]

In 1910, several members of the National Assembly of Panama, demanded that Cromwell be bonded, but the motion failed. "Cromwell continued to serve as Panama's fiscal agent until 1937. At that time, Cromwell and J.P. Morgan turned over the constitutional funds invested in more than a hundred New York City mortgages to the Chase Manhattan Bank." [9]

CROMWELL, J.P. MORGAN, AND PANAMA

Previously, the question was raised by historians of why Cromwell and J.P. Morgan would still be involved in the Panama Canal issue after they effectively drained it dry.

Most historians attribute Cromwell's extended involvement in Panama to his thirst for power and control, and his obsession for secrecy. The same has been said for J.P. Morgan. Certainly, there is enough documentation to support those assumptions. Power, control, and secrecy were merely the tools used by Cromwell and J.P. Morgan to enrich themselves.

They gained their power, and their control of events, by enlisting other influential businessmen, bankers, and politicians in the United States, Panama, and Colombia as full partners, or at least sympathizers, in their financial schemes. Cromwell's obsession with secrecy was an integral part of his financial schemes. This web of Cromwell's partners and sympathizers could not stand public exposure of the part they played in these schemes.

In short, without this secrecy Cromwell and J.P. Morgan were able to obtain when promoting their schemes, it is doubtful they would have succeeded.

J.P. Morgan's financial activities started long before Cromwell became active in the railroad business. Most historians look to J.P. Morgan and Rothschild's bonding scheme to bail out the treasury of the United States during the 1893 financial panic. Few people bothered to look into the fact that J.P. Morgan was

---

[8] 2003, Ovidio Diaz Espino, How Wall Street Created A Nation, pp. 194-195.
[9] 2003, Ovidio Diaz Espino, How Wall Street Created A Nation, pp. 194-195.

engaged in competition and, in some cases, partnership with J. Gould, in buying up failed railroad and financial institutions at predatory prices.

Cromwell's first noted contact with J.P. Morgan came when he obtained a loan for his employer from J.P. Morgan that eventually led to the total control of the Northern Pacific Railroad Company by Cromwell and J.P. Morgan.

It was Cromwell's creation of the "holding company" concept, and the secrecy it provided to those companies, that helped J.P. Morgan create his vast banking interests in New York. It was the 1880 J.P. Morgan financial syndicate buyout of the Panama Canal Railroad Company that first brought J.P. Morgan into the Panama Canal issue.

This was de Lesseps's secret deal with the United States banking industry for their support of his French Panama Canal. It was also the first congressional investigation of the scandal that surfaced after word leaked out over this secret deal.

It was Cromwell's 1893 appointment as legal counsel, and stockholder, of the Panama Canal Railroad Company that helped him consolidate his control over the Railroad Company, and eventually the Panama Canal Company. It was Cromwell's $60,000-dollar donation to the Republican campaign committee that helped turn the Republican Senate, especially Senator Hanna, from the Nicaragua route to the Panama route. It was the public exposure of this Cromwell donation, an embezzlement, which caused Cromwell to temporarily lose his position of counsel for the New Panama Canal Company.

It was Hanna's banker, J.S. Edward Simmons, which convinced Hanna to seek Cromwell's re-appointment as counsel to the New Panama Canal Company. It was Cromwell that finally convinced the New Panama Canal Company to sell its property to the United States for $40,000,000 dollars. It was Cromwell that worked to insert the financial protections of the New Panama Canal Company within the negotiations between the United States and Colombia, leading up to the Hay–Herran Treaty.

It was these protections, and the issue of sovereignty, that helped cause the Colombian legislature to reject that treaty. It was Cromwell that attempted to apply the same subversive activities regarding the Hay–Bunau-Varilla Treaty.

It was Cromwell that initially convinced the Panama rebels to move against the Colombian government. It was Cromwell that, ostensibly, abandoned the leaders of the Panama Revolution, and it was Cromwell that later was able to convince these same rebels, especially Amador, to appoint him as the special counsel to Panama.

In January 1904, before the Hay–Bunau-Varilla Treaty was even ratified by the United States, it was Cromwell, in secret—and apparently acting on behalf of Panama, General Reyes, the Colombian representative, J.P. Morgan, and, allegedly, the representative of the United States, President Roosevelt—that put together the framework of the Tripartite Treaty that the United States, Colombia, and Panama finally agreed to in 1921. At its base was an apology to Colombia, recognition of Panama by Colombia, the method of payment of Colombia's third-party debts, and financial incentives to Colombia.

It was Cromwell that, with his handpicked French attorney, worked to defeat the Colombian suit in Paris. It was Cromwell, working with the representatives of the United States and Panama, which removed all the legal obstacles to turning over of the New Panama Canal Company and Panama Railroad Company to the United States.

Working with his attorney, who was soon to become president of France, Cromwell ensured that, except for the disciplinary bondholders, none of the recipients of the $40,000,000 dollars paid to the French liquidator and the representatives of the New and Old Panama Canal Company, including the Panama Canal Railroad Company, were ever known.

It was Cromwell that produced and controlled all of the documents, wrote all of the contracts, and arranged for the transfer of all of the property that was turned over to the United States. It was Cromwell that ensured that the Panama Canal Company archives were never released to the United States, as required. It was Cromwell that proposed and worked to ensure that the J.P. Morgan banking firm would act as the fiscal agent of the United States when distributing these funds. It was Cromwell that convinced representatives of the United States that they should distribute those funds, through J.P. Morgan in the United States, to the Bank of France, and eventually to the liquidator and the Canal Company representatives.

It was Cromwell and J.P. Morgan's representative that invested Panama's $6,000,000 dollars in stocks and bonds and real estate, through President Roosevelt's brother-in-law, a J.P. Morgan banker.

As noted above, all of Cromwell's activities were conducted in secret, only to come to light many years later. Exposed early to public scrutiny, he could not have succeeded, and most likely there would not have been a Panama Canal.

Cromwell's activities after the ratification of the Bunau-Varilla Treaty were best described in the 1906 Senate hearing describing Cromwell's control in the United States, Panama, and the Canal Zone: "...and having been general counsel of the Republic of Panama, representing it in a diplomatic sense in making agreements with the President of the United States while he still held his offices and relations above stated; and being the fiscal agent of the Republic Of Panama in control of certain large investments in bonds and stocks held in the United States; and being the counsel of the legation of Panama to the United States, all of which offices and appointments he still holds; and being the confidential advisor and informant of the secretary of war and the President of the United States in very important affairs relating to the Panama Railroad and the conduct of all the operations of the government in the Canal Zone connected with the organization of the forces and the qualification of appointees for doing the work of construction, sanitation, and preparation; and having been actively engaged at the request of this government, in making agreements with the government of Panama for changes in the postal affairs of the United States and Panama; and in enacting a tariff law for the Canal Zone; and in arranging with bankers of Panama for supplying coin for the payment of officers, clerks, and laborers who were doing service in Panama for the United States; and in making agreements with Panama in reference to supplying food for persons so employed; and in many other matters disclosed in Cromwell's testimony..."[10]

Cromwell's control of the affairs of Panama, after the Hay–Bunau-Varilla Treaty can be best said by Panama's ambassador to the United States, Pablo Arosemena. In a letter he wrote to his government on January 8, 1908, he stated: "Cromwell is persuaded that he has a monopoly on everything related to Panama, and assumes that any action taken without previously having consulted with him, and received his consent, is wrong." [11]

Cromwell proved this statement to be true, when in November 1910, the simple matter of bonding Cromwell, no different than that which was done in the case of J.P. Morgan in 1904, was defeated in Panama's legislature.[12]

Cromwell's control in the United States and the Canal Zone can best be described by the first Canal Zone chief engineer, John F. Wallace: On November 27, 1904, Secretary of War Taft, accompanied by Admiral Walker, head of the Canal Commission, and Cromwell, arrived in Colon, Panama. Taft took up residence in the home of Mr. Wallace. During Taft's whole trip to the Canal Zone, Wallace was unable to discuss the issues of the Canal with Taft alone. When finally the opportunity arose, Taft "interrupted to let him know that he had promised Cromwell to have him present." Cromwell was at the front door when they got up in the

---

[10] Committee on foreign affairs, House of Representatives, Feb. 9,12, 1912, entitled "the story of Panama". p. 532.

[11] 2003, Ovidio Diaz Espino, How Wall Street Created A Nation, p. 195.

[12] Ibid, p.194.

morning and was with the secretary until late at night. [13]

THE CANAL RAILROAD EMPLOYEES' REWARD

In his Data for a History, Senator Arango, a key figure in the Panama Revolution, described Captain Beers, the freight agent and port captain for Panama City for the Panama Railroad Company, as "a man of sane and clear views, of absolute probity and honor," and one who, of course, possessed of the confidence of William Nelson Cromwell.

In clear contrast of Arango's description, Cromwell had promised Beers that once the Panama Treaty was ratified, he would take care of Beers and other employees of the Panama Railroad Company. Cromwell was aware that without the cooperation of the railroad employees in Panama, a revolution in Panama was next to impossible.

Beers went to New York, even before Amador, to confer with Cromwell, while Arango and Amador stoked the fires of discontent in Panama. It was Cromwell that provided Beers with a codebook in which to secretly communicate.

Early in 1903, the rebels were aware that they had no hope of a revolution without the financial support of Cromwell. In fact, by several knowledgeable accounts, it was Cromwell that sent for his "eyes and ears" in Panama. It was Beers that first suggested the revolution to Arango and convinced the rebels that they could count on Cromwell's support.[14] Not all, but most of the American co-conspirators were Panama Railroad employee's intent on getting their reward for their cooperation in the revolution. Just some of these local co-conspirators were Herbert G. Prescott, assistant superintendent, and Colonel Shaler, superintendent of the Panama Railroad, Hezekiah A. Gruger, then American consul general in Panama, Gabriel Duque, Major William Murray Black, and his assistant Lieutenant Mark Brooke of the U.S. Army Engineer Corps, who was in charge of inspection of Canal excavation of the French Canal Company on behalf of the Isthmian Canal Commission, Felix Ehrman, senior partner of the bank of Ehrman, and U.S. consul Mr. Drake, vice president of the Panama Railroad Company.

On February 23, 1904, Dr. Amador was sworn in as president of Panama. That same day Amador's son, Dr. Raoul A. Amador gave a luncheon at the Waldorf

---

[13] 1947, Miles P. DuVal, Jr., And the Mountains will Move, p. 149.
[14] Committee on foreign affairs, House of Representatives, Feb. 9,12, 1912, entitled "the story of Panama". pp. 348-350.

Astoria in New York, for the men to whom his father felt most indebted. Apart from Cromwell, those men attending that luncheon were George H. Sullivan, E.B. Hill, S. Deming, R.L. Walker, E.A. Drake, Charles Paine, William J. Curtis, R.L. Farnham, and Mr. M.J. Echeverria.

Before the letter of December 30, 1903—the letter sent by Mr. Drake—Captain Beers, while still in New York, and at the direction of Cromwell, wrote eight to ten letters to his friends in Panama, urging them to undermine Bunau-Varilla's influence with the newly created government of Panama. In his letter to Mr. Prescott he indicated that he believed "Cromwell has several enterprises in view for the Isthmus, in which you and our Panama friends will be considered." [15]

Except where he profited directly, Cromwell's promises were spotty at best. One of these enterprises alluded to by Beers was the transfer of Panama's gambling concession.

Prior to the revolution, Governor Alban of Panama granted the concession to Hezekiah A. Grudger, who transferred it to Pratt & Seymour for $5,000 dollars. Perhaps this was the center of the discussion in Cromwell's office when Grudger visited New York with Mr. Prescott. According to Mr. Grudger, this private meeting was not about the revolution. Prescott, Beers, and Jessy Hyatt, the American vice consul of Colon, Panama, immediately after the revolution, obtained the concession in their own names, and sold it back to Pratt & Seymour for $60,000 dollars. Why Pratt & Seymour would buy the concession from Grudger, sell it to Prescott and Beers, and buy it back within months is another story.

However, in the end, because the United States intervened to protect the interests of its workforce, the government of Panama denied the concession. Pratt & Seymour, an American company, was left holding the bag.

Whitley, Drake, and Farnham, created a land-and-lumber syndicate that took form in 1908. When Jones Whitley, the press agent of Cromwell, attempted to control all the Atlantic watersheds of Panama, President Amador publicly accused Farnham of bribing him in exchange for Amador's approval of this concession.

Cromwell invested $45,000 dollars in the public utilities in Panama and became the largest single stockholder in that enterprise.

Another promise made by Cromwell was to appoint Captain Beers as the general manager of the transportation line Cromwell expected to organize. To do this, the United States had to be induced to abandon the steamship business of the Panama Railroad.

---

[15] Ibid, pp. 726-727.

In his annual 1904 report, the first governor of the Canal Zone, and a member of the seven-man Isthmian Canal Commission, along with the first chief engineer of the Canal Zone, Mr. Wallace, recommended "strongly" that the steamship line be abandoned, and the enterprise left to "private enterprise." It was the governor and Mr. Wallace who recommended that the United States buy up the remaining shares of the Panama Railroad Company in order to gain complete control of this company. Cromwell was commissioned by Secretary Taft to accomplish this task. What a surprise! Based upon what was discovered by the Senate investigative committee in 1906, it was Cromwell that helped cause the problems that forced the United States to take these actions in the first place.[16]

THE WORM TURNED ON CROMWELL

Sometimes, a person believes that he is too smart for his own good. Cromwell was that person. He made promises he could not keep, and the people he made promises to turned against him. That is why in 1908, Cromwell sent his attorney to the attorney general of New York to complain that he was being blackmailed by several Panamanians that felt they were not rewarded enough for their participation in the revolution of 1903.

That is why Cromwell sent his press agent, Mr. Whitley, to the World newspaper to try to spin a story Cromwell thought was about to be published. That is why Cromwell himself added to the problem when he apparently thought Whitley did not clearly represent him. It was this incident, which occurred in 1908, that blew the roof off Cromwell's secrecy, and eventually exposed the people that supported his schemes.

THE GREAT HOG OF THE NORTH

The phrase "The Hog of the North" was a familiar and derogatory phrase uttered by many in Central and South America to imply that the United States was an imperial nation, bent on taking advantage of its neighbors to the south. Putting aside any other international issue related to the activities of the United States and its southern neighbors, the issue of a Canal treaty in Panama was, by far, the basis for this phrase, and could not have been further from the truth.

In the case of Colombia, in 1902–1903, controlled by a virtual Conservative dictatorship, the issue of an Isthmian canal, centered on sovereignty and money.

---

[16] Ibid, pp. 726-727

After Colombia rejected the Hay–Herran Treaty, the dictatorship decided to settle on the money.

The idea of sovereignty became a distraction, a legal argument, in which to regain control of the District of Panama, and in turn, the money offered by the United States.

Colombia's negotiations with the United States, before and during the Hay–Herran Treaty, were being conducted while Colombia was still engaged in a civil war with the Liberal faction of that country. It was a civil war that the Conservatives were initially losing, until they agreed to a backdoor treaty with the United States in return for support in ending the war. It was because of this civil war, and this agreement, that in 1902, the United States sent troops to Panama, ostensibly to protect the property of the Panama Railroad Company, pursuant to the 1846 treaty with Colombia.

After defeating the Liberals, a shaky defeat at best, the government of Colombia was not in a political position to accept a treaty with the United States that would cede power and control of the Canal to the United States. Even if it was similar to the treaty of 1846, and the concessions they gave to France and the Panama Railroad Company, Colombia was not in a political position to ratify it. Sovereignty became a new buzzword, stirred up by detractors of a canal in Panama, and the government of Colombia itself.

In the case of Panama, the issue, initially, centered solely on independence, protection, and the money. A small cadre of rebels was intent on using the power of the United States in order to break away from Colombia and secure their independence, and of course, the money promised by the United States for that treaty.

Their principal promise was a treaty with the United States. These rebels were fully aware that a treaty with the United States meant the exclusive construction, control, and protection of the Canal in Panama by the United States. Most of these rebels, Panamanian and U.S., alike, lived and worked for the Panama Canal Railroad for many years, and under the very same conditions provided by the 1846 treaty.

The collapse of the French Canal, and the creation of the Transcontinental Railroad in the United States, reduced the District of Panama, and the Panama Railroad Company located in Panama, to a desperate state of poverty. The issue of sovereignty was not an issue before or during the treaty ratified by Panama.

The mere fact that the rebellion was caused by the rejection of the Hay–Herran Treaty between Colombia and the United States is the simple proof of this statement. This same cadre of rebels was perfectly content to live under the same repressive government of Colombia when the French were building their canal. Likewise, had the Hay–Herran Treaty passed, there would not have been a rebellion.

Again, like Colombia, the issue of Panama sovereignty became a distraction after the ratification of the Hay–Bunau-Varilla Treaty. The issue of sovereignty was, and has always been, a vehicle by the government of Panama to extract more money and concessions from the United States when their own government, periodically, comes under economic pressure from their own corruption.

In the case of the United States, the Canal issue had always been a need for economic growth and strategic protection. Upon the creation of the Transcontinental Railroad in the 1860s, the United States economic reliance upon an Isthmian canal became a lesser, but still important, issue for the United States.

The strategic issue of protection of both coasts of the United States has always been a paramount issue for the United States, since as far back as the Spanish–American War. A canal in Panama or Nicaragua was the solution. The United States was motivated, not just to build an Isthmian canal, and not just to figure out where to build that canal, but most importantly, the United States was motivated to have, and in fact required, exclusive control and protection of that canal. Without these three factors, exclusivity, control, and protection, the United States government knew that they could never guarantee the protection of its own borders.

That government, under President Roosevelt, who had participated in the Spanish–American War, was acutely aware of the requirements the United States needed to attain its goal. Roosevelt was willing to pay for the right to build and exclusively control and protect the Canal. After Colombia rejected the Hay–Herran Treaty, he had even contemplated gaining the Canal through international eminent domain. In the end, he settled for the outcome of the Panama revolution, and relied upon the rights given to the United States under the 1846 treaty with Colombia.

By the year 1903, Colombia, Panama, and for that matter, the whole Western world, knew that the United States, and only the United States, would build a canal in Panama or Nicaragua. Anyone that could read knew that the United States would not build that canal unless the United States had exclusive protection and control of that canal.

For over fifty years, the British, by the Clayton–Bulwer Treaty, blocked the United States from building a canal in either Panama or Nicaragua, free from outside interference. Roosevelt was determined to correct that problem, and he did.

If one wants to argue that the United States was the great Hog of the North, one must admit that the leaders of Colombia and Panama happily fed at the same trough provided by that Great Hog of the North.

CHAPTER TWELVE
POLITICS TRUMP PERSONAL POWER

FINALLY, THE UNITED STATES WAS FREE TO BUILD THE CANAL, OR WAS IT?

I DO NOT INTEND to spend much time describing how the United States spent ten years building the Panama Canal. There have been many more capable writers that have described this subject in detail, including Miles DuVal, who I will quote liberally.

With few exceptions, the citations I have credited to Mr. DuVal are also contained in the Senate hearings of 1906, and the House hearings of 1912. However, I would be remiss if I did not discuss the politics, personalities, and difficulties involved in the process that went into building that canal.

At the time, building the Panama Canal was such a monumental project for any country, that it was, and still is, beyond description. The men that built the canal have never been able to fully describe the difficulty and hardship involved in the project. The men and women that have worked in the Panama Canal have never been able to fully describe the enormity of the project. Unless one stands on the floor of an empty lock, walks through the lock tunnels, views the enormity of the valves, and understands the complexity, and at the same time simplicity of the lock operation, one will never understand why the Panama Canal has been described as one of the few wonders of the world.

THE FIRST COMMISSION IS CREATED BY ACT OF CONGRESS

Pursuant to the Spooner Act of 1902, President Roosevelt appointed a seven-member commission to build the Panama Canal. Admiral John G. Walker was appointed chairman of the commission. William H. Burr, Carl E. Grunsky, William B. Parsons, Benjamin M. Harrod, and Frank J. Hecker were also appointed commissioners.

On April 5, 1904, the commission, accompanied by Colonel William C. Gorgas, arrived at Colon, Panama. Colonel Gorgas had been appointed as chief sanitary officer of the Canal Zone. Gorgas had distinguished himself in helping to eradicate yellow fever and malaria in Cuba.

On May 6, 1904, John F. Wallace was offered the position of chief engineer, at a salary of $25,000 dollars, effective June 1, 1904. Captain George R. Shanton was appointed chief of police. Captain Shanton had served with Roosevelt during the Spanish–American War. Wallace was well known and respected within the world of railroad engineers. He rose from the lowest ranks to chief engineer, became the general manager of the Illinois Central, and had been the president of the American Society of Civil Engineers. However, he had little or no experience building a canal in the mountains, swamps, and jungles of an area like Panama. He "felt" that he could quickly gain that experience, and "serve as a valuable member of the commission."

On May 9, 1904, under an executive order signed by President Roosevelt, the commission was placed under the supervision of the secretary of war, Mr. Taft.

This executive order gave the commission the right to legislate the military, civil, and judicial affairs in the Canal Zone. The order gave the commission the power to build the Canal and appointed the commissioners as directors of the Panama Railroad, and, in effect, gave the commission "almost autocratic power" within the Canal Zone until the close of the 58th Congress. Major General George W. Davis was appointed the first governor of the Canal Zone. He was appointed because of his extensive administrative experience in Cuba, Puerto Rico, and the Philippines.

Photo of president Taft

Photo of fist governor of the Canal Zone George W. Davis

On May 17, 1904, General Davis arrived in Colon, Panama, with the first permanent party; Major Black, Ernest Lagarde, Jr., Paymaster E.C. Tobey, Dr. R.L. Sutton, Captain Shanton, the first Canal Zone chief of police, and M.E. Mitchell. They were met by a boarding committee headed by Tracy Robinson, one of the co-conspirators of the revolution, named by Colombia in 1903. Mr. Robinson was a local merchant eager to benefit from the needs of the Canal employee.

Upon his arrival in Panama, Governor Davis issued a proclamation of occupation in the Canal Zone. He immediately set about appointing the civil officers of the Canal Zone government. Major Black was appointed head of the engineering department; Harry Reed was appointed the first executive secretary; E.C. Tobey was appointed head of the accounts and material department; and the buildings and grounds department was headed by the Frenchman C.F. Bertoncini.

Governor Davis was immediately met with several problems. Because Panama did not enforce its own quarantine regulations, Governor Davis's first action was to bring the duties of inspecting vessels, and quarantine regulations under the control of the Canal Commission.

In addition, Davis found that Panama claimed the port of Laboca, located in the Canal Zone, as the port of Panama City. He eventually was able to negotiate an agreement with Panama that solved this problem in favor of the United States.

When it came time to make a payroll, Davis decided to publicly request open bids for silver needed. The local bankers were used to secret bidding and objected. In the end, Davis got his way, and the local employee was paid in silver, and the American employee was paid in gold. The phrase "gold and silver rolls" long stood, at least for the last fifty years of U.S. control, as a symbol of local and American employee payment within the Canal Zone, and early on was equated to the difference of race. [1]

Davis emphasized the urgent need for sanitation, sewage, and a water supply for the cities of Panama, and Colon. These cities were viewed as nothing more than muddy cesspools. In the United States, temperance groups were working to make the Canal a "dry" community. The "friends of labor," the American Boycott Association, were lobbying Admiral Walker to reduce the workday from ten hours to eight hours. In addition, a decision had to be made between Bohio and Colon as the Atlantic terminal.

The commission was finding it difficult recruiting enough engineers to work in Panama, because of the reputation of yellow fever and malaria. Upon returning to the United States, from his first Canal visit, Colonel Gorgas published an arti-

---

[1] 1947, Miles P. DuVal, Jr., And the Mountains will Move, pp. 129-139.

cle describing how safe it was living in the Canal Zone, given certain precautions such as drinking boiled water, sleeping under mosquito nets, and sleeping away from the native malaria carriers.

When Wallace arrived in Panama, with the returning Gorgas and sixteen nurses, he brought with him two "fine metallic caskets." He was obviously worried about his future health. This was not a good sign to project to the rest of the workforce.

As the workforce increased, the supply for food and housing became scarce, and when obtained, more expensive. This problem continued to get worse as time went on.

Wallace found the French equipment and buildings covered with jungle growth, rot, and rust. The equipment, adequate in 1888, was almost useless in 1904, some sixteen years later. The only work being done, and by hand at that, was the excavation in the Culebra Cut near Gold Hill, the only place where employment could be had. Most men applying for a job were looking for employment as "watchmen, timekeepers, or foremen." [2]

Wallace had been reluctant to accept his position. He was obviously afraid of the health hazards associated with working in the Canal Zone. But just as important, he did not like the idea of working under seven people who may be giving him conflicting and unworkable directions. All but two of the commissioners were engineers in their own right.

Wallace took the position under the condition that he would answer to Admiral Walker, chairman of the commission, and that he, Wallace, would have full control of building the Canal in Panama. Wallace was convinced that eventually he could replace Admiral Walker as the chairman of the commission.

Upon his arrival in Panama, Wallace confronted Governor Davis, expecting to take over control of the Canal functions. Governor Davis explained that he had been commissioned as the "managing representative." Davis stated that he would turn over the engineering work to Wallace, but that his commission "practically leaves me in charge of the work, as I hold the purse strings." [3]

Shocked at first, Wallace reluctantly decided to accept his situation and bide his time. Colonel Black was relieved of his position as acting chief engineer by Davis and was sent back to the States.

After inspecting the Canal facilities, Wallace immediately got to work rebuilding buildings and roads within the Canal Zone. His first effort, possibly as a

---

[2] Ibid, pp. 139-140.
[3] Ibid, pp. 140-142.

result of his own health fears, was directed toward the Ancon hospital. In order to provide living conditions of potential future employees, Wallace also decided to create two hotels, one in Corozal, and the other in Culebra. No sooner had Wallace gotten to work than he found that he could not obtain enough material to keep his carpenters working. He had to seek material on the open market. When he sent requisitions to Washington, he was met with extensive delays regardless of the urgency. Confronted with bureaucratic delay in Washington, Wallace was also faced with the same problems within the Canal Zone.

When he had the need to advance payment to local contract agents, Governor Davis's paymaster, Mr. Tobey, informed Wallace that he, Tobey, had to comply with the commission regulations. In addition, Tobey informed Wallace that the commission had appointed him independent of the chief engineer.

The public was demanding that work on the Canal should begin, and Davis, and Wallace were under pressure to make "the dirt fly." However, the conditions within the Canal Zone made it impossible for that to happen.

In addition, Wallace, in July of 1904, undecided on the merits of a lock canal, or a sea-level canal, started experimental excavations to determine the unit cost of different excavation yardage. The French had done extensive experiments on this subject many years before, and Wallace's work, which lasted for months, was considered redundant.

Gorgas, expecting to complete his sanitation work within fourteen months, was also confronted with similar problems to those experienced by Wallace. The chief engineer and the chief sanitary officer needed more power to satisfactorily complete their job. It was clear, that they could not do their job with a commission sitting 2000 miles away in Washington.

On August 3, 1904, the commission returned to the Isthmus, accompanied by their general counsel Judge Charles E. Magoon. Governor Davis left the same day to visit his wife in the United States. Admiral Walker took his place as governor of the Canal Zone, as well as retaining his position as chairman of the commission.

As the volume of employees increased, rents and food prices increased. It became increasingly more difficult to live within their income. There was no cold storage in the Canal Zone. All meat was bought fresh, and vegetables if they could be had, would quickly rot, or had to come from cans. Local bread, when obtained, was dirty. There was no ice, no fresh milk, and no fresh butter. Water was the greatest problem early in the construction. There was no electricity. Vessels returning to the States carried back many disillusioned employees.

On August 31, 1904, Governor Davis returned to the Canal Zone, aware of all of these problems, and he proposed that the commission appoint one head on the Isthmus, similar to what the French had done, but his proposal was turned down. The commission decided to revoke his previous instructions, leaving him as the executive officer of the commission, and personal representative of President Roosevelt, and placed Wallace in sole charge of all construction on the Isthmus. In addition, the commission created the Canal Zone Code, and Commissioner Grunsky created the Department of Health organization. On September 7, 1904, the commission returned to the United States. [4]

When Admiral Walker arrived in the United States, he stated that the work on the Canal was proceeding, and ready for "real work, health excellent, and sanitary measures taken." A week after the commission left the Canal Zone, Wallace also left the Isthmus and traveled to New York. He indicated that it would be eight months before there would be water in Panama, and when he checked on the requisition of pipes he had ordered in August 1904, he found nothing had been done. The pipes did not arrive until January 1905.

Wallace, more interested in a sea-level canal, indicated that the "Culebra Cut" was the key to making that happen. He seemed to disregard completely the influence of the Chagres River on the Canal construction, whether it was a lock canal or a sea-level canal. He stated publicly that he wanted a full year of experience before presenting his final plan.

While Wallace was in the States, ships loaded with cargo and destined for Panama were stacking up at the docks. There were not enough men to unload them, and not enough railroad cars to handle the traffic. By November 11, 1904, the first U.S. steam shovel arrived on the Isthmus.

On November 16, 1904, Commissioner Hecker, a businessman, resigned his position, citing that the Panama climate was detrimental to his health. He understood the futility of the business plan being applied to the Canal project and wanted no part of it. To make matters worse, relations between the government of Panama and Governor Davis were cold at best. The government of Panama was complaining that Governor Davis was interfering with their treaty rights, a familiar refrain since November 1903.

On November 27, 1904, Wallace returned to the Isthmus with his wife prior to the visit by Secretary Taft, accompanied by Admiral Walker and William Nelson Cromwell. It was on this visit by Taft, while residing in Wallace's home, that Taft, at the request of Cromwell, refused to privately discuss the Canal problems. Wallace wanted to bring up these problems without Cromwell's presence. It was

---

[4] Ibid, pp. 144-146.

Wallace that brought up this frustrating problem to the Senate in 1906. It was Wallace that, in 1906, informed the Senate that Cromwell had wrongly provided a windfall profit for the stockholders of the Panama Canal Railroad, prior to the sale of the railroad to the United States. It was Wallace that informed the Senate, in 1906, that Cromwell charged the United States for the exorbitant repair of two ships, prior to the sale of the Canal to the United States. Perhaps Cromwell was afraid Wallace wanted to bring these issues to the attention of Taft, and he wanted to be present to defend himself.

Taft's refusal to accept Wallace's request was strange at best. Taft's reputation was dependent upon the success of Wallace, his chief engineer. He readily admitted that he was impressed by Wallace's "earnestness and interest in the work, his ability, his facility of expression, his power of planning ahead, and his experience…on the Illinois Central." [5] And yet, Taft refused to discuss matters with Wallace without the presence of Cromwell.

Before leaving the Canal, Taft received an executive order from President Roosevelt, dated December 3, 1904, that was purported to resolve the complaints presented by the Panama government.

To present his views, which he wanted to express privately, Wallace was forced to send Taft several letters after he left the Isthmus. Those letters included documents that referred to conditions within the Canal, Wallace's relations with Governor Davis, the problem with and the need to have complete control over the Panama Canal Railroad, the problem of having seven commissioners to answer to, the need to have those engineers as consultants rather than members of the commission, and the need to have the commission reduced to three members: the chairman in Washington, and then the governor and the chief engineer, located on the Isthmus.

Governor Davis also wrote Taft, describing Wallace as a "very superior man, and he ought to be retained." Davis suggested that the office of the minister to Panama and the governor's office should be combined, to remove the friction that had developed between him and the minister's office. While Wallace and Davis were writing letters to Taft, Canal employees were also writing letters, describing the poor working and living conditions in the Canal. They particularly resented the semi-military lifestyle, under Governor Davis. "They wanted civilian control."

In December 1904, Secretary Taft requested that Dr. C.A.L. Reed present him with a report on the "hygienic conditions" in the Canal Zone. Dr. Reed praised Gorgas for his work, and lambasted the commission, and especially Commis-

---

[5] Ibid, pp. 147-149, Taft's statement, April 19, 1906 (hearing s No. 18, III, 2557)

sioner Grunsky, for the deplorable conditions he found in the Canal Zone. Commissioner Grunsky had prepared the Health Department Organization.

Reed suggested that the sanitation department should be removed from the control of the governor, and that Canal doctors should not be placed in a position of competition with Panamanian doctors. Taft secretly turned over the report to Admiral Walker, who provided the commission's rebuttal, citing that Reeds points were "ludicrous" and published "without official authority."

To make matters worse, yellow fever was starting to take its toll on the Canal employee morale, and by January 1905, a minor panic was developing due to exaggerated local news stories.

As the year 1905 rolled around, Wallace was having some success with the Culebra Cut and work was improving. He had increased his workforce from 500 in July 1904 to 1,200 men in January 1905. He had assigned two French excavators, and one American steam shovel to the task. However, he was still having trouble attracting qualified supervisors to lead the work gangs, and Wallace was still having major problems with the Panama Railroad Company.

He had forced the Railroad Company to replace the old superintendent, J.R. Shaler, with a new superintendent, H.G. Prescott, in the hope that the railroad service would improve. Apparently, Wallace was unaware that both Shaler and Prescott had played an integral part in the Panama Revolution, and any action they took would have to be approved by Cromwell. If the railroad service was causing problems, it was because Cromwell wanted it that way.

Although the United States had bought most of the shares of the railroad when they bought the French Panama Canal Company, there were still 1,013 shares outstanding. Most, if not all, of those shares Cromwell, apparently, still owned. Cromwell bought those shares in 1893, to gain control of the railroad, and there is no documentation to show that he ever sold them. If that is the case, it just shows one more duplicitous act by Cromwell to squeeze money out of the United States.

In January 1905, Taft took up Wallace's request, and assigned Cromwell, still the Panama Canal Railroad Company's general counsel, to buy up the remaining stock of the railroad, at par plus five. It is interesting to note here that in 1893, this stock was next to worthless, due to the 1893 financial panic, and the collapse of the French Panama Canal Company in 1888. In 1905, as you can imagine, that stock was worth a lot of money.

JOHN F. WALLACE

Photo of Wallace

On January 17, 1905, Cromwell advertised worldwide that the United States intended to buy the outstanding stock of the railroad, and implied legal proceedings if these phantom shareholders did not sell. By late May, Cromwell reported to Taft that all of the shares had been bought. As a result of Cromwell's action, Taft wrote a letter of commendation, praising Cromwell for his "patriotism and unselfishness" in securing the stock, and Cromwell's refusal to accept compensation for his actions. If that is not a kick in the pants, perhaps the next part of this story is.

After gaining complete financial control of the Panama Railroad Company, Wallace was appointed as general superintendent of the railroad. Wallace was insulted. He expected to be appointed general manager, with Prescott as superintendent. Wallace did not want to report to the vice president of the railroad, who was still located in New York. He lamented that he had held "more responsible positions on railroads in the United States." Wallace strongly protested to Taft and Walker. Walker placed the appointment in abeyance, and considered the issue "highly irregular." It was later discovered that Cromwell had engineered the whole issue. Cromwell was still not through with this issue. [6]

As time went on, Wallace began hearing rumors that he was about to be replaced by a younger and less experienced man to build the Canal. In fact, President Roosevelt wanted Elihu Root to take charge of the Canal. He had even written Taft, stating that he would consider employing Root at a salary of $50,000

---

[6] Ibid, pp. 149-155.

or even $100,000 dollars to take complete charge and run this whole business." [7]

On January 13, 1905, President Roosevelt sent a special message to Congress recommending that the president be given more power regarding the Canal, and that the commission be reduced to five, or even three commissioners to help eliminate the problems of a seven-member commission. By February 4, 1905, President Roosevelt wrote a letter to Secretary Taft, indicating that Admiral Walker would "have to go."

Wallace had to know, at least in early March 1905, that Roosevelt was planning to replace him. He informed Admiral Walker that he wanted to take leave in May or June 1905, before starting his second year in office.

In the meantime, the House of Representatives passed a bill incorporating Roosevelt's recommendations, but the Senate failed to act prior to adjournment. The Canal Zone was left with no government, and the authority of the commission under the act of April 28, 1904, expired upon the inaction of the Congress as of March 4, 1905.

THE SECOND COMMISSION WAS CREATED BY EXECUTIVE ORDER

Roosevelt and Taft, informed Governor Davis to continue the Canal Zone government as if the law of 1904 had not expired. On March 24, 1905, the secretary informed Wallace that they had adopted almost all his recommendations.

In addition, Secretary Taft ordered Wallace to return to Washington to assist in the reorganization. The next day, Wallace, elated, cabled the secretary expressing his thanks. On March 30, 1905, Wallace journeyed to New York, expecting to finally have a free hand in building the Canal. That was not going to happen. Nor was Wallace's aspiration to eventually replace Admiral Walker going to happen.

On April 1, 1905, President Roosevelt signed an executive order designating Mr. Shonts as chairman of the newly formed three-member commission. Mr. Charles E. Magoon was designated as the new governor, and Mr. Wallace was designated as the chief engineer. Shonts, Magoon, and Wallace were designated as the executive committee of the commission. In addition, the executive order required that Rear Admiral Mordecai T. Endicott, Brigadier General Peter C. Hains, Colonel Oswald H. Ernst, and Benjamin M. Harrod—all commissioners, all engineers under the control of Wallace—should study the best type of canal for submission to the board of consulting engineers. The engineering commis-

---

[7] Roosevelt to Taft, February 4, 1905 (Taft Papers: Taft-Roosevelt, Box II) (MS)

sioners were to be paid $7,500 dollars each; the governor was to be paid $17,500; the chairman $30,000; and the chief engineer $25,000.

The engineering commissioners immediately objected to their subordinate position, and Taft, in response, informed them that they would not be subordinate to the chief engineer. To emphasize his position and dismiss their objections, Taft sent copies of his response to Shonts and Wallace.

For whatever reason, President Roosevelt was unable to appoint his first choice, Mr. Root, as chairman of the commission. His second choice, Mr. Shonts, was a hard-hitting railroad man, a classmate, and considered friendly to Wallace. Mr. Magoon was an intimate associate to Taft, and a former adviser to Secretary Root. Roosevelt had promised Shonts a "free hand in carrying out his policies."

Even before Wallace arrived in New York, Shonts was busy replacing the requisition clerk and the purchasing officer in Washington, and the materials and supplies officer in the Canal Zone. While Shonts stated that these men did their best, he emphasized that they were unable to perform the duties required on such a large project like the Panama Canal.

When Wallace arrived in New York, he was met by Cromwell's secretary, who informed him that it was necessary to be sworn in as a commissioner immediately, in Cromwell's office.

Shock of all shocks, Wallace found that the new executive order was written "with conditions different" than what he had expected. It provided for the spreading of authority rather than the single control he wanted. In addition, it required that "Mr. Shonts spend some time on the Isthmus. Apparently, one of the few gains Wallace received from his trip to the States was to change his position as superintendent of the railroad to vice president and general manager of the railroad, in charge of "all affairs of the railroad and its steamship line." [8]

After helping to reorganize the new commission, Wallace decided to take two weeks' vacation.

No sooner had the commission been created than Taft received word from the Canal Zone, with alarming reports of yellow fever. He advised Wallace to return to the Isthmus immediately. Wallace ignored Taft's advice. General Davis, still acting as governor also "implored" Wallace to return to the Isthmus. On May 4, 1905, Davis cabled Taft urging him to have Wallace return to the Isthmus, stating Wallace's absence was "detrimental to the Canal." The yellow fever problem was just beginning. There was no leadership that the employee could look to,

---

[8] Panama Railroad, general order No. 8, April 17, 1905 (P.C. Rec. Bur., File Personnel, Wallace) (MS)

and to make matters worse, Davis, soon after, came down with malaria and was ordered back to the United States by Secretary Taft. On May 9, 1905, Davis left the Canal for good. Colonel Gorgas was forced to perform the duties as governor after Davis left.

Upon his return from vacation, Wallace had a conference with Secretary Taft, in which he expressed his gratitude. Wallace also met with Mr. Shonts, who told him that the president had given him, Shonts, absolute power as chairman of the new commission. Wallace took this statement to mean that Shonts intended to "run the job." It was not a good start for Wallace's future. At New York, he was entertained at Cromwell's home. During his conversation with Cromwell, Wallace was convinced that Cromwell intended to interfere in Wallace's own "prerogatives as chief engineer." Wallace bluntly let Cromwell know that he would not allow that to happen. In short, Wallace was returning to the Canal with disturbing thoughts that clearly indicated his position as chief engineer would be threatened, and there was no hope of attaining the position of chairman of the commission, which was ultimately what he wanted. Accompanied by Governor Magoon, on the trip back to the Isthmus, Wallace, apparently, decided not to continue in the position of chief engineer to look elsewhere for work.

On May 25, 1905, Governor Magoon was inaugurated as governor, and as the minister of the United States to Panama. He was sworn in by Judge Gudger, the chief justice of the Canal Zone Supreme Court. Judge Grudger was another co-conspirator of the Panama Revolution, and obviously a friend of Cromwell.

Within days of his arrival, Wallace wrote Cromwell, explaining that he may have appeared too blunt, and he was impressed by the wisdom of president's "privy council."

No sooner had Wallace arrived on the Isthmus and started to reorganize the engineering department than he was met with opposition from his assistants. They emphasized that preparation was "of paramount importance," and in contrast, he wanted to press for the actual construction and preparation at the same time. The rainy season had begun in the Canal Zone and neither preparation nor construction was possible. Work on sanitation continued, but the number of yellow fever cases continued to rise. Magoon reported that the executive committee had decided to curb, pave, and gutter the streets of Panama as a measure of sanitation, but there was no panic. He obviously did not speak for Wallace.

On June 4, 1905, frustrated with the progress he was making, Wallace wrote Secretary Taft that "certain complications" in his personal affairs would make it necessary to return to the States. He followed up this letter with a cable the next day indicating that some "important business matter" that could not be handled by correspondence might affect his position as chief engineer, and required his immediate return to the United States. He requested that the secretary order him to return to the United States in order not to panic the workforce. Wallace had confided with Governor Magoon that he had been offered a position in the States at a salary of $50,000–$60,000 dollars. Governor Magoon cabled Taft with this information. Among the reasons given for wanting to leave were that he was at the breaking point with Cromwell and Shonts. He felt that Shonts wanted to dominate the work in building the Canal.

Prior to leaving the Isthmus, Wallace had established an eight-hour day, 7 to 11 A.M., and 1 to 5 P.M.; he set up a reward system based upon merit; and divided the canal into construction divisions, like what the French had done. Hotels at Cristobal and La Boca were finished, ten more were planned, and the New Commission Hotel at Corozal was in the process of completion. Dock facilities at Cristobal and La Boca were being enlarged. Double tracking of the Panama Railroad was started. The Culebra Cut had eight steam shovels, and three French excavators working. Main shops for locomotive repair were at "Matachin," and a machine shop was located at Culebra, Cristobal, and Empire.

SHONTS, TAFT, CROMWELL, WALLACE, AND THE NEW YORK MEETING

Secretary Taft was upset after receiving the messages of Wallace and Magoon. He was scheduled to visit the Philippines, but decided to postpone his trip until he met with Wallace in New York. Shonts also came to New York to meet Wallace.

On June 21, 1905, Cromwell, up to his old tricks, visited Shonts at his hotel, and suggested that Wallace was coming up to take Shonts' place. "They don't want you to know that he is coming up here to get your job, until after they've disposed of him."

On June 22, 1905, Wallace arrived in New York. He was met at his hotel by Cromwell, who stated that he was instructed by Taft to find out the reasons for Wallace's return to the States and discuss them. Wallace refused to discuss his reasons with Cromwell, and told him that he wanted to discuss the matter with the secretary in strict privacy. Cromwell suggested that they could hold the meeting at the Manhattan hotel where Taft was residing, or they could meet at his home.

On June 25, 1905, Cromwell arranged a meeting with the secretary at the

Manhattan hotel. Again Taft refused to meet with Wallace alone, and insisted that Cromwell should be present. After a heated discussion, Taft insisted that Wallace resign on the spot, and stated that he did not want any of Wallace's reports, nor did he have any use for Wallace or any of his "counsel or advice" and the matter was settled.

Wallace submitted his resignation to the president on June 26, 1905, effective at the "convenience of the President." Roosevelt accepted the resignation effective June 28, 1905. Taft released a public statement castigating Wallace "seldom seen in official public life."[9]

GORGAS, MAGOON, AND THE YELLOW FEVER SCARE

By the time Wallace left the Isthmus, the yellow fever scare was at its height. In May, absentees and desertions were so frequent little work could be done. 500 men returned to the States in April, May, and June. Wallace's name was associated with death, because of the coffins he originally brought with him. Wallace's resignation helped precipitate that panic. When Magoon arrived on the Isthmus, he found an American Canal force that was "ill-paid, over-worked, ill-housed, ill-fed, and subjected to the hazards of yellow fever, and malarial fever." As governor of the Canal Zone, Magoon was responsible for the government and the sanitation of the Canal. Magoon went to work and ordered all that Gorgas had been asking for. Within days, the supplies were delivered. Until the arrival of Magoon, Gorgas was unable to make much progress on fumigation of the Isthmus. Magoon ordered fumigation on all houses, and daily house-to-house inspection. Doors and windows were screened. All building crevices were sealed by paper. All streets, and buildings were sprayed. Magoon hired Panamanian doctors as inspectors, and paid $50.00 dollars for every discovery of unreported cases of yellow fever. By July 1905, the work showed success. The number of cases dropped to forty-one, and continued to drop until the epidemic was over. What were the real casualties from this epidemic?

Thanks to Magoon and Gorgas, from July 1, 1904, to January 31, 1906, there were 134 cases with thirty-four deaths attributed to Canal employees. The number of Canal native cases during the same period was 112 cases and fifty deaths. The last case occurred on December 11, 1905. More people were affected by malaria, than by yellow fever. By the 4th of July 1904, the waterworks were finished, and the worst was over. Taft cabled Magoon that a new engineer was coming. "Shonts, and Stevens will soon be with you, and the mountains will move."[10]

[9] 1947, Miles P. DuVal, Jr., And the Mountains will Move, pp. 155-176.
[10] Ibid, 177-181, Taft to Magoon, June 30, 1905 (P.C. Rec. Bur., File 2-C-4) (MS)

JOHN F. STEVENS REPLACES WALLACE

Wallace submitted his resignation on June 26, 1905. Roosevelt accepted that resignation on June 28, 1905, and Stevens accepted his appointment, reluctantly, on June 30, 1905, at $30,000 dollars a year, effective July 1, 1905.

After Wallace's resignation, and the brutal and public criticism Taft directed toward him, Taft and Shonts immediately examined the engineering records of several men in the transportation industry.

James J. Hill, the famous railroad builder, had recommended Stevens to Taft. He stated that there was no better man found in the country to build the Canal. Taft sent Cromwell to convince Stevens to take the job. Stevens was already employed as the railroad expert for the Philippine Commission, was in Chicago, and about to depart for his assignment.

Photo of John F. Stevens

Interestingly, on the same day that Stevens accepted his appointment, Taft, at the suggestion of Chairman Shonts, wrote a letter to the chief of staff, and the chief of engineers, suggesting that Major G.W. Goethals be assigned as one of the chief assistant engineers on the Canal. On July 5, 1905, Shonts brought this suggestion up to Stevens, who turned down the suggestion.

Stevens was a well-known and respected railroad engineer in his own right. With no formal education, he had worked with James J. Hill. Among the many railroad companies, he had worked, he was famous for becoming the chief engineer of the Great Northern Railroad that was built over the Rockies to the Pacific, and through the Marias pass that Stevens himself discovered. "His record was known to every engineer on the Isthmus." [11]

---
[11] 1947, Miles P. DuVal, Jr., And the Mountains will Move, pp. 182-184.

Unlike Wallace, Stevens was uniquely conditioned to overcome the rigors and the fears of the Isthmus. He had withstood the cold and mountains of the Northwest, "for three years, the chills and fever of Mexico," and "the wet skies of the western plains." To Stevens, the Isthmus could be no worse than that found in the Philippines.

Stevens was empathetic to the problems faced by Wallace. He had studied almost everything written on the Canal since the time of Phillip II of Spain. If nothing else, he was not about to receive the same fate as Wallace. He had been given a free hand by Shonts, and immediately went to Washington to organize a corps of engineers based upon their fitness.

When confronted by the "American Federation of Labor" in their effort to convince him to set up a "closed" shop, Stevens refused. When the union representative "threatened to take the matter to the president," Stevens stated, "that he could take it to the Lord, if he chose, but that would make no difference, and to close the door when he went out." [12]

Stevens, acutely aware of the assurances given to Wallace by Walker, was not content with the assurances given to him by Shonts and called on the president at Oyster Bay. Roosevelt told Stevens that the Isthmus was a mess. In turn, Stevens told the president that he would accept the position on the condition that he be given a "free hand in all matters" and not be hampered by anyone in authority. He told Roosevelt that he would remain until the "success or failure" of the project, based upon his own judgment.

Roosevelt agreed to those terms, and informed Stevens to communicate with him directly, instead of through official channels. Stevens, aware of Wallace's problems with the War Department and Cromwell, pointed out this possible conflict. Roosevelt dismissed Stevens's worries, and informed him that everyone knew his views. Armed with these assurances, Stevens set sail for Panama with Chairman Shonts and Colonel Ernst.

Upon their arrival in Colon on July 25, 1905, Stevens and Shonts changed the primary objectives set out by Wallace. Instead of emphasizing both construction and preparation working in unison, they emphasized preparation, employee food, housing, and sanitation. Governor Magoon informed Stevens and Shonts that each time pay raises had been granted, food prices were raised by the Panama merchants. More men were leaving the Canal than were arriving. The employees had to go into the jungle for bananas and sugar cane in order to sustain life under their present pay level. Shonts directed that commissaries would be opened to resolve the problem.

---

[12] Stevens, The Panama Canal." A. S. C.E., Transactions, XCI, 950.

Magoon informed him that his decision would be against the orders of the War Department. Shonts ordered Stevens to load a rail car at Colon, and pick out, and condemn a building along the rail line, and sell the food at cost. When Magoon cautioned him that the merchants would object, Shonts, again, ignored his warning, and stated that he would go to the Congress if necessary.

Turning to the issue of sanitation, Shonts found that the fight against yellow fever had not progressed as expected, and the employees were not convinced that Gorgas's theory of mosquito propagation was the cause of the disease. High and low, Gorgas was considered a "crank," and "wasting money in trying to drain pools, cutting grass and weeds, and insisting that every house and quarters should be screened." Shonts promised that Gorgas's orders would be prioritized by cable and delivered on the next steamer.

Work on the Canal, which was generally limited to the Culebra Cut, was suspended, and Stevens reorganized the workforce into track gangs to install a double-track system that he planned. Excess men were sent back to the United States. Both Shonts and Stevens felt that Wallace would have been better off not starting any operation at all than utilizing the antiquated French equipment that he had been using.

When Stevens arrived on the Isthmus, 350 of the 2,100 French houses had been repaired, because of the delays of lumber and other equipment. There was insufficient labor to unload the ships on the docks, which had caused a great deal of congestion. To solve the problem, Shonts transferred 125 men working on the governor's mansion, and assigned them to unloading ships. Within a week the "commission decided to double track the Panama Canal railroad, order new terminal equipment, place all available workers on sanitary work, establish commissaries for all employees, construct the Tivoli Hotel as a temporary employee quarters, measure and then erect permanent quarters, and make thorough preparation of levels at the Culebra Cut that would receive the greatest number of steam shovels." [13]

The only early disagreement between Shonts and Stevens came when Shonts informed Stevens that Gorgas would be replaced by a "young osteopathist." Stevens strongly opposed the decision and saved Gorgas's job, and worked with him to eventually eradicate the yellow fever problem. On August 1, 1905, all Canal excavation ceased. Shonts returned to the United States, and Stevens was left in full charge of the Canal.

Working with Shonts, Stevens placed the division of materials and supplies

---

[13] Ibid., pp. 188-189.

under a new man. They replaced paymaster Tobey with W.G. Tubby, recently the general storekeeper of the Great Northern, at $9,000 dollars a year, and they employed E.J. Williams of the Chicago and Northwestern Railroad as the disbursing officer.

The Panama Railroad still remained a major problem. Part of the problem was that the local merchants were using railroad property for storage, and material for the Canal was stacking up at the docks, sometimes for months at a time. Within a month, Stevens replaced the old railroad manager with W.G. Bierd. He convinced the "steamer lines to take portions of the delayed freight, locate the owners, and make deliveries. By December 1905, the congestion problem was solved.

Stevens then set out to restore morale among the Canal employees. Stevens soon found that the commissary reorganization was not working as expected. The workers were still finding themselves out of food and the auditor in charge of the commissary at "Empire" refused to open the store. To show he was serious, Stevens traveled to the Empire commissary, on a special train, overruled the auditor, and personally opened the store. He installed cold storage equipment on the Panama Railroad steamers, a cold storage plant was built in Colon, and refrigerator cars were bought for the railroad. Soon, for the first time, perishable food and ice were available across the Isthmus. The Panamanian merchants protested to no avail. Even the Panama government ignored their protests.

Stevens still had to feed the workforce. He set up mess halls all along the Isthmus and found that he could feed the gold personnel for thirty cents a meal, or $27.50 dollars a month. While Stevens was feeding his employees, Washington received contract bids for setting up mess halls and feeding the Canal employee. The lowest bid was from a friend of Wallace, Jacob E. Markel, who put in a bid of $36.00 a month.

After explaining the extensive and self-sustaining food supply system he projected, and that would be in the Canal Zone, Markel canceled his bid. Markel stated that it would be impossible to do the work expected with Stevens "cutting his bowels out." [14]

On September 1905, a sanatorium for recuperating employees was set up at the old French "Aspinwall House" on the island of Taboga.

Stevens also began ordering construction equipment a month after his arrival. He placed orders for 120 locomotives, 800 flatcars with steam-operated plows for unloading wet material and installed an eight-mile airline at the Culebra Cut

---

[14] Markel's statement, March 2, 1906 (Hearings No. 18, II, 1290-1291).

for drilling. In October, he ordered sixty steam shovels, and planned to have one hundred—eighty working, and twenty in repair or service.

He could not make the decision on what type of canal would be adopted, so he provided three sets of plans for any decision the Congress decided.

Stevens was also aware that the employees had no means of recreation, except to visit Panama, and decided to set up "clubhouses" at Cristobal, Gorgona, Empire, and Culebra, where the employee could play cards, billiards, bowl, read, and smoke, without fighting the mosquitos. By November 1905, the yellow fever problem was nearly eliminated. That month there were only three cases.

TAFT RETURNS TO PANAMA WITH GOETHALS

On November 2, 1905, Secretary Taft made his second trip to Panama to assess the progress being made by Stevens, and clear up issues related to the security of the Canal. He was accompanied by General John P. Story, chief of artillery, Colonel Clarence R. Edwards, chief of the Insular Bureau, Lieutenant Colonel W. M. Black, Lieutenant Mark Brooke, and Major George W. Goethals.

Taft brought Goethals along on this trip as his special assistant and advisor on Isthmian affairs. Goethals knew little or nothing about the Canal and seemed indifferent to the issues surrounding the Canal. Goethals was heard to have said that the prospect of a Canal seemed "rather hopeless."

THE SEA-LEVEL CANAL OR THE LOCKS CANAL WAS SOON TO BE DECIDED

Prior to his arrival in the Canal, Stevens was inclined to agree with Wallace that a sea-level canal should be built on the Isthmus. Soon after his arrival, and discussing the issue with the other Canal engineers, Stevens was convinced that a locks canal was the preferred system. His decision was based upon the power of the Chagres River and its tributaries during the rainy season. Wallace's sea-level planning had completely disregarded this problem. Stevens also settled on the idea of an eighty-five-foot high-level lock system. On this matter he stood alone. Most, if not all, of the Canal engineers thought the idea was foolish. Most felt that he had set himself up for failure. His reply was "Well, we'll see."

By December 1905, Stevens thought that his preparation stage had gone as far as possible without knowing which type of canal the Congress wanted to build. By the end of the year, 1,000 French houses had been rebuilt, there were

2,600 employees working at the Culebra Cut, a good deal of double tracking had been laid, employee morale and working conditions had been restored, sanitation conditions had drastically improved, and the administrative organization of the Canal was almost complete.

On December 5, 1905, President Roosevelt informed the Congress, during his yearly address, that there had been "gratifying progress" made in the Canal, "especially during the last four months." [15]

Stevens was called back to Washington to testify in Congress. On December 12, 1905, Stevens reluctantly left the Canal. Convinced that the Congress would choose a lock system, Stevens chose Joseph Ripley, the lock superintendent of the Sault Saint Marie lock system, as the designer of the Panama Canal lock system. However, he held the position in abeyance until the Congress made their final decision. While testifying in Washington, he objected to the eight-hour workday initiated by Wallace, advocated a ten-hour workday, and suggested the introduction of Chinese labor into the workforce.

The first commission—created in 1904 by Congress—in March of 1905, accepted its engineering committee's recommendation for a sea-level canal, on the suggestions outlined by Wallace. They recommended "a sea-level canal with a bottom of 150 feet, a minimum depth of 35 feet, with twin tidal locks at Miraflores 1,000 feet long, 100 feet wide, and a great dam at Gamboa." They set the cost at $230,500,000.00 dollars. On March 29, 1905, the commission, among other business, authorized the design of the Canal Zone seal, with the inscribed words "The Land Divided–The World United," and adjourned.

In April 1905, President Roosevelt reorganized a new commission, by executive order, and also created another engineering committee to study the type of canal best suited for Panama. That committee was comprised of well-known engineers from around the world, including Bunau-Varilla.

In addition to his final decision on an eighty-five-foot lock system, Stevens set out to determine the best spot to establish an Atlantic dam. In 1902, the Walker Commission had determined that the dam should be located at Bohio. After making extensive test borings at Gatun, where none had been made previously, he decided that the best location for the dam should be located at Gatun. Stevens decided that the dam at Gatun would handle the torrential rains of the Chagres and its tributaries more effectively than at Bohio.

The board met with President Roosevelt on September 11, 1905, and finally

---

[15] 1947, Miles P. DuVal, Jr., And the Mountains will Move, pp. 190-200.; Messages and papers of the President, X, 7021 (US)

voted on the issue on November 18, 1905, in favor of a sea-level canal. On January 10, 1906, a minority and majority report were submitted to the commission. The commission approved the minority report and submitted their recommendation to the president. The advice given by the only engineer that had any first-hand experience in building the Canal, Bunau-Varilla, was rejected as "inexpedient." It had always been Bunau-Varilla's position that the Canal should first be created as a lock system, and later create a sea-level system. Bunau-Varilla also advocated wet dredging as the most economical system. He also opposed the location, and type of the Gatun Dam, and the depth of the cut at Culebra as proposed.

On January 11, 1906, the Congress took up the matter. Stevens testified in favor of his eighty-five-foot lock system, an earth and rock dam at Gatun, opposed changing the present five-foot gauge rail system of the Panama Railroad, to the standard gauge system, and he adamantly opposed the idea of a set of locks, and a lake at Sosa Hill. Stevens recommended that there should be a double three-level set of locks made of one structure at Gatun and Miraflores.

Both Wallace, and Parsons, a member of the president's engineering committee, also testified in the congressional hearings in favor of the sea-level canal. Parsons went further and objected to the idea of a locks system in Miraflores, and especially at Gatun. It was Parsons's position that a single-lock system at Gatun was not large enough, as a matter of safety. He stated that it would take longer to build a lock system, due to the complexity of lock machinery. Shonts and Stevens pushed back by asserting that a, triple-level, single-lock system at each end of the Canal was the perfect system. At the request of Taft, Stevens revisited his boring tests at Gatun to prove that the system was safe. After attending committee hearings, Stevens returned to the Canal on February 5, 1906.

President Roosevelt decided that the minority report was the superior system. On February 19, 1906, he submitted his recommendation for a lock system to the Congress.

In March 1906, Wallace again testified. He stated that a dam, and a three-level locks system at Gatun, where there was no rock foundation, would cause seepage, and was dangerous unless there was a uniform settlement over the projected one-mile lock structure. Shonts inserted a statement by Stevens, who had returned to the Canal, indicating that there was no possibility, that the Gatun locks system "absolutely prohibit the slightest chance of any settlement." [16] On May 17, 1906, the Senate committee reported to the full Senate with a six-to-five vote, recommending a sea-level canal.

---

[16] Hains' statement, March 27, 1906 (hearings No. 18, III, 2111) (US)

Stevens again returned to Washington and testified before the House committee on June 5, 1906. He stated that "if the sea-level canal, as imagined by many people, could be built for $404,000,000 dollars in ten or twelve years, I would say to build it that way and drop all other plans; but you cannot do it." [17]

On June 15, 1906, the House passed the Canal Appropriation Bill, with an amendment prohibiting any funds to be provided for the use of a sea-level canal.

On June 21, 1906, the Senate passed the bill thirty-six to thirty-one. The House approved the bill on June 27, 1906, and the president signed the bill into law on June 29, 1906. The law provided for an eighty-five-foot-summit, high-level lock system.

It also provided for a summit-level lake on the Atlantic by damming the Chagres River at Gatun, a 200-foot cut through the central mass, and an intermediate-level lake, Sosa, on the Pacific side of the Isthmus. The law provided for locks to be located at Sosa Hill, Gatun, and Pedro Miguel. In short, except for the lake on the Pacific side of the Canal, this system was the same as that advanced by the Frenchman Godin de Lepinay, in 1879. [18]

Stevens again returned to the Isthmus with Mr. Shonts on July 4, 1906. He directed Joseph Ripley to organize a group to design locks and dams by August 1906. By June 30, 1906, the total workforce in the Canal was about 19,600 men, and the reorganization was almost complete. By July 1906, work was started to locate the railroad tracks on the east side of the Canal, and at the request of the assistant chief engineer, Mr. John G. Sullivan, on July 7, 1906, Stevens established an office of engineers. Shonts recommended that the governorship should be separated from the minister to Panama and placed under the commission. Magoon was not in favor of some of these changes and requested that Taft not proceed with these changes until he could discuss the issues with him. He stated that he saw no reason to make changes since things were going well. Taft agreed with Magoon and told Magoon that he wanted to speak with the president about the matter before the reorganization was put into place. Taft stated that he agreed with much of what Stevens and Shonts had proposed, but that there were "some aspects of it that they do not fully appreciate the importance of."

---

[17] Stevens' Statement, June 5, 1906 (Hearings No. 10, p.32) (US)
[18] 1947, Miles P. DuVal, Jr., And the Mountains will Move, pp. 212-221.

MAGOON IS REMOVED TO OCCUPY A HIGHER OFFICE

Returning to Washington, Shonts wrote back to Stevens, indicating that Taft and Roosevelt agreed with their reorganization plan. The problem with Magoon was solved when a revolution broke out in Cuba, and the United States was forced to occupy it.

On September 25, 1906, Magoon was sent to Cuba as the provisional governor, a better position, in recognition of his work in the Canal. He turned over his duties to his executive secretary, Harry D. Reed. Because of an earlier vacancy by Colonel Ernst, who had resigned, and no indication that position was going to be filled any time soon, the commission was left to Shonts and Stevens. Shonts, as chairman, spent most of his time in Washington, and Stevens, in the Canal, controlled all day-to-day activities. There was no impediment left to overcome, and Stevens predicted that the Canal would be completed by January 1, 1915.

The preparation was done, the work was to begin. Steam shovels, unloaders, and spreaders were being assembled as they arrived on the Isthmus. John G. Sullivan and George D. Brooke devised the side extension of the "Lidgerwood" flat cars that was used to dump spoil well off the track. Another unique machine devised by W.G. Bierd, the general manager of the railroad, was the track shifter. In October 1906, the yardage removal at the Culebra Cut was 327,009.

Little did Stevens know that politics and personal aggrandizement would raise their ugly heads, just as most of the major problems were coming under control.

As employee working conditions improved, labor–management relations became an increasing distraction. Stevens approached the problem, much the same way he approached the national union demands in Washington, D.C. He simply removed a problem employee from the Canal. His actions were severely criticized by the national media, and it was brought to the attention of Taft and Roosevelt.

POLITICS SURFACES AGAIN

Apparently, Taft's return to the Canal, with Colonel Goethals, on November 2, 1905, was not only for assessing the security of the Canal. His back and forth communication with Magoon, and Shonts, in July 1906, further indicates that Taft was uncomfortable with the power created by Stevens and Shonts, as it related to Panama. He was afraid that they would take the same attitude toward labor that they would, had they been working for Hill on the Great Northern Railroad. Taft knew that Stevens was a product of Hill, and the Great Northern Railroad, and he didn't want any more problems. Roosevelt, although an admirer of Stevens, noted that Stevens didn't provide for any replacement, and seemed indifferent to the Congress and Panama as representatives of the public. He wrote Taft on August 27, 1906, stating that Stevens "could render himself worse than valueless in just one way, and that is by thinking himself indispensable."[19] Based upon other information previously presented in this book, Cromwell may have been the origin of these fears by Taft and Roosevelt. However, it should also be said that many of the high officials close to Roosevelt, and Taft, were also either close to or else former employees of J.P. Morgan and Cromwell.

Roosevelt was clearly getting advice that was contrary to the commitment he made to both Wallace and Stevens. Regardless of the origin of this issue, Stevens, like Wallace, was not long for the Canal, and neither was Shonts. Again, Secretary of State Root, was offered the job as chairman, and again he turned the offer down. He offered an explanation to a friend by stating that the road to political and personal ruin led to the Canal.

ROOSEVELT VISITS THE CANAL

On June 25, 1906, the White House announced that Roosevelt, accompanied by Shonts and Taft, would visit Panama in November 1906. Roosevelt felt the need to answer some of his Canal critics, during a mid-year election season, and he wanted to do so from his first-hand experience during the rainy season, the worst part of the year. Roosevelt also decided to make his final decision on Stevens's and Shonts 'reorganization plan, after he observed the progress on the Canal. This was to be Roosevelt's signature project of his presidency, and he knew that, to own it, he had to at least once visit it. Ironically, to do so, Roosevelt broke a long-standing precedent that the president never leaves the country. He was strongly criticized for his action.

The problem with this plan was that while Roosevelt insisted that he remain ashore during his visit. The Tivoli Hotel, located on the Pacific side of the Canal, was the only hotel large enough to accommodate the president and his companions, and was not yet completed. Upon notification of Roosevelt's visit, Shonts and Stevens spent a great deal of their time frantically preparing the Tivoli for the president's visit. Stevens assured Shonts that it would be ready, and it was.

---

[19] Roosevelt to Taft, August 27, 1906 (Taft Papers: Taft-Roosevelt, Box II) (MS)

Prior to the president's visit, Stevens received word that the secretary of state, Elihu Root, would visit. This visit, made on September 21, 1906, was seen as a prelude to Roosevelt's visit, and the Canal Zone government spared no effort to make him comfortable. Although Root was impressed by the progress made on the Canal, it did not change his mind about rejecting the position as chairman of the Canal Commission.

At 1:00 P.M., November 14, 1906, President Roosevelt arrived at Colon, Panama, aboard the U.S.S. Louisiana, and was given a twenty-one-gun salute. He was expected to arrive on the 15th of November, when pomp and ceremony were considered the order of the day.

Roosevelt set aside three days for his visit, and he was not about to waste any more time than necessary on receptions and ceremonies. On the 14th, he remained on the Louisiana, got up early the next morning and met President Amador, Shonts, Stevens, and Bierd on the Colon dock. He had already been up and walking along the pier for two hours. The reception was brief. He rode horseback through Colon to the train station, and by 8:10 A.M., he boarded a train to Panama City. At 11:00 A.M., he arrived at the Tivoli train station, and toured the Ancon Hospital, with Police Chief Shanton. After the hospital tour, he went to Balboa, boarded the tugboat Bolivar, and toured the Islands of Naos, Perico, and Flamenco to observe the approaches to the Canal. When he returned to La Boca, he spent the afternoon at the La Boca Hotel visiting with the Canal employees, listened to their complaints, and advice, inspected the kitchen, and finally returned to his room at the Tivoli Hotel. [20]

By 4:00 P.M., Roosevelt was riding a carriage with President Amador toward the Cathedral Plaza, where the Panama government provided a great ceremony in his honor.

Roosevelt reminded the procession that it was the first time a United States President had set foot on foreign soil since President Washington. Roosevelt became the new hero of Panama, replacing de Lesseps. That evening Roosevelt attended a state dinner, complete with fireworks, dancing, and festivities.

The next morning, Roosevelt got up at 6:30 A.M., and vigorously set off on his inspection trips. Within the limit of his three-day trip, Roosevelt inspected every aspect of the Canal construction. On November 17, 1906, his last day of the Canal trip, Roosevelt signed an executive order, giving Stevens and Shonts all that they asked for to create a centralized management within the Canal Zone.

On November 19, 1906, Shonts appointed Stevens as chief engineer and

---

[20] Panama Star and Herald, November 26, and December 17, 1906.

head of the engineering department, R.R. Rogers as general counsel, Gorgas as chief sanitary officer, E.J. Williams as disbursing officer, D.W. Ross as purchasing officer, and Jackson Smith as manager of labor, subsistence, and quarters. Shonts emphasized that Stevens would govern all work in the Canal, subject to his own absence. Finally, the management system created by the French, was re-created by the United States.[21]

Upon his return to Washington, on December 17, 1906, Roosevelt presented a special message to Congress, complete with illustrations, which dispelled most of the public criticism that had been generated during the 1906 midterm election season.[22] That year, Senator Morgan, a Democrat, had held extensive hearings to expose the corruption related to the Panama Canal, and Nelson Cromwell's secret syndicate's connection to the Roosevelt administration.

THE CONTRACT THAT BROKE STEVENS'S BACK

In Steven's mind, everything he had been working for had finally fallen into place. With his preparations well underway, Stevens was left with constructing the Canal by "day labor" under direct supervision, or by "contract." Stevens and Shonts, both railroad men, favored the contract method. The French used the contract method, and the contract method was used to build the Transcontinental Railroad, and was favored by every major railroad company in the United States. It was thought that by using that method of construction, the Panama Canal Company could draw from the experience of employees, foremen, administrators, and engineers from the already established construction industry.

Stevens was also firm in his belief that the work on the Canal should not be done by one contractor alone. After consulting with Walston H. Brown, he wrote Shonts with a plan for an association of ten or fifteen railroad and construction contractors. They were to have a capital of $25,000,000 dollars, and a bond of $10,000,000. The work would include the dredging and sea-level portion, construction of the locks, dams, and excavation from Gatun to the Pacific, including the Culebra Cut, and the relocation of the Panama Railroad.

It put each contract on a percentage profit, and overrun deduction basis. In addition, he provided for a bonus for each month saved. Most important, Stevens provided that the commission retain control of the Canal Zone government, san-

---

[21] 1947, Miles P. DuVal, Jr., And the Mountains will Move, pp. 228-242.
[22] President Roosevelt, special message to Congress Concerning the Panama Canal ..., December 17, 1906, p. 28 (U.S.)

itation, engineering, supplies, waterworks, building construction, labor, quarters, and repair of machinery. Stevens was uniquely familiar with this plan of construction, and had used it before. He also knew the pitfalls. He was strongly opposed to letting the entire contract, by bid or otherwise, to one single contractor. He emphasized that the control should be under the direction of the commission engineers, in short, himself, as chief engineer. Stevens was also opposed to an open bidding system and emphasized that each contractor should be qualified by their financial ability, as well as their "nature, experience, or achievement." He emphasized that his plan should be approved by mid-October 1906.

When Shonts received Stevens's plan, he agreed, and promised to submit it to Taft, and President Roosevelt. By August 14, 1906, Shonts wrote Stevens that the president had approved of his plan. While the framework of the contract plan was conceived by Stevens, the awarding of the contracts was in the hands of Taft, and the president. All that Stevens was promised was that he would be consulted before making any awards.

While waiting on the outcome of the contracts, work on the Canal continued, and Canal living conditions by the Canal employee continued to improve. The streets of Panama City, and Colon were paved, and by January 1907 electricity at Culebra had been installed. By January 1907, large-scale excavation at the Culebra Cut had begun. Along with better living and working conditions, came labor problems.

The "Spaniards" refused to work under black foremen, and the workforce had to be reorganized. Stevens found that he could solve most of his vexing problems by simply sending problem employees, and their dependents, back to the States. This practice, in one form or another, was continued, throughout the years, by Canal Zone governors, at least, until 1964.

When the steam-shovel engineers, considered on a par with the locomotive engineers, informed Stevens that they would go on strike if they were not paid as much, Stevens refused to give into their demands. They went back to work, but they also took their demands to the president. It was because of these incidents and others that Taft and Roosevelt began to have some political misgivings with Stevens. To some degree, especially in the North, the Republican Party was dependent upon the national unions for support during an election year.

While Stevens was adamant about the contractor bidding conditions, Shonts was not so strongly persuaded. Stevens had previous experience as an engineer in this matter, while Shonts had little. He was not an engineer. He spent his career as a railroad manager, and was more sensitive to the politics in Washington, where he spent most of his time.

By the time the president had approved Stevens's plan, Shonts believed most of the Canal problems had been resolved, and the only thing left to do was to provide an "endless chain of constantly moving trains" working with the steam shovels to remove the excavation spoil. [23] Progress on the Canal, under the direction of Stevens, proceeded to the point that some considered there was no need for contract bidding.

Stevens's plan was soon to be modified. On August 22, 1906, at the suggestion of Secretary Taft, who wanted "an element of competition," Shonts advised Stevens that he and R.R. Rogers had decided to modify the contract draft. Later, he sent Stevens a copy of the revised draft, warning him that Speaker Spooner, and Cannon, powerful Republican senators, had informed him that Stevens's first proposals might have political repercussions if they were not modified to include open advertising for the contract bidding.

In September, Shonts wrote Stevens informing him that the president had taken the advice of Secretary Taft, regarding an open advertisement of contracts. On October 2, 1906, Stevens wrote Shonts, informing him that the bidding process would end in "endless complications and entanglements." Stevens also thought that Secretary Root's influence in changing the contract framework would result in "endless friction and conflicts of authority." [24]

Proposals for bids were advertised on October 9, 1906. On December 12, 1906, Stevens attended a meeting with Shonts, Taft, Root, and R.R. Rogers to discuss the contract-bidding process. After some of his objections were overruled, Stevens's contract-bidding plan was fundamentally modified, but he was assured that he would have the last word on the contract bidding.

The opening of all bids was set for January 12, 1907. On January 12, 1907, only four contractors responded. The North American Dredging Company of San Francisco put in a bid for 28 %, the MacArthur–Gillespie Company from Chicago put in a bid of 12.50 %, George Pierce and Company from Frankfort, Maine, put in a bid of 7.19 %, and William J. Oliver and Anson M. Bangs of New York City put in a bid of 6.75 %. On January 15–16, 1907, Shonts asked Stevens what he thought of the proposals. Stevens replied, "The lowest bid was too high," and requested to know what capacity, and experience these companies had. Immediately after receiving the bids, Shonts conferred with Roosevelt and

---

[23] Shonts' Statement, February 9, 1907 (hearings No. 7, p. 894) (U.S.)

[24] Stevens to Shonts, October 2, 1906 (P.C. Rec. Bur., File 9-A-4) (MS), 1947, Miles P. DuVal, Jr., And the Mountains will Move, pp. 250-252.

Taft, without first consulting with Stevens, as he had promised.

They agreed to award the bid to Oliver and Bangs, from New York. Ten days later, it was decided to allow W.J. Oliver to qualify with new associates in a $5,000,000-dollar corporation. Bangs was eliminated as an associate. On January 18–19, 1907, Shonts informed Stevens of the president's decision.

On January 29, 1907, Stevens again cabled Shonts, informing him that it would be a mistake to award the contract to Oliver. Stevens considered Oliver unqualified by "nature, experience, or achievement." [25] He further stated that by changing associates, it allowed Oliver a new bidding, a right the other bidders did not have. In addition on the same date, Stevens cabled Taft with the same general message.

THE RESIGNATION OF SHONTS

This one issue, the contractor bidding, set in motion the resignation of Shonts. There was immediate speculation regarding Shonts' resignation. There were those that thought that Shonts believed that he was being pushed aside in favor of Steven.

Shonts publicly stated that his reason for his resignation was that he had been offered a position in a transportation merger in New York City. In addition, he reminded Roosevelt of his April 1905 agreement to release Shonts when excavation of the Culebra Cut began. To his friends, Shonts stated that he was repulsed by "Washington red tape and Washington political interference." Based upon the public record, this latter statement seems closer to the truth. [26] There is no doubt that, because he spent most of his time in Washington, Shonts was intimately more sensitive to the politics generated in Washington.

On January 22, 1907, Roosevelt accepted Shonts' resignation, effective March 4, 1907. Ironically, Roosevelt did not treat Shonts with the same demeaning manner he did with Wallace. Instead, Roosevelt and Taft set out to lionize Shonts. Roosevelt stated that Shonts carried out his responsibilities with "energy, administrative capacity, fertility of resource and judgment." [27]

Certainly, regardless of what public condemnation Wallace may have received from his resignation, the political, and public perception of completing the Canal received a major setback, because of his resignation. Taft, and especial-

---

[25] 1947, Miles P. DuVal, Jr., And the Mountains will Move, pp. 253-254.
[26] Panama Star and Herald, February 7, 1907.
[27] Roosevelt to Shonts, January 22, 1907; quoted in Pepperman, op, cit., pp. 16-17.

ly Roosevelt, while the major cause of this problem, did not want another public perception of failure in their effort to building a Canal in Panama.

CRONY CAPITALISM REARS ITS HEAD ONCE, AGAIN AND STEVENS'S RESIGNATION

Stevens knew by December 12, 1907, that his contractor plan had been neutered by the politics in Washington. On January 24, 1907, by the time he learned that Shonts had resigned, Stevens decided to take his objection of the bidding selection of Oliver to a higher, more forceful level. In addition, on January 24, 1907, Stevens cabled President Roosevelt, with little effect, requesting that he take "no action until matter thoroughly discussed."

On January 25, 1907, Roosevelt cabled a reply, and agreed to take no action until he heard from Stevens. [28]

On January 29, 1907, after receiving Stevens's cable, asserting that it would be a mistake to award Oliver the Canal contract, Taft requested that he explain his reasons.[29]

On January 30, 1907, Stevens cabled Taft with a detailed, confidential explanation for his objections. He stated the bid should have been awarded based upon ability, and fitness, not money. He stated that Oliver was not fitted by "nature, experience or achievement," and that changing of associates was equivalent of a new bid. He further stated that the "contract should never have been advertised" and the best result should have been to make the contractors agents of the commission.[30] This latter statement was personally directed at Secretary Taft who decided to open the bidding to the public, and certainly had a major influence in selecting Oliver as the final selection in that bidding.

In addition to his cable to Taft on January 30, 1907, Stevens also sent a six-page letter to President Roosevelt in which he stated he wanted to leave the Canal and return to the railroad environment. His letter did not reach the White House until February 12, 1907.

While waiting for Roosevelt's reply, Stevens continued to provide information to Taft and, eventually, Roosevelt, as to why he objected to the Oliver contract appointment.

---

[28] Stevens to Roosevelt, January 24, 1907 cable, (P.C. Rec. Bur., File 9-A-4), (MS).

[29] Roosevelt to Stevens, January 25, 1907 cable, (P.C. Rec. Bur., File 9-A-4), (MS).

[30] Stevens to Secretary Taft, January 30, 1907 cable, (P.C. Rec. Bur., File 9-A-4) (MS); 1947, Miles P. DuVal, Jr., And the Mountains will Move, p. 255.

Undaunted, Taft cabled Stevens, requesting that he explain what published interviews Oliver made that convinced Stevens he was unqualified. On January 31, 1907, Stevens replied that "a Napoleon is not needed here, but such an organization as outlined in my letter of July 27 to Chairman." [31]

On February 3–4 1907, Taft again cabled Stevens stating that Oliver would include John B. MacDonald, a New York subway contractor, John Pierce, a masonry contractor from Maine, and the Milan Dredging Company of Baltimore as associates, and Oliver stated that the reported press releases were unfounded. However, in response to Stevens's cables, he held the "final acceptance of Oliver in abeyance." [32]

For the next several days, there was a constant back-and-forth conversation between Stevens and Taft surrounding the qualification of Oliver's Canal construction bid. It was obvious that Taft was determined to award Oliver the contract, and it should have been obvious to Taft that Stevens was adamantly opposed to awarding the contract to Oliver. By February 4, 1907, Stevens's cables to Taft had made his position clear.[33]

Finally, on February 8, 1907, President Roosevelt cabled Stevens, and confidentially requested that Stevens explain his position on the matter, and his knowledge of Oliver's associates. Roosevelt indicated his surprise that Stevens would have objected to the Oliver contract process, since it was processed in accordance to Stevens's request, in the presence of Root, Shonts, Taft, and R.R. Rogers, on December 12, 1906. Roosevelt further stated that "I would not be willing now to alter this policy entered into with deliberation, save for grave reasons which can be stated publicly, and verified." [34]

Roosevelt further stated that: "I need your assistance in carrying the policy through and I wish full comment from you." It should be noted that Roosevelt's present position on the matter was in direct contrast to the early discussions that were predicated upon Stevens's agreement on the contract award. [35]

On February 9, 1907, Stevens responded to Roosevelt's request by stating that the contract would result in a one-man project. Stevens stated that the points that differed from his original plan were that "the capital was one fifth, the bond was

---

[31] 1947, Miles P. DuVal, Jr., And the Mountains will Move, p. 256.

[32] Taft to Stevens, February 3-4, 1907, 1947, Miles P. DuVal, Jr., And the Mountains will Move, p. 256.

[33] Miles P. Duval, Jr., Ibid, pp. 258-259.

[34] Miles P. Duval, Jr., Ibid, p. 257.

[35] Roosevelt to Steven, February 8, 1907, confidential cable (P.C. Rec. Bur., File 9-A-4), (MS).

one half, the payment was to be one percent, and the contractor was to supply all labor." He stated that he did not know the associate personnel well enough to give the president advice on their qualifications, but that the process of the contract should be considered as a new bid.

Finally, he stated, regarding the December 12, 1906, meeting, he objected to the "last two points in the December 12 meeting but was overruled, and his silence was mistaken as "explicit approval." Stevens added that "you should receive personal letter tomorrow which may clarify situation." That personal letter was Stevens's resignation.[36]

Stevens's letter, written on January 30, 1907, arrived in Washington on February 12, 1907. The content of that letter was even more vitriolic and personal than his letter to Roosevelt on February 9, 1907. He told President Roosevelt that he initially took his position purely as a business proposition, but found he was confronted by "enemies from the rear." He stated that he had been in a "continuous battle with people that "I would not wipe my boots on in the United States." He claimed that he had been losing $100,000 dollars a year working in the Canal, and the honor of building the Canal did not appeal to him. He stated that he could return to positions that he "would prefer to hold, if you will pardon my candor, then the Presidency of the United States." Obviously from the content of his January 30, 1907, letter, Stevens knew his position on this matter was a lost cause.

Stevens's letter of January 30, 1907 caused Roosevelt to become furious. On February 12, 1907, Roosevelt immediately, sent a letter to Taft stating that "Stevens must get out at once." He indicated that he would not reconsider his position, because of the tone of Stevens's letter, but would consider a solution provided it met "his wishes."

Roosevelt expressed his frustration by stating that he could not finish the Canal with chief engineers that resign every year, and he wanted someone who would stay on the job until "I get tired of having them there, or till I say they may abandon it. I shall turn it over to the Army." [37]

Taft consulted General Alexander Mackenzie, the chief of engineers, who recommended Major Goethals, as the best man from the Corps of Engineers, as chief engineer of the Canal. Considering that Goethals was Taft's special advisor on the Canal, this seemed more like a pro-forma act. In addition, it was against the policy of appointing members of the commission. The next day, Taft met

---

[36] Stevens to Roosevelt, February 9, 1907 (P.C. Rec. Bur., File 9-A-4), (MS).
[37] Roosevelt to Taft, February 12, 1907 (Taft Papers: Taft-Roosevelt, Box III) (MS)

with Roosevelt and the president accepted Taft's selection of Goethals as chief engineer of the Canal.

On February 14, 1907, Roosevelt cabled Stevens, accepting his request to resign as soon as a replacement could be appointed and could become familiar with the work.[38] The same day Roosevelt sent a recess appointment to the Senate for members of the Canal Commission, which included Goethals as chief engineer, Gorgas as chief health officer, and Jackson Smith as manager of labor, quarters, and subsistence.

On February 18, 1907, President Roosevelt met with Goethals, discussed the resignation of Stevens, and told him that he wanted to establish "continuity of leadership" without these constant changes. He wanted to eliminate the constant friction of leadership by combining the office of chief engineer, and the chairman of the Canal Commission. He further told Goethals that he, Roosevelt, would "assume powers that the law did not give, but which it did not forbid him to exercise." [39]

---

[38] Roosevelt to Steven, February 14, 1907, cable (P.C. Rec. Bur., File 9-A-4), (MS).

[39] 1947, Miles P. DuVal, Jr., And the Mountains will Move, p. 261; Goethals; quoted in J.B. and F. Bishop, op. Cit., p. 144.

CHAPTER THIRTEEN
PERSONAL POWER AND INCOMPETENCE RULE

THE DAY GOETHALS REPLACES STEVENS AS CHIEF ENGINEER OF THE CANAL

SINCE HIS GRADUATION FROM West Point in 1880, Goethals had acquired an excellent military record within the Corps of Engineers, but he had no experience building any project even close to the magnitude of the Panama Canal. He was Taft's man, and that was enough. Goethals understood that he would work under the direction of Stevens, until he was ready to take over the full control of the Canal project.

Roosevelt then directed his attention to the problem of the bidding that caused Stevens to resign. On February 26, he wrote Shonts, stating that because Stevens had objected to the contract awards, and it would have been his duty to supervise the work, there would be no need to award these contracts. Roosevelt recommended that the commission reject all of the bids and added that none of them fulfilled the purpose of the contract. The president requested that the commission appoint Goethals as chief engineer of the Canal and added that he would be accompanied by Majors D.D. Gaillard, and W.L. Silbert. The Commission followed Roosevelt's recommendation on February 27, 1907, and appointed Goethals as "chief engineer, vice John F. Stevens." [1]

To clear up any misunderstanding of the wishes of the president, and to vent

---

[1] I.C.C. Minutes, 121st meeting, February 27, 1907, pp. 33-34 (U.S.); Miles P. Duval, Jr., Ibid, p. 262.

his anger, Taft cabled Stevens to inform him that he would be expected to "assist in the substitution of Goethals with "as little friction and as little loss of efficiency in the organization which you have created," and that he, Stevens, would remain in charge as long as he and Goethals should desire.[2]

On March 4, 1907, President Roosevelt signed an executive order appointing Stevens chairman and chief engineer of the Panama Canal. Stevens got his way, but he lost his job in the process.

Stevens's resignation was a complete surprise to the Canal workers, the public, and to the news media. The news media was on the hunt. When questioned, Stevens referred to the president, and refused to give a reason.

Stevens would only state that he did not attempt to bluff the president in order to gain some advantage. He further stated that, his reason for resigning was a private matter, and that there was no friction between himself and the president.

Secretary Taft's reply to Steven's resignation was to state that "nervous strain" caused him to insist on leaving the Canal work. Goethals implied that Stevens had a nervous breakdown because of his responsibilities and attention to the details of the work. Of course, none of these public statements by Taft and Goethals were true.

Goethals and Gaillard arrived on the Isthmus on March 12, 1907, and were greeted by Stevens, members of the commission, and the press. When asked what changes he intended to make, Goethals stated that he would follow Stevens's plan in every way. He further stated that Stevens had done "an immense amount of work," and compared this progress to what he had seen during his first visit in 1905.[3]

On March 21, 1907, Goethals and Stevens agreed that they would transfer responsibility of the Canal on April 1, 1907.

After acquainting Goethals with the work necessary to complete the Canal, on March 27, 1907, Chairman Stevens held his last commission meeting and formally submitted his resignation, effective April 1, 1907. Also, during that meeting, the commission reaffirmed Goethals's appointment to be effective on the same date, April 1, 1907.

On March 30, 1907, Secretary Taft arrived on the Isthmus to inspect the progress of the work done on the Canal. On March 31, 1907, Stevens was relieved as chairman and chief engineer of the Panama Canal. He left the Isthmus late on April 7, 1907.

---

[2] Taft to Stevens, cable, February 27, 1907 P.C. Rec. Bur., File 9-A-4) (MS)
[3] Goethals; quoted in J.B. and F. Bishop, op. Cit., p. 150.

GOETHALS'S FIRST LABOR–MANAGEMENT CONFRONTATION AND HOW IT WAS HANDLED

By the time Goethals took over the job of the Canal chief engineer, most of the plan set out by Stevens was well organized, well equipped, and well manned. Housing, recreation, meals, and health facilities, all established within the Canal Zone, were plentiful and affordable for the silver and gold employees. Yellow fever and malaria were, essentially, things of the past. In Goethals's mind, what was left that needed his attention was the work on the locks and dams, where little work had been done, and the completion of which, he thought was more important to the completion of the Canal than the Culebra Cut. The transportation system was completed, and work at Culebra was proceeding quickly. [4]

On April 2, 1907, no sooner had Stevens left the Canal than Secretary Taft signed an executive order, by direction of the president, appointing Goethals chief engineer, chairman of the commission, and governor of the Canal Zone. Goethals was, at least publicly, answerable only to the president, and secretary of war.[5] Directed by the president, the commission members were required to reside on the Isthmus. Sibert was assigned to lock and dam construction. Gaillard was assigned to excavation and dredging. Rousseau was assigned to municipal engineering, motive power and machinery, and building construction." Gorgas was assigned as chief sanitary officer. Jackson Smith was assigned as chief of labor, quarters, and subsistence, Joseph Ripley was assigned as special designing engineer, and H.F. Hodges was assigned as general purchasing officer, located in Washington. The organization of the construction divisions remained within the same framework as planned by Stevens. The commission remained in "continuous session." Only Ripley, who had been assigned as assistant chief engineer by Stevens, quickly resigned his proposed position.

THE FIRST STEAM-SHOVEL STRIKE

Like Stevens, before him, Goethals first labor–management problem met him at the door, so to speak. As stated above, Stevens solved his early labor–management problem by giving an ultimatum to his employees, "go back to work or leave the Canal." Stevens's attitude did not go over too well with the national labor unions, the Canal steam-shovel employees, the press, or, more importantly, progressive

---

[4] 1947, Miles P. DuVal, Jr., And the Mountains will Move, pp. 273-274.

[5] Executive Order of April 2, 1907, signed by Taft by direction of President (P.C. Rec. Bur. File 2-C-13) (MS)

politicians seeking labor votes.

But there is no doubt he conveyed a message to the Canal workforce, which eventually gained their respect. Stevens did not face any further serious labor problems during his tenure as chief engineer.

Stevens's actions did not help his cause with the Roosevelt administration. It should be clear by now that Roosevelt was pragmatic when it came to be building the Canal, but he was a committed progressive politician in every other way. More important, Roosevelt was intent on limiting bad publicity related to his signature legislation, the Panama Canal.

In 1906, Stevens's actions were exacerbating that problem. Taft's position was simple. Advised by Cromwell, Taft was intent on creating crony capitalism, and Stevens was in the way.

In 1907, in contrast, Goethals, met by the same problems, by many of the same employee groups, decided not to follow Stevens's example. While ushering Taft around the Canal to inspect various facilities and worksites, Goethals was confronted by the steam-shovel employees, locomotive engineers, and conductor, demanding that they be given pay increases, or they would resign.

Photo of Goethals

Instead of solving the problem himself, Goethals passed the problem on to Secretary Taft. Ironically, President Roosevelt had directed Taft to visit the Canal with engineers to inspect rock foundations for the locks, but also to investigate and resolve the complaints of the "steam-shovel men." At the time, the steam-shovel men were the highest paid employee group in the Canal workforce, $210.00 dollars a month. All other employees' salaries were based upon the steam-shovel workers' wage base. They were demanding an increase to $300.00 a month. The workforce in 1906 was about 19,600 employees. In June 30, 1907, the workforce was 29,446 employees.

Progressive administration or not, there was no way the Roosevelt administration could increase the wage base of the Canal workforce by $90.00 dollars, even if it was restricted to the higher wage base of the steam-shovel and locomotive engineers. In addition, 1907 was not an election year, and the administration must have felt that they had more time in which to make a political decision on the matter, not necessarily favorable to the workforce.

Taft decided not to decide until after he returned to the United States and further consult the president. Under the circumstances, these employees were left to wait until a decision was made in Washington.

On May 5, 1907, Secretary Taft published his decision. He ordered that the steam-shovel and locomotive engineers be paid the same salary. He authorized an increase in transportation crews, and set a 5% increase in salary for the first year, and 3% increase for each succeeding year. [6]Goethals considered Taft's decision as little more than an appeasement, a "sop" to the workforce. His interest was directed to reducing the cost of the workforce, not maintaining that cost.

Instead of solving the problem, at least temporarily, Taft's ultimatum forced the steam-shovel men to strike, and the number of operating steam shovels was reduced from sixty-eight to thirteen. In January 1907, the Canal workforce excavated over 500,000 cubic yards, in February the excavation increased to over 600,000 cubic yards, and by March it rose to over 800,000 cubic yards. After the strike, excavation at Culebra Cut was reduced to 624,586 cubic yards. Many of the strikers left the Canal. [7]

As a union representative, I was fascinated by the dichotomy of Stevens's approach to labor management and Goethals's approach to that same labor force. Stevens had extensive experience in a civilian workforce, while Goethals, an army officer had literally no experience with civilian workers. Left to Secretary Taft,

---

[6] 1947, Miles P. DuVal, Jr., And the Mountains will Move, pp. 277-278.
[7] Ibid, p.278-279.

a political solution was attempted to solve the labor problem in 1907. One can only wonder if left to Secretary Taft and President Roosevelt, the same political solution would have been made in 1906, during a midterm election year.

Of course it didn't happen, and the Roosevelt administration hid behind the actions of Stevens in 1906, while criticizing him for his actions. The labor force then, as now, fell into making demands that they should have known could not be attained. They relied on the false premise that they could not be replaced. They refused to consider alternative and reasonable demands that could have generated political support from the public and the Congress. They still may not have succeeded, but at least they would have stood a better chance of succeeding than how they went about making their demands in 1906 and 1907.

Goethals was forced to recruit and train new employees, and eventually, the excavation yardage slowly increased. By August of 1907, Goethals reported that excavation yardage was at 1,274,404. Roosevelt congratulated Goethals on the turnaround. [8]

CRONY CAPITALISM AGAIN RETURNS TO THE FRAY

Goethals next major problem was how to address the private contractor issue, which never went away, even though publicly, because of the actions of Stevens, it seemed a dead issue. Taft was not through with this issue. He did all he could to eliminate Stevens from the Canal, in order, he thought, to usher in the private contractors he thought would help him win the presidential election in 1908. In addition, Taft was not only the secretary of war. He was the man Roosevelt had decided would replace him in 1908, and Roosevelt went to the extreme of taking over Taft's presidential campaign to ensure that would happen. In turn, Taft was of the opinion that Goethals, like Cromwell, was his man.

Almost from the beginning, Goethals, like Cromwell, accompanied Taft on almost every one of his visits to the Canal. Early on, Taft appointed Cromwell and Goethals as his special advisors. Taft recommended that Goethals replace Stevens as the chief engineer of the Canal. Taft appointed Goethals, at the direction of Roosevelt, as the chairman, chief engineer, and governor of the Canal. There is no reason for an outsider to think that Goethals was anything but Taft's man. However, there was more to Goethals than even Taft, and just as likely Cromwell, had ever considered.

First, Roosevelt had gone through two well-known and respected chief engi-

---

[8] Roosevelt to Goethals, September 5, 1907, Canal Record, September 11, 1907, pp. I,9, (U.S.)

neers. In doing so, Roosevelt had gone to great effort to limit the adverse publicity attached to Wallace, and Stevens, and he was not about to fight that war again with Goethals, so close to another presidential election if it could be avoided. He was stuck with Goethals, and Goethals, and Taft knew it.

Second, Goethals was also a politician of sorts. He was a career soldier and a bureaucrat. He knew how to work within the federal system; he knew how to work with the Congress; and unlike Stevens, he knew how to get other people to do his bidding, without becoming directly involved.

Third, he was a fast learner, and he was convinced that Stevens's plan was the right plan to finish the Canal. Goethals, like Stevens, also knew that if he allowed the Canal to be taken over by private contractors, the power of the commission, and more importantly, his own power would eventually become subordinate to these private contractors.

Like he did with the employee problem of 1907, Goethals did not confront the contractor issue head-on, instead he pushed off the issue to the Canal Engineering Committee, headed by Gaillard, Rousseau, and Sibert. They, in turn, provided a report that shot down the idea of finishing the Canal through private contractors.[9]

That report allowed Goethals to write Taft and explain that the Canal workforce was divided into dry excavation by steam shovel at the Culebra Cut, dredging at the sea-level portions of the Canal, and construction of the locks, dams, terminals, and the relocation of the railroad. He further stated that eighty percent of the plant was in place or would be in place shortly, over the entire excavation of the Canal. To placate Taft, he stated that it may be better to hire private contractors to construct the locks and operating machinery. However, he further stated that the work could be done "better, cheaper, and more quickly by building the Canal by the Government."[10] For all practical purposes, the issue of the private contractors was dead, at least through the 1908 election year.

GOETHALS THROWS HIS WORKFORCE UNDER THE BUS

Goethals objective was to bring the Canal construction to completion, and just as important, under budget. To do that, Goethals needed to reduce the wage level of the entire Canal workforce. That opportunity rose late in 1907.

---

[9] I.C.C. Engineering Committee, Report, June 24, 1907.
[10] Goethals to Taft, July 30, 1907 (p.C. Rec. Bur., File 9-A-4) (U. S.)

On November 7, 1907, the House committee on appropriations decided to visit the Canal, and conducted a hearing for the 1909 Canal financial estimates. John A. Tawney was the chairman.

The committee members were given a "cool" reception by the members of the Canal Commission. Goethals presented his present organization and the work for the year. The congressmen were critical of the "employee privileges" they observed, and specifically pointed to the fact that the employees did not pay for their residence, their wages seemed excessive, and they seemed to be wasting electricity. On one occasion, while scheduling an afternoon meeting, the congressional committee observed every employee front porch light was lit on their route to the hearing. Some of the congressional members were also critical of the housing assignment, which was based upon the Canal employee salary level.

Of importance, Goethals was asked at that hearing how a reduction of personnel would be handled if salaries were cut. Goethals answered by stating it would be better for Congress to take that action rather than leave it to him "to discover the way of doing it." [11]

Goethals, as he did previously on other sensitive issues, did not want his fingerprints on any action that would directly affect the workforce wage level. When asked if he thought that the employee should continue the privileges they had, Goethals replied, "I do not. Personally, I think they are getting too much." [12] Goethals further stated that the steam-shovel men were getting too much and were the basis of agitation among others.

When asked if a wage reduction would cause a strike, Goethals answered, "All right, suppose they do, we will get additional men. We had that trouble in May. We will have some trouble so long as these steam-shovel men are on the Isthmus. There may be men that will leave, but we will not have any strikes." [13] The committee members went on to criticize the number of hospitals spread out within the Canal. They wanted a centralized system where an employee could be sent to a "terminal hospital" and eliminate unnecessary hospitals.

As critical as the congressional committee was on the Isthmus, they were more generous upon returning to the States, stating that conditions in Panama were in "excellent shape." [14] It took several subsequent hearings before the "Panama Canal Act" was approved on August 24, 1912. That act established the title

---

[11] Goethals Statement, November 11, 1907 (Hearings No. 1, p. 96) (U.S.)

[12] Ibid, p. 97.

[13] Ibid, p. 98.

[14] Panama Star and Herald, December 5, 1907; 1947, Miles P. DuVal, Jr., And the Mountains will Move, pp. 282-283.

of governor as the operating head of the Canal, and at a salary of $10,000 dollars. The salary of employees was established at no more than 25% above comparable wages paid to employees doing similar work in the United States. Of interest to some, it was because of this act, that the wage base of the Canal Zone police was tied to the Washington, D.C., Park Police, at the time one of the lowest police wage bases in the United States. The Park Police, like the Canal Zone Police, until it was abolished, was considered a federal police force.

GOETHALS IS READY TO TAKE COMPLETE CONTROL OF THE CANAL

In late 1907, the president was intent on centralizing the general Canal organization. He had solicited the Congress to appoint the Canal work under one man, but they refused to act on his request. However, he also did not want Congress to pass legislation that would interfere with the Canal Zone government, and he did not want the Canal commissioners to cause problems. Apparently, the president was aware that Goethals was getting kickback from some of the Canal commissioners, especially Gorgas and Sibert, both on the job and in testimony before Congress. Gorgas and Sibert were, in fact, working together to remove Goethals as chairman.

Prior to having completed his administrative organization, Goethals set about preparations for the necessary construction of the Atlantic and Pacific locks and dams. He needed to have the plant in place by the beginning of 1908, to start pouring the concrete at the Gatun locks, and the Gatun Dam spillway. Goethals requested $8,000,000 dollars from Taft to accelerate the work, and in August 1907, the president approved the request. [15]

Unsettled by late 1907 was the location and configuration of the Pacific locks and dam. The Congress had adopted a lock system at Sosa Hill, and Pedro Miguel, with an intermediate-level lake for the Pacific terminal. The dam was started by Stevens, who objected to it because he thought it was subject to attack by ships from the shore. Nevertheless, Goethals continued the Sosa Dam construction, until he ran into major problems.

He immediately shut the project down and appointed a board to recommend the best configuration and location for the Pacific locks and dam. On December 9, Goethals recommended that the president approve a single-level locks at Pe-

---

[15] Acting Secretary of War to Goethals, August 26-27, 1907, Canal Record. September 11, 1907, I, 9 (U.S.)

dro Miguel, and a double-lift lock system at Miraflores. Neither configuration or location was supported by Stevens or Sibert. The president approved of the plan on December 20, 1907. True to form, while attending a congressional hearing in 1909, Goethals was asked who suggested the changes that were made to the Sosa locks. Goethals answered that "the first mention of the change was from Mr. John F. Stevens." [16]

GOETHALS'S ADMINISTRATIVE REORGANIZATION

In January 1908, Goethals decided it was time he consolidated his control within the Canal, and at the same time, put his personal stamp on the organization of the Canal. Upon his visit to Washington, Goethals carried a draft of an executive order, prepared by R.R. Rogers, the Canal general counsel, which proposed greater strength to the original Stevens order by increasing the power of the chairman in appointing department heads, and adjusting duties among the members. It required that the commission reside on the Isthmus.

When Goethals submitted the draft to Taft, he requested that the president know that while the order was "what we'd like, it isn't in accordance with the law." Roosevelt's response was typical. "I don't give a damn for the law; I want the Canal built!" [17] Roosevelt signed the order on January 6, 1908. The order put all power in the hands of Goethals, and relegated the other members to a position of impotency.

By May 1908, Goethals had his reorganization plan ready to be implemented, and explained it to Secretary Taft. At the time, Taft was visiting the Canal, on a specific task to remove Jackson Smith as head of labor, quarters, and subsistence. Smith had earned the displeasure of the national unions, and therefore, was a liability to the Taft Election of 1908. Hodges was appointed to the commission in his stead.

Goethals wanted to "divide the function of labor, quarters, and subsistence." He made no attempt to change the department of sanitation, except to assign grass cutting to the quartermaster, and sanitary-ditch digging to the construction forces. In June, Goethals abolished the Department of Lock and Dam Construction, effective July 1, 1908, and formed a new Atlantic Division, to include all of

---

[16] Goethals Statement, January 7, 1909 (Hearings No. 12, p.122) (U.S.)
[17] Goethals to Mark Sullivan, April 12, 1926; quoted in J.B. and F. Bishop. Goethals, Genius of the Panama Canal: a biography, p. 193.

the territory north of Tavernilla, headed by Major Sibert. [18]

The relocation of the Sosa Locks to Miraflores enabled Goethals to create a new Pacific Division of Lock and Dam Construction, headed by Sydney B. Williamson, a civilian and a longtime friend of Goethals. The dredging and excavation from Miraflores to the sea was appointed to W. G. Comber. Mr. H.F. Hodges was assigned as the general purchasing officer in Washington and was additionally assigned to the design of lock gates. [19]

In July, Goethals issued a second circular abolishing the Excavation and Dredging Division, and formed a Central Division, headed by Major Gaillard, with Mr. L.K. Rourke as his assistant division engineer. Goethals divided the Departments of Motive Power and Machinery, Municipal Engineering, and Building Construction was divided among the three major division.[20]

Photo of Major Gaillard

---

[18] Official Circular No. 183; quoted in the Canal Record, June 24, 1908, pp. I,342. (U.S.). 1947, Miles P. DuVal, Jr., And the Mountains will Move, pp. 286-283.

[19] Ibid; 1947, Miles DuVal, And the Mountains Will Move, p. 286

[20] Ibid; 1947, Miles DuVal, p. 288

THE CANAL RECORD

Just as important to Goethals's success finishing the Canal as his administrative re-organization and his plant preparations was the creation of the Canal Record.

In September 1907, Miss Gertrude Beeks, a Canal social worker, suggested that Goethals create a local newspaper to inform the workers about "decisions, and the progress of the work." The matter was brought up and approved by the commission. Free, weekly distribution became available, not just to the Canal workers, but to the Congress, the national media, and the public at large. It was intended to be a source of accurate information that heretofore had been more a sea of propaganda, misinformation, and rumor. It was the Canal Record, which helped Goethals establish himself as first in the building of the Canal, and relegated Wallace, and Stevens as "preparers and supporters" of Goethals's final work.[21]

In addition to the location and type of lift settled for the locks, was the problem of the width of the locks. The navy wanted a width of no less than 110 feet to accommodate any future warships. Goethals did not think that any future warship would ever exceed a hundred-foot-wide lock. In his message to Congress, dated December 3, 1907, Roosevelt suggested that the locks width should be 120 feet. However, the commission and the president finally sided with the navy, and President Roosevelt approved of the recommendation to establish the locks width at 110 feet, on January 15, 1908.[22]

This issue, like several others issues, was criticized by Bunau-Varilla as not forward thinking enough, if the builders were considering a perpetual locks system. He cited the continual creation of larger commercial, and military ships, which would make the permanent lock system canal obsolete before it was finished. Even today, as the Republic of Panama builds its "third locks" system to accommodate larger ships, more ships will be built to carry more cargo tonnage than can be accommodated by the Panama "third locks." Already China is considering building a sea-level canal in Nicaragua. China and Russia have shown interest in a "forth locks."

Goethals decided on three other changes to ensure that ships would pass through the Canal without damage. Originally planned as a dump at La Boca, the first change was the construction of a breakwater running from La Boca to Naos Island. Residents referred to this breakwater as the "causeway." It was a solution to a problem of a low tide level at La Boca, while the depth of water around the Naos Island was always sufficient for ships entering or leaving the Canal. The

---

[21] Ibid; 1947, Miles DuVal, pp. 279-281.
[22] Messages and Papers of the Presidents, XVI, 7101 (U.S.).

Naos side of the causeway was eventually used as a pickup and release point for boarding officers, "pilots and ad-measurers," for ships entering and departing the Pacific end of the Canal. The Naos Island was converted into defensive artillery batteries, and the whole complex eventually was named Fort Amador, after the first president of Panama. After the death of President Amador, on May 2, 1909, the town of La Boca was renamed Balboa, by direction of President Roosevelt. [23]

The second change was a breakwater change at Colon that ran from Toro Point eastward across Limon Bay. The third change came when Goethals recommended an increase in the "bottom width" of Culebra Cut from 200 feet to 300 feet to prevent groundings, and damage to larger ships. The president approved of Goethals's plan on October 23, 1908. Goethals estimated that these changes increased the total cost of the Canal by $250,000,000 dollars.[24] These changes were made because of perceived problems by Goethals, but they were not the only problems, both major and minor, he was to face in the coming years. Most of these problems, I might add, he had been warned would happen years before he took office as chief engineer.

Men working on the Culebra Cut With bucket Dredge

---
[23] Canal Record, May 5, 1909, II, pp. 281-282 (U.S.)
[24] Canal Record, May 5, 1909, II, pp. 281-282 (U.S.)

Emplacement of Canal Gates

Men working on Track System

Men working in Disposal of Spoil

THE HISTORY OF THE THREE IDEAS REVISITED

Except for the initial support of Wallace, and to some extent Major Sibert, the one engineer that was the most qualified, had the most hands-on experience, and engineering knowledge in building the Panama Canal was virtually the most ignored by the American Canal builders.

That person, of course, was Philippe Bunau-Varilla. After signing the Hay–Bunau-Varilla Treaty, Bunau-Varilla never lost interest in the method used, and the type of canal the United States would build in Panama. His frustration at being ignored caused him to include a chapter in his book Panama: The Creation, Destruction, And Resurrection that illustrated some of the problems, financial and otherwise, that the United States would encounter in their permanent lock system, and method of "dry" excavation in building the Canal. As an answer to why his advice was virtually ignored, Bunau-Varilla turned to the teachings of the philosophers "Bacon and Descartes" by stating, "Bacon gave us the exclusive faith in facts revealed by experience, and the method of induction by which we can rise from the facts themselves to the laws which governs them." Bunau-Varilla went on to express, in the eloquent prose of his time, that "Descartes tore from our eyes the bandage which the Spirit of Authority has bound over them."

In short, the engineers of the day, Stevens, Goethals, and others, refused to accept the proven methods of modern engineering Bunau-Varilla helped invent, perfected, and proposed. Bunau-Varilla commended these engineers for their organizational expertise, and persistence, but he was quick to fault them on their refusal to accept provable, modern engineering methods. Bunau-Varilla understood that these engineers were not innovative thinkers. Wallace and Stevens were well known in the railroad industry, but they had little or no experience in canal building, and especially in an area like Panama. Their canal building experience was done by trial and error. What success they had in the Canal was made possible due to the eventual eradication of yellow fever and malaria.

Goethals was even less equipped to build the Canal in an effective, and economical manner. He was an army engineer with a very limited engineering body of work to recommend him for the job of building the Panama Canal. All three of these engineers were comfortable in working within the engineering practices of the day. They showed that they were extremely uncomfortable working with modern engineering practices posed by Bunau-Varilla. Obviously, all three of these engineers thought of Bunau-Varilla as a French diplomat, a revolutionary, even an opportunist, and possibly a mediocre engineer.

At best, they considered Bunau-Varilla as one of their peers, with no better skills than their own. In fact, Bunau-Varilla proved himself to be, first, a brilliant, innovative engineer, second, an innovative French diplomat, and third, an innovative revolutionary.

As a young engineer, at the age of twenty-one, Bunau-Varilla, solved the Naos–La Boca breakwater problem, his first assignment, while other more experienced engineers, considered that the problem had no solution. He solved that problem some thirty years before Goethals was even aware of the problem.

Bunau-Varilla solved the Cucaracha slide problem, manifested at the Culebra Cut, that practically shut down the very idea of a sea-level canal by the French in 1885. Bunau-Varilla became the chief engineer of the French Panama Canal at the age of twenty-five. His excavation method, with the use of explosives and dredging, made Bunau-Varilla a rich man as a private contractor for the French Canal Company. Bunau-Varilla worked on almost every problem related to the Panama Canal, some thirty years before an American ever set foot in the Canal. Unlike Stevens and Goethals, he did it while in the pestilence that was the Canal. He deserved a voice in their decision-making.

THE HISTORY OF BUNAU-VARILLA'S METHOD AND THE COST OF DREDGING

To understand the error of the American engineering position, one must go back to the history of the three types of canals studied, and the one eventually proposed by the International Congress of 1879. At issue was the so-called Ferdinand de Lesseps idea, "the sea-level canal," the Godin de Lepinay idea, "the locks canal," and the Bunau-Varilla idea, "an eventual transition from a locks system to an eventual sea-level system." The sea-level system was adopted by the International Congress in 1879, and the locks system was all but ignored. Bunau-Varilla's transition system initially drew some interest but eventually was also ignored because of the perceived cost. It was this perceived cost in the type and method of Bunau-Varilla's system that doomed it to failure when the United States took up the issue. It was a perception that Bunau-Varilla set out to prove was a false perception, and he did so with the detail he was known to possess.

In 1890, the Guillemain Commission, appointed by the receiver of the Old Panama Canal Company, refused to accept the Bunau-Varilla system, and the proven reduced cost of a so called "wet excavation system" in favor of the more expensive "dry excavation system." Their final assertion was that it was impossible to "dredge rock." By 1901, the Panama Canal locks system became the favored system, excavated in the "dry," with a dam projected at Bohio.

The 1901 Isthmian Canal Commission listed standard excavation prices of rock at:

"Removal of hard rock per cubic yard…$1.15"

"Removal of soft rock per cubic yard…$0.80"

"Removal of rock underwater per cubic yard…$4.75"

Bunau-Varilla argued that the International Congress of 1879 and the Guillemain Commission of 1890 may have had reason to dismiss his canal system by reason of the "spirit of authority" he alluded to when discussing the philosophy of Bacon and Descartes, but the 1901, Isthmian Canal Commission dismissed his system through ignorance of his work done on the Canal precisely with that system in 1885. Bunau-Varilla went on to quote Wallace, in 1905, when he stated that a perpetual lock canal was an absurdity. Later, on February 1, 1905, Wallace, relying on his perceived idea of the cost of Bunau-Varilla's excavation method and canal system stated, "Any lowering of the summit level was impossible, on account of the cost of such operation and of the necessity of closing the Canal to traffic for a long time during this process."

It was this very issue that Bunau-Varilla fully addressed when discussing his wet dredging process years before. The cost of that system was projected by Bunau-Varilla at less than $0.50 for hard rock underwater per cubic yard with the modern equipment available in 1905. It is interesting to note that, today, this very process is going on, while Canal ship traffic is virtually unhindered, and while the Republic of Panama builds the proposed third locks. But it isn't necessary to project ahead to today, or even 1905. Bunau-Varilla was performing that process, at that cost, as a private contractor on the original French Panama Canal in 1885, and deriving an enormous profit doing so.

On March 27, 1905, Bunau-Varilla met with Secretary Taft, and President Roosevelt, and convinced Roosevelt that his canal system, and method of dredging, was the correct process in which to build the Canal. In August 1905, Bunau-Varilla published the content of the discussion he had with Secretary Taft, President Roosevelt, and the follow-up note he sent to President Roosevelt. The title of the publication was "Locks First, Sea Level Canal Afterwards: The Minimum of Difficulties in the Near Future—the Maximum of Perfection in the Distant Future." Bunau-Varilla emphasized the extreme risk of "digging the Culebra Cut in the dry." He recommended drilling wells every hundred feet, as a means of studying the ground structure at Culebra. It was a method of removing the necessary tonnage of ground necessary for the stability of the side slopes in order to avoid slides. Of course, none of his recommendations were accepted by Stevens or Goethals. On September 1, 1905, after meeting with Bunau-Varilla, the president created the International Consulting Board, and reconstituted the Isthmian Canal Commission.

THE LOBNITZ DREDGE

At about the same time Bunau-Varilla was using explosives to break up rock in his dredging system in 1885, another innovator, by the name of M. Lobnitz, a dredge builder from Scotland, was working on a concussion rock-breaking machine. In 1886, he took out several patents on his invention. By 1905, the Lobnitz system was adequately advanced that it could replace Bunau-Varilla's explosive dredging system. In addition, Mr. Bunau-Varilla was familiar with a French engineer by the name of M. Quellennec who had been the chief engineer at the Suez Canal, and was, at the time, a technical consultant to that Canal administration. Early in this writing, mention was made that the area of the Suez Canal between the Bitter Lakes and the Red Sea consisted in rock at the bottom. In 1895, at the recommendation of M. Quellennec, and his familiarity with this Lobnitz dredging system, and the low cost of that system, the Suez Canal employed this system to eliminate the rock bottom at that location.

On May 5, 1905, Bunau-Varilla wrote to President Roosevelt, and recommended M. Quellennec be appointed to the consulting board set up by Roosevelt. On July 12, 1905, Roosevelt appointed M. Quellennec to the board.

MEMBERS OF THE BOARD

Members of the International Consulting Board were considered eminent engineers from five different countries: The United States, Great Britain, France, Germany, and Holland; two of those members were previous members of the 1901 Isthmian Canal Commission, and they signed off on the document proposing the cost of rock-breaking underwater at $4.75 dollars a cubic yard. Four years later, they signed off on the consulting board's document proposing that rock-breaking excavation underwater would cost $2.50 a cubic yard, less than half of their original proposal, without any engineering basis for their change, far less than what the 1901 Isthmian Committee projected, but still far greater than the projection they made for the dry excavation.

In October 1905, M. Quellennec created a document he expected to give to the other members of the Consulting Board that showed that the average cost of rock breaking on the "Suez Canal from January 1, 1904, to June 30, 1905, had been twenty-five cents per cubic yard." M. Quellennec gave Bunau-Varilla a copy of that document. The Consulting Board failed to include M. Quellennec's document in their "appendices" among all the other documents prepared for the members of the board. In addition, verbal mention of these figures were never reproduced in their report.

Even worse, the British representative, the chief engineer of the Manchester Ship Canal, also signed off on the cost of $2.50 per cubic yards to excavate any rock underwater in the Panama Canal. "He had just completed a project for the deepening of the Manchester Ship Canal, removing several hundred thousand cubic yards of submerged rock," and had calculated the price for this project at "$0.50 cents a cubic yard." Bunau-Varilla further stated that "the average so-called rock in the Panama excavation is softer than that of the Manchester Canal, and is, therefore, cheaper to break; a great part of it is even dredge-able direct, by means of our powerful modern dredges, without mechanical or other disintegration!"

The Consulting Board declared that the cost of excavation of "any class of rock below water was…two dollars and a half a cubic yard." They declared that it would cost "fifteen cents for the cost of dredging loose ground."

ROOSEVELT'S REQUEST

On September 11, 1905, President Roosevelt requested the Consulting Board of 1905, to inform him "if you recommend a high-level multi-lock canal, it will be possible, after it is completed, to turn it into and to substitute for it, in time, a sea-level canal without interrupting the traffic upon it."

BUNAU-VARILLA'S RESPONSE TO THE ROOSEVELT REQUEST "THE KEY TO THE SECRET OF THE STRAITS"

Bunau-Varilla's answer to that question was based first, upon the enormous improvement of the modern ladder dredge, the improvement of mechanical concussion machines, and second, based upon the easy disposal of the massive material excavated. The first combination of these tools, the modern dredge and concussion tool, was also proven on the Eala River in Spain in 1895 by the Dutch. The Dutch delegate, M. Welcker, confirmed Bunau-Varilla's contention, by proving that dredge excavation, and concussion machines, even by steam engine, could be done at a cost of 3.5 cents per cubic yards, some ten years after Bunau-Varilla used his explosive dredging system. Bunau-Varilla went further to state that 90% of rock on the Isthmus "scarcely deserve such a name." The cost of the system could be done even cheaper if powered by electric dredges, and electric concussion machines.

The second factor described by Bunau-Varilla, was the easy disposal of the spoils, deposited in barges, that could be disposed of within a ten-mile distance in a man-made lake created by a dam built near Gamboa. He proposed that a simple disposal system be set up, using the waters of the Chagres River, the power of the Canal, to pass over that dam, and use the spill water to be used as the electricity to power the electric concussion machines, the dredges, and the electric barges used to break up and dredge the rock, deposit the spoils in barges, and dump the spoils at a designated location in the 150-foot deep lake, all without interfering with the free flow of existing ship traffic. Of course, Bunau-Varilla went into much greater detail on how this system would work in his own writing.

Again, it cannot be stated enough: Bunau-Varilla's system would not interfere in building a lock system in Panama. His proposal was to create a sea-level canal after that lock system was created and collecting tolls.

Unsaid is the obvious motivation to avoid the enormous maintenance cost of a lock system, compared to the low maintenance cost of a sea-level canal. Bunau-Varilla compared his proposal to the need for tens of thousands of employees working to produce a sea-level canal with a dry excavation system proposed by the Isthmian Canal Commission.

He stated that his proposal could be done without "postponing for a single hour the opening to traffic, and without disturbing this traffic for an hour during its work." Bunau-Varilla went on to state, "Here is the key of the secret of the straits, in search of which Charles the Fifth sent Hernando Cortes in 1523. … Humanity has vainly looked for it during centuries in the geography of the Isthmus. The secret lay in its hydraulics. … For centuries, and even up to the present day, mankind has believed that the Chagres was the terrible enemy of the great undertaking. It was the mysterious enigma which has hitherto baffled human sagacity, but it was also the gigantic workman placed by providence for the realization of the 'straits.'" Bunau-Varilla compared what occurred at Salamanca in 1487–1490—which dictated the "dogma of the Church of that day against the mathematical proofs of astronomy, and geography—to the "Spirit of Authority," or engineering dogma, taken up by the Consulting Board of 1905–1906.

Having lost the support of the 1905 consulting board, Bunau-Varilla was not finished arguing the merits of his Canal System. In 1907, he was invited to speak about technical problems in Panama at the London Royal Society of Arts, an organization "almost exclusively devoted to applied sciences." The meeting was held by Sir John Wolfe Barry, considered the "most celebrated English engineer of his day." Sir Barry considered the cost of $2.50 adopted for excavation of rock underwater in Panama "startling," when compared to the cost obtained at the Suez Canal and the Manchester Canal. Because of his presentation, and the position of Sir Barry, in June of 1907, Bunau-Varilla was asked to speak at the engineering conference of the Institution of Civil Engineers in London. "The question of removal of rock underwater was put on the programme."

M. Quellennec, unable to attend, sent a note to Bunau-Varilla, reproducing the figures he presented the consulting board in 1905. These figures showed that the average breaking of rock in the Suez Canal was $0.25 cents per cubic yard (After deducting the time lost for passages of ships). Mr. Sandeman, the chief engineer of the Harbour of Blyth, presented similar results. Mr. Hunter, in a "verbal report," stated that the effective cost of breaking 280,000 cubic yards of rock on the "Manchester Ship Canal was just a little below $0.12 cents per cubic yard." [25]

PRESIDENT TAFT AND COLONEL GOETHALS RESPOND TO THE BUNAU-VARILLA DREDGING SYSTEM

Sometime after Bunau-Varilla addressed the engineering conference of the Institution of Civil Engineers in Great Britain, the American government purchased a Lobnitz rock breaking machine, and set up a test at Panama to determine the cost and ability of this machine to efficiently break rock underwater.

Panama was known to have the hardest rock on the Isthmus, and the most unfavorable variations of water level due to the tides, which would hinder the work. The American government fully expected the test to fail. On March 16, 1909, Goethals spoke to the Manufacturers Association in Chicago, and stated: "The variation in the character of the rock on the Isthmus from soft argillaceous sandstone to hard trap are such as to make the use of such devices very problematical. ... Experiments are now being made on the Isthmus with one of these rock-crushing devices, but thus far the results are not promising." [26] In May 1909,

---

[25] 1912, Bunau-Varilla, Panama: The Creation, Destruction, And Resurrection, pp. 444-460.

[26] Canal Record, March 31, 1909.

President Taft published an article in the McClure's Magazine stating: "The Lobnitz method of excavating rock underwater is on trial to-day on the Pacific side of the Isthmus of Panama, and the result of the work there confirms the judgment of practical engineers elsewhere that the machine will work in comparatively soft rock with thin laminations, but that it will not work in hard rock or in rock in which the strata are widely separated, of which there is much to be excavated in constructing the Panama Canal."

The Canal Record reported that the machine began working on August 21, 1909, and detailed records were being kept, and would be released when the work had been completed. Neither the Canal Record, nor the yearly reports of the secretary of war, up to the year 1912, ever published the results of this test.

This zone of silence was not sufficient to keep Bunau-Varilla from learning and exposing the truth. His approach to this problem illustrates how innovative Bunau-Varilla really was. Bunau-Varilla stated that "the machine left traces of its activity on the ground and consequently in the statistics published by the reports." "The figures…could be extracted from the statistics of the official reports as an unknown quantity can be extracted from an equation." "This machine, which these two high authorities had announced would fail to attack the hard trap, broke and rendered dredge-able, despite the difficulties due to a water level constantly varying, a mass of hard rock, the hardest on the Isthmus, amounting to 2,514 cubic yards, during the first month of its work. The cost price was $0.58 cents." In April 1911, under the same conditions, with less-than-hard trap rock, the rock-breaker produced "7,275 cubic yards, at a cost of $0.19 cents per cubic yard."

Bunau-Varilla went further. He stated that his old explosive system and the concussion system were used together on the Pacific side of the Isthmus, on the Barge Teredo, between July 1910 and June 1911, and dredged 145,000 cubic yards of rock at a cost of $0.45 cents per cubic yard. Major Sibert, in charge of these tests, produced similar results on the Atlantic side of the Isthmus. It was Bunau-Varilla's view that the cost of his system would have fallen to $0.25 cents per cubic yard, if modern, more powerful dredges were used. Until March 1912, the United States refused to order any ladder dredges, settling on the dipper-dredges, the very best of which were considered inferior, even to the ladder dredges used by the French twenty-five years previously. When a modern ladder dredge did arrive, the Canal Record voiced surprise that it could dredge soft rock without any preparation. It was used to finish off the Culebra Cut. The name was changed to the Gaillard Cut.

The argument over what system to use to dig the Canal had already been decided in 1909 by Goethals, when he decided to excavate through the rocky Mindi Hills. He stated: "As the material can be removed more cheaply by the shovels than by dredging, excavation in the dry was continued." In his report, he cited the cost of excavating the Mindi Hills at "$0.55 cents per cubic yard, dirt and rock." Of course, based upon the above information, that statement was patently not true. Putting aside the reason why Goethals's statement was not true, one should ask, if Goethals lied about other issues related to his duties as chief engineer of the Panama Canal, what other issues did he mislead the public and Congress that, in the end, wasted an enormous amount of taxpayer funds and time in building that Canal.

First, Goethals did not make any decisions, if he could avoid it, that would contradict the wishes of Secretary Taft. For example, the minority of the Consulting Board had recommended a dam on the Pacific side of the Isthmus, close to the ocean on top of "a broad flat formed by a blue grey marine, clayish silt, plastic and slippery, covering a table of rock or hard clay."

In 1907, the secretary of war went to the Isthmus personally to inspect the site, with an advisory board consisting of Mr. Noble, Stearns, and Mr. Freeman, all eminent American engineers. They made the following statement: "For the dam construction, we do not think it will be necessary to remove the soft material…the softest material will be either displaced or consolidated by the material disposed on it."

On December 9, 1907, after problems surfaced, Colonel Goethals stopped work, and reported to the secretary, stating: "The investigations clearly demonstrate that the construction of dams which would remain in place after the lake is filled can be accomplished only by the removal of all the material overlying the rock." A copy of his statement was inserted in the Canal Record, on December 25, 1907. However, Goethals contradicted his own 1907 statement by inserting the following statement in the March 31, 1909, Canal Record: "I know that the La Boca dams could be built to withstand safely the heads of water in the resulting lake by adopting either the method of dredging out the ooze or by giving massive dimensions to the superimposed structure."

Bunau-Varilla illustrated the folly of building a dam at La Boca when he cited what happened to the American Panama Railroad wharf. On August 17, 1912, the wharf not only collapsed, but it also sunk the steamer Newport. The wharf was erected on the same material on which the board recommended the La Boca dams were to be built. The French wharf, erected next to the American wharf, was built on caissons and resting on bedrock, and never showed any weakness. In the end, Goethals moved the dam, and relocated the Pacific locks to Miraflores, the site Bunau-Varilla had selected when he worked for the French Canal Company.

When Goethals was asked, by a member of Congress, "Who suggested the changes in the placement of the Sosa locks?" Goethals stated that he thought Stevens first mentioned the idea. [27]Goethals would not even admit his own formal recommendations that were previously signed off on through an executive order by President Roosevelt. Perhaps because Goethals estimated that all of his changes would increase the cost of the Canal by $250,000,000 dollars. While it is true that Stevens discussed the security, problems associated with the dam and the Sosa lock, in fact, in 1905, Bunau-Varilla had mentioned to President Roosevelt, Secretary Taft, and the International Consulting Board, the dangers in placing the dam and lock system at La Boca, much earlier than Stevens, not just for security reasons, but also because of the safety problems.

BUNAU-VARILLA'S WARNING OF THE GATUN DAM PROBLEMS

In 1906, the minority, from the International Consulting Board changed the 1901 Isthmian Canal Committee proposal by substituting a dam at Gatun instead of at Bohio, "some ten miles lower down, the width of the valley." This change increased the length of the dam from 1,300 to 7,700 feet. It increased the depth to bedrock from 158 to 255 feet below sea level.

In 1892, Bunau-Varilla suggested a small earthen dam at Bohio, using the same process, one he devised, and one used by the builders of the Gatun Dam. However, Bunau-Varilla cautioned against the problem of earthquakes, and the location of the dam, which was partially sitting on "plastic, blue clay." On March 5, 1906, Bunau-Varilla wrote an open letter in the Sun, to President Roosevelt, stating: "I consider such a structure as a highly dangerous one in view of the softness of its mass, if one considers the light earthquakes which are frequent and must be constantly expected on the Isthmus. … They often cause the fall of glasses on the tables and such inclinations of the ground will determine successive compressions and depressions in the soft and extremely long mass which will cause ruptures of continuity and immediate wash-out."

Bunau-Varilla did not make these statements without substance. The 1901 Isthmian Canal Commission cited an earthquake that occurred in 1882, that

---

[27] Goethals, Statement, January 7, 1909 (Hearings No. 12, p. 122) (U.S.)

opened crevices "in the ground in Colon." In just two years, 1909–1910, the Canal Record cited three earthquakes, August 30, 1909, April 13, 1910, and December 20, 1910, that were at least sufficient to cause crevices at Gatun. Having lived in the Canal Zone from 1964–1984, I have personally experienced many earthquakes, a few much stronger than the ones described by Bunau-Varilla.

How did the minority members of the 1905 International Consulting Board respond to Bunau-Varilla's open letter? They proposed a long soft dam at Gatun, 135 feet above sea level, 50 feet above the level of the Gatun Lake, which was projected to be 85 feet deep. In a letter dated May 18, 1906, Mr. Frederic P. Stearns, a leading member of the board, believed that the dam would be protected against earthquakes. He stated: "It is my opinion that a dam so designed is earthquake-proof, by reason of the great height to which it is built above the level of the water in the proposed lake. …if a… line of rupture should occur passing directly through the dam the pressure of the superincumbent earth would, in my opinion, squeeze the sides of the fissure together, so that no water could pass out of the lake…but if any one questioned the certainty of this action, the weight could be increased without materially increasing the cost of the Canal by building the high portions of the dam up to 100 or 150 ft. above the water line." [28]

He thought that the heavier the dam, the less likely it would be affected by earthquakes. He failed to consider, or ignored the fact, that the dam was partially lying on 255 feet of plastic blue clay. In November 1907, during the congressional hearing in which he threw his employees under the bus, Goethals was quick to correct a response Major Sibert made to a congressional question: "Were there any differences of opinion as to the stability of Gatun dam?" Sibert answered, "I think not." Goethals interceded by stating, "I can say that there is not." On August 25, 1908, Goethals reported on the earth below the dam: "The material encountered is of such nature as to be amply strong for supporting the proposed structure." On November 11, 1908, the Canal Record reported that the Gatun Dam had been completed, at a required height of sixty feet above the proposed lake level. On November 21, 1908, after a heavy rain, the upstream rock connection, or "toe," of the dam slid. On November 25, 1908, the dam sunk twenty feet over a length of 200 feet. Shortly after, the whole world was aware of the Gatun slide. If the dam gave way, the Canal would be ruined. On December 12, 1908, the New York Herald published a front-page article, based upon a Bunau-Varilla wire interview entitled: "The Panama Canal May Be History's Greatest Ruin, Says M. Bunau-Varilla."

---

[28] Sen. Doc. 3626, 59th Congress, 1st session.

President Taft announced that he would leave Washington to investigate the problem. On December 30, 1908, The New York Herald published the names of the experts, Mr. Stearns, Mr. Freeman, and Mr. Randolph, that would accompany Mr. Taft on his trip to the Isthmus. Mr. Stearns and Mr. Freeman signed off on the 1907 recommendation regarding the dam, and Mr. Randolph was an original member of the International Consulting Board that recommended the dam. According to the New York Herald, these three experts were recommended by Mr. Noble, who was the most influential member of the minority, and a co-signer with Mr. Stearns and Mr. Randolph on the Gatun Dam project. The two dangers related to this dam were the problem of earthquakes, and the weight of the dam partially sitting on a plastic blue clay stratum. Basically, the Gatun Dam problem was very similar to the Sosa Dam problem. Goethals solved the Sosa dam problem, by moving the Sosa Dam to a more favorable location.

As a result of the New York Herald article, Colonel Goethals was requested to answer the charges of the instability of the dam. On January 6 and 7, 1909, a committee of the House of Representatives held a hearing on the problem. Representative Each asked Major Harding, a Canal engineer, "Would that diminution in height lessen the security of the structure?" Major Harding answered: "I think it may possibly increase the stability of the structure. … Then if we lower the level of the crest of the dam 20 ft., we take off a ton to the square foot of the base of the dam underlying the part that is taken off."

On January 10, 1909, Colonel Goethals published a report addressing the collapse of the toe, stating: "In sinking, it has squeezed out and pushed up the clay underneath it..." Goethals went on to state: "The stratum of blue clay, which M. Bunau-Varilla mentions as a danger at Gatun, exists chiefly in two deep gorges in the rock which are crossed to about right angles by the axis of the dam, and where crossed are about 1900 ft. and 950 ft. wide, respectively, at sea level. … It requires only to be held in place to form a reliable foundation, for an earth-dam of suitable cross section." Goethals's statement in January 1909 was opposite to his statements made in August 1908 and November 1907.

The Taft Commission addressed the problem by recommending the reduction in the height of the dam from fifty to thirty feet above the water level. They reduced the altitude of the crest from 135 feet to 115 feet above sea level, and retained the projected depth of the lake to 85 feet. Mr. Stearns was a signature to this report. In addressing the issue of the material underlying the dam, the report stated: "Nor are they so soft as to be liable to be pushed aside by the weight of the proposed dam, so as to cause dangerous settlement."

The justification for making these changes are contained in the March 3, 1909, Canal Record: "We were requested to consider the proper height of the crest of the Gatun Dam, and after consideration concluded that it could be safely reduced 20 ft. from that originally proposed…" "Changes in this respect will facilitate the work of construction and will reduce somewhat the cost of the proposed work." The Taft Commission report was also in contradiction to the January 10, 1909, statement by Colonel Goethals.

On February 17, 1909, President Roosevelt stated, in support of the Taft Commission: "As to the Gatun dam itself they (the engineers) show that not only is the dam safe, but that, on the whole, the plan already adopted would make it needlessly high and strong, and accordingly they recommend that the height be reduced by 20 ft., which change in the plans I have accordingly directed." In fact, the commission, through their report, compromised the safety of the dam if earthquakes should occur. The possibility that the dam could sink, and could break apart of its own weight, would be due to the underlying unstable clay surface.

"On October 12, 1911, a movement again occurred in the east half of the dam, on the North (downstream) side. For a length of approximately 1000 ft., the top of the dry fill settled four or five feet." On February 21, 1912, the Canal Record, referring to the western part of the dam, reported: "Its length is to be 8000 ft., its greatest width 3000 ft., and its final elevation about 105 ft. above sea level." In short, in contrast to the Roosevelt executive order of 1909, the assurances of the Taft Commission, and Goethals himself, Colonel Goethals reduced the height of the dam by an additional ten feet. [29]

BUNAU-VARILLA'S WARNING REGARDING THE CULEBRA CUT

As the assigned engineer of the Cut, under Ferdinand de Lesseps, and as the chief engineer of the French Canal, and even later, as the private contractor assigned to work on the Culebra Cut, Bunau-Varilla was intimately familiar with the slides at the Culebra Cut.

In a note Bunau-Varilla gave President Roosevelt in March 1905, and which he also gave to the Consulting Board in September 1905, he stated: "The question of the stability of the slopes of the great Culebra Cut will be of paramount

---

[29] 1912, Bunau-Varilla, Panama: The Creation, Destruction, And Resurrection, pp. 480-488.

importance. Whatever process of excavation will be adopted, shovels on rails or dredgers on water, no slices of ground will be attacked before its nature and stability be recognized by open-air wells through the said slice, along the foot-line of the lateral slopes every hundred feet. If the nature of the ground so recognized makes it necessary to soften the slopes, or to increase the width, or to make any kinds of works to ensure the stability of the cut, that will mean simply delay in the completion of the transformation, but no harm to international navigation."

The Consulting Board's reply was: "Inasmuch as by far the greatest part of the under-water excavation in his (M. Bunau-Varilla's) process of transformation, would be made in material classed as rock, large portions of the side slopes might be as steep as four verticals on one horizontal and a very small portion, if any, of them will be less steep than three verticals on two horizontals." [30]Bunau-Varilla suggested a summit level cut of a hundred feet above sea level, and went further, stating, "It would be better to adopt a higher altitude such as 140."

Based upon their response, the board concluded that the Culebra Cut consisted of stable rock formation, and could be excavated at a steep angle, and much deeper. The Consulting Board majority concluded that the cut could be excavated down to forty feet below sea level, or 140 feet below where Bunau-Varilla had set as a safe limit for the excavation. The Consulting Board minority concluded that the cut could be made at forty feet above sea level, or 60 feet below what Bunau-Varilla suggested. Again, on March 5, 1906, Bunau-Varilla wrote an open letter to President Roosevelt, again stating his suggestion that the cut should be no more than one hundred feet above sea level, saying, "It is recommended by all considerations of logic and experience." The conclusions of the Consulting Board minority prevailed. On October 27, 1909, the level of the Culebra Cut was eighteen feet below the hundred-foot level suggested by Bunau-Varilla.

In December 1909, the first slides began. To prove his suggestion, correct, Bunau-Varilla cited the approximate percentage of slides due to excavation when the cut reached a hundred feet, on July 31, 1909, it was 8.5 %. From July 1909 to June 1910, it was 17%. From July 1910 to June 1911, it was 36%. From 1911 to June 1912, it was 53 %. Ironically, the final work on the cut, by dry excavation, was abandoned, and the work on the cut was finished by the process of underwater excavation suggested by Bunau-Varilla. He stated that the Canal could have been completed in 1909 if his suggestions had been accepted.

---

[30] Ibid, p.471.

NO SURPRISE THE ORIGINAL COST OF THE CANAL WAS INCORRECT

In January 1906, the Consulting Board minority estimated that the cost of the Canal would be $139,705,209 dollars. In December 12, 1908, published in the New York Herald, Bunau-Varilla suggested that the real cost of the Canal would be in excess of $280,000,000 dollars. The board revised its estimate some weeks later to $282,766,000. Due to Goethals changes, approved by President Roosevelt, the cost was estimated to be $297,766,000.

WATER AVAILABLE FOR CANAL TRAFFIC

Even the crucial issue of how much water was available for ship traffic through the Canal, projected by the Consulting Board minority, was incorrect. The minority declared that after reviewing documents over a period of fifteen years, there was a flow of 1250 cubic feet per second "during the driest three months." "They provided for a flow of 20% less for still drier periods," and stated that 1000 cubic feet per second was "an entirely safe quantity for the three driest months of any year in the future."

In 1908, the flow at Gatun was 930 cubic feet per second during the driest three months. In 1912, the flow was 608 cubic feet per second during the three driest three months. The minority apparently relied upon the calculations given by General Abbott, when he stated the yearly flow of water could be expected to be 5,730 cubic feet per second "as the minimum annual contribution which may confidently be expected from the Chagres and its tributaries at Gatun." The Canal Record gave the average discharge in May 1905 to April 1906 at 4526 cubic feet per second, and for the same period, from 1911 to 1912, at 4626. [31]

Bunau-Varilla suggested that it takes just under 38,000 cubic feet per second of water for the lockage of forty-eight ships through the Canal per day. Therefore, there is not much room for error. Considering the increase in tonnage over the years, ships transiting the Canal will reach a limit before it becomes obsolete as a perpetual lock canal. He was right.

---

[31] September 18, 1912, The Canal Record.

THE GATUN LAKE STORED WATER LOSS WAS ANOTHER PROBLEM IGNORED BY THE CONSULTING BOARD MINORITY

Again, in February 1909, Bunau-Varilla pointed out that the lake area in front of the Gatun Dam and lock was in danger of losing water due to the fissures in the hills forming the rim of the lake. Bunau-Varilla considered this problem unique to the Gatun Dam area, because the rest of the Canal had hills that are "of solid, compact, and stable rock." The hills around Gatun "are formed by sand surrounded by clayish elements. It is a kind of intermediary between rock and earth." Bunau-Varilla was not alone in his opinion. On January 7 and 8, 1909, Major Sibert, when questioned by a member of the committee of the House in the Panama Canal, he stated: "Yes, Sir, the country is fissured." He went on to demonstrate that after digging a well, and pumping water, the level of all these boreholes was lowered in the vicinity. Some of these holes were at 2000 feet. He went on to state that "curtains of masonry had to be established in front of the locks, through the subsoil, in order to try to remove from below the foundations these dangerous underground currents." He went on to state: "Personally, I do not think it practicable to cut off this flow entirely, because we do not know the depth of these fissures."

Of course, the Consulting Board minority's answer to all of this was to state: "From our examinations in the neighborhood of Gatun Dam, we can find no reason to apprehend important loss of water by seepage through the ridges surrounding the lake." [32]

THE ARGUMENT AGAINST A SEA-LEVEL CANAL BY ROOSEVELT, GOETHALS, AND TAFT; BUNAU-VARILLA'S ANSWER

In his congressional message of February 17, 1909, after receiving an engineering report submitted by President-elect Taft, and after he visited the Isthmus, President Roosevelt stated: "In fact, this report not only determines definitely the type of canal but makes it evident that hereafter attack on this type—the lock type—is merely attack upon the policy of building any canal at all. … I am happy to report to you that the accompanying document shows…that it would be an inexcusable folly to change from the proposed canal to a sea-level canal."

---

[32] 1912, Bunau-Varilla, Panama: The Creation, Destruction, And Resurrection, pp. 488 -490.

In a lecture he made at Chicago in March 1909, and contrary to his statement he made in 1907 regarding the Sosa Dam, Goethals stated, "The charge that the dam (at Laboca) could not be constructed is not true." Regarding the idea of a sea-level canal, Goethals stated, "There is no data for such a canal. With mountains instead of hills to be removed, estimates are of course impossible." Goethals referred to the sea-level canal as "a precise and well-defined scheme of a cut 500 feet wide at the bottom to be carried out by a powerful and well-experimented process—as a thing impossible even to conceive—as a thing belonging exclusively to the domain of the Ideal." He also dismissed the ability of the use of the rock-breaking machine in Panama. Finally, Goethals suggested that the supporters of the sea-level canal did not take into consideration how they would divert or control the Chagres River.

Bunau-Varilla reminded his readers that Goethals himself was building the "canal with an overall 300-foot-wide bottom, and a 500-foot-wide bottom from "the foot of the locks to the sea." In addition, the Consulting Board minority specifically approved of the dimensions suggested by Bunau-Varilla when constructing the sea-level portions of the Canal. Bunau-Varilla answered the issue of the Chagres current in a more scientific method than the simple estimates he had previously provided.

He "discovered and formulated the general mathematical laws governing the maximum velocity of currents at any point or any hour in any canal of any width or length, connecting a sea without tides with a sea having tides out of the same mean level." On May 3, 1909, Mr. Paul Painleve, an esteemed mathematician of his day, sanctioned and presented these laws to the Academy of Sciences. In addition, on June 27, 1909, Mr. Painleve presented a second law dealing with a new hydraulics law, also devised by Bunau-Varilla. "These laws made it possible to calculate the highest tides of the Pacific Ocean, and the greatest floods of the Chagres." Bunau-Varilla was then able to answer Goethals definitively: "The mouth of the Chagres is transferred from the shores of the Atlantic ocean to the place where it enters the Straits of Panama." [33]

President Taft's May 1909 published statements to the McClure's Magazine members was in answer to the one Bunau-Varilla made to the members of the Outlook Magazine that same month. Taft's article was less problematic than the speech given by Goethals, because Goethals was considered an accomplished engineer, while President Taft's article was replete with several glaring, factual errors, errors that Bunau-Varilla was quick to point out. Taft wrote: "The dam

---

[33] Ibid, pp. 491-493.

projected is a masonry dam…with a level of the water 170 feet against the dam and above the bedrock of the stream. It would be the highest known dam in the world." Bunau-Varilla stated: "Mr. President—A dam retaining water 170 feet above the foundation is not the highest dam in the world. At the new Croton Dam, erected for the waterworks in New York, the water level is 300 feet above the foundation. The first theoretically calculated masonry dam, the Furens Dam, near St. Etienne, France, retains the water 164 feet above the foundation. It was built half a century ago."

Taft wrote: "Another difficulty about the sea-level canal, but one rarely referred to, is the obstacle to its construction in the Black Swamp between Gatun and Bohio, this would probably necessitate retaining walls or the draining of the swamp with such an extended area as to make the task a huge one." Bunau-Varilla answered by stating: "Mr. President—The Black Swamp is not on the Canal line, it is on the railroad line, which is some miles away on the east side and widely separated from the canal by hills."

Taft again wrote: "The criticism of gentlemen…who institute comparisons between the present type of canal and the sea-level type of 300 to 600ft. in width, that never has been or will be on sea or land, cannot disturb the even tenor of those charged with the responsibility of constructing the canal." Bunau-Varilla answered by stating: "Mr. President—After I proposed to the Consulting Board the 'Straits of Panama,' 500 ft. wide at the bottom, the minority of the board adopted for the sea-level sections of its plan a width of 500 ft. at the bottom. … Such a channel, which you have been told never will exist on sea or land, will, therefore, exist at Panama from the foot of the locks to the end of the excavation… say seven miles on the Atlantic side and eight miles on the Pacific side." About fifteen miles out of the fifty miles projected for the Canal.

Bunau-Varilla was convinced that President Taft was discussing a topic he knew nothing about. What Bunau-Varilla failed to realize was that most presidents discuss subjects they know nothing about. They rely on the advice of others, about subjects these advisers may know nothing about.

In contrast, Bunau-Varilla did not just formulate a theory to support his position. Bunau-Varilla created new scientific laws to prove that his position was correct. He had his laws tested by Mr. Paul Painleve, an esteemed mathematician of his day, who sanctioned and presented these laws to the Academy of Sciences. In addition, on June 27, 1909, Mr. Painleve presented a second law dealing with a new hydraulics law, also devised by Bunau-Varilla. "These laws made it possible to calculate the highest tides of the Pacific Ocean, and the greatest floods of the Chagres."

MORE PROBLEMS AND ODD DECISIONS MADE BY GOETHALS

Goethals was in fact an administrator, quick to put off his engineering problems on his subordinates, or committees. Even so, on more than a few instances, his committees or boards advised against Goethals's recommendations. The few independent decisions he did make, invariably led to further engineering problems, or were political in nature. For example, Goethals stated that "I do not impose the employment of any man on any division engineer."[34] In short, he holds his engineers accountable for the work, and he does not interfere. However, at a hearing held on November 17, 1909, in response to a congressional suggestion that he was a "young Czar…and everything had to go his way in the canal." Goethals stated: "I can issue instructions with a view to bringing about results, but I am not in a position to take hold of the details and attend to their execution so as to secure results." [35]

Early in this writing, I mentioned that Goethals did not get along with either Gorgas or Sibert. His issues with Sibert appeared to reflect Goethals lack of engineering skills, or decisions. For example, after the work stoppage at the Sosa Dam, Goethals appointed a board to recommend a final location of the Pacific locks. Goethals had gone ahead with the construction of the dams at Sosa, despite the warnings made by Bunau-Varilla, and the recommendation made by Sibert, and only stopped work when a trestle toppled over, and the fill sank eight feet. The next morning, the tracks sank six feet after a train passed over them at the same location.

Both Stevens, William Gerig, and Sibert recommended a double lift at Miraflores, and a single lift at Pedro Miguel. Goethals wanted a combined lock at Miraflores but discovered it would take a prohibitively large concrete foundation fill. Sibert was not against combining the Pacific locks, and in fact submitted a formal plan to do so.[36] His intention was to obtain an anchorage above the locks, at "what is now Miraflores Lake" so that ships entering or leaving the Culebra Cut at Pedro Miguel could anchor safely. If adopted, Sibert's plan would have improved the operation of the Canal considerably. Goethals assigned Colonel Hodges to review Sibert's plan. Hodges was opposed to the idea, and stated he was in favor of a "division of lifts" for safety reasons. [37] In the end, Goethals agreed

---

[34] Goethals' Statement, January 7, 1909 (Hearings No. 12, p. 140) (U.S.)
[35] Goethals' Statement, November 18, 1912 (Hearings No. 4, pp. 69-70) (U.S.)
[36] W.L. Sibert to D.D. Gaillard, January 31, 1908 (P.C. Rec. Bur., File 9-A-11)
[37] Hodges to Goethals, November 17, 1908 (P.C. Rec. Bur., 9-D-17) (MS)

with Hodges, and he finally recommended the single-lift Pedro Miguel and double-lift Miraflores locks.

The issue took on new life when the Congress became aware of Sibert's plan and held hearings on the matter. Goethals submitted the issue to a board, which recommended in favor of Sibert's plan, and the combination of the Pacific locks, similar to the Atlantic locks. Goethals argued that this change would cause a "delay" in the "opening of the canal" and that the recommendation of the "board" could not be adopted "when it was proposed."[38]

Goethals made sure that the Congress knew, first, that the idea of a separation and relocation of locks was first proposed by Stevens, and second, that the report was submitted to President Roosevelt before he had made his decision on the matter. This was obviously Goethals way of insulating himself from any criticism on the matter. These two issues, a Pacific anchorage, and a single Pacific lockage, by all accounts today, unrealized major improvements in the "design of the Canal" could have been adopted by Goethals but were rejected for political reasons. It would have "delayed the opening of the Canal." There are plenty of historians that would forgive Goethals for not accepting his own board's recommendations, but to ignore the recommendations of Bunau-Varilla, the board, Sibert, and even Stevens on such a serious matter, exposes Goethals as incompetent at best, and a political hack at worse.

After work began on the Pedro Miguel locks, the Gatun locks, and the Gatun Dam in 1909, and the Miraflores locks in 1910, Goethals appointed another board to determine his preference to have the Pacific division ship sand to the Atlantic division. Goethals submitted that sand from the Atlantic side costs $1.25 per cubic yard. Sand from the Pacific costs less. Sibert was against such a decision. The board appointed by Goethals recommended in favor of Sibert. At the hearing of November 18, 1909, Goethals simply stated: they wanted to retain "everything under their own control."[39] At a later hearing in 1912, Goethals stated it was a mistake not to have followed his recommendation. At the same hearing, Sibert argued against that recommendation. "In fact, it would have been impossible for the Panama Railroad to haul the sand and rock for the Atlantic locks and Gatun spillway from the Pacific end of the Canal." [40]

Before the Canal could be opened, the Panama Canal Railroad tracks had to be relocated. The general manager of the Railroad, H.J. Slifer, presented Goethals

---

[38] Goethals to J.R. Freeman, June 18, 1909 (ibid), Sibert and Stevens, Construction of the Panama Canal, pp. 139-144.

[39] Goethals' Statement, November 17, 1909 (hearings No. 2, pp. 8-9) (U.S.)

[40] 1947, Miles P. DuVal, Jr., And the Mountains will Move, p. 300.

with three alternatives. The engineers wanted the best location for the railroad line, with a plan to run the line through the Culebra Cut on the East berm. Slifer recommended one plan to run from Frijoles directly to Mount Hope, with a spur running to Gatun. The third plan, one Slifer thought was purely "sentimental," ran directly from Gatun.[41] Without explaining himself, Goethals chose the Gatun route as the "final location of the railroad line."[42]

THE COMPLETION OF THE CANAL

As the completion of the Canal became imminent, three major problems surfaced.

The first problem was the transition from a construction workforce to an operating workforce, and the agency that would be in control of the Canal. The second problem was the Canal tolls issue, and the Panama Canal Railroad issue. The third was the safe transit of ships through the Canal. In 1911, Goethals brought his ideas to the attention of the Congress.

His initial thoughts were that there should be a single head of the Canal, an army engineer. Confident that he would be chosen for the job, he insisted that his assistant be an army engineer. Goethals again brought up the wage base of the employees that would be operating the Canal. He suggested that they should receive no better financial treatment than employees in Puerto Rico, or the Philippines, who received 25% higher wages than employees in the United States doing the same job. He further suggested that the operating force be selected by seniority, and that they pay for their housing, and lighting "to make the employees realize that they were not getting something for nothing." [43]

At the October hearing, Goethals suggested the organization of the Canal should be divided into five departments: the operating department, the engineering department, the quartermaster department, the electrical and mechanical department, and the accounting department.

In the December 17, 1911, hearing, Goethals suggested that the town of Balboa be located on the dump near La Boca, and the town of Cristobal be designated as the Atlantic terminal city.

Several committee members objected to this suggestion and argued that his suggestion making civilian cities at the terminals would defeat the military pur-

---

[41] H. J. Slifer to Goethals, July 9, 1908 (P.C. Rec. Bur., File 45 G-7) (MS)

[42] Goethals to H. J. Slifer, July 20, 1908 (P.C. Rec. Bur., File 45 G-7(MS)

[43] Goethals Statement, October 26, 1911 (Hearing No. 20, p.11) (U.S.)

pose of the Canal. [44]

Goethals reply was forceful, lengthy, and to the point: "The construction of the canal is not a military proposition; it is a civil and commercial proposition. The fact that I am in the Army does not alter that situation at all. I look upon the operation and maintenance of the canal as a distinctly civil and commercial function, and that the reason for our being here is for the operation and maintenance of the canal, and after its construction this should be a civil function. But we should create such an entity here that in time of war the military necessities of the situation would predominate, and the operation and maintenance of the canal will be subordinate to those military features." During his testimony, Goethals again emphasized that the wage base of the operating employees should be reduced. He advocated cutting from the "top down," starting with his own salary.

At the same hearing, but given on December 22, 1911, regarding the tolls issue, Goethals stated that he was aware that a board had been appointed, and he was against appointment of a board, and recommended that Professor Emory R. Johnson, "the eminent student of canal tolls," make the study. Goethals stated: "In the Army a board is considered as long, narrow, and wooden, and that has been my experience with boards as a rule." [45] This was a strange statement for Goethals to make, considering his whole history as chief engineer of the Canal was not making a major decision regarding the construction of the Canal without first appointing a board or committee to advise him on alternative decisions regarding the matter. Perhaps it was because those boards or committees frequently advised against his suggestions.

Goethals ended his testimony by requesting that a law be passed providing for the "permanent organization and government of the Canal Zone." During the construction phase, the Canal was governed by the Spooner Act of 1902, and various presidential orders, and Goethals indicated, when that phase is terminated, there would be no law to govern the operation of the Canal, unless the Congress acted beforehand. Goethals wanted an army engineer to be the head of the Canal, appointed by the president, and naval officers to run the Canal.

At the March hearing the following year, Goethals again urged quick action by the Congress on his request for a law governing the operation of the Canal, and a decision on the tolls. The Panama Canal Act was passed in the summer of 1912, and finally approved on August 24, 1912. Most of what Goethals requested was included in the act.

---

[44] Goethals Statement, December 19, 1911 (Hearing No. 15, I, 215) (U.S.)
[45] Goethals Statement, December 22, 1911 Hearings No. 15, I, 410) (U.S.)

THE TOLLS ISSUE WAS A CONGRESSIONAL AND INTERNATIONAL PROBLEM

When presenting this problem, I have followed closely the history presented by Bunau-Varilla, if for no other reason than he has supported his statements with ample citations from the congressional record.

The issue of the tolls has little to do with the cost of a ship passing through the Canal. The Canal hired personnel called "ad-measurers," employees that measure the interior space of every type of ship passing through the Canal. A record is kept of that ship, and when it passes through the Canal again, it is charged the same price based on the type of ship, and cargo that ship carries.

The tolls problem was an international argument between the Congress and primarily the European powers over the issue of the neutrality of the Canal. You would think that because the United States built the Canal, we should have the right to charge or not charge ships passing through the Canal. Well, you would be wrong.

The whole reason that the United States was able to build the Canal was because the United States was able to remove the Clayton–Bulwer Treaty, signed in 1850. This treaty blocked the ability of the United States to independently build any canal on the Isthmus, without the agreement or participation of the British. This treaty remained in place for fifty years. In its place, the British and the United States signed the Hay–Pauncefote Treaty, on November 18, 1901.

The Hay–Bunau-Varilla Treaty was signed on November 18, 1903, giving the United States the right to build a canal in Panama. The Hay–Bunau-Varilla Treaty included an article of neutrality, declaring that the Canal be open, based upon the terms and condition provided by Section 1 of Article 3 of the treaty entered by the United States and Britain "on November 18, 1901" (the Hay–Pauncefote Treaty).

Interestingly, both treaties were linked to the principles of the Convention of Constantinople, signed on October 29, 1888, regarding the Suez Canal. This treaty, in Article 1 and Article 12, clearly mandates that no signatories be given any more commercial advantage or privilege than any other country, and that the Canal will be open to all countries in peace and in war "without any distinction as to the flag."

The Congress of the United States demanded, early on, that the warships of the United States would have priority in time of war. But they also wanted to exempt United States coastwise shipping from toll payments, or have the right to subsidize that shipping.

THE HISTORY OF THE TOLLS PROBLEM

In December 1908, Rear Admiral Robley, U.S.N. retired, in Hampton's Magazine, proposed the free passage of American coastwise ships through the Panama Canal. He acknowledged the restriction posed by the Hay–Pauncefote Treaty to his suggestion. His solution was: "It annoys us. Well! Let us change it."

On December 7, 1910, the senator from Maine, Frye, proposed a bill ordering the reimbursement by the treasury for toll payments for all American flagships. On November 15, 1911, Mr. Stimson, the secretary of war, declared that the United States had an "absolute right in spite of the Hay–Pauncefote Treaty, to reimburse the tolls paid by American ships." He argued the reimbursement was the same as a subsidy, and it was the right of any nation to subsidize its own shipping. In his message to Congress, On December 21, 1911, President Taft declared, "We own the Canal. It was our money that built it." On February 2, 1912, press releases indicated that the New York Chamber of Commerce voted to oppose the subsidizing of tolls as long as the Hay–Pauncefote Treaty was not abrogated.

Bunau-Varilla, who had an interest in the matter, wrote to the New York Herald, and explained that abrogating the Hay–Pauncefote Treaty would not solve the problem, "because it was a condition of the charter of the Canal."

On February 12, 1912, the secretary of war, declared that the government no longer exempted coastwise shipping from the tolls, nor would they reimburse or subsidize coastwise shipping if they paid the tolls. On the 9th of March 1912, a bill was approved by the committee of the House that provided no special favors to any American ships, except that it provided for an exemption from tolls for United States and Panamanian owned ships. On 23, May 1912, the House adopted the "Doremus" amendment that gave free passage to American coastwise shipping. It also authorized the president the right to extend this exemption to any other American ships, provided it did not violate the Hay–Pauncefote Treaty. In early June 1912, the House passed a bill exempting American coastwise shipping from the tolls.

On July 10, 1912, the British chargé d'affaires, Mr. Innis, objected to the House vote, and requested that the State Department intervene in any Senate vote, and hold the matter in abeyance until he received the formal protest papers from his government.

On August 9, 1912, the Senate voted to exempt American coastwise shipping, and exempted any American ship if it could be used in time of war by the United States.

Both Bills went to a conference committee. The conference committee retained the exemption of coastwise shipping but removed the exemption of American shipping in time of war.

On August 16, 1912, Bunau-Varilla, in an interview published by the London Daily Express, suggested that the matter should be presented to the United States Supreme Court for adjudication. On August 19, 1912, President Taft recommended that the Congress reconsider the bill voted out by the conference committee, and he also suggested that the bill should be reviewed by the Supreme Court.

On August 21, 1912, the Senate committee on interoceanic canals rejected the president's suggestion. The committee of the house did not even take the issue up for consideration. Although embarrassed by the congressional snub, Taft signed the bill on August 24, 1912.

Protests were made in England and the United States. On August 29, 1912, the Tribune reported that the president would refuse to submit the law to arbitration. The Panama Canal Act was set in stone. Or was it?

Bunau-Varilla, true to form, submitted three letters to the Shipping World, reproduced by the New York Sun, outlining the issue in detail, and declaring that the Panama Canal Act violated the spirit and letter of the Hay–Pauncefote Treaty and the Hay–Bunau-Varilla Treaty. The first letter was written in Paris on August 24, 1912 and published on August 28, 1912. The second letter was written on August 31, 1912, in Paris, and published on September 4, 1912. The third letter was written on September 7, 1912, and published on September 11, 1912. In addition, Bunau-Varilla sent a letter written on September 10, 1912, in Paris, to the publisher of the New York Sun, which was published on September 19, 1912, that also went into detail and was entitled "The Trustee of Humanity." This fourth letter was in response to the Sun editor's comment that "if the United States had received a trusteeship to build the canal, the proceeds thus far had been nothing but debts."

Anyone reading the arguments made by Bunau-Varilla cannot but agree with his position. However, Bunau-Varilla's arguments were in direct conflict with "real politic." "Real politic" won the day. [46]

---

[46] 1912, Bunau-Varilla, Panama: The Creation, Destruction, And Resurrection, pp.505-524.

THE FIGHT OVER THE CONTROL OF THE CANAL OPERATION

By 1913, control of the Canal became a major issue, between the army and the navy, at the highest levels, and even the Department of the Treasury becoming involved.

Contrary to what he had told the Congress in 1911, Goethals appointed a committee, headed by Gaillard, and containing Sibert, Gorgas, and Thatcher, for the purpose of forming a permanent organization for the Panama Canal. The committee worked on the problem from May through August. When Gaillard became sick, Colonel Sibert took over until Colonel Hodges was made permanent chairman. [47] Goethals expected that he would get competition from other agencies of the federal government, and he wanted to be able to respond to any objections they may have. He was right.

On April 18, 1913, the president of the general board considered the Panama Canal as a "great naval asset," and thought the operation of the Canal should be under the control of naval officers always.

"Active management and control of the finished canal belongs to the naval branch of the government." [48]

The new secretary of war, Lindley M. Garrison, became interested in the issue, and visited the Canal in October of 1913. Goethals convinced Garrison that President Wilson should appoint him as governor, and establish a permanent organization, as soon as possible. Garrison consulted Judge Frank Feuille and asked him to "draw up a memorandum giving reasons why Goethals should be appointed governor.

The secretary endorsed the memorandum and sent it to the president. When Garrison returned to Washington, he sent a cable to Goethals, inquiring if he would remain at his post for two years. Goethals answered that he would remain "as long as the President ordered him to stay."[49] A proposed executive order for the president's signature was drafted, and organizational diagrams were written and sent to the secretary of war on November 14, 1913.

Included was a detailed explanation of the proposed canal organization, emphasizing that the governor should be an army engineer and "put in charge of maintenance, naval officers as port captains, army doctors as chief health officers,

---

[47] Goethals to Hodges, August 26, 1913 (P.C. Rec. Bur., File 2-C-124) (MS)
[48] President of General Board to Secretary of the Navy, April 18,1913 (P.C. Rec. Bur., File 2-C-124) (M.S.)
[49] 1947, Miles P. DuVal, Jr., And the Mountains will Move, pp. 324-325.

and public health service officers as chief quarantine officers." [50]

On November 9, Goethals received a letter from General Leonard Wood, chief of staff of the army, informing him that the navy was about to submit a plan to take control of the Canal.

In the letter, Wood assured Goethals that the plan would not prevail. [51] When the joint army and navy board met on October 9, 1913, Admiral Dewy asked that Colonel Goethals determine the "proper measure" of naval control on the Canal. At the request of the Joint Board, General Wood, in his letter, informed Goethals of their discussions, and suggested that the navy wanted the Canal in "their hands."

TROUBLE WITHIN THE CANAL COMMISSION

While Goethals's commission was conducting their work, Thatcher resigned, and he was replaced by Richard Lee Metcalfe, the editor of the Commoner, which was founded by Secretary of State Bryan. [52]

Before Metcalfe was due to replace Thatcher, he submitted a plan to the secretary of war, suggesting a permanent organization of a three-man commission, composed of a chief engineer in charge of operations, a governor, and a chief sanitary officer, holding monthly meetings under the chairmanship of the chief engineer. He also suggested separating the railroad from the Canal, and that the commissaries should be under private control.[53] In short, Metcalfe's plan was all that Goethals, Wallace, and Stevens had been working against, and not much different than the organization under Shonts.

Three questions should be asked about the Metcalfe appointment to the Canal Committee, charged with forming a permanent organization for the Panama Canal.

The first question is, how is it possible that a newspaper editor from Lincoln, Nebraska, got an appointment to a committee primarily composed of engineers? The second question is how is it possible that a man, not yet a member of the committee, could have sufficient confidence to think that his opinion would be seriously considered? The third question is why would anyone seriously listen to a man that gives advice on a subject when he has not yet been appointed to

---

[50] Goethals to Garrison, November 14, 1913 (P.C. Rec. Bur., File 2-C-124) (MS)
[51] Wood to Goethals, October 9, 1913 (P.C. Rec. Bur., File 2-C-124) (MS)
[52] 1947, Miles P. DuVal, Jr., And the Mountains will Move, p. 324.
[53] R. L Metcalfe to Goethals, October 1, 1913, (P.C. Rec. Bur., File 2-C-124) (MS)

study that subject? The other committee members, Sibert, Gorgas, Hodges, and Gaillard, and even Thatcher, the man Metcalfe was to replace, had spent months working on the issue. They were given the benefit of Canal organizational history, and other government organizational structures, for the sole purpose of giving the right advice regarding the matter. The answer to all three of these questions, of course, was that Metcalfe was the first Wilson administration appointment to the Canal, a political appointment, handpicked by Secretary of State Bryan.

Despite the Panama Canal Act of 1912, Secretary of War Garrison not only accepted Metcalfe's advice, but he embarked on an effort to retain Metcalfe after the commission was abolished but was legally blocked from doing so by the advice given to him by Judge Feuille. Why would Garrison do this? Perhaps he did it as a political favor for Secretary Byron. He certainly did it at the request of President Wilson. Why else would Garrison apologize to the president for failing to accomplish the retention of the commission, for "sentimental reasons," after the proposed opening of the Canal in 1915? [54]

THE SECRETARY OF THE TREASURY WANTED A PIECE OF THE PIE

In October 1913, Secretary of the Treasury W.G. McAdoo wrote the president, suggesting that control of the toll collection should be given to his department. [55]

The secretary of war, in favor of Metcalfe's plan, requested a legal opinion from the head of the Department of Law in Ancon, Judge Frank Feuille.[56] Garrison wanted to hold the commissioner over, with positions in the permanent organization, until the formal opening of the Canal in 1915, so that they could participate in the celebration. Judge Feuille answered that the president was not authorized to operate the Canal until the commission was abolished. [57]

On December 4, 1913, the secretary of war submitted Goethals's plan with its proposed executive order to the president, requesting quick action. [58]

Finally, on January 27, 1914, President Wilson signed the executive order proposed by Goethals, with little or no changes, to be effective April 1, 1914. Wilson nominated Goethals as the first governor of the Panama Canal. In addition,

---

[54] Garrison to President Wilson, Dec. 4, 1913(P.C. Rec. Bur., File 2-C-124) (MS)
[55] McAdoo to President, October 17, 1913 (P.C. Rec. Bur., File 2-C-124) (MS)
[56] L. M. Garrison to Frank Feuille, Nov. 1, 1913 (P.C. Rec. Bur., File 2-C- 124) (MS)
[57] Feuille to Garrison, Nov. 11, 1913 (P.C. Rec. Bur., File 2-C-124) (MS)
[58] Garrison to President, Dec. 4, 1913 (ibid)

Wilson, added a memorandum directing that the "permanent operation" of the Canal be under the direction of the secretary of war, that "an army engineer be assigned as the maintenance engineer, naval line officers be assigned as marine superintendents, and port captains, naval constructors as superintendents of mechanical division, Public Health Service officers as chief quarantine officers, and army medical officers as chief health officers." [59]

The secretary of the navy, Josephus Daniels, was not at all happy with the duties assigned to the naval officers and cabled his objections to Captain Hugh Rodman. Rodman was assigned to the Canal as the marine superintendent and was on the Isthmus organizing the marine division. Daniels wanted the shops and dry docks under the operating division. Goethals wanted them placed under maintenance.[60]

Rodman passed on Daniels's objection to Goethals, who, as expected, assigned Colonel Hodges to make a recommendation on the matter. In the end, shops and dry docks were placed under a separate mechanical division, reporting directly to the governor. As Goethals finalized the permanent organization of the Canal, he recommended the appointment of Hodges as engineer of maintenance and left Sibert out in the cold with no assignment. So much for independent thinking.

GOETHALS'S PROMOTION

On March 4, 1914, the Senate confirmed Colonel Goethals's appointment as major general. For Goethals to pass over other colonels, and especially brigadier generals, the Senate had to pass a special law that was "forced" through the Congress "by pressure placed on the members." Goethals indicated that he was embarrassed by the way his promotion was engineered, but he accepted the promotion anyway.

He stated it deprived him of the "so-called reward of any sweetness or gratification." [61]

---

[59] Wilson's Memorandum, Jan. 27, 1914 (ibid)
[60] Cable from Daniels to Rodman, Feb. 2, 1914 (ibid)
[61] Cable from Daniels to Rodman, Feb. 2, 1914 (ibid)

THE SAFE LOCKAGE THROUGH THE CANAL

Even as the construction of the Canal was complete, Goethals showed his engineering incompetence. This time, instead of arguing with Sibert, Goethals went head to head with Captain Rodman. It was Goethals's position that ships entering the Canal would first tie up to the approach wall. The lock personnel would then take charge of passing the ship through the lock, a man on the bridge, and another in the engine room, with cables from towing locomotives attached to the ship, and the ship slowly towed through the lock, without the use of the ship engine.

Captain Rodman, who arrived on the Isthmus in early 1913, suggested several minor safety issues, but most importantly, insisted that control of the vessel should "absolutely be in the hands of the Canal pilots," with the ship's master on the bridge "ready to give advice." Rodman objected to the use of towing locomotives as the independent power when moving vessels into the locks, and instead suggested using locomotives as moving Capstans while the ship is in the locks. He wanted to have the ship enter the lock under its own power. He also recommended installing "ranges at center lines of narrow reaches," the rounding off the "ends of the approach walls," and that vessels should "sound whistles before sharp turns in the canal."

Rodman's objection to the towing locomotive could not have been welcome to the inventor of the towing locomotive, Edward Schildhauer, one of the Canal engineers.

During the beginning lockages, composed of small vessels, Rodman's objections were ignored, and the procedure outlined by Goethals in 1911 was generally followed. In May 1914, the authorization of the lockages was turned over to the marine division. On May 18, 1914, Rodman was even more opposed to using locks personnel from controlling ships passing through the locks, and considered the practice by these personnel "neither legally nor professionally qualified." He also considered the practice would lead to "delay, confusion and danger."

He suggested the towing locomotives be used as "traveling capstans" rather than towing locomotives, and that the vessel "not stop at the approach walls, and instead keep moving while entering the lock chamber."

Goethals referred Rodman's objections to a three-man board of engineers. Hodges answered Rodman's objections by stating that more lock accidents occurred when using the ships' engines and advised the continued use of tying ships up to the approach wall before entering the locks.

Rodman followed up his letter of May 18, 1914, with another stronger letter, indicating he wanted the lockage operation under one person to avoid "delays and misunderstandings." He objected to "continually consult, request, or require," and he suggested that navigation in the locks should be placed under the marine superintendent.

Goethals wrote Rodman, noting the reason for caution, and stated that the "plan proposed and adopted by Congress" would be carried out unless actual practice should show another to be preferable.

It is true that Congress adopted Goethals plan, but it was not true that Congress proposed that plan, and it is absurd to imply that they did. True or false, Goethals knew he was on solid ground, and dogmatically refused to accept the advice of Rodman, who obviously knew more about the intricacies of ship movements in close quarters than Goethals or his engineering board, would ever know.

On August 3, 1914, the first large ship to pass through the Canal, the Cristobal, a Panama Railroad ship, was a practice run. Goethals wanted to be sure there would be no problems at the expected formal opening of the Canal. He invited several employees and engineers that were long-time associates with the Canal. Bunau-Varilla "was standing on the boat deck" while the Cristóbal passed through the Canal. August 3, 1914, was also the date of a banner headline announcing the war between Germany and France. Bunau-Varilla stated, after reading the headlines: "Gentlemen, the two great and consuming ambitions of my life are realized on the same day: the first, to sail through the Panama Canal on the first ocean liner; the second, to see France at war with Germany."

In addition to his detailed history of his activities related to the Canal, Bunau-Varilla also wrote an analysis of what Germany did to interfere in the Hay–Herran Treaty.

After being released from the lock wall, at Gatun, and under the control of the lock personnel, the Cristobal was caught in turbulence caused by the mixing of salt water and fresh water from the lake. The result was that one of the towing locomotives burned out an engine. When the Cristobal reached the Pedro Miguel locks, Goethals was standing on the lock wall when a cable parted from one of the locomotives, and he was afraid that the ship would strike the gates before it could be stopped. There was no problem when the ship entered the Miraflores locks.

Goethals realized that he had made a major mistake, and immediately ordered that pilots "take charge of towing and handling ships" in the locks. Captain Rodman directed that pilots should not tie up to the lock approach wall, that they not leave the vessel until they cleared the locks, and he also directed that he wanted vessels to pass through the locks without "touching any of the walls." This is the same problem that may occur when the third locks are completed.

AUGUST 15, 1914, FORMAL OPENING OF THE CANAL

The first large ship to transit the Canal at the formal opening was the Panama Railroad ship Ancon. Of note, the dredging at the Cucaracha slide continued from the time it closed the Canal. As the Ancon passed the Gaillard Cut, the channel was 150 feet wide, and 35 feet deep. Slides continued at the cut long after the Canal opened. From beginning to end, the construction of the Canal was not done based upon marine engineering experience. If there was a fault made in its construction, it was because the Canal was built by railroad and army engineers that rejected modern concepts of marine engineering. Because of this fault, the Canal was considered obsolete even before it was completed.

THE ACQUISITION SUMMARY

The origin of the corruption, crony capitalism, and incompetence related to the Panama Canal didn't begin with the Roosevelt Administration. In fact, it began, at least, in the early 1860s. Let me explain, before you accuse me of absurdity.

In 1860, the Republican Party was in total control of the Congress, and Abraham Lincoln was president. The Congress decided that there was a need for the "Transcontinental Railroad," if for no other reason than to help win the Civil War.

The Congress decided, for the first time that I am aware of, to create a public–private partnership to construct that railroad. To do so, they opened the Treasury of the United States, by subsidizing the railroad companies that participated in that endeavor. In addition, the Congress left to the president the power to select which company would benefit the most from this joint venture.

President Lincoln, a railroad lawyer, and a previous associate with the Durant syndicate and railroad company, and having represented them on several occasions, decided to select Mr. Durant's railroad for this project. Crony capitalism was not first born with Lincoln's action, but it was flagrantly expressed. Durant immediately set about devising every corrupt scheme he could imagine to squeeze money from the United States Treasury. When the corruption became publicly known, Lincoln enlisted another of his political friends, Oaks Ames, to correct the problem. Instead of helping Lincoln, his friend Oaks Ames took it upon himself to take over the Durant business model and run the scam himself.

Eventually, Oaks Ames was forced to resign from the Congress because of his misdeeds. The Transcontinental Railroad scandal was considered the greatest scandal of its time. It was one of several issues that almost cost President Johnson his presidency. Johnson succeeded Lincoln after his death.

In December 1865, Andrew Johnson introduced his "Reconstruction Plan," which restored the southern property rights. Many in the North vehemently objected to his leniency.

On December 6, 1865, the Congress passed the 13th Amendment, abolishing slavery. In April, the Congress passed the Civil Rights Act of 1866. On July 9, the Congress passed the 14th Amendment, denying the States the right to deprive life, liberty, or property without due process. On February 24, 1868, Andrew Johnson was impeached. On April 13, 1868, the trial began. The Senate failed to impeach Johnson by two votes. Johnson finished his term, and was forgotten.

While this scandal was smoldering, in 1869, the United States signed a treaty with Colombia, giving the United States the sole right to build a canal in Colombia. President Johnson submitted the treaty to the Senate. Because of the scandal, and the other issues I described, the Senate failed to ratify the treaty.

The consequences of this scandal was more far-reaching than the impeachment of a president, or than the failure of this treaty. It resulted in the repudiation of the Republican Party. The railroads and financial institutions were coming under increased pressure.

Many of these railroads, and the banks that financed them, were going bankrupt. In came Cromwell. In 1890, Cromwell was just coming into his own. In 1893, he invented the "holding company" and convinced the New Jersey Legislature to incorporate the holding company bylaws into their own corporate laws. The holding company could set up any number of subordinate companies, some without assets, without the parent company being accountable for their actions, and in turn, by law, hide the assets and actions of the parent company.

Cromwell teamed up with J.P. Morgan and used the Oregon & Transcontinental Railroad as a vehicle to consolidate control of the Northern Pacific Company. Based upon their historic relationship, no doubt J.P. Morgan was the senior partner, although that term was never used by J.P. Morgan. He held the paper to all of these transactions.

In 1893, a devastating financial depression occurred during the second Cleveland presidency, primarily because of the railroad companies' overbuilding and financial failures. J.P. Morgan, and the Rothschild syndicate became partners with the United States government. They provided the United States Treasury with 3.5 million ounces of gold for a thirty-year bond issue.

In one stroke, Cleveland, who was considered "an honest Democrat," had set up a public–private enterprise, and had engaged in crony capitalism at the same time. Cleveland obviously made this deal to shorten the depression, but the public outcry turned it into a major scandal. To add fuel to the fire, the French Canal scandal was getting public notice. It was disclosed that ex-Navy Secretary Thompson was paid $25,000 dollars just to promote and act as chairman of a committee supporting the de Lesseps canal.

Thompson resigned his position in order to take the job. De Lesseps also paid $1,200,000 dollars to the banking firms of J.M. Seligman, Drexel Morgan & Co., and Winslow Lanier in commissions solely for their public support within the United States.

In addition, the Panama Railroad Company, anxious to sell out to de Lesseps, was accused of colluding with the Pacific Mail Co. For the last fifteen years, they had been restricting commerce between New York and San Francisco. The same financial institutions who had been paid by de Lesseps for doing nothing bought up most of the Panama Railroad Company stock, pennies on the dollar, and eventually sold it back to the French Panama Canal Company at an enormous profit. Because of the competition from the Transcontinental Railroad, the Panama Railroad was close to bankruptcy.

All these public accusations and scandals caused these New York financial institutions to throw their support to McKinley and Roosevelt, and the rest is history.

When McKinley died, Roosevelt became president, but the cabinet officers surrounding McKinley remained in place when Roosevelt took office. Roosevelt, at forty-two, was the youngest president to take office. Much of his cabinet consisted of associates, or ex-employees of J.P. Morgan. The corruption that occurred between the time Roosevelt became president and when the Congress ratified the Hay–Bunau-Varilla Treaty was beyond compare.

The first and greatest mistake the United States made was to enter into treaty negotiations while being advised by the crony capitalists Cromwell and J.P. Morgan, who were also advising the officials of the other country, first Colombia, and later Panama.

Roosevelt's second mistake was to make significant decisions related to the Canal solely based upon his political future.

Roosevelt's third mistake was to surround himself with family, associates, and ex-employees of J.P. Morgan.

The fourth mistake Roosevelt made was to hire railroad and army engineers to build the Canal, when it was obvious that he should have hired a marine engineer that was familiar with modern hydraulic engineering techniques. It was only through the primarily obstinate actions of Stevens, and to some extent Wallace, and Goethals, that the Canal did not become a public–private enterprise like the Transcontinental Railroad.

However, not to let them off the hook, their opposition to Taft's desire to turn the Canal into his crony capitalist empire, with Cromwell as his advisor, was solely rooted in their desire to maintain total control of the Canal. The incompetence, and the cover-up that followed, admittedly, resulted in millions of wasted dollars, and time that could have been used to improve the efficiency of the Canal. Roosevelt, and later Taft, listened to and ignored the one person, Bunau-Varilla, which was uniquely qualified to give them proven engineering advice on the Canal. Wallace, Stevens, and especially Goethals approached their work in the Canal as good organizers, but lacking in experience, open-mindedness, and knowledge of modern hydraulic engineering techniques. Bunau-Varilla was endowed with all four of these qualifications, but his advice was never accepted.

CHAPTER FOURTEEN

THE AGREEMENT CONCEIVED IN 1904 WAS RATIFIED IN 1926

THE TRI-PARTITE AGREEMENT

AFTER FAILING TO CONVINCE the French, that the United States violated the 1848 treaty, and the 1878 concession, the government of Columbia decided to again appeal to the United States for reparations. General Rafael Reyes, left Paris, and replaced General Marroquin, as president of Columbia. Both men were conservative politicians, and effectively dictators of Columbia. The United States appointed Mr. Russell as minister to Columbia. The republican party controlled the United States government.

Initially, Columbia put forward a lengthy letter of protest from their minister of Foreign Relations, Mr. Luis Carlos Rico, dated April 12, 1904, to Mr. Alban G. Snyder, the minister of the United States in Columbia. The letter contained a detailed history of Columbia, the early canal issues, and the events leading up to the Panama revolution. His claim made was that the United States violated the treaty of 1848; the violation of the neutrality laws established by international right; and the law of concessions made between the Panama Canal Company and Columbia.[1]

In October 21, 1905, Mr. Diego Mendoza Perez, the minister of Columbia in Washington, sent a letter to Mr. Elihu Root, the United States secretary of State, a letter demanding Arbitration on the matters presented by Mr. Rico, in

---

[1] Committee on foreign affairs, House of Representatives, Feb. 9,12, 1912, entitled "the story of Panama". pp. 594-612.

1904. Both letters were dismissed by Secretary Root. In 1906 The United States sent Minister John Barrett to Columbia. President Reyes instructed his Minister Valencia, a delegate to the Rio conference, to ask for renegotiations with the United States, and discussions of mutual matters with Secretary Root. Realizing that Minister Mendoza was getting nowhere, Reyes announced an early appointment of Enrique Cortes, as Columbia's minister in Washington, with instructions to suggest a new treaty to replace the 1846 treaty, with the same privileges enjoyed by Panama. In turn, Columbia would recognize Panama, and Panama's assumption of a proportionate share of the national debt it accrued when it broke away from Columbia.

Minister Cortes negotiated these terms from 1906 until 1909. In February 1909, the United States signed the treaty. The United States sent Mr. Thomas Dawson to Columbia with the treaty. The Columbian Congress was to meet on February 22, 1909 to discuss and ratify the treaty. Not surprising, the Columbian Congress erupted in turmoil. Some delegates were opposed to the terms of the treaty. Some delegates were insulted by the offer of $2,500,000 dollars that the United States had offered as part of the treaty. Other delegates were intent on using the treaty to overthrow General Reyes' dictatorship.

Because of this turmoil the Columbian congress was dissolved, and a new congress was expected to convene on July 20, 1909. Before that could happen, a bloodless coup took place. In 1910, through a popular election, Carlos E. Restrepo, a conservative, became President of Columbia. He set about reorganizing the government and reintroduced the treaty. One of the terms of the Columbian acceptance of that treaty, was an apology from the United States.

In 1910, the Republican party was still in control of the United States government, and an apology, which is what the Columbian government wanted, was not going to happen. By 1911, Theodore Roosevelt, a true progressive, became disappointed with President William Taft, and split the Republican party. He gained support from a group of Ohio republicans, from Taft's home state. The 1912 primaries went for Taft. Undeterred, Roosevelt ran as a "progressive" and created the "Bull Moose" party. After an assassination attempt, Roosevelt was forced to remove himself from the campaign, and eventually lost the election. Taft, a single term President, lost to Wilson.

In 1913 the United States submitted the following proposals to Columbia: recognition of Panama; the granting of coaling stations in San Andres to the United States; and cede to the United States the option to build another canal along the Atrato route.

In return, the United States would pay Columbia $10,000,000 dollars, and grant Columbia special privileges related to the Panama Canal. In addition, the United States would agree to Arbitration, with the possibility of $49,000,000 dollars going to Columbia. The offer ended with a veiled threat that if Columbia did not agree to these proposals, the Atrato district could go the way of the Panama district. Of course, Columbia rejected these proposals. Columbia responded by insisting on an apology, and $50,000,000 dollars. The United States rejected the Columbian counter proposal.[2]

In 1914, the democrat, Woodrow Wilson, had no problem inserting an apology into the treaty proposals. He appointed William Jennings Bryan, as secretary of State. Bryan had been a recurrent Presidential nominee and was previously defeated by Taft in 1908. In addition to the apology, Bryan gave Columbia special privileges in the use of the Panama Canal and promised to pay Columbia $25,000,000 dollars. These special privileges would have been in violation of the 1903 Hay-Bunau-Varilla treaty, as well as the 1901 Hay-Pauncefote Treaty, and the principles of the 1888 Convention of Constantinople. Obviously, the Wilson was not concerned with previous commitments made by the United States.

Columbia quickly ratified the treaty. The United States House of Representatives also ratified the treaty. However, The United States Senate, sufficiently controlled by the Republicans, rejected it. The treaty was sent to the Committee on Foreign Affairs and buried. The Columbian Minister, Betancourt, and others tried to revitalize the treaty with little success. In 1915, Minister Betancourt threatened to withdraw Columbia from the Pan American Union, if the United States didn't act on the matter. On December 15, 1915 he was assured the United States would act soon.

In 1916, when the Committee on Foreign Affairs finally reported the treaty out, they reduced the payment to $15,000,000 dollars, and made the apology an expression of mutual regret. Columbia felt insulted again.

Between 1916 and 1919 Columbia discovered Oil. The rush was on to obtain oil drilling concessions from Columbia. However, Columbia made it clear that there would be no concessions given to American companies, until the treaty was resolved in favor of Columbia.

As Secretary of State, Bryan set about concluding the treaty, however, the 1st World War broke out, and the treaty was put on a back burner. The treaty was finally ratified on April 4, 1921. From 1903 until 1921, the United States, and

---

[2] E. Taylor Parks, The United States and Columbia, 1765-1934, Durham, N.C., 1935, pp.429,430,433, 435.

Columbia had no direct relations, unless it was connected to the Panama Canal question.[3]

The origin of this treaty can be traced back to the meeting Cromwell allegedly had with General Reyes, in 1904. It is safe to say, for Mr. Cromwell, and General Reyes, it was all about the money.

---

[3] J. F. Rippy, The Capitalists and Columbia (New York: Vanguard Press, 1931) pp.103-121: Louis Martin Sears, A History of American Foreign Relations, New York, 1927, p.566.

INDEX

THE QUEST

A

Accessary Transit Company 74
Admiral Ammen 97
Alexander Von Humboldt 53
Alonzo de Hojedo 35
Ambrose Thompson 94
American Atlantic Ship Canal Company 66, 73, 87
Anglo–American Convention 61
Aroostook War 61
Asa Whitney 88
Atrato River 24, 37, 218

B

Bartholomew Dias 31, 32
Bastidas 34
battle of Antietam 86
Bay of Fonseca 62, 67, 73
Benjamin Franklin 48
Bluefields Lagoon 44

C

Caledonia Bay 35, 45
Canas–Jerez Treaty 79, 80, 114
Casas 38
Castillo del Oro 35
Central Pacific 88, 90, 91
Chagres River 68, 69, 279, 292, 295, 327, 338
Chancellorate of Guatemala 42
Charles III of Spain 46
Chiriquí improvement Company 94
Christopher Columbus 27, 33
Civil War 63, 82, 85, 87, 88, 89, 90, 93, 94, 95, 114, 118, 119, 126, 353
Claudius Ptolemy 25
Clayton–Bulwer Treaty 73, 74, 75, 79, 96, 97, 106, 112, 113, 114, 117, 121, 122, 124, 126, 136, 270, 344

Colonel George W. Hughes 67
Colonel Macdonald 60, 62, 64
Colonel Totten 68, 69, 70
congressman Oakes Ames 92
Conti 31
Contreras 42
Cortez, the conqueror of Mexico 38
Credit Mobilier 91, 92
Cristoval Olid 38
Cushing Convention 97

D

Dallas–Clarendon Treaty 78, 79
Davila 35, 36, 37, 38, 42
de Lesseps 80, 101, 102, 103, 104, 105, 106, 107, 108, 109, 111, 124, 125, 179, 233, 263, 298, 323, 334, 355
Description of The World 28
Dickinson–Ayon Convention 97
Diego de Nicuesa 35
Don Antonio José Canaz 58
Dred Scott decision 84, 85
Dr. Geoffrey Chambers 24
Dr. John Hessler 26

E

Elijah Hise 66
Emancipation Proclamation 82, 86, 93, 94
English freebooters 43, 45
English woodcutters 44, 46
Ephraim G. Squier 66

F

French and Indian War 45, 46

G

Gabriel Novick 24
Gavin Menzies 24
General Filisola 54

361

General Stephen Hurlbut 97
George Washington 19, 46
Gorgona 69, 292
Grenville M. Dodge 89, 90
Greytown 67, 74, 75, 98, 115

H

Henry Chauncey 68
Henry of Portugal 31
Henry S. McComb 93
Herbert Hoxie 91
Hernandez de Cordova 37, 38
Holy Alliance 55

J

Jaun de Francisco Martin 68
Jaun Diaz de Solis 37
Jay Gould 93, 113
John L. Stevens 60, 68, 69
Juan de Grijalva 37

K

Kansas Pacific rail 91
Khubilai Khan 28
King Charles of Spain 37
Kingdom of New Granada 41
King Ferdinand 35
King Phillip II of Spain 43

L

Limon Bay 68, 69, 319

M

Magalhaens 34, 35
Mallarino–Bidlack Treaty 66, 67
Mandeville 31
Manuel Galisteo 46
Manzanillo Island 68, 69
Marco Polo 2, 28, 29, 31, 123
Mateo Klein 68
Mexican–American War 62, 65, 66
Millard Fillmore 73
Monroe 55, 56, 57, 58, 59, 61, 73, 76, 77, 79, 80, 81, 82, 103, 104, 106, 118, 122, 123
Monroe Doctrine 56, 57, 58, 59, 61, 73, 76, 77, 79, 80, 81, 82, 103, 104, 106, 118, 122, 123
Morazon 60
Moscoes Indians 44
Mosquera 95
Mosquitoland 44, 46, 60, 73
Mr. Dickinson 95

N

Napoleonic Wars 52
Nicaragua route to the East Indies 46
Nombre de Dios 35, 38

O

Oregon Territory 63, 64, 65, 87
Oregon Treaty 65

P

Panama Railroad Company 67, 68, 105, 132, 152, 162, 168, 183, 193, 194, 209, 231, 232, 233, 240, 244, 245, 246, 258, 264, 266, 268, 269, 281, 282, 355
Pascual de Andagoya 39
Patrick Walker 60
Pedro Arias de Avila 35
Perlas Islands 36
Peter Cabal 34
Pierce government 95
Pierre-Andre Garza 48
Polk administration 62, 63, 65, 66
President Adams 56, 58
President Buchanan 78, 79, 81, 82
President Grant 102
President Jackson 59
President Lincoln 83, 89, 92, 353
President Taylor 72, 73, 74
Projet de Paix Perpetuelle, par P.A.G 48

Q

Queen Elizabeth 43

R

Revolutionary War 47, 48, 50, 61
Robert Charles Frederick 60
Rush–Baget Treaty 51

Rustichello 28

S

San Juan River 33, 34, 38, 42, 44, 47, 61, 62, 66, 74, 81
Santa Anna 54
Secretary of State Clay 58
Secretary of State Seward 86
Seilor Cardenas 97
Senator Conness 97
Simon Bolivar 54, 59
slavery 54, 56, 57, 63, 73, 76, 83, 84, 85, 86, 93, 95, 354
Solicitor of the Treasury Jordan 94
Spanish king Phillip II 41
Suez Canal 80, 103, 104, 108, 109, 122, 127, 325, 326, 328, 344

T

Tehuantepec route 42
Texas–Mexican War of independence 63
The government of New Granada 95
Theodore Judah 88
Thomas C. Durant 89
Thomas Jefferson 49, 55
Tiger Island 67, 73
transcontinental railroad 87, 88
Trautwine 68

Treaty of Gent 51
Treaty of Guadalupe Hidalgo 63
Treaty of Madrid 53
Treaty of Paris 46, 61, 119
Treaty of Peace, Friendship, Commerce, and Navigation 66
Treaty of Tordesillas 34
Treaty of Versailles 47
Tulio Arends 24

U

Union Pacific 88, 89, 90, 91, 92, 93, 113, 117
United States of Colombia 95

V

Vasco Nunez de Balboa 35
Vespucci 34
Victoriano de Diego Paredes 69

W

Waldseemueller 34
War of 1812 50, 51, 52
West Indies 43, 44, 53, 80
Whigs 63, 66, 72, 83, 84
William Henry Aspinwall 68
William Paterson 45
William Walker 76, 77

THE ACQUISITION

A

Admiral Glass 180, 219
Admiral Walker 122, 136, 138, 143, 265, 276, 277, 278, 279, 281, 283
Algernon Sullivan 132
Americanization project 136
Anglo-Dutch contractors 107
Aristides Fernandez 151
Arthur Grudger, the United States consul general in Panama 160
assault on San Juan Hill 119
August Belmont 137

Auguste Larent Burdeau 125

B

banker, Kuhn 137
banking firms of J.M. Seligman, Drexel Morgan and Co., and Winslow Lanier 105
Baron de Reinach 124, 125
Bowling Green Trust Company 174, 177, 206, 228
BUNAU-VARILLA COMES TO TOWN, AND THE REVOLUTION IS SAVED 169

C

Canas–Jerez 79, 80, 114
Captain Humphrey 179
Captain J.R. de la Mar 137
Carlos Arosemena 160, 195
Cathedral Plaza 183, 188, 298
chargé d'affaires, Mr. White 121
Charles Burdett Hart 165, 226
Charles de Lesseps 111
Charles P. Flint 137
Chauncey M. Depew 140
Chester Arthur presidency 112
Colombia rejected the Hay–Herran Treaty 157, 160, 269, 270
Colonel Eliseo Torres 187, 189
Colonel Hains 136
Colonel Hepburn 142
Colonel James R. Shaler, superintendent of the Railroad Company 168
Colonel Myron T. Herrick 127
Commander Hubbard 185, 187, 188, 189, 191, 193
Concha, the chargé d'affaires of Colombia 148
Credit Lyonnaise 174
Culebra Company 124, 125
Culebra Cut 15, 107, 111, 124, 125, 177, 277, 279, 281, 286, 290, 291, 293, 296, 299, 300, 302, 309, 311, 313, 319, 323, 324, 329, 334, 335, 340, 342

D

de Lesseps's sea-level canal 109
Doctor Albert Shaw 171
Douglas Robinson 140, 226, 250, 252

E

Eads 105, 106
E.C. Converse 137
engenieurs de Ponts et Chaussees 108

F

Felix Ehrman 174, 188, 190, 191, 266
first Hay–Pauncefote Treaty 122
Francis B. Loomis 127
Frank D. Pavey 127
Frederico Boyd 160, 183, 195
Frelinghuysen–Zavala Treaty 112, 113
French Panama Canal 117, 124, 131, 134, 143, 148, 160, 176, 178, 180, 209, 220, 222, 224, 229, 263, 281, 323, 324, 355

G

Garfield administration 106
General Huertas 186, 190, 191, 258, 259
General Juan B. Tovar 181
General Nel Ospina 155, 159
General Pedro Cuadras 189
General Ramon G. Amaya 181
General Ruben Varon 181
George R. Sheldon 137
Godin de Lepinay's lock canal 109
Guarantee Bill of 1892 117
G.W. Perkins 140

H

Hay–Concha Treaty 148, 152, 154
Hay–Herran Treaty 11, 141, 142, 157, 159, 160, 161, 162, 163, 165, 166, 169, 179, 181, 189, 195, 198, 201, 202, 211, 212, 220, 224, 227, 242, 263, 269, 270, 352
Heidlebach, Ikleheimer & Company 174
Henry W. Taft 140
Herbert Prescott, assistant superintendent of the Panama Railroad 160
H.J. Satterlee 140
holding company 133, 137, 225, 263, 354
H.W. Seligman 137

I

Isaac Brandon & Brothers 174, 206
Island of Naos 108
Isthmian Canal Commission 122, 127, 135, 143, 256, 261, 266, 268, 324, 325, 327, 331

J

J. Edward Simmons 137, 147, 209
J.E. Simmons 140

John Biglow 121, 126
John Foster Dulles 134
Jonas Whitley, an employee of Nelson Cromwell 175
José Agustin Arango 160, 161, 195, 257
José Gabriel Duque 160
J.P. Morgan 105, 117, 128, 132, 133, 134, 140, 141, 195, 199, 220, 221, 225, 226, 227, 228, 229, 230, 232, 233, 234, 235, 239, 240, 243, 244, 246, 247, 248, 249, 252, 254, 255, 257, 258, 259, 260, 261, 262, 263, 264, 265, 297, 354, 355
J.R. Hill 140

L

Le Matin 125, 143, 145, 169, 172, 212
Levi Morton 137
Lieutenant Commander Asher Baker 127
Lieutenant Commander Asher C. Baker 127
Lieutenant Murphy 180
Lord Lansdowne 123
Lorenzo Marroquin 151
Lucien Napoleon Bonaparte Wyse 101

M

Manual Espinosa 160
Maurice Bunau-Varilla 111
Maurice Hutin 139
mouth of the Rio Grande 108
Mr. Artigue 111
Mr. Cannon, chairman of the ways and means committee 127
Mr. Carlos Lievano 150
Mr. Couvreux 107
Mr. Dingler 108
Mr. Don Porfirio Melendez 185
Mr. Edward B. Hill 168
Mr. Hersent 107
Mr. Hutin 110, 135
Mr. Loomis 127, 172, 173, 191, 224
Mr. Mancini, the Canal Company agent in Colombia 157
Mr. Martinez Silva 149
Mr. Ovidio Diaz Espino 176
Mr. Pauncefote 121
Mr. Percy Peixotto 127
Mr. Petit 110
Mr. Roger Farnham 165
Mrs. Espinosa 188
Mr. Severiano de Heredia 124
Mrs. Lefevre 188
Mr. Sonderegger 111
Mr. Sordoillet 110
Mr. William J. Curtis 133

N

New Jersey State corporate laws 133
New Panama Canal Company 132, 135, 136, 137, 138, 139, 140, 141, 143, 145, 146, 147, 148, 149, 150, 152, 159, 163, 174, 176, 177, 178, 185, 209, 221, 229, 231, 232, 233, 234, 243, 245, 246, 247, 248, 249, 250, 253, 263, 264
Nicanor de Obarrio 160
Nicaragua route 42, 43, 46, 53, 60, 97, 102, 106, 126, 127, 138, 139, 142, 143, 145, 146, 149, 153, 156, 162, 212, 263

O

Oregon 61, 63, 64, 65, 68, 87, 119, 122, 133, 136, 354

P

Paris Geographic Society 101
Penonome 181, 187, 191
Philippe Bunau-Varilla 107, 169, 170, 171, 172, 173, 174, 177, 179, 180, 184, 185, 194, 255, 322
Piza, Nephews & Company 174, 227, 228, 229
Ponts Chaussees 108
President Barrios of Guatemala 114
President Marroquin 147, 148, 149, 150, 152, 153, 155, 156, 157, 161, 163, 164, 181
President McKinley 118, 121, 122, 123, 127, 136, 138, 142, 143

President Roosevelt 123, 128, 132, 143, 155, 156, 162, 169, 170, 171, 175, 176, 179, 208, 214, 216, 219, 224, 225, 226, 227, 239, 241, 242, 243, 248, 250, 251, 252, 260, 264, 270, 274, 279, 280, 282, 283, 284, 293, 294, 298, 299, 300, 303, 304, 305, 306, 308, 311, 312, 318, 319, 324, 325, 326, 331, 334, 335, 336, 337, 341
Professor Haupt 136

R

Rainey resolution 135, 136, 137, 138, 139, 140, 142, 148, 149, 151, 152, 157, 161, 162, 166, 170, 173, 174, 179, 180, 181, 182, 184, 185, 186, 187, 188, 190, 192, 197, 205, 218, 219
Ricardo de la Espriella 195
Richardo Arias 160
Richard W. Thompson 104, 233
Rothschild syndicate 117, 354

S

Salsipuedes Street 193
Secretary of State Hay 121, 149, 152, 167, 173, 224
Secretary of State Richard Olney 121
Secretary of the Navy William E. Chandler 113
Senator John T. Morgan 142
Senator Spooner 145, 146, 216
Senorita Maria Amelia de la Ossa 188
Sherman Anti-Trust Act 115, 133

Sir Edwin Dawes 127
Societe Civile Internationale de Canal Interoceanique 101
Speaker of the House, James G. Blaine 113
Spooner 145, 146, 147, 148, 153, 157, 162, 171, 179, 216, 237, 238, 239, 247, 254, 274, 301, 343
Statement on Behalf of Historical Truth 135, 140, 147, 148, 170, 174, 176
Stewart Woodford 118

T

The civil unrest in Colombia 150
The Panic of 1893 116
The Treaty of Peace 151

U

United States at the Bay of Manila 119
U.S.S. Dixie 180, 193

V

Vernon M. Brown 137

W

Waldorf Astoria 170, 172, 266
Warner Van Worder 137
William Nelson Cromwell 128, 131, 132, 133, 134, 228, 231, 240, 252, 266, 279
Winslow Lanier and Company 140

Y

Yellow fever 69, 107, 309

THE ACQUISITION

A

Achille Monchicourt 230
Admiral Coghlin 219
Atrato River 24, 37, 218

B

Bacon and Descartes 322, 324

Barranquilla, Colombia 161, 219

C

Canal steam-shovel employees 309
Canal Zone chief engineer, John F. Wallace 265
Captain Beers 206, 221, 227, 266, 267

Captain Rodman 351, 352
Charles E. Magoon 278, 283
Comptoir National d' Escompte 245

D

Deputy Attorney General Stuart Mc-Namara 252

E

Earl Harding 215, 224, 241, 259
Edward Schildhauer 351

F

Frank Feuille 347, 349

G

Gamboa 293, 327
General Reyes 200, 203, 207, 208, 216, 217, 218, 220, 221, 264, 358, 360
George W. Davis 274, 275
Goethals 288, 292, 296, 305, 306, 307, 308, 309, 310, 311, 312, 313, 314, 315, 316, 317, 318, 319, 322, 323, 325, 328, 330, 331, 332, 333, 334, 336, 338, 340, 341, 342, 343, 347, 348, 349, 350, 351, 352, 356

H

H.J. Slifer 341

I

Isadoro Hazera 258

J

James J. Hill 288
John F. Stevens 288, 307, 316
Jonas Whitley 175, 215, 249, 363
Joseph Ripley 293, 295, 309

M

Major Gaillard 317
Mandingo Indians 219
Miraflores 293, 294, 316, 317, 331, 340, 341, 352
M. Lobnitz 325
Mr. Alban G. Snyder 357
Mr. Boyard 233
Mr. Caleb M. Van Hamm 251

Mr. Diego Mendoza Perez 357
Mr. Gautron 230, 245
Mr. George W. Perkins 225
Mr. John G. Sullivan 295
Mr. Joseph Pulitzer 224, 251
Mr. Lemarquis 230, 245
Mr. Paul Painleve 338, 339
Mr. Root 217, 284
Mr. Shonts 283, 284, 285, 295

P

Police Chief Shanton 298
port of Laboca 276
President Wilson 347, 349
progressivism 225

R

Robert H. Lyman 251
Rough Rider 225

S

sea-level canal 102, 103, 109, 159, 278, 279, 292, 293, 294, 295, 318, 323, 326, 327, 337, 338, 339
Secretary of the Treasury Shaw 247
Senate voted to accept the Panama Treaty, sixty-six to fourteen, without amendments 224
Sosa Locks 317
speak softly and carry a big stick 225
Square Deal 225
Stock-Gambler's Plan to Make Millions 215

T

The Panama Revolution, A 12, 215
Titumati 218
Tivoli Hotel 290, 297, 298
Tribunal Civile de la Seine 230, 237
trust busting 225

W

W.G. McAdoo 349
W.L. Silbert 307

Y

Yavisa 219

Milton Keynes UK
Ingram Content Group UK Ltd.
UKHW032352050124
435497UK00005B/156